# SOCIAL ENTREPRENEURSHIP AND SUSTAINABLE DEVELOPMENT

This volume discusses the seminal interface between social entrepreneurship and sustainable development along with their inter-linkages. It traces the role of social entrepreneurship and innovations in societal transformation in creating sustainable societies, especially in developing nations. It explores how social entrepreneurship and enterprise is integral to the promise of fostering opportunities for socially disadvantaged groups (including the poor, women, and young people), as well as in addressing environmental and ecological issues apart from wealth creation.

The book presents key concepts, case studies, and multiple innovative models involving social entrepreneurship, such as green financing, serial social entrepreneurship, sustainable livelihood creation, and well-being, in addition to highlighting global sustainable development goals of the United Nations. The chapters are organised under the broad themes of sustainability of the organisation, sustainability of the community, sustainability of the development, and sustainability of the community–organisation interface. They examine social change, social innovation, social enterprise, small and micro-enterprises, microfinance institutions, inclusive growth, education, productivity, physical health, waste management, energy retention, self-reliance, and corporate social responsibility. They contain emerging research issues in the field as well as critical assessments while bringing together theoretical and practitioners' perspectives.

This book will be useful to scholars and researchers of development studies, social entrepreneurship, sustainable development, environmental studies, public policy, and political sociology. It will also greatly interest professionals from non-profit, corporate, and public sectors, other development practitioners, and international bodies.

**Archana Singh** is Assistant Professor at the Centre for Social Entrepreneurship, School of Management and Labour Studies, Tata Institute of Social Sciences (TISS),

Mumbai, India. She teaches social entrepreneurship, social sector perspectives and interventions, qualitative research, and corporate social responsibility at the postgraduate level. She has also taught at Kennesaw State University, Atlanta, Georgia, in 2016. She earned her PhD in social work from TISS in 2014, her M. Phil in social work from the same institute in 2008, and her master of social work from Dr B. R. Ambedkar University, Agra, India in 1998. Prior to this, she worked at the ground level on various social issues, such as AIDS awareness, women's self-help groups, women's empowerment, in rural and urban areas, etc. She has presented several papers at conferences, published papers in international journals, and contributed chapters to edited volumes. She has also published the book *The Process of Social Value Creation: A Multiple Case Study on Social Entrepreneurship in India* (2016). Her research interests include social work, social change, social value, and women's empowerment.

**Edakkandi Meethal Reji** is Assistant Professor at the Centre for Social Entrepreneurship, School of Management and Labour Studies, Tata Institute of Social Sciences, Mumbai, India. He completed his PhD from the School of Management and Labour Studies, Tata Institute of Social Sciences. His doctoral thesis dealt with value chains and small enterprises. He has more than 15 years of experience in teaching, research, and consultancy in the areas of business and development management. His current teaching and research interests include public policy, inclusive value chains, small enterprise development, inclusive innovations and livelihoods, sustainable development, rural development, and public policies. He has worked as a team member for the Need Assessment Study and Corporate Social Responsibility Policy for L&T Finance Ltd, 2014–2015. He also drafted a comprehensive district plan for Gajapati District for the years 2008–2012, a project sanctioned by the State Planning and Co-ordination Department, Government of Orissa. He has organised conferences, presented papers, and has several publications in reputed journals.

## Towards Sustainable Futures

The Sustainable Development Goals (SDGs) were adopted by all United Nations Member States in 2015 as a universal call to action to end poverty, protect the planet, and ensure that all people enjoy peace and prosperity by 2030. The 17 SDGs are integrated, that is, they recognize that action in one area will affect outcomes in others, and that development must balance social, economic and environmental sustainability. The volumes in this series critically engage with the contemporary debates and discussions around development and sustainability. The series includes interdisciplinary and topical books presenting new perspectives for a sustainable future.

**Social Entrepreneurship and Sustainable Development**
*Edited by Archana Singh and Edakkandi Meethal Reji*

For more information about this series, please visit: https://www.routledge.com/Towards-Sustainable-Futures/book-series/TSF

# SOCIAL ENTREPRENEURSHIP AND SUSTAINABLE DEVELOPMENT

*Edited by Archana Singh and Edakkandi Meethal Reji*

LONDON AND NEW YORK

First published 2021
by Routledge
2 Park Square, Milton Park, Abingdon, Oxon OX14 4RN

and by Routledge
52 Vanderbilt Avenue, New York, NY 10017

*Routledge is an imprint of the Taylor & Francis Group, an informa business*



*British Library Cataloguing-in-Publication Data*
A catalogue record for this book is available from the British Library

*Library of Congress Cataloging-in-Publication Data*
A catalog record for this book has been requested

ISBN: 978-0-8153-9468-6 (hbk)
ISBN: 978-0-367-50176-1 (pbk)
ISBN: 978-1-003-04239-6 (ebk)

Typeset in Bembo
by Apex CoVantage, LLC

# CONTENTS

*List of figures* *x*
*List of tables* *xi*
*Foreword by Satyajit Majumdar* *xiiii*
*List of contributors* *xix*
*List of abbreviations* *xxii*

Introduction 1
*Archana Singh and Edakkandi Meethal Reji*

**PART 1**
**Sustainability of organisation** **23**

1 Social entrepreneurship and sustainable development: emerging research issues 25
*Archana Singh*

2 Madhav Sathe: social entrepreneur seeking opportunity in problems 41
*Satyajit Majumdar and Bina Ajay*

3 Business services for small enterprise development: emerging theory and practices 53
*Edakkandi Meethal Reji*

**PART 2**
**SUSTAINABILITY OF COMMUNITY** **71**

4 Case studies on utilisation of community radio in achieving sustainable development 73
*Amolina Ray*

5 Sustainable development and indigenous entrepreneurship: a case study of Santhei Natural Park 88
*Jackson Khumukcham, Satyajit Majumdar, and Samapti Guha*

6 Napasar: an approach to sustainable livelihood 115
*Anu Sharma, Simmi Bhagat, and Mona Suri*

**PART 3**
**SUSTAINABILITY OF DEVELOPMENT** **131**

7 Role of social enterprises in the creation of sustainable livelihood: the case of microfinance institutions in the slums of Mumbai 133
*Chandralekha Ghosh and Samapti Guha*

8 Social entrepreneurship through the lenses of wellbeing and sustainable development: a critique 155
*Samapti Guha*

9 Sustainable development and green financing: a study on the banking sector in Bangladesh 170
*Dewan Muktadir-Al-Mukit and M. Ashraf Hossain*

**PART 4**
**SUSTAINABILITY OF COMMUNITY AND ORGANISATION INTERFACE** **189**

10 Social enterprises and inclusive societies: a SAATH perspective 191
*Archana Singh, Gladwin Issac, and Shrinivas Sinha*

11 Is serial social entrepreneurship leading towards sustainable development? A case of Annapurna Pariwar 207
*Samapti Guha, Medha Purao Samant, and Edakkandi Meethal Reji*

12 Integrating corporate social responsibility (CSR) and social entrepreneurship (SE): a conceptual framework for social value creation 227
*Archana Singh*

*Glossary* *242*
*Index* *246*

# FIGURES


| | | |
|---|---|---|
| 1.1 | Model of the contribution of social entrepreneurship (SE) to sustainable development (SD) | 28 |
| 6.1 | Napasar organisational chart | 120 |
| 6.2 | SWOC chart of Napasar cluster | 122 |
| 7.1 | Conceptual framework developed by the authors | 138 |
| 8.1 | Sustainable development, wellbeing, and social entrepreneurship | 159 |
| 9.1 | Three phases of green banking policy implementation | 175 |
| 9.2 | Green financing at a glance | 176 |
| 9.3 | Three domains of sustainable development | 177 |
| 9.4a, b, & c | Utilisation of funds for green finance | 179 |
| 9.5 | Sector-wise contribution of banks towards green financing | 182 |
| 9.6 | Financing projects after environmental risk rating in 2011 and 2012 | 183 |
| 9.7 | Top 12 banks in allocation of budget for green finance during 2012 | 185 |
| 9.8 | Top 12 banks in budget utilisation for green finance in 2012 | 186 |
| 11.1 | Organogram of Annapurna Pariwar | 213 |
| 12.1 | Conceptual framework: integrating CSR and SE for social value creation | 232 |

# TABLES


| | | |
|---|---|---|
| 1.1 | Selected sample cases for the study | 30 |
| 2.1 | Comparison between 1985–1986 and 2014–2015 | 48 |
| 4.1 | Details of community radio stations | 80 |
| 7.1 | Socio-economic profile | 141 |
| 7.2 | Asset and loan profile | 142 |
| 7.3 | Enterprise profile | 143 |
| 7.4 | Description of the variables | 144 |
| 7.5 | Tobit Model I: determinants of loan size | 145 |
| 7.6 | Tobit Model II: role of MFI on loan size | 145 |
| 7A.1 | Descriptive statistics between MFI loans and informal loans | 149 |
| 7A.1a | Association between financial asset and MFI dummy | 149 |
| 7A.1b | Association between capital asset and MFI dummy | 150 |
| 7A.2 | Descriptive statistics of profit level, revenue level, and income level | 150 |
| 7A.3 | Kolmogorov-Smirnov test of sales per month, profit per month, and income level | 151 |
| 7A.3a | Frequency distribution of sales per month, profit per month, and income level | 151 |
| 7A.3b | Test statistics of sales per month, profit per month, and income level | 151 |
| 9.1 | Utilisation of fund for green banking (amount in million Taka) | 174 |
| 9.2 | Allocation of funds for green banking and green financing in 2012 | 178 |
| 9.3 | Utilisation of funds for direct and indirect green finance in 2012 (amount in million Taka) | 178 |
| 9.4 | Direct and indirect green finance of SCBs in 2012 (amount in million Taka) | 180 |

9.5 Direct and indirect green finance of SDBs in 2012 (amount in million Taka) 180
9.6 Direct and indirect green finance of FCBs in 2012 (amount in million Taka) 181
9.7 Top six PCBs for direct and indirect green finance in 2012 (amount in million Taka) 181
9.8 Sector-wise contribution of banks towards green financing (amount in million Taka) 182
9.9 Financing projects after environmental risk rating in 2011 and 2012 183

# FOREWORD

I feel happy to write this Foreword for this edited volume from our Centre for Social Entrepreneurship, School of Management and Labour Studies, Tata Institute of Social Sciences, Mumbai, India. Our centre has pioneered developing the curriculum on social entrepreneurship while not limiting the attention towards enterprise creation or the heroic personalities of social entrepreneurs; rather, we have taken a broader view and explored multiple domains which can contribute to the knowledge and practice of social entrepreneurship to bring sustainable and desirable social change. Interestingly, the design and development of our two-year master's programme has been an entrepreneurial journey wherein we have considered social entrepreneurship in specific and responsible entrepreneurship in general a process of social value creation. We have designed the programme while mapping two major decision logics—effectual and causal.[1] We have also rejected the debate on the definition of social entrepreneurship which, we believe, is context-dependent and hence would remain inclusive.[2] We proposed, in a given context, that we need freedom to define and take a position on social entrepreneurship. There are other domains too in which we can search for the process of social value creation: corporate social responsibility (CSR), innovation, and sustainable development are prominent among them.

This edited volume is profiled on our visualisation of the contribution social entrepreneurship can make in sustainable development. It presents a wide coverage of themes—from the concepts of sustainability and sustainable development to various methods and technologies. The institutional framework is the highlight of this volume, ranging from country-specific subjects to organisational variables. It also includes both meta-analyses and the contextual dimensions of sustainable development.

## Sustainable development

The conflict between ecology/environment and development has been a matter of worry for all those who believe in a happy and just society. Soon, we have realised that rapid progress in the present at the cost of the future is not going to lead us to real growth. Sustainable development has thus emerged as a strong developmental discourse, which has drawn the attention of not only the people who were raising their voices about the way countries were adopting economic development policies but also scholars who were considering alternate theories in development economics.

While an economically sustainable system considers production of goods and services at manageable levels without extremities and imbalances, an environmentally sustainable system demands a stable resource base, prevention of over-exploitation with maintenance of biodiversity, and avoidance of climatic changes. The third dimension—a socially sustainable system—expects participation of stakeholders in the entire process of development; equity among genders, castes, classes, communities, and races; and provision of basic human services such as health and education with political accountability.

## Structural adjustment of the 1980s—a critique

The 'structural adjustment' policies adopted during the 1980s led to several major new measures of liberalised policies in almost every part of the globe. Political decisions were taken to make governance efficient with less interference and with adoption of market-led policies. Many 'correction' initiatives were taken to facilitate barrier-free economic development. Though this new discourse of development brought free trade, cross-border exchanges of labor, knowledge, goods, and services, it also brought inequality and hardship for the poor. The human development approach emphasizing the basic needs and equity is well-grounded in the history of economic theory, wherein Amartya Sen and others have expressed concerns that the wealth maximisation approach has dominated modern economics. We have witnessed a tension between the efficiency pull of the free market and deprivation and a cry for fulfilment of basic needs of the millions of poor people. Now, the uneven distribution of the benefits of development with income inequalities is evident. On the one hand, the middle-class population has become affluent; on the other hand, the numbers of extremely poor and malnourished people have not only remained high but have also increased in some areas. This has adversely impacted indigenous people and traditional societies due to excessive exploitation of forests, water, and intensive fisheries. Gross adverse impacts such as on pollution and inadequate transportation, water, and sewer infrastructure are also visible in urban areas.

## Theories, concepts, and knowledge gaps

In neoclassical economic theory, sustainability can be defined in terms of 'maximisation of welfare over time', whereas for operational advantage it can be simplified as 'maximisation of welfare with the maximisation of utility derived from consumption'. This may be oversimplified as a concept, but this approach provides the means to measure human welfare such as food, clothing, housing, transportation, health, and education services.

The other concept is natural capital, which consists of the natural resources and environmental services of the planet. Also, the 'other capital' is human-made capital, which is contested for substitutability of natural capital. For example, cutting down forests to construct roads would offer economic value. There are also critiques on this view that human-made and natural capital complements and marginally substitutes.

In this situation, Toman's suggested decision framework on the role of moral imperatives, public decision-making, and formation of social values become important for us. It does not appear in the neo-classical economic model, wherein markets are accepted to be the basis for resource allocators and market imperfection is corrected by the appropriate role for government. Rather, this framework leads to the importance of sustainability as an independent concept, explicitly normative and socially determined process of decision-making. This has been a fundamental shift. Sustainability as a social goal places a new complexity in the relationship between human economic activity and the environment. Market, though an essential means, does not determine the ends and is a social decision process. This provides an opportunity for interdisciplinary work to address the critical issues related to sustainability—defining objectives, identifying constraints, and resolving the relevant disagreements. Economists, social scientists, ecologists, and other disciplines have roles to play to resolve the issues discussed here. An indicative list of knowledge gaps could be: population and consumption, biological systems, planet, choice of goods and technology, social actions, governance, and regulations.

## Knowledge gaps in sustainable development

I propose that sustainable development is a new paradigm of development. For example, to achieve food security and adequate clean water supplies may require changes in land usage, which may affect the biodiversity. Also, non-polluting energy sources could be more expensive for the poor population to afford.

If we take a deeper view of some other important sectors such as food and agriculture, we face the challenge of feeding an expanding population at higher per capita levels of consumption that is straining soil and water systems. The current high-input technologies in agriculture are resulting in soil degradation and water pollution. In this context the subjects of soil rebuilding, integrated pest management, and efficient irrigation need no explanation. Greater reliance on local knowledge and participatory input into the development of agricultural techniques also provides means for newer solutions. On the consumption side, limits on population growth and greater equity and efficiency in food distribution are of central importance considering the issues related to resource limitations on production.

Similarly, in the energy sector supply gaps, environmental impacts, especially the accumulation of greenhouse gases, dominates the discourse of development, and the need for transition away from fossil fuels is critical. Migration to non-fossil energy systems is a major subject to deal with the issues of ever-increasing demand of energy, and hence focus is shifting towards decentralised wind, biomass, and off-grid solar power systems. This also raises challenges in mobilisation of capital for renewable energy development.

Every such area has unique challenges which are social, institutional, as well as economic. It is clear that the social component of sustainability is not just an idealised goal but a necessity for achieving the economic and ecological components of growth. Institutions of all kinds—corporations, local and national governments, and transnational organisations—will have to adapt to the requirements of sustainable development before the problems which motivated the developmental concepts do not grow worse. Democratic governance, participation, and satisfaction of the basic needs are thus essential parts of the new development synthesis.

In sum, in the new paradigm of sustainable development, the social component of development is essential. The three elements of sustainability—economic, social, and environmental—pose a complex nature of operational challenges, and their multidimensional nature raises difficulties in achieving balanced objectives of development.

## New practice and knowledge of intervention—social entrepreneurship

Considering the need to search for a balanced approach with three developmental principles (social, economic, and environmental), we feel motivated to search for newer ways of achieving the goals of human development.

Making people capable of participating in the market by building their capacities, by facilitating linkages with the market, by providing timely credit and information, etc. seems to be the new approach of development. Developmental funding is increasingly seen as social investment, where social mission and social change are not the only objectives of investment, but the financial sustainability of such initiatives is also considered to be important. Thus, social and financial (environmental inclusive) returns on investments are becoming the indicators of sustainable development. In this situation social entrepreneurs are the professionals to manage investments of financial and social capital to bring social change through market-driven mechanisms. Despite that, social entrepreneurship is equally pursued by governments from across the globe as drivers of innovation to solve complex social problems that the countries face today. Now we understand that social entrepreneurship: a) is an alternative to the existing economic order that maximises financial returns on investment while considering the market dynamics and opportunities; b) emphasises sustainability; and c) addresses the needs of a scattered society and struggles among various sections and communities. Due to its inherent nature to deal with complexities in a reasonably sustained way, social entrepreneurship has been gaining acceptance to be an innovative and game-changing approach to development.

It is natural that social entrepreneurship as a discipline has received valuable attention from academicians and researchers. It provides a possibility to encounter several socio-economic gaps created by the traditional models of economic development due to the market-led growth mechanisms. Of late there has been a significant amount of faith and hope generated in this field due to historical evidence in countries such as India with a wide geographic spread, diversified culture, and economic development status. The practice of social entrepreneurship (especially in India) is age-old, whereas the field is new as a scholarly inquiry. Academic programmes developed in this field emerged from multiple disciplines—social science, management, public policy, health systems, and technology to name a few. Therefore, academic and practice professionals have made significant efforts to document case studies and to derive theoretical perspectives.

## Themes in this edited volume

I feel happy that this edited volume is yet another attempt to compile research papers and case-based studies on social entrepreneurship on relevant themes which are of great value in advancing the knowledge in this discipline.

To write this Foreword, and as a scholar myself, I have been curious to know the patterns of the research papers and the thematic considerations the research scholars have made in their respective chapters. I believe the scholarly advancement is also a function of the sensitivity (of the researchers) to search for new knowledge and theories. Theorising new practices and developing scholarly insights are critical not only for (theoretical) generalisation but also for developing frameworks or points of view to question 'the future', wherein the scholarly research has an important role to play.

This edited volume would be of great value to readers who want to know about the spectrum of research areas. The context of sustainable development is critical, and the research gaps are efficiently presented here. This, in my opinion, would also provide a broad direction for future research.

I have been experiencing the 'cry' for large data-based studies in social entrepreneurship to draw patterns while seeking the possibilities of generalisation; on the other hand, I also feel the need for 'enough' evidence-based or case-based studies to design this broad agenda for future research. This volume has taken a responsible position to act as a bridge to provide the needed research direction. The chapters on social enterprises and their patterns and the case studies are good sources to form the basis for the desired large data-based studies of the future. The volume provides new themes such as finding opportunity for social enterprise in problems including livelihood and indigenous entrepreneurship. Specific studies on micro and green finance, community and cluster approaches, and the process of social enterprise creation provide valuable insights to be pursued in future research. Technology adoption for social value creation is yet another area with which this volume has aptly dealt. The research methodological discussion, though not presented as an exclusive agenda, remains a matter of investigation. The volume submits that we have arrived at a situation when we also need clearer direction(s) on the research methodology at the intersection of disciplines of sustainable development and social entrepreneurship because social entrepreneurship is fast emerging as an effective way to create sustainable development.

To conclude, we have some general principles and also specific requirements of sustainable development. Development theory has always been normative as well as positive in its analytical vision, and so is the role of social entrepreneurship. However, we need direction to search for newer approaches and principles of economic, political, and social theories while combining them with traditional wisdom and modern technology. This volume is one such important step in this direction.

The volume has been efficiently anchored and edited by my colleagues Archana Singh and Edakkandi Meethal Reji. I compliment them and also the authors for their valuable contributions to the advancement of knowledge.

**Satyajit Majumdar**
Professor, Centre for Social Entrepreneurship, School of Management and Labour Studies, Tata Institute of Social Sciences, Mumbai, India

## Notes

1 An entrepreneur as a decision-maker makes decisions to create (and to grow) enterprise. Based on our experience in teaching and research on entrepreneurship, and mentoring and guiding social and business enterprises, we have developed a different view on the entrepreneur and enterprise creation. The entrepreneur or the person does not always have a great idea to start an enterprise. Rather, he/she develops deep understanding of a problem or gap and also a strong emotional connection to take that up to resolve. This also explains the reason why entrepreneurs demonstrate the behaviour of 'not giving up' despite several odds. The strong desire to solve the problem with an unlimited number of experimental attempts is also evident for the same reason. This process of non-linearity is the science of 'entrepreneurship', which the individual entrepreneur develops for self. We are thankful to our friend and one of the most-cited scholars, Professor Saras D. Sarasvathy from the Darden School of Business, The University of Virginia (USA) for provoking us to take this position. This has immensely helped to carry forward our work with social, business, and technology entrepreneurs. Personally, I had several discussions with her on this subject, although not in all such discussions did we have a very sharp conclusion or agreement.

2 Nia Choi and I published a paper in the *Journal of Business Venturing* titled "Social Entrepreneurship as an Essentially Contested Concept: Opening a New Avenue for Systematic Future Research" in Volume 29 (2014) to present our argument that social entrepreneurship is a cluster concept and hence does not need definition. Scholars have found our work useful to advance the knowledge of social entrepreneurship, evidenced by more than 225 citations. Essentially, the contested concept was first proposed by Walter Bryce Gallie in 1956.

# CONTRIBUTORS

**Bina Ajay** is a doctoral student at the University of Cincinnati's Carl H. Lindner College of Business, USA. She has a bachelor of commerce degree from University of Mumbai, India. She is also an associate member of the Institute of Chartered Accountants of India. Prior to joining the doctoral program, she worked in the industry for many years and has experience in capital budgeting, strategy, business planning, project finance, accounting, taxation, audit, and fund management.

**Simmi Bhagat** is Associate Professor at the Department of Fabric and Apparel Science, Lady Irwin College, Delhi University, India. She did her Ph.D. in textiles and clothing from the same department. She has more than 22 years of teaching experience, and her areas of interest, research, and publications are design, textile conservation, traditional textiles, and illustrations. She guides doctoral research theses and dissertations along with those at postgraduate and graduate levels.

**Chandralekha Ghosh** is Assistant Professor in the Department of Economics in West Bengal State University, India. She obtained her PhD from the Department of Economics, Jadavpur University, Kolkata, India. Her areas of interest are agriculture economics, productivity and efficiency analysis, microfinance, as well as microenterprise-related issues and financial inclusion-related issues. She has published several research articles in national and international journals.

**Samapti Guha** is Professor at the Centre for Social Entrepreneurship, Tata Institute of Social Sciences. She did her PhD in economics from Jadavpur University, India, in 2004, and her postdoctoral study at the London School of Economics and Political Science, UK in 2006. In 2007, she joined the Tata Institute of Social Sciences and launched a new MA programme in Social Entrepreneurship. Her areas of research are microfinance, social entrepreneurship, and development.

**M. Ashraf Hossain** is Professor of Business Administration and Director of Institutional Quality Assurance Cell (IQAC), Eastern University, Dhaka, Bangladesh, and previously was Chairman and Acting Dean. He is a development economist and management consultant with 30 years of experience in education, training, and field-level research on financing and strengthening small enterprises and integrated farming systems for poverty alleviation and nutritional security. He was a researcher/trainer at the United Nations Centre for Research and Development (UNCRD) and faculty/researcher in Japanese universities, and has track records as team leader of various local, United States Agency for International Development (USAID), and UN projects in many Asian countries.

**Gladwin Issac** is a final-year undergraduate student of law and social work at the Gujarat National Law University, Gandhinagar, India. He is also a researcher with the International Institute of Sustainable Development's Investment for Sustainable Development program.

**Jackson Khumukcham** is a doctoral candidate at the Tata Institute of Social Sciences. His work mainly focuses on entrepreneurship and indigenous entrepreneurship. He has a diverse background in social work and cultural studies. He studied the problem faced by traditional performing artists in his M.Phil. dissertation. He is a Dalai Lama Fellow (2013) and has been honoured with the Bal Shree Award (2000) by the then president of India for his creative performance in the field of traditional performing art.

**Satyajit Majumdar** is Chairperson and Professor at the Centre for Social Entrepreneurship in the School of Management and Labour Studies of Tata Institute of Social Sciences, and teaches entrepreneurship, growth and technology strategy, corporate social responsibility, and service operations management. He has published research papers and case studies in the areas of entrepreneurship, social entrepreneurship, small business, growth strategy, and corporate social responsibility. He mentors young entrepreneurs, participates in activities related to building an entrepreneurship ecosystem, and reviews research papers for international journals.

**Dewan Muktadir-Al-Mukit** is Assistant Professor in the Faculty of Business Administration, Eastern University, Dhaka, Bangladesh. He received his master's and bachelor degrees in finance from the University of Dhaka. He is an expert in the field of corporate governance, social business, and the stock market, and has published a number of papers in professional journals. He is a regular participant in local and international conferences and a recipient of the Best Research Paper presenter award. He has successfully completed several funded research projects, including a government project under the Planning Ministry of the country. He is the trainer of the Social Business short course at Eastern University and also instructor of the Social Business module of 'Business Schools for Impact', the United Nations Conference on Trade and Development (UNCTAD), Geneva.

**Amolina Ray** has worked as a project fellow in Community Radio in India at Jadavpur University, which was part of the scheme "University with Potential for Excellence–Phase II" funded by the University Grants Commission, for nearly three years. She also has operational knowledge of Community Radio, having worked as Programme Manager in Community Radio at Jadavpur University for four years.

**Medha Purao Samant** is Chairperson and Managing Director of Annapurna Pariwar, a conglomerate of five non-profit organisations, working for the empowerment of poor self-employed women in the slums in Pune and 600 slums in Mumbai. She has completed her PhD in social work and a special course on Gender and Development at the Institute of Development Studies, Sussex, UK. She has received several important national and international awards for her contribution to women's empowerment.

**Anu Sharma** is a doctoral research scholar in the Department of Fabric and Apparel Science, Lady Irwin College, Delhi University, India. With an M. Des. in textile design from the National Institute of Fashion Technology (NIFT), New Delhi, her areas of interest, research, and publications are design, textiles, and design management. Her field of experience encompasses national and international projects related to designing, artisan skill development, forecast interpretation, and teaching over 14 years.

**Shrinivas Sinha** is a final-year law student pursuing a B.S.W. LL.B (Hons.) from Gujarat National Law University, Gandhinagar, India. He was previously associated with the Unique Identification Authority of India (UIDAI) and has a keen interest in policy making.

**Mona Suri** is Academic Vice President and Associate Professor at Royal University for Women, Kingdom of Bahrain. She completed her Ph.D. in textiles and clothing from the Department of Fabric and Apparel Science, Lady Irwin College, Delhi University, India. She has more than 28 years of teaching experience, and her areas of interest are design, textile technology, textile finishing, and protective clothing. She has successfully guided six Ph.D. research scholars, more than 50 dissertations of postgraduate students, and has many publications to her credit.

# ABBREVIATIONS

| | |
|---|---|
| ACDI | Agricultural Co-operative Development International |
| ADB | Asian Development Bank |
| AIDS | Acquired Immune Deficiency Syndrome |
| AIR | All India Radio |
| AMARC | Association of Community Radio Broadcasters |
| AMCCSL | Annapurna Mahila Credit Cooperative Society Limited |
| AMR | antimicrobial resistance |
| APVS | Annapurna Pariwar Vikas Samvardhan |
| BAI | Broadcasting Authority of India |
| BASIC | Bank of Small Industries and Commerce |
| BDBL | Bangladesh Development Bank Limited |
| BDS | Business Development Services |
| BKB | Bangladesh Krishi Bank |
| BMC | Bombay Municipal Corporation |
| BMCWS | Bombay Mothers and Children Welfare Society |
| BMO | business membership organisations |
| BRAC | Bangladesh Rural Advancement Committee |
| BRIC | Brazil Russia, India, and China |
| CAPART | Council for Advancement of People's Action and Rural Technology |
| CBE | community-based enterprises |
| CD | compact disc |
| CDA | Centro de Desarrollo de Agronegocios (Agribusiness Development Center) |
| CII | Confederations of Indian Industries |
| CR | community radio |
| CRY | Child Rights and You |

| | |
|---|---|
| CSE | corporate social entrepreneurship |
| CSP | corporate social performance |
| CSR | corporate social responsibility |
| CYSD | Centre for Youth and Social Development |
| DDS | Deccan Development Society |
| DESA | (United Nations) Department of Economic and Social Affairs |
| DFID | Department of Finance and International Development (UK) |
| DSMS | District Supply and Marketing Societies |
| DST | Department of Science and Technology |
| DWCRA | Development of Women and Children in Rural Areas |
| ECC | essentially contested concept |
| ETP | effluent treatment plant |
| FCB | foreign commercial bank |
| FIT | farm implements and tools |
| FM | frequency modulation |
| FSF | Family Security Fund |
| GDP | gross domestic product |
| GTZ | German Organisation for Technical Cooperation |
| HEPC | Handloom Export Promotion Council |
| HHK | Hybrid Hoffman Kiln |
| HIV | Human Immunodeficiency Virus |
| HMF | Health Mutual Fund |
| IADB | Inter-American Development Bank |
| IBEF | India Brand Equity Foundation |
| ICITP | Indian Council of Indigenous and Tribal Peoples |
| ICT | information and communication technologies |
| IDE | International Development Enterprise |
| IFC | International Finance Corporation |
| IGP | Income Generation Programme |
| IISCO | Indian Iron and Steel Company |
| ILO | International Labour Organisation |
| INR | Indian National Rupee |
| IPCC | Intergovernmental Panel on Climate Change |
| IRDA | Insurance Regulatory and Development Authority |
| IRDP | Integrated Rural Development Programme |
| KB | Krishak Bahandu |
| LIC | Life Insurance Corporation |
| LMF | Life Mutual Fund |
| LPG | liberalisation, privatisation, and globalisation |
| LPG | liquefied petroleum gas |
| MDG | millennium development goals |
| MGF | matching grant fund |
| MHz | megahertz |
| MoU | memorandum of understanding |

| | |
|---|---|
| MPDF | Mekong Project Development Facility |
| MSE | micro and small enterprises |
| MSME | Ministry of Micro, Small and Medium Enterprises |
| NBFI | non-banking financial institution |
| NCC | National Cadet Corps |
| NCSTC | National Council for Science and Technology Communication |
| NGO | non-governmental organisation |
| NIACL | New India Assurance Company Limited |
| NIVH | National Institute for the Visually Handicapped |
| NSDC | National Skill Development Corporation |
| OASiS | Organisation for Awareness of Integrated Social Security |
| PCB | private commercial bank |
| PIL | public interest litigation |
| PRA | participatory rural appraisal |
| RAKUB | Rajshahi Krishi Unnayan Bank |
| ROSCA | Rotating, Saving, and Credit Association |
| SAIL | Steel Authority of India Limited |
| SCB | state-owned commercial bank |
| SCP | sustainable corporate performance |
| SD | sustainable development |
| SDGs | sustainable development goals |
| SE | social entrepreneurship/enterprise |
| SEEP | Social Enterprise Education Programme |
| SEV | social entrepreneurial ventures |
| SEWA | Self-Employed Women's Association |
| SHGs | self-help groups |
| SI | social innovation |
| SLA | sustainable livelihood approach |
| SMCR | Sender Message Channel Receiver |
| SRREOSHI | Society for Research and Rudimentary Education on Social and Health Issues |
| SWOC | strengths, weaknesses, opportunities, and challenges |
| TB | tuberculosis |
| TBL | Triple Bottom Line |
| TISS | Tata Institute of Social Sciences |
| Triple P | profit, planet, people |
| UN | United Nations |
| UNCTAD | United Nations Conference on Trade and Development |
| UNDP | United Nations Development Programme |
| UNESCO | United Nations Educational, Scientific, and Cultural Organisation |
| UNICEF | United Nations Children's Education Fund |
| UNIDO | United Nations Industrial Development Organisation |

| | |
|---|---|
| USA | United States of America |
| VOCA | Volunteers in Overseas Co-operative Assistance |
| WCED | World Commission on Environment and Development |
| WBRYC | Western Baruni Road Youth Club |
| WEF | World Economic Forum |
| WHO | World Health Organisation |

# INTRODUCTION

*Archana Singh and Edakkandi Meethal Reji*

Entrepreneurship and innovations have long been recognised as vehicles for societal transformation (Dean & McMullen, 2007; Cohen & Winn, 2007; Hall, Daneke, & Lenox, 2010). Beyond its contribution to wealth creation, entrepreneurship is also identified with the promise of fostering opportunities for socially disadvantaged groups, including the poor, women, and young people and addressing environmental and ecological issues (Prahalad, 2004; Brugmann & Prahalad, 2007; Hart & Christensen, 2002). In this process social entrepreneurs[1] are at the forefront to create a sustainable society by creating both economic and social value (Seelos & Mair, 2005; Bornstein, 2007; Bornstein & Davis, 2010). As change agents they create organisations to achieve their social mission and operate business-like to address social and/or environmental problems and function within the guided philosophy of sustainable development. They take up innovative practices to enhance the socio-economic status of marginalised people, access to education, health, conserving natural resources, waste management, renewable energy, and self-reliance of individuals and societies (Mulgan, Tucker, Ali, & Sanders, 2007; Phillips, Lee, Ghobadian, O'Regan, & James, 2015).

The pressing need to address the global social problems and environmental challenges has led to an increasing interest in social entrepreneurship among practitioners, academics, and policymakers (Weerawardena & Mort, 2006). Scholars from a wide variety of disciplines, including economics, sociology, anthropology, entrepreneurship, business management, and politics, engage in social entrepreneurship research because it is an interdisciplinary field. In this context, it is important to understand the emergent practices in these diverse fields for addressing sustainable development challenges. Although popular writers and practitioners make claims about the potential role of social entrepreneurship in addressing sustainability challenges, including poverty reduction, gender inequality, health, education, and other social and environmental issues, very little is known about the role of social entrepreneurship in sustainable development in the academic literature. Against this background, this edited volume brings the interface between social entrepreneurship and sustainable development to the fore. Broadly, this volume addresses the following two research questions: 1) Whether and/or how can social entrepreneurship contribute to addressing the sustainable development challenges? and 2) What are the emergent practices and what can be learnt from these practices? The chapters in this volume bring together interdisciplinary themes in economics, sociology, anthropology, management, entrepreneurship, social entrepreneurship, and sustainable development. It also discusses the emerging research issues in this area and presents a critical view on social entrepreneurship and sustainable development.

## The concept and evolution of sustainable development

The concept of sustainable development began as a development process compatible with ecosystem. It is conceived as "a development process that meets the needs of the present without compromising the ability of future generations to meet their own needs" (WCED, 1987, p. 43). Sustainable development acknowledges the nexus between environment and development and securing development objectives in a sustainable manner (Jabareen, 2006). The concept received international attention with the United Nations Conference on Human Environment in Stockholm, 1972, the United Nations Conference on Environment and Development in Rio de Janeiro, 1992, the World Summit on Sustainable Development in Johannesburg, 2002, and the United Nations Conference on Sustainable Development in Rio de Janeiro, 2012.

Ever since the concept has been introduced, there are diverse and competing views on what constitutes sustainability or sustainable development. Some of these are contested (Springett, 2015) as being 'an oxymoron' (Redclift, 2005), 'disturbingly muddled' (Munn, 1988), and a 'contradiction in terms' (O'Riordan, 1985). Sustainability and more often sustainable development is used interchangeably with 'ecologically sustainable' or 'environmentally sound development' (Lele, 1991). The economists view sustainable development as 'sustained growth' or 'sustained change' and more recently 'sustainable human development' with associated development objectives such as expansion of choice, freedom and capabilities, wellbeing, democracy, human rights, equity, and justice (Anand & Sen, 2000; Sen, 2000; Solow, 1991).

Robert Solow clarifies that sustainability is simply a matter of distributional equity, about sharing the capacity for wellbeing between present people and future people. Solow states that

> it is an obligation to conduct ourselves so that we leave to the future the option or the capacity to be as well off as we are. It is not clear [to me] that one can be more precise than that. Sustainability is an injunction not to satisfy ourselves by impoverishing our successors.
>
> *(Solow, 1991, p. 3)*

Solow's formulation of sustainable development captures the percept that the possibilities open to people tomorrow should not differ from those open today (UNDP, 2011). For Solow sustainable development is something more than a vague emotional commitment, which requires something to be conserved for the very long run. Solow clarifies that "a sustainable path for an economy not necessarily that conserve everything but conserving the generalised capacity to produce economic well-being" (Solow, 1993, p. 168). Building on the works of Solow (1991, 1993) and Anand and Sen (2000), the United Nations Development Programme (UNDP) defines sustainable human development as "the expansion of the substantive freedoms of people today while making reasonable efforts to avoid seriously compromising those of future generations" (UNDP, 2011, p. 30).

This inter-generational aspect of sustainable development implies the confluence of diverse economic, social, and environmental objectives. However, the primacy of an economic approach to development provides very little emphasis on the environmental and ecological dimensions of development. With the increasing realisation that not all of society's functions and goals can and should be defined through economic methods alone, the social scientists were confronted with the centrality of environment and sustainability (Redclift, 2005). Some feared that the major environmental problems of the 1970s are associated with resource scarcities that underline the difficulty in reconciling development with sustainability (Meadows, Meadows, Randers, & Beherens, 1972). It was increasingly realised that in pursuit of economic growth, industrialisation, and urbanisation, the scale of exploitation of natural resources including land, minerals, and energy resources has soared, leading to increasing environmental pollution and weakening ecosystem functions and resulting in irreparable damages to the environment and ecology (Norgaard, 1988; Munda, 1997; Haque, 2000). Scholars with environmental and ecological backgrounds point out that many of the current development challenges, including global warming and unprecedented natural disasters, are direct consequences of the development process, and they argue that development is not sustainable if it is not ecologically sustainable (Holden, Linnerud, & Banister, 2014). This increasing recognition that the overall goals of environmental conservation and economic development are not conflicting but can be naturally reinforcing has prompted calls for environmentally sustainable economic development (Barbier, 1987). These scholars view sustainable development as the optimal level of interaction among three systems—biological, economic, and social—a level which is achieved through a dynamic and adaptive process of trade-offs (Barbier, 1989). Environmental economists continue to emphasise this trade-off between systems or between present and future needs, as the key issue and argue that sustainable development involves maximising the net benefits of economic development, subject to maintaining the services and the quality of natural resources over time (Barbier, Markandya, & Pearce, 1990). Yet, the concept remained vague with the questions of what is to be sustained or what is to be developed (Daly, 1991). Some argue that the natural stock of resources or critical natural capital needs to be given priority as it cannot be substituted by human-made capital, and others argue that the present (or future) levels of production (or consumption) need to be sustained.

These contrasting views lead to conceptual paradigms like 'strong sustainability' and 'weak sustainability' (ibid.). The concept of weak sustainability relies on the assumption that human-made capital can replace natural resources and ecosystem services with a high degree of substitutability. Strong sustainability, in contrast, takes the view that certain critical natural stocks such as biodiversity and climate systems can't be replaced by human-made capital and must be maintained (Neumayer, 2010). A related issue is whether one should evaluate development only in terms of human wellbeing, which depends on environmental services, or also account for natural systems as intrinsically valuable (Attfield, 2008).

Over the years, sustainable development has been conceptualised beyond securing basic needs and preserving the environment and involving three pillars of sustainability: environment, economic, and social aspects (Elkington, 1997). Related development included the emergence of concepts like 'Green Development' (Adams, 1990), 'Sustainable Business/Triple Bottom Line' (Elkington, 1997), 'Clean Technologies' and 'Ecological Modernisation' (Spaargaren & Mol, 1992).

Amidst these contestations and diversity, sustainable development has become an aspiration for a good society. The most widely discussed definition of sustainable development is "development which meets the needs of current generations without compromising the ability of future generations to meet their own needs" (WCED, 1987, p. 43). It emphasised satisfying basic human needs, safeguarding long-term ecological sustainability, and promoting inter-generational and intra-generational equity. It views that development is only sustainable when it takes into consideration both human needs and long-term ecological sustainability. It also covers a spectrum of issues including political, social, economic, and cultural as essential for sustainable development. It has adopted the view that

> sustainable development is a process in which the exploitation of resources, the direction of investments, the orientation of technological development and institutional change are all in harmony, and enhance both current and future potential to meet human needs and aspirations.'
>
> *(WCED, 1987, p. 46)*

Taking cognition of this, the United Nations Declaration on Sustainable Development states that "sustainable development is not a destination, but a dynamic process of adaptation, learning and action. It is about recognising, understanding and acting on interconnections—above all those between the economy, society and the natural environment" (United Nations, 2012). This makes an integrated conception of sustainable development taking into account the interconnection among environmental, social, and economic dimensions and underlines the need to strengthen participation, to safeguard social cohesion, to limit the consumption of environmental resources, and to foster economic competitiveness (Springett, 2015; Sachs, 2015).

Sustainable development offers a vision for a good society. This global vision is built on the consideration of five pillars of sustainable development: people, planet, prosperity, peace, and partnership (United Nations, 2012). It aspires to a world free of hunger and poverty and a world devoid of terrorism, violence and conflicts, epidemics, natural resource depletion, global warming, and climate change issues. It is also about reducing inequality and bringing equity within and among countries. The outcome document adopted by the United Nations Conference on Sustainable Development reiterates that

> We recognise that eradicating poverty in all its forms and dimensions, including extreme poverty is the greatest global challenge and an indispensable requirement for sustainable development. We are committed to achieving sustainable development in its three dimensions—economic, social and environmental—in an integrated manner.
>
> *(United Nations, 2015, p. 6)*

Reaffirming its commitment to achieving sustainable development, the UN has adopted 17 Sustainable Development Goals with 169 target points that will guide all major development decisions until 2030.

## Development challenges

Development challenges are many and diverse. A recent review of Millennium Development Goals (MDG) indicates that although significant achievements have been made on many of the MDG targets worldwide, the poorest and most vulnerable people are left behind (United Nations, 2015). Several regions and countries are still falling behind in achieving the targets. Globally, around 836 million people are suffering from extreme poverty and hunger. More than a billion people worldwide have no access to an improved water source; more than 2.5 billion people do not have access to improved sanitation; one in four children under 5 years old worldwide has stunted growth (ibid.). These challenges are further aggravated by extreme violence and conflicts that cause millions of people to be pushed into extreme poverty and destitution. Besides, big gaps exist between the poorest and the richest households and between the rural and urban areas. Mortality rates for children under 5 years old are almost twice as high for children in the poorest households as for children in the richest. In rural areas, only 56 percent of births are attended by skilled health personnel, compared with 87 percent in urban areas. About 16 percent of the rural population does not have access to improved drinking water sources, compared to 4 percent in urban areas (United Nations, 2015).

Poverty is persistent and being poor is a highly shameful experience, degrading one's dignity and sense of self-worth (World Bank, 2015; Roelen, 2017). A recent study showed that the shame associated with crop losses and financial stress has pushed farmers to suicide in India (Mathew, 2010). In Tanzania, researchers studying bilingual education have found that fear of being mocked can prevent students with weaker English skills from participating in class. And in Uganda, poor high school students say the inability to pay fees, purchase uniforms, or obtain school supplies is a constant source of humiliation (Kyomuhendo, Muhanguzi, & Chase, 2017).

Gender inequality remains another challenge. There is widespread gender discrimination in many societies. This is related to the systematic unfavourable treatment of individuals on the basis of their gender, which denies their rights, opportunities, or resources (World Bank, 2011). This happens at all levels—public and private—and is further compounded by factors such as race, economic, and education status. Gender bias is reflected in measuring women's contribution to development. In many societies women lack control over resources and lack involvement in key decision-making both in the household and community. There is discrimination in pursuing opportunities such as education, employment, and receiving remuneration for their work. Women are paid less compared to men for even comparable jobs. Their role in family and farm are unrecognised and unaccounted for (Duflo, 2012).

The global health threats caused by intense outbreaks of both communicable and non-communicable diseases, including HIV, malaria, TB, dengue, flu, ebola, and other infectious diseases, add to the miseries of the poor. A major challenge in global public health is the threat caused by antimicrobial resistance (AMR). A recent report of the World Health Organisation (WHO) reveals that globally 480,000 people develop multi-drug-resistant TB each year, and drug resistance is starting to complicate the fight against HIV and malaria as well (WHO, 2017).

Global warming and climate change have emerged as one of the toughest public policy problems of the 21st century. Global greenhouse gas emissions continue to rise and are now more than 50 percent higher than the 1990 level (United Nations, 2015). It is imperative that climate change will affect development policies that critically establish carbon emission paths, ability to adapt sustainable adaptation and mitigation options, and to build overall adaptive capacity (Sachs, 2015). There is increasing evidence on the impact of climate change in both urban and rural areas. In urban areas some of the issues related to climate change include heat stress, inland and coastal flooding, air pollution, drought, water scarcity, sea-level rise, and storm surges. In rural areas it affects water availability and supply, food security, infrastructure and agricultural income, and shifts in production areas of food and non-crop products. Hence, limiting the effects of climate change is necessary to achieve sustainable development and equity, including poverty eradication (IPCC, 2015).

## Social entrepreneurship and sustainable development

Social problems are numerous, complex, and multidisciplinary in nature. Addressing the growing social and environmental problems is unavoidable for meeting the goals of sustainable development (Hall et al., 2010; Barrutia & Echebarria, 2012). Sustainability is not the responsibility of any single country, region, or group but a shared responsibility (Barrutia & Echebarria, 2012), which requires co-operation from all the sectors: non-profit, for-profit, and public (Hutt, 2016). In addition, innovation and community action are essential for achieving sustainable development (Seyfang & Smith, 2007).

The traditional and old ways of looking for solutions to the deep-rooted problems of society do not offer sustainable solutions. In this context, entrepreneurship is increasingly being recognised as a tool to foster sustainable development. Entrepreneurs are creating sustainable products/services and processes and new ventures to address many social and environmental concerns (Hall et al., 2010). There is increasing consensus that entrepreneurship and intrapreneurship with a focus on solving social and environmental issues can stimulate the larger industry to be sustainable (Lange & Dodds, 2017). Social entrepreneurs have created and implemented effective, scalable, and sustainable solutions to the most basic of human challenges, and they are making a huge difference for the underserved population around the world (Cuta, 2017). Using creativity, innovation, and developing partnerships and networking, social entrepreneurs are providing sustainable solutions to diverse social and environmental problems worldwide, both in developing as well as developed countries. For this, entrepreneurial efforts are targeted at three different levels: basic social needs of individuals, societies' needs for structures and capacity to build sustainable communities, and the needs of future generations to inherit a minimum of constraints (Seelos & Mair, 2005).

## The concept of social entrepreneurship

Social entrepreneurship mainly focuses on two things: social mission and entrepreneurship. In this way, two cultures, namely, culture of charity and culture of entrepreneurial problem solving, play roles simultaneously in the field of social entrepreneurship (Dees, 2012). However, it does not have a unified definition, because scholars have developed definitions in multiple domains, such as non-profits, for-profits, and the public sector, and also a combination of all three (Short, Moss, & Lumpkin, 2009). It means different things to different people (Dees, 1998). Choi and Majundar (2014) submitted that a uniformly accepted definition of social entrepreneurship is hardly possible, because it is an essentially contested concept (ECC)—a cluster concept, which includes other sub-concepts within it. However, despite multiple views, there is an agreement that social value creation is central to social entrepreneurship (Singh, 2016).

Social entrepreneurs seek answers to social problems by identifying and delivering new services that improve the quality of life of individuals, communities, and society at large (Fields, 2016). Being highly socially oriented, they use their entrepreneurial skills to solve the social problems or meet the unmet needs of the people and achieve their social mission. Both social entrepreneurship literature and practice indicate the importance of social innovation in the process of addressing social and/or environmental problems. Witkamp, Raven, and Royakkers (2011) observe that being socio-technical in nature, the innovative element mainly pertains to its social dimensions in the context of social entrepreneurship. Innovation in social entrepreneurship is aimed at fulfilling a primary social mission to create social value (Weerawardena & Mort, 2006). They are most commonly known as 'change agents' in the social sector (Nicholls, 2006). As change agents, social entrepreneurs harness innovation at a systemic level to bring about a change in social equilibrium (Phills, Deiglmeier, & Miller 2008; Phillips et al., 2015).

Social entrepreneurs create organisations to achieve their social mission and value creation. From the social entrepreneurs' perspective, 'social value creation' is about bringing the desired social change or creating social impact/social outcomes through a resolution of social problems/issues. These include a range of impacts such as increasing awareness, empowering the beneficiaries, creating and providing socio-economic benefits to them, impacting their lives, bringing a change in their perception, attitudes, and behaviour, and finally, changes in norms, which occur at the institutional, individual, community, state, and international levels (Singh, 2016, pp. 109–110).

## Development of social entrepreneurship globally

Social entrepreneurship is not new. Dees (1998) acknowledges that "the language of social entrepreneurship may be new, but the phenomenon is not; we have always had social entrepreneurs, even if we did not call them that" (p. 1). Bornstein and Davis (2010, p. 2) elaborated that,

> Social entrepreneurs have always existed. But in the past they were called visionaries, humanitarians, philanthropists, reformers, saints, or simply great leaders. Attention was paid to their courage, compassion, and vision but rarely to the practical aspects of their accomplishments. Thus, people may know Mahatma Gandhi for demonstrations of nonviolent resistance, but not for building a decentralized political apparatus that enabled India to make a successful transition to self-rule.

The new name is important because it implies a blurring of sector boundaries, ranging from innovative not-for-profit ventures to social purpose business ventures and hybrid organisations mixing not-for-profit and for-profit elements. In this situation, the new language helps to broaden the playing field (Dees, 1998). Although the practice existed for many years, the concepts of 'social entrepreneur' and 'social entrepreneurship' are relatively new and popularised by Ashoka[2] (founded by Bill Drayton) during the 1980s and 1990s (Bornstein & Davis, 2010).

Social entrepreneurship is emerging globally to bridge the increasing gap between demand for social and environmental needs and the supply of resources to meet these needs (Singh, 2016). It is expected to grow further, because non-profit organisations, entrepreneurial firms, governments, and public agencies are recognising its significant contribution towards the development of world-class competitive services (Christie & Honig, 2006). Perhaps the role played by social entrepreneurs in addressing social problems globally is the reason behind its popularity (Singh, 2016). It is attracting the attention of not only practitioners but also academicians (Bielefeld, 2009). However, as an emerging field of academic enquiry, social entrepreneurship research has gained the significant attention of scholars, only since the late 1980s (Short et al., 2009; Dees & Anderson, 2003; Nicholls, 2010).

In the last few decades, there has been a rising interest in social entrepreneurship across Asia, Europe, and the Americas (Huang & Donner, 2018). However, the context of development of social entrepreneurship differs in different countries. There are different historical, socio-economic, and political contexts behind its emergence and development in different countries. Some of these are examined here.

Asia has several factors that are conducive for social business to take off. One of them is the prevalence of a number of social problems, which is beyond the public sector's capacity to fully handle—poverty, unemployment, rural development, environmental degradation, improving the livelihoods of women, and waste management, etc. The gap between public service and demand is especially acute in large developing countries such as India and Indonesia (Kikuchi, 2017). In India, government, private, and voluntary sectors contribute to solve social and environmental problems, but many problems still remain unaddressed (Singh, 2016). Social entrepreneurs have emerged to bridge this gap between demand of increasing needs and diminishing supply of resources. The positive and supportive ecosystem created by the Government of India and also the interest of the corporate sector in promoting entrepreneurship in the country contributed significantly to entrepreneurship development in India (Singh & Majumdar, 2019). These days many highly educated youths are opting for entrepreneurship/social entrepreneurship as their career choices in India. Several social entrepreneurs have already provided sustainable solutions through their innovative approaches.

In Nepal, youths who returned back to their country after completing their higher education or having working experience from Western countries are inspired to see the success of the entrepreneurs of Western countries. Due to this and also lack of employment opportunities in Nepal, they opted for entrepreneurial careers, if not social entrepreneurship in particular.

Bangladesh's story is slightly different from these countries. In Bangladesh, due to widespread poverty and unemployment problems in the country, micro entrepreneurs are emerging. Globalisation has resulted in many entrepreneurial opportunities. For the poor people of Bangladesh, entrepreneurship is their livelihood option (ibid.), and in order to support them, many social business models have emerged there. Kikuchi (2017) also observed this changing trend in the Asian social entrepreneurship space. There are a growing number of social enterprises—companies, in Asia, that measure success not just by the profits they make but also by the good they do in the world. For example, Narayana Hrudayalaya (Founder Dr Devi Shetty) addresses a huge gap in India's health care services, where millions of low-income patients have been underserved, especially when it comes to expensive treatments such as heart operations. Narayana makes a good case for investors looking to pair long-term returns and social impact. There are signs that the 'creating shared value' (CSV) concept is spreading in Asia. The CSV concept, created by Harvard University professor Michael Porter, implies that companies aiming to improve society are more sustainable and profitable in the long term than those focused on creating profits for shareholders. However, it is acknowledged that balancing profitability with social impact—all while expanding business scale—is a challenging task for social enterprises. The networks of global social entrepreneurs are also growing. There are about 800 Fellows in Asia supported by Ashoka, out of 2,962 Fellows globally (ibid.).

In the context of Western countries, both the United States and Europe have experienced simultaneous development of social enterprises since the 1980s (Kerlin, 2006), but the context of its development is different in European countries than in the United States. European welfare states have a long tradition of partnership with third-sector organisations, even if the relationships vary according to the type of welfare mix (Defourny & Nyssens, 2010). Thus, the development of social entrepreneurship and social enterprises can be understood in a context of changing forms of government's support to third-sector organisations to reduce state budget deficits and to address new emerging social needs, especially unemployment. In Western Europe, the economic downturn of the 1970s was the cause of the emergence of the contemporary social enterprise sector (Poon, 2011). The economic downturn led to decreased economic growth and increased unemployment, which placed a major strain on the welfare state system. Soon, Work Integration Social Enterprises (WISE) emerged throughout the region with an employment-creation focus to help the poorly qualified unemployed in society to gain employment. In this context, European social enterprises most often combine income from sales with public subsidies linked to their social mission and private donations and/or volunteering (Defourny & Nyssens, 2010). Government saw social enterprises as partners through which they could address the socio-economic problems brought about by the economic circumstances which their welfare states were unable to effectively address, and thus, the social enterprises received strong supports from governments, which helped to foster their growth and development (Poon, 2011).

In the United Kingdom (UK), the social enterprise sector is seen by government as another important vehicle for delivering public services, and thus, this sector is going through a period of rapid growth (Spear, Cornforth, & Aiken, 2009). This clearly contrasts with a strong US tendency to define social enterprises as non-profit organisations that are more oriented towards the market and developing 'earned income strategies' as a response to decreasing public subsidies and to the limits of private grants from foundations (Defourny & Nyssens, 2010).

Poon (2011) mentioned that the emergence of the social enterprise sector in the US was largely driven by the political withdrawal of the state due to economic conditions, the cultural context characterised by the prominence of business approaches, and also a well-developed ecosystem supported by private foundations and academic institutions. Especially with a lack of political and economic support for non-governmental organisations, social enterprise emerged as an alternative in

America (Huang & Donner, 2018). Similarly, the emergence of the social enterprise sector in Africa was also largely due to withdrawal of the state's funding for related activities. The market-based form of social enterprises emerged in North America and Africa, whereas the hybrid-based form emerged in Europe and Latin America (Poon, 2011).

The role of social entrepreneurship in fostering the socio-economic development of the nations is evolving continuously. It is developing rapidly worldwide without any doubt, but social entrepreneurship policies are yet to be crafted in most countries, though there is a significant increase in the policy development efforts from governments of certain developed countries. In many European and non-European countries, social entrepreneurship has acquired tremendous thrust in policy debates (Satar, 2016). The UK has more than 70,000 registered social enterprises, which contribute £24 billion annually to the UK economy. The sector is well protected and supported by government policy (British Council, 2015).

However, there are little or no concerns for social entrepreneurship policy framework in a majority of developing countries, including India. The social enterprise context in India is diverse and growing in size and capacity (Satar, 2016). The ecosystem in India is relatively well developed, with social enterprises active across all major sectors of the economy without specific government support, but most stakeholders recognise that there is value in identifying bottlenecks which government could help address through policies, strategy documents, dialogue, practical activities, and programmes at the state and local levels. There is currently no formal *social enterprise policy* at the national or state level (British Council, 2015). The Indian social enterprises lack sectorial recognition, and there is no uniform understanding of the concept of social entrepreneurship in India as of yet. There is an absence of a regulatory framework or any formal recognition system for social enterprises in India. The social entrepreneurs are majorly deprived of formal sectorial benefits such as tax breaks or incentives in India.

In recent years, the Government of India is playing a critical role in the development of social entrepreneurship in India. Many policies are shaped up in India. These include the Micro, Small, and Medium Enterprises (MSMEs) Act, 2006, the India Inclusive Innovation Fund (IIIF), and the National Policy for Skill Development and Entrepreneurship, 2015. It is important to note that, "Unlike traditional policies which had an 'enterprise focus', the present policy carries an 'individual focus' to drive motivation, awareness, networking, skills and opportunity with the individuals with the expectation of fostering an entrepreneurship movement within the country" (Satar, 2016). The British Council (2015) has made recommendations in terms of policy engagement and potential government support in India. Some of these are that: government can play a leading role in bringing together key stakeholders to build consensus around a definition of social enterprise; situating responsibility for social enterprise within government is important; there is considerable energy around 'social innovation' and 'social entrepreneurship' in India that can be capitalised upon, etc. Through clear social entrepreneurship policy, governments can certainly encourage growth of this sector in some countries.

## Role of social entrepreneurship in sustainable development: evidence from practice

Several successful initiatives combine social innovations and entrepreneurship for solving social problems. For example, Bangladesh Rural Advancement Committee (BRAC) provides a range of services, such as rural capacity building, education, health services, and micro-credit to over 5 million rural people for breaking the cycle of poverty in Bangladesh. BRAC is working in conditions where formal institutions, governments, or markets have failed to ensure social justice. It aims to address the '3Ps': serving the 'people', benefiting the 'planet', and making 'profit'. In India, innovative models of Narayana Hrudayalaya (founded by Dr Devi Shetty) and Aravind Eye Care (founded by Dr Govindappa Venkataswamy) have been consistently providing accessible and affordable health care services to the masses, irrespective of their capacity to pay. Narayana Hrudayalaya's affordable, no-frills medical service has attracted patients both at home and abroad. Narayana now runs 24 hospitals with more than 7,000 beds in India and the Cayman Islands, and has conducted more than 16,000 cardiac surgeries in the year ended in March 2017 (Kikuchi, 2017).

It is not a case of a well-run and innovative charity or state-backed health company. In fact, Narayana is a public company, backed by investors including JP Morgan, which began investing in the company as early as 2008. After it listed its shares in 2016, Narayana's market capitalisation touched $1 billion, and it posted earnings and revenue growth in its first year as a listed company. Key to this success is a focus on keeping costs low following 'economy of scale'. Narayana uses disposable surgical gowns, offers bare-minimum group rooms for patients, and maximises efficiency on surgical procedures so that Shetty and his colleagues can perform at least one or two heart surgeries per day. The hospitals' high volume of patients allows young doctors to gain experience and hone their skills quickly, making Narayana an attractive career choice for doctors (ibid.).

One of the foci of social entrepreneurship is also green economy/ green energy technologies (www.selco-india.com, 2019). For example, SELCO, a social enterprise based in Bengaluru (India), works on solar energy. It tries to break 'myths' such as that poor people cannot afford sustainable technologies, poor people cannot maintain sustainable technologies, and social ventures cannot be run as commercial entities (www.selco-india.com, 2019). SELCO views energy access as an underlying precondition to catalyze progress related to health, education, livelihoods, financial inclusion, and so on, leading to overall improvement in quality of life. It understands the root of the problem within the context and then assesses how energy can resolve it. Its solutions are designed based on the needs of the poor, and the poor are looked at as partners, innovators, inventors, and enterprise owners in order to develop solutions that are truly inclusive and not designed based on assumptions of what the poor need. SELCO has carefully structured its investment journey to achieve financial sustainability and retain its social mission (ibid.).

Other examples include Shri Mahila Griha Udyog Lijjat Papad, popularly known as 'Lijjat', and the Self-Employed Women's Association (SEWA). Lijjat was founded in 1959 on the Gandhian Sarvodaya ideology of trusteeship, with its core principles of self-reliance, collective ownership, profit sharing, and co-operation (Chaudhary, 2005; Datta & Gailey, 2012). Lijjat is organised as a for-profit worker's cooperative, where ownership is restricted to its working women members, who are addressed as 'Lijjat sisters'. It has provided self-employment opportunities to mostly poor urban women. It has a non-hierarchical organisation structure. Decision making in the organisation is based on consensus. Its sister members are typically unskilled women hailing from poor to lower-middle-class backgrounds. Membership in Lijjat is open to any woman, irrespective of class or caste or religion, who is willing to work in any capacity (Datta & Gailey, 2012).

The core product of Lijjat is papad (or poppadum), a popular savoury snack in India, which is now being exported worldwide. Besides the daily rolling charges, the sister members earn distributed profits. As collective owners, each sister member gets an equal share of profits and losses, regardless of her work, seniority, or responsibility. Lijjat provides a number of welfare measures to its women members such as daily transportation from home in company buses, health check-ups, scholarships for sisters' children, literacy campaigns, computer training for sisters' children, and a savings/borrowings scheme (ibid.). Over five decades, the enterprise has grown rapidly into a large-scale organisation, with its Central Office at Mumbai and its 81 branches in different states of India, and membership of 43,000 sisters throughout India (www.lijjat.com). In 2009, Lijjat's financial turnover was Rs. 5 billion ($111 million) with profits of Rs. 200 million ($4.4 million) (Datta & Gailey, 2012). Datta and Gailey (2012) found that the collective form of entrepreneurship has empowered sister members in three ways: economic security, development of entrepreneurial behaviour, and increased contributions to the family.

SEWA was born as a trade union for poor self-employed women workers in 1972 in Ahmedabad, Gujarat in India. These are women who earn a living through their own labour or small businesses. Gandhian thinking is the guiding force for SEWA's efforts towards organising poor, self-employed members for social change (www.sewa.org). Ms. Ela Bhatt was one of the founders of the organisation and a force behind the movement. As part of its integrated model, SEWA has helped women workers create more cooperatives. It has transformed itself from a trade union organisation to a labour cooperative and women's movement, which has contributed significantly to the economic and social wellbeing of large numbers of women and households (Datta, 2003). It also provides various services such as banking, child care, legal aid, and vocational instruction. SEWA provided women the opportunity to take charge of their economic activities, demand fair wages, and make decisions within the household, and also created leaders. SEWA's model transmits a fundamental but simple message that women have to find suitable strategies for themselves (ibid.). SEWA's initiatives and strategies have paved the road for women's empowerment. Its membership has grown rapidly and reached to

1.3 million in 2006 (www.sewa.org). Both Lijjat and SEWA use models that are innovative and also inclusive' in nature.

Similarly, Dr Medha Samant used (Singh, 2017) 'financial inclusion' as a tool to empower women in the slums of Pune and Mumbai (Maharashtra, India) and founded the Annapurna Mahila Multi-State Cooperative Credit Society in 1986. Because empowerment only through the provision of financial and services is unlikely to lead to wider changes in gender inequality unless programmes strategically combine credit with other vital services (Krenz, Gilbert, & Mandayam, 2014), she started with providing financial services (savings and credit) to these women, and later entered into providing various non-financial services in order to empower them (Singh, 2017). Recent research has also experimented with integrating social entrepreneurship and conflict engagement for regional development in divided societies (Friedman & Desivilya, 2010).

Not only the social entrepreneurs but also professionals from diverse fields and sectors (non-profit, for-profit, and public) are hopeful about the potential of the social entrepreneurial approach in creating sustainable social impact. Hence there is growing interest in social entrepreneurship and the activities of social entrepreneurs in all sectors. Even the corporate sector explores the potential of social entrepreneurship. Performance on all three parameters of the 'Triple Bottom Line'—financial, social, and environmental—has become crucial for corporate sustainability, and thus, the corporate sector is constantly looking for innovative models of integrating Corporate Social Responsibility (CSR) and social entrepreneurship (Singh, Majumdar, & Saini, 2017). A recent study on 32 managers from 15 organisations already witnessed that corporate involvement in social responsibility initiatives improved positioning in the marketplace, which could reflect increased consumer loyalty and also increased motivation of employees (Miragaia, Martins, Kluka, & Havens, 2015). Many corporations are making partnerships with the social enterprises for this purpose.

It is worthwhile to note that the social entrepreneurship approach has not remained restricted to social enterprises now, but corporations are also using the social entrepreneurship approach in their businesses to increase their profit and to solve social and/or environmental problems simultaneously. Hindustan Unilever Limited's (HUL) 'Sustainable Living Plan' and ITC's e-Chaupal initiative are a few excellent examples of corporations using the social entrepreneurship approach. HUL is following a green economy, by reducing emissions and use of energy-efficient technologies in their operations. Besides, HUL is committed to operate and grow its business in a socially responsible way. With the vision to grow the business whilst reducing the environmental impact of operations and increasing its positive social impact, it aims to achieve responsible growth. To achieve this, HUL has embraced the 'Unilever Sustainable Living Plan' (USLP), which is the blueprint for its sustainable growth. This Plan sets out three big goals: 1) improving health and wellbeing, 2) reducing environmental impact, and 3) enhancing livelihoods. This Plan is helping to drive profitable growth for HUL brands, save costs, and fuel innovation (www.hul.co.in, 2019).

Similarly, 'e-Choupal' has been conceived by ITC's Agri Business Division as a more efficient supply chain aimed at delivering value to its customers around the world on a sustainable basis (www.itcportal.com, 2019). The e-Choupal model has been specifically designed to tackle the challenges posed by the unique features of Indian agriculture, characterised by fragmented farms, weak infrastructure, and the involvement of numerous intermediaries. Real-time information and customised knowledge provided by e-Choupal enhance the ability of farmers to make decisions and align their farm output with market demand and secure quality and productivity. While the farmers benefit through enhanced farm productivity and higher farm gate prices, ITC benefits from the lower net cost of procurement (despite offering better prices to the farmer) due to eliminated costs in the supply chain that do not add value. Launched in June 2000, e-Choupal services today reach out to more than 4 million farmers growing a range of crops in over 35,000 villages through 6,100 kiosks across 10 states (Madhya Pradesh, Haryana, Uttarakhand, Uttar Pradesh, Rajasthan, Karnataka, Kerala, Maharashtra, Andhra Pradesh and Tamil Nadu) (ibid.). All of these initiatives contribute to more inclusive and sustainable development.

## Chapters in this volume

This edited volume contains 12 chapters organised into four thematic areas: sustainability of organisation, sustainability of community, sustainability of development, and sustainability of community and organisation interface. The chapters in Part 1 broadly focus on sustainability of organisations. In Chapter 1, Archana Singh examines sustainability in different types of social enterprises. A framework for sustainable development has been presented and nine cases in social entrepreneurship are examined for their contribution to sustainable development. This study illustrates that the poor can also access quality services including health, education, and livelihood supports if they are provided through appropriate models with innovations in the delivery of services. This study also raises several research issues related to sustainability in the context of social entrepreneurship. The theme of Chapter 2 is the journey of a social entrepreneur in transforming an ailing social enterprise into a self-sustainable social venture. In this chapter, Satyajit Majumdar and Bina Ajay explain the decision logic and the process adopted by the social entrepreneur in understanding and tracking opportunities and the logic used to exploit them. Their analysis is anchored on three debates of entrepreneurship theory: 1) opportunity discovery versus creation, 2) inherent versus learned entrepreneurial capabilities, and 3) causal versus effectual decision processes. Through this study they argue that social entrepreneurship is not a single decision of founding a new venture; instead, it is a series of steps taken to evaluate and exploit opportunities—discovered and/or created. Edakkandi Meethal Reji provides an analysis of the sustainability of micro and small enterprises in Chapter 3. The key focus of this study is the strategies, approaches, and the emerging business models of business services for small enterprises. This study highlights the importance of BDS provision and design of appropriate delivery models for addressing a vital missing link in small enterprise development.

The chapters in Part 2 deal with the sustainability of community. Amolina Ray, in Chapter 4, traces the evolution of community radio stations in India and analyses its potential for bringing sustainable development. Amolina explains that community radio is an alternate communication media in rural areas providing opportunities for the people to be their own agents of change—to act individually and collectively using their own ideas, practices, and knowledge and own their means of communication and participate in the decision-making. The findings of this study suggest that by giving 'voice to the voiceless', the community radio enhances the cultural identity and quality of life of the population through improving mental wellbeing, social justice, participation, and freedom of speech. Chapter 5 is about entrepreneurship within an indigenous community. Jackson Khumukcham, Satyajit Majumdar, and Samapti Guha analyse the role of indigenous entrepreneurship in the Loi community in the Andro village of Santhei Natural Park in Manipur. Based on an ethnography of the Loi community, this chapter concludes that with a focus on preserving the traditions and immersed in the social and cultural context, the indigenous entrepreneurship practiced by the community contributes to sustainable development while preserving the natural environment. In Chapter 6, Anu Sharma, Simmi Bhagat, and Mona Suri present an analysis of the Napasar cluster of Rajasthan (India)—a hub of weavers and spinners community to identify the prospects for attaining sustainable livelihood for this cluster. Based on the case study, the authors highlighted the drawbacks and strengths of the Napasar handloom cluster, and also envisaged the importance of revival of old traditions in Napasar to protect them from being lost forever.

Part 3 focuses on sustainability of development. Chandralekha Ghosh and Samapti Guha analyse the role of community-based microfinance institutions in creating sustainable livelihoods for people in the slums of Mumbai, India (Chapter 7). The theme of Chapter 8 is social entrepreneurship and community well-being. Based on three case studies of social entrepreneurship, Samapti Guha submits that the social entrepreneurship approach has helped in addressing local issues of wellbeing of the communities they serve. Dewan Muktadir-Al-Mukit and M. Ashraf Hossain (Chapter 9) discuss 'green banking', a new concept of conducting the banking business, which requires the banks to consider environmental and ecological factors in their operations. In particular, they present the status of green financing activities in different types of banks operating in Bangladesh, and also explore their effectiveness.

Part 4 deals with sustainability of the community and organisation interface. In Chapter 10, Archana Singh, Gladwin Issac, and Shrinivas Sinha analyse the innovative model of 'SAATH', a social enterprise engaged in promoting a sustainable livelihood for the urban poor in the Gujarat state of India. This study also explains the challenges in the sustainability and scalability of the social enterprise and also strategies for creating inclusive societies. Chapter 11 explains the role of serial social entrepreneurship in sustainable development. Based on the case study of 'Annapurna Pariwar', Samapti Guha, Medha Purao Samant, and Edakkandi Meethal Reji tell us that serial social entrepreneurship can address some of the most pressing development challenges at the grassroots and make development more inclusive and sustainable. The final chapter is by Archana Singh, in which she analyses the interface between corporate social responsibility (CSR) and social entrepreneurship (SE) in social value creation. She presents a conceptual framework for social value creation by integrating CSR and SE and also discusses various ways of combining CSR and SE which could inspire future direction of research is social entrepreneurship and sustainable development.

## Notes

1 Social entrepreneurs are reformers and revolutionaries with a social mission. They make fundamental changes in the way things are seen and done in the social space (Dees, 1998). Social entrepreneurs make social change with innovative solutions for the societal problems they come across.
2 A group that identifies and invests in social entrepreneurs.

## References


Adams, W. M. (1990). *Green development: Environment and sustainability in the Third World*. London: Routledge.

Anand, S., & Sen, A. (2000). Human development and economic sustainability. *World Development, 28*(12), 2029–2049.

Attfield, R. (Ed.). (2008). *The ethics of the environment* (620p.). Farnham and Burlington, VT: Ashgate. ISBN:9780754627869.

Barbier, E. (1987). The concept of sustainable economic development. *Environmental Conservation, 14*(2), 101–110.

Barbier, E. (1989). *Economics, natural resource scarcity and development*. London: Earthscan.

Barbier, E. B., Markandya, A., & Pearce, D. W. (1990). Environmental sustainability and cost-benefit analysis. *Environment and Planning A, 22*(9), 1259–1266.

Barrutia, J. M., & Echebarria, C. (2012). Greening regions: The effect of social entrepreneurship, co-decision and co-creation on the embrace of good sustainable development practices. *Journal of Environmental Planning and Management, 55*(10), 1348–1368.

Bielefeld, W. (2009). Issues in social enterprise and social entrepreneurship. *Journal of Public Affairs Education, 15*(1), 69–86.

Bornstein, D. (2007). *How to change the world: Social entrepreneurs and the power of new ideas*. New York: Oxford University Press.

Bornstein, D., & Davis, S. (2010). *Social entrepreneurship: What everyone need to know?* New York: Oxford University Press.

British Council. (2015). *Social enterprise: An overview of the policy framework in India*. Retrieved July 31, 2019 from www.britishcouncil.in/sites/default/files/social_enterprise_policy_landscape_in_india_0.pdf

Brugmann, J., & Prahalad, C. (2007). Cocreating business's new social compact. *Harvard Business Review, 85*(2), 80–90.

Chaudhary, R. (2005). Lijjat and women's empowerment: Beyond the obvious. *Economic and Political Weekly, 40*(6), 579–583.

Choi, N., & Majundar, S. (2014). Social entrepreneurship as an essentially contested concept: Opening a new avenue for systematic future research. *Journal of Business Venturing, 29*(3), 363–376.

Christie, M. J., & Honig, B. (2006). Social entrepreneurship: New research findings. *Journal of World Business*, *41*, 1–5.

Cohen, B., & Winn, M. I. (2007). Market imperfections, opportunity and sustainable entrepreneurship. *Journal of Business Venturing*, *22*(1), 29–49.

Cuta, N. (2017). Book review. Teresa Chahine: *Introduction to social entrepreneurship*, CRC Press, Boca Raton, FL, 2016, Textbook—292 pp. *Voluntas*, *28*, 2807–2808. https://doi.org/10.1007/s11266-017-9834-4

Daly Herman, E. (1991). Operationalising sustainable development by investing in natural capital. In A.M. Jansson, M. Hammer, C. Folke, & R. Costanza (Eds.), *Investing in natural capital: The ecological economics approach to sustainability* (pp. 22–37). Washington, DC: Island Press.

Datta, P. B., & Gailey, R. (2012, May). Empowering women through social entrepreneurship: Case study of a women's co-operative in India. *Entrepreneurship: Theory and Practice*, 569–587. https://doi.org/10.1111/j.1540-6520.2012.00505.x

Datta, R. (2003). From development to empowerment: The self-employed women's association in India. *International Journal of Politics, Culture and Society*, *16*(3), 351–368.

Dean, T. J., & McMullen, J. (2007). Toward a theory of sustainable entrepreneurship: Reducing environmental degradation through entrepreneurial action. *Journal of Business Venturing*, *22*(1), 50–76.

Dees, J. G. (1998). *The meaning of social entrepreneurship*. Retrieved July 30, 2019 from https://docs.google.com/viewerng/viewer?url=https://community-wealth.org/sites/clone.community-wealth.org/files/downloads/paper-dees.pdf

Dees, J. G. (2012). A tale of two cultures: Charity, problem solving, and the future of social entrepreneurship. *Journal of Business Ethics*, *111*, 321–334. https://doi.org/10.1007/s10551-012-1412-5

Dees, J. G., & Anderson, B. B. (2003). For-profit social ventures. *International Journal of Entrepreneurship Education*, Special Issue on Social Entrepreneurship, *2*, 1–26.

Defourny, J., & Nyssens, M. (2010). Social enterprise in Europe: At the crossroads of market, public policies and third sector. *Policy and Society*, *29*, 231–242. https://doi.org/10.1016/j.polsoc.2010.07.002

Duflo, E. (2012). Women empowerment and economic development. *Journal of Economic Literature*, *50*(4), 1051–1079.

Elkington, J. (1997). *Canibals with forks: The triple bottom line of 21st century business*. Oxford: Capstone.

Fields, Z. (2016). *Using creativity and social innovation to create social value and change*. Retrieved January 1, 2018 from Using_Creativity_and_Social_Innovation_to_Create_Social_Value_and_Change/links/5673bafa08ae04d9b09bd910.pdf

Friedman, V. J., & Desivilya, H. (2010). Integrating social entrepreneurship and conflict engagement for regional development in divided societies. *Entrepreneurship & Regional Development*, *22*(6), 495–514.

Hall, J. K., Daneke, G. A., & Lenox, M. J. (2010). Sustainable development and entrepreneurship: Past contributions and future directions. *Journal of Business Venturing*, *25*, 439–448. https://doi.org/10.1016/j.jbusvent.2010.01.002

Haque, S. M. (2000). Environmental discourse and sustainable development. *Ethics and the Environment*, *5*(1), 3–21.

Hart, S., & Christensen, C. (2002). The great leap: Driving innovation from the base of the pyramid. *MIT Sloan Management Review*, *44*(1), 51–56.

Holden, E., Linnerud, K., & Banister, D. (2014). Sustainable development: Our common future revisited. *Global Environmental Change*, *26*, 130–139.

Huang, C.-C., & Donner, B. (2018). *The development of social enterprise: Evidence from Europe, North America, and Asia*. Retrieved July 17, 2019 from https://socialwork.rutgers.edu/sites/default/files/report_40.pdf.

Hutt, R. (2016). *What are the 10 biggest global challenges*? Retrieved January 5, 2018 from www.weforum.org/agenda/2016/01/what-are-the-10-biggest-global-challenges/

Intergovernmental Panel on Climate Change (IPCC) (2015). *Climate change 2014: Impacts, adaptation, and vulnerability*. Retrieved September 10, 2017 from www.ipcc.ch/report/ar5/wg2/

Jabareen, Y. (2006). A new conceptual framework for sustainable development. *Environment, Development and Sustainability, 10*, 179–192. https://doi.org/10.1007/s10668-006-9058-z. ISSN:1387–585X, 1573–2975.

Kerlin, J. A. (2006). Social enterprise in the United States and Europe: Understanding and learning from the differences. *International Journal of Voluntary and Nonprofit Organizations, 17*(3), 247–263.

Kikuchi, T. (2017). *'Social enterprises' rise in Asia amid scepticism: New breed of company aims to help the world—and make money*. Retrieved July 30, 2019 from https://asia.nikkei.com/Spotlight/Cover-Story/Social-enterprises-rise-in-Asia-amid-skepticism2

Krenz, K., Gilbert, D. J., & Mandayam, G. (2014). Exploring women's empowerment through "credit plus" microfinance in India. *Affilia, 29*(3), 310–325.

Kyomuhendo, G. B., Muhanguzi, F. K., & Chase, E. (2017). Children's experiences of poverty-related shame: Implications for anti-poverty policies. Paper presented at the Putting Children First Conference, 23–25 October 2017, Addis Ababa. Retrieved April 15, 2020 from https://www.theimpactinitiative.net/sites/default/files/Session%201.6.B%20Elaine%20Chase,%20Grace%20Bantebya%20&%20Florence%20Muhanguzi%20-%20Shame-proofing%20anti-poverty%20programmes%20%5b23-Oct-17%5d_0.pdf

Lange, D. D., & Dodds, R. (2017). Increasing sustainable tourism through social entrepreneurship. *International Journal of Contemporary Hospitality Management, 29*(7), 1977–2002. https://doi.org/10.1108/IJCHM-02-2016-0096

Lele, S. M. (1991). Sustainable development: A critical review. *World Development, 19*(6), 607–621.

Mathew, L. (2010). Coping with shame and poverty: Analysis of farmer's distress. *Psychology and Developing Societies, 22*(2), 385–407.

Meadows, D. H., Meadows, D. L., Randers, J., & Beherens, F. (1972). *The limits to growth*. London: Pan.

Miragaia, D. A. M., Martins, C. I. N., Kluka, D. A., & Havens, A. (2015). Corporate social responsibility, social entrepreneurship and sport programs to develop social capital at community level. *International Review on Public Nonprofit Marketing, 12*, 141–154. https://doi.org/10.1007/s12208-015-0131-x

Mulgan, G., Tucker, S., Ali, R., & Sanders, B. (2007). *Social innovation: What it is, why it matters and how it can be accelerated*. Working Paper, Skoll Centre for Social Entrepreneurship.

Munda, G. (1997). Environmental economics, ecological economics, and the concept of sustainable development. *Environmental Values, 6*(2), 213–233.

Munn, R. E. (1988). *Towards sustainable development: An environmental perspective*. Paper presented at the International Conference on Environment and Development, 24–26 March, Milan, Italy.

Neumayer, E. (2010). *Weak versus strong sustainability: Exploring the limits of two opposing paradigms* (272p.). Cheltenham and Northampton, MA: Edward Elgar. ISBN:9781848448728.

Nicholls, A. (2006). Introduction. In A. Nicholls (Ed.), *Social entrepreneurship: New models of sustainable change* (pp. 1–35). New York: Oxford University Press.

Nicholls, A. (2010). The legitimacy of social entrepreneurship: Reflexive isomorphism in a pre-paradigmatic field. *Entrepreneurship Theory and Practice*, *34*(4), 611–633.
Norgaard, R. (1988). Sustainable development: A co-evolutionary view. *Futures*, *20*(6), 606–620.
O'Riordan, T. (1985). Future directions in environmental policy. *Journal of Environment and Planning*, *17*, 1431–1446.
Phillips, W., Lee, H., Ghobadian, A., O'Regan, N., & James, P. (2015). Social innovation and social entrepreneurship: A systematic review. *Group & Organisation Management*, *40*(3), 428–461. https://doi.org/10.1177/1059601114560063
Phills, J. A., Deiglmeier, K., & Miller, D. T. (2008). Rediscovering social innovation. *Stanford Social Innovation Review*, *6*(4), 34–43.
Poon, D. (2011). *The emergence and development of social enterprise sectors*. Social Impact Research Experience (SIRE). Retrieved July 17, 2019 from http://repository.upenn.edu/sire/8
Prahalad, C. K. (2004). *The fortune at the bottom of the pyramid: Eradicating poverty through profits*. Philadelphia, PA: Wharton School Publishing.
Redclift, M. (1991). The multiple dimensions of sustainable development. *Geography*, *76*(1), 36–42.
Redclift, M. (2005). Sustainable development (1987–2005): An oxymoron comes of age. *Sustainable Development*, *13*, 212–227.
Roelen, K. (2017). *Shame, poverty and social protection*. IDS Working Paper-489, Institute of Development Studies, Brighton, UK.
Sachs, J. D. (2015). *The age of sustainable development*. New York: Columbia University Press.
Satar, M. S. (2016). A policy framework for soacil entrepreneurship in India. *IOSR Journal of Business and Management*, *18*(9), 30–43.
Seelos, C., & Mair, J. (2005). *Sustainable development: How social entrepreneurs make it happen*. Working Paper No. 611, IESE Business School, University of Navarra, Spain.
Sen, A. (2000). *Development as freedom*. New York: Oxford University Press.
Seyfang, G., & Smith, A. (2007). Grassroots innovations for sustainable development: Towards a new research and policy agenda. *Environmental Politics*, *16*(4), 584–603.
Short, J. C., Moss, T. W., & Lumpkin, G. T. (2009). Research in social entrepreneurship: Past contributions and future Opportunities. *Strategic Entrepreneurship Journal*, *3*, 161–194.
Singh, A. (2016). *The process of social value creation: A multiple case study on social entrepreneurship in India*. New Delhi: Springer.
Singh, A. (2017). Social entrepreneurship as a tool for women empowerment though financial inclusion: The role of values in ethical decision making. In L. Karczewski & H. A. Kretek (Eds.), *Cultural, social, legal and ethical aspects of management and economics* (pp. 249–267). Raciborz: PWSZ w Raciborzu.
Singh, A., & Majumdar, S. (2019). Entrepreneurship: Nation as a context. In S. Majumdar & E. M. Reji (Eds.), *Methodological issues in social entrepreneurship knowledge and practice*. Singapore: Springer.
Singh, A., Majumdar, S., & Saini, G. K. (2017). Corporate social responsibility and social entrepreneurship: An Indian context. *Journal of Entrepreneurship and Innovation in Emerging Economies*, *3*(1), 71–76.
Solow, R. M. (1991). *Sustainability: An economist's perspective*. Paper presented at the Eighteenth J. Seward Johnson Lecture to the Marine Policy Centre, June 14, Woods Hole Oceanographic Institution at the Woods Hole, MA.
Solow, R. M. (1993). An almost practical step toward sustainability. *Resources Policy*, *19*(3), 162–172.
Spaargaren, G., & Mol, A. P. J. (1992). Sociology, environment, and modernity: Ecological modernisation as theory of social change. *Society and Natural Resources*, *5*, 323–344.

Spear, R., Cornforth, C., & Aiken, M. (2009). The governance challenges of social enterprises: Evidence from a UK empirical study. *Annals of Public and Cooperative Economics, 80*(2), 247–273.

Springett, D. (2015). Editorial: Critical perspectives on sustainable development. *Sustainable Development, 21*, 73–82.

United Nations. (2012). *The future we want: Resolution adopted by the General Assembly on 27 July 2012*. Retrieved September 12, 2016 from www.un.org/ga/search/view_doc.asp?symbol=A/RES/66/288&Lang=E

United Nations. (2015). *Transforming our world: The 2030 agenda for sustainable development*. Retrieved January 10, 2017 from https://sustainabledevelopment.un.org/content/documents/21252030%20Agenda%20for%20Sustainable%20Development%20web.pdf

United Nations Development Programme (UNDP). (2011). *Human development report 2011, sustainability and equity: A better future for all*. New York: United Nations Development Programme.

Weerawardena, J., & Mort, G. S. (2006). Investigating social entrepreneurship: A multidimensional model. *Journal of World Business, 41*(1), 21–35.

WHO. (2017). Retrieved December 15, 2017 from www.sho.int/mediacentre/factsheets/fs194/en/

Witkamp, M. J., Raven, R. P. J. M., & Royakkers, L. M. M. (2011). Strategic niche management of social innovations: The case of social entrepreneurship. *Technology Analysis & Strategic Management, 23*(6), 667–681. https://doi.org/10.1080/09537325.2011.585

World Bank. (2011). *World development report 2012: Gender equality and development*. Washington, DC: World Bank.

World Bank. (2015). *World development report 2015: Mind, society and behaviour*. Washington, DC: World Bank.

World Commission on Environment and Development. (1987). *Our common future*. London: Oxford University Press.

## Websites

www.hul.co.in/sustainable-living/india-sustainability-initiatives/. Retrieved August 1, 2019.
www.itcportal.com/businesses/agri-business/e-choupal.aspx. Retrieved August 1, 2019.
www.lijjat.com. Retrieved January 24, 2018.
www.selco-india.com/who-we-are. Retrieved August 1, 2019.
www.sewa.org. Retrieved January 24, 2018.

# PART 1
# Sustainability of organisation

The chapters in this section focus on the sustainability of organisations. Sustainability in an organisational context implies the initiatives for enhancing the societal, environmental, and economic systems within which a business operates. It also denotes 'actions of organising something sustainably'. In this process organisations need to be sustainable. Organisations are increasingly focusing on developing a 'culture of sustainability' by recognising the importance of environmental, social, and financial performance (Triple Bottom Line). Sustainability organisations adopt environmentally friendly or green practices and ensure that all the process and products adequately address environmental concerns and still remain profitable. In this sense, their business activities adhere to the most acceptable definitions of sustainable development—a business that meets the needs of the present world without compromising the ability of the future generations to meet their own needs. An increasing number of organisations and networks are integrating sustainability into their central goals and contributing to environmentally and socially responsible business. Sustainability organisations are not limited to implementing sustainability strategies which provide environmental and economic benefits. For them, sustainability is an end in itself. Sustainability strategies allow them to generate long-term growth and profitability along with preservation and enhancement of financial, environmental, and social capital.

# 1

# SOCIAL ENTREPRENEURSHIP AND SUSTAINABLE DEVELOPMENT

## Emerging research issues

*Archana Singh*

### Introduction

The concept of sustainable development (SD) has received multidisciplinary attention since it appeared in the 1987 United Nations Brundtland Report (Shao, Li, & Tang, 2011). SD has been defined in many ways. One of the most commonly used definitions of SD is that "sustainable development is development that meets the needs of the present without compromising the ability of future generations to meet their own needs" (WCED, 1987, p. 41). In general, SD encompasses three interrelated fundamental approaches—economic, environmental, and social development—which are complementary (Shao et al., 2011). Hence, SD can be conceived of in terms of increases in the quality of life which are equitable (Qizilbash, 2001). Unfortunately, that did not happen in many of the poorest countries across the globe (Pritchett, 1997; Gottschalk & Smeeding, 1997 mentioned in Seelos & Mair, 2005b) or even in developed countries like the USA, UK, and Australia (Diesendorf, 1999). Despite impressive economic growth since the 1990s, inclusive growth has not been achieved in developing countries (UN, 2017). It is clear that sustainable development, involving improvements to the natural environment and in the social and economic domains, is needed in the 'rich' countries as well as in the poor (Diesendorf, 1999). However, a lot of studies (Pandey, Mukherjee, & Kumar, 2009; Dale & Sparkes, 2011; Ashoka, n.d.) witnessed the contribution of social entrepreneurs towards achieving the goal of sustainable development, especially in the poor-country context (Seelos & Mair, 2005a). They contribute to sustainable development by creating innovative organisations and new models for the provision of products and services that cater directly to the social needs underlying sustainable development goals (ibid.). Social entrepreneurship has the potential to address social problems, reduce inequality and poverty, and also tackle environmental challenges (UN, 2017).

The scholars see social enterprise (SE) as an enterprise with a purpose that helps a large number of people in a positive way, and while doing so, it may or may not earn surpluses (Sriram, 2011). For the purpose of this chapter, the organisation created by a social entrepreneur to create social change and social impact is termed as 'social enterprise'. However, it is important to emphasise here that unlike traditional entrepreneurs, the motivation of social entrepreneurs is not the creation of an organisation, but the creation of a path defined so that participants can alleviate a complex social problem (Dorado, 2006). So, they may or may not create an organisation, because creating social change is the most important goal for them. From the perspective of the value creation model in social entrepreneurship, social activism is also a form of social entrepreneurship. Martin and Osberg (2007) mentioned, "social activists may or may not create ventures or organisations to advance the changes they seek" (p. 38).

Social entrepreneurs follow an entrepreneurial approach or activities to meet social goals (Nicholls, 2006), and for sustainable entrepreneurship towards meeting societal goals and changing market contexts, sustainability innovation is emphasised (Schaltegger & Wagner, 2010). 'Sustainable entrepreneurship' focuses on the preservation of nature, life support, and community in the pursuit of perceived opportunities to bring into existence future products, processes, and services for gain, where gain is broadly construed to include economic and non-economic gains to individuals, the economy, and society (ibid.). Haldar (2019) studied how social enterprises generated innovations aimed at sustainability. In this context, sustainability of the social enterprises or the process of creating social value and bringing about social change (i.e. social entrepreneurship) becomes significant to attain its social and environmental goals in order to contribute towards sustainable development. How can one achieve the goal of sustainable development through social entrepreneurship without having sustainability in their approach? Thus, 'sustainability' becomes an essential part of the practical process of working towards sustainable development. Foster, Kim, and Christiansen (2009) also mentioned that most of the time, even donors want to partner with and invest in sustainable projects rather than simply give money to the needy organisations.

Thus, recognising the importance of 'sustainability' of social enterprises for them to play a role in sustainable development, and also due to my awareness that social entrepreneurship can emerge across all the sectors—non-profits (including charitable), public, for-profit, and cross-sector partnerships (Nicholls, 2006)—with the condition of its primary focus on social mission, the concept of 'sustainability' in the context of social enterprises or social entrepreneurship caught my attention. When, I looked at the definition of SD mentioned in the Brundtland Report for clarity on 'sustainability', I found that it gives little interpretation of the concept of 'sustainability' in the context of the process of achieving sustainable development goals. Diesendorf (1999) clearly mentioned that this definition only emphasises the long-term aspect of the concept of sustainability and introduces the ethical principle of achieving equity between the present and future generations. Although, other SD literature discussed sustainability by focusing on what is to be sustained, namely, nature, life support systems, and community, and what is to be developed, namely, individuals, the economy, and society (Shepherd & Patzelt, 2011), but that too does not give any clear interpretation of sustainability in the context of efforts of social enterprises to attain the goal of sustainable development.

Sustainability is about an organisation's capacity to endure over time (Burkett, n.d., p. 1). In the context of social enterprises, sustainability has two sides: first, an enterprise needs to be able to survive and endure financially over time, and second, it needs to maintain or deepen its impact over time. Impact and financial sustainability cannot be separated in social enterprises (Burkett, n.d.). Moddie (n.d.) further clarified the concept of 'sustainability' in the context of social entrepreneurship and social enterprises. She mentioned four critical elements for sustainability in the change-making process: a) benefit sustainability (activities continue to be felt by beneficiaries), b) organisational sustainability (enabling environment inside the project), c) financial sustainability, and d) community sustainability (capacity to sustain itself).

Using this conceptual understanding, this chapter explores sustainability in different types of social enterprises supporting sustainable development goals. Despite my belief in the social value creation model of social entrepreneurship, not in the enterprise model, I have purposely restricted the discussion of sustainability to enterprise models only for better clarity and understanding. The multiple case studies provided context to discuss this issue. This chapter aims to bring to the forefront emerging research issues in this context. I suggest several research issues related to sustainability in the efforts of social entrepreneurs to attain the goal of sustainable development, which emerged from the grounded data of multiple case studies of social entrepreneurship. I believe it will help future scholars to explore sustainability in-depth in the context of social entrepreneurship to contribute towards sustainable development in the real sense.

## Theoretical underpinning

This chapter is guided by the theoretical framework of social entrepreneurship and sustainable development (Seelos & Mair, 2004, 2005b): "Social entrepreneurs find new and efficient ways to create products and services that directly cater to social needs that remain unsatisfied by current economic and social institutions" (Seelos & Mair, 2004, p. 4). Observing the positive social impact of entrepreneurs catering to basic needs, the framework recognised their unique role in efficiently contributing to the achievement of sustainable development goals (refer to Figure 1.1). To contribute to sustainable development is defined as the purpose of social entrepreneurship. The notion of SD is divided into three distinct sets of activities, aimed at: 1) satisfying basic human needs; 2) creating communities that establish norms, rights, and collaborative behaviour as a prerequisite for participating in social and economic development; and 3) translating the more abstract needs of future generations into action today (Seelos & Mair, 2005b). In other words, entrepreneurial efforts are targeted at three different levels—basic social needs of

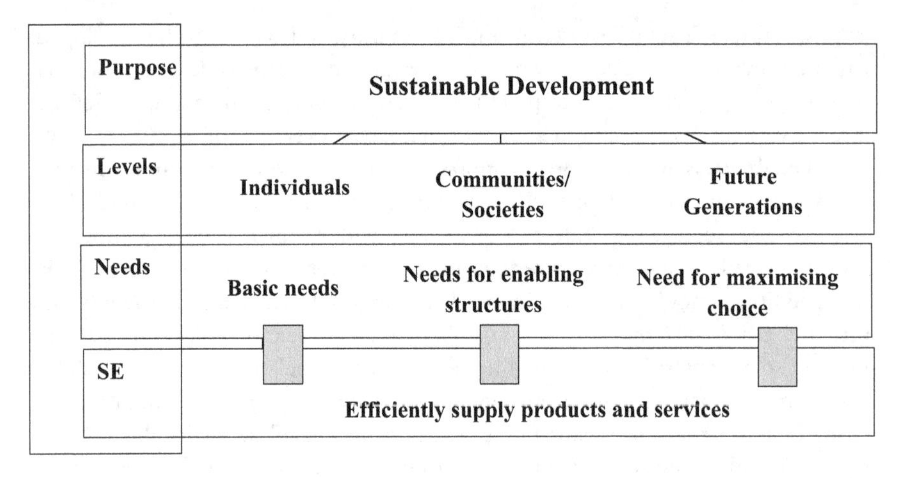


**FIGURE 1.1** Model of the contribution of social entrepreneurship (SE) to sustainable development (SD)

*Source*: Seelos and Mair (2005b)

individuals, large communities' or whole societies' needs for structures and capacity to build sustainable communities, and the need for future generations to inherit a minimum of constraints (e.g. polluted environment that demands high levels of investment for clean-up), so as to maximise the choices they have to fulfil their own needs and desires (Seelos & Mair, 2004). Social entrepreneurs contributed to sustainable development by creating innovative organisations and service provision models and by catering to various levels of needs—the basic needs of the individuals, the institutional needs of the communities, and the needs of the future generations. They created social and economic development in a poor-country context (Seelos and Mair, 2005b). Thus, they suggested that development processes need to consider the link between social and economic development.

## Methodology

Social entrepreneurship (SE) is a context-based phenomenon: "The case-study is a method of choice, when the phenomenon under study is not readily distinguished from its context" (Yin, 1993, p. 3). Social entrepreneurial ventures can emerge in a variety of structures—non-profit, the public sector, for-profit sector, and a combination of these three sectors (Christie & Honig, 2006). Thus, in order to identify the research issues in all types of social entrepreneurial ventures, a 'multiple-case study' approach (Yin, 2003) was used in the study, and social entrepreneur was the unit of analysis. Due to strong linkages of three sectors—health, education, and livelihood in fighting poverty—nine social entrepreneurs as cases were selected. Only Ashoka[1] Fellows were selected, as Ashoka has pioneered the term 'social entrepreneurship' during the 1980s, and till the mid to late 1990s that several other organisations adopted a similar terminology (Grenier, 2006). They select only those social entrepreneurs as Ashoka Fellows who have created great social impact with their efforts. As the purpose was to explore sustainability in different types of social enterprises engaged in achieving the goal of sustainable development, samples were selected from three types of organisations: 1) charitable; 2) self-sustainable organisations of the not-for-profit sector or sustainable with mixed income, i.e. donation and generated income; and 3) 'for-profit' social enterprises. Thus, a theoretical sampling was used for sample selection. Filtering all of the boundaries, the final list of selected samples is given in Table 1.1.

The primary data were collected through interviews and observation. Interviews were conducted with the principal founders to understand efforts made by their social enterprises to achieve the goal of sustainable development. If founders were busy and not able to give sufficient time for interviews, management personnel were also interviewed to supplement the interviews of founders. Data were collected for six months (from 1 January 2012 to 7 July 2012).

All of the interviews were tape recorded and transcribed. The transcribed data were coded and analysed to develop subthemes and themes. These data were supplemented with secondary data from secondary sources of data collection such as annual reports, their websites, brochures, etc. in the final level of analysis.

These multiple cases provided a context for discussing 'sustainability' in a social entrepreneur's efforts to achieve the goal of sustainable development. Based on the findings of the study, I pose a series of research issues that emerged from the grounded data for future studies in social entrepreneurship contributing to sustainable development. It involves both rethinking and re-evaluation of existing social entrepreneurship practices for sustainable development, and reformulation of models to confront and overcome the difficulties faced by some of the existing categories of social enterprises. In other words, the emerging research issues I pose are aimed at moving us toward a more sustainable approach of social entrepreneurship for achieving the goal of sustainable development.

## Emerging research issue 1: *is the approach of charitable social enterprises really sustainable in the long run for achieving the goal of sustainable development?*

It is argued that charitable organisations also are included in the realm of social entrepreneurship, if they are engaged in entrepreneurial activities to solve social problems, address social needs, and create social value. Ashoka Innovators for the Public is the global association of the world's leading social entrepreneurs—men and women with system-changing solutions that address the world's most urgent social challenges (opportunity identification, resourcefulness, innovation) for social value creation and bringing social change to attain the goal of sustainable development.

However, the question arises: 'Is their approach really sustainable in the long run for achieving the goal of sustainable development?' The study showed that although all the founders of charitable social enterprises (Dr Armida Fernandez,

**TABLE 1.1** Selected sample cases for the study

| Sector | Non-profit social enterprises depended on external funding such as charity, donations, and also grants and subsidies from the government | Sustainable non-profit social enterprises with combined income of charity, grant, and own generated income; not-for-profit self-sustainable social enterprise, or hybrid social enterprise | For-profit social enterprises (social enterprises registered as private limited companies, but their primary mission is solving a social problem, creating social value, and bringing social change) |
|---|---|---|---|
| Health | SNEHA: Society for Nutrition, Education and Health Action, Mumbai (Dr. Armida Fernandez, Founder) | Narayana Hrudyalaya Pvt. Ltd., Bengaluru (Dr. Devi Shetty, Founder) | Vaatsalya Healthcare Solutions Pvt. Ltd, Bengaluru (Dr. Ashwin Naik, Founder) |
| | SNEHA's initiatives target both care seekers and care providers in order to improve urban health standards. On the one hand, SNEHA worked at the community level to empower women and slum communities to be catalysts of change in their own right. On the other hand, SNEHA collaborated with existing public systems and care providers to create sustainable improvements in urban health. The head office of SNEHA is located in Dharavi, Mumbai (Maharashtra). | In order to achieve his aim of providing affordable and accessible health care delivery for the masses worldwide, Dr Shetty is following a hybrid model and relying on economies of scale. He has three types of packages for the patients: general, charitable, and patients insured under govt's micro health insurance programmes. However, the quality of services was the same across all types of patients in all the network hospitals of NH. The headquarter of Narayana Hrudayalaya Hospitals is in Bengaluru. | Started in 2005 as India's first hospital network focused on tier-two and tier-three towns, Vaatsalya has grown to a total of 17 hospitals across Karnataka and Andhra Pradesh. Their four main focus areas are gynaecology, paediatrics, general surgery, and general medicine. Apart from these, they also provide nephrology/dialysis in some of the hospitals, wherever required. |
| Education | Akanksha Foundation, Mumbai (Ms. Shaheen Mistri, Founder) | Kathalaya, Bengaluru (Ms. Geeta Ramanujam, Founder) | BookBox Pvt. Ltd., Pondicherry (Dr. Brij Kothari, Founder) |
| | The Akanksha Foundation is working with a mission to maximise the potential of every child and transform their lives. Its vision is to provide the highest quality of education to every child in the country. They were doing it largely by running 'after-school centres' and 'schools' directly for children of low-income | Kathalaya Trust uses storytelling as an educational and communicative tool to affect change in society. They introduced stories related to the curriculum in the classroom with the aim of enriching the curriculum. Weekly storytelling sessions are held for children in primary classes (class one to five) in schools, along with other | In 2004, after winning a one-year fellowship at a business plan competition at Stanford University, Dr Brij Kothari, along with his team members, founded BookBox Inc., a for-profit social enterprise in Pondicherry. The mission of the BookBox is to create content or produce animated stories to help improve reading skills and |

| | | | |
|---|---|---|---|
| | families in Mumbai and Pune (Maharashtra). Initially, Akanksha started after-school centres for its students, with a focus on English, Mathematics, Values, and Extra-curricular Activities, and then changed its model to running schools in partnership with the government. It has 47 centres and nine schools between Mumbai and Pune and reached out to over 4,000 children through these two models. | activities mentioned in the curriculum. The schools are from both categories: private and government-aided rural schools in the outskirts of Bengaluru (Karnataka). They teach mainly two subjects through storytelling, namely, EVS and languages. Kathalaya also conducts short-term and long-term certificate courses in storytelling and is affiliated with the International Institute of Storytelling, Tennessee, USA. | language learning, ultimately promoting a love for reading. This scientifically tested and proven innovative approach of same language subtitling (SLS) is at the heart of BookBox's strategy. BookBox aims to provide access to reading content or a 'book' for every child in his/her own language, and through 'edutainment', a mix of education and entertainment. |
| Livelihood | SAATH, Ahmedabad (Mr. Rajendra Joshi, Founder) | SammaaN Foundation, Patna (Mr. Irfan Alam, Founder) | KnidsGreen Pvt. Ltd., Patna (Mr. Kaushalenrda Kumar, Founder) |
| | Since the poor often have many needs at once, SAATH created one-stop centres, through which slum residents and those in vulnerable situations had access to services such as health, education, and affordable housing, micro-finance and livelihood options. Communities co-invested with SAATH and the donors, by paying for, deciding, and implementing programmes. All SAATH programmes are funded by the government (60%), private funding (30%) and beneficiaries (10%). SAATH's one-stop, integrated services reached over one lakh slum dwellers in Ahmedabad and many more in the states of Gujarat and Rajasthan. | The idea at the core of SammaaN Foundation is to organise a micro public transport sector, i.e. rickshaw pulling, and convert this potential sector into a promising earning source, thereby enhancing the standard of living of the families of the cycle rickshaw pullers. Initially, SammaaN Foundation started by giving them rickshaws, uniforms, bank accounts, identity cards, and accidental insurance for the rickshaws, rickshaw pullers, and their passengers as well. Later it also included rickshaw pullers' health insurance. Through this model, SammaaN Foundation is able to provide them access to finance, insurance, and health care services. It also provides their children access to education. | KnidsGreen aims to give equal benefits to all its stakeholders—farmers (small, marginal and landless: SMAL vegetable growers), the poor vendors at the two ends of the vegetable value chain, and lastly, the consumers. In other words, its aim is to benefit the farmers, vendors, and consumers and also generate employment at the grassroots level. He had put a system in place which brought together SMAL growers, value-adding intermediaries, vendors and consumers on one platform, and developed a formal vegetable supply chain. The government of India adopted Kaushalendra's integrated and inclusive model for vegetable value chain and tried to replicate it in the form of the National Vegetable Initiative (NVI) project in eight states of India. |

*Source*: Singh, Saini, and Majumdar (2015)

Shaheen Mistri, Rajendra Joshi) and partly funded charitable social enterprises (Geeta Ramanujam) started the process of social change with the sole purpose of maximising social value creation, after some time they all had to face a sustainability problem. Though they all managed to do so, they accepted that they had to struggle a lot to obtain sustainable funds for their social enterprises. Facing the same problem, Geeta Ramanujam had to think of some alternative to support Kathalaya partly with generated finances and her own funds as well. Therefore, later she started a separate for-profit social enterprise, Academy for Story Telling, to substitute the funding of Kathalaya. However, sustenance of both Kathalaya and Academy for Story Telling was again a challenge for her. She said that: "It is very difficult when you get [a] grant for one year. It gets exhausted in no time. When you take a grant from then you build up something that, you don't know how to sustain".

Most often, due to the dependency entirely on external funds, the charitable social enterprises are compelled to modify their models and sacrifice their own goals to satisfy the donors. These enterprises face the pressure of working in accordance with the requirement or demands of the fund providers, but how much to compromise with the model and goals? Rajendra Joshi said,

> Overall . . . yes, generally what happens is that there can be changes, but there won't be too many changes in what people want. Changes in our case what Ahmedabad Municipal corporation wants to do, what our partners want to do, what our funders would want to do and accordingly we would have to change our strategies.

Here, it is important to mention that, even if the social enterprises were able to design effective and sustainable social programmes to achieve their social mission, getting timely and sustainable funds was often a real challenge. For example, Dr Armida Fernandez mentioned that she had sustainability in work, because she did not create a parallel system like a dispensary or hospital (nature of work) and also worked in partnership with the government and made use of the existing infrastructure, yet she had to struggle for financial sustainability. It is rightly said that for an organisation's capacity to endure over time, both forms of sustainability—impact and financial—is required.

Thus, despite being engaged in sincere efforts towards sustainable development, whose sustainability itself is at stake in the long run, their contribution towards sustainable development poses a question. Schorr (2011) also observed that the absence of strategic frameworks to help structure non-profit leaders' thinking and planning for sustainability certainly has not helped. Foster et al. (2009) also found that rarely do the non-profits engage in clear and succinct conversations about an organisation's long-term funding strategy. They clearly mentioned, "that is because the different types of funding that fuel nonprofits have never been clearly defined" (pp. 32–34). Surely, we need to think seriously about a way out of this issue.

## Emerging research issue 2: *are alternatives available to charitable social enterprises to bring sustainability in their approaches to contribute to sustainable development?*

I have already discussed the research issue related to the sustainability problem faced by charitable social enterprises. Now, it generates another question: 'Is there no option available to these charitable social enterprises except for continuous struggling for sustainable funds to attain the goal of sustainable development?', or 'Is there any alternative left to the existing charitable social enterprises, so that they could also get sustainability in their efforts towards contributing to sustainable development?' This discussion is important if we are putting sincere efforts to attain the goals of sustainable development through a charitable approach (which face a sustainability problem in the long run). The study found that at the initial level, founders of all the charitable social enterprises did not think of this issue. Only after some time, when they started facing this problem of getting sustainable funds, they started to think of other alternatives in order to get sustainability of their services provided by the organisations and the financial sustainability of their social enterprises. It was found in the course of the study that multiple alternatives were used by these organisations in order to get sustainability in their services. The important strategies used by these organisations in this regard included registration of a self-sustaining programme under Section 25 of The Companies Act, 1956,[2] or as a for-profit enterprise, and creation of a new for-profit social enterprise to substitute the funding of a charitable social enterprise. For example, SAATH registered its self-sustaining livelihood generation programme for poor women of slums, i.e. Urmila, as a for-profit enterprise Empower Pragati and made it a separate entity. SAATH is operating its youth livelihood programme Udaan under Saath Livelihood Services registered under Section 25. Similarly, Geeta Ramanujam started the Academy for Story Telling, a for-profit social enterprise, to sustain Kathalaya. She mentioned:

> The sustainability part every time, when funds were not there, we used to feel, what to do? We have to again employ people. So, I thought, why not start something, which will sustain both the organisation and me. So, that's when I started 'Academy for Story Telling'.

Ly (2012) also mentioned that amidst pressure to become self-financing, NGOs (non-governmental organisations) have become increasingly involved in profit-generating business ventures. Other strategies used by the social entrepreneurs are creation of a corpus fund with a purpose to face an emergency fund crisis, focus on diversification of funding sources (combination of corporate funding in the form of CSR, individual donors, institutional donors etc.), focus on building multiple partnerships and alliances within sectors and cross-sectors (government, not-for-profit, and for-profit). "Strategic alliances are an important source of resources, learning, and thereby competitive advantage" (Ireland, Hitt, & Vaidyanath, 2002,

p. 413). It was found in the study that municipal corporations provided space to all of the charitable social enterprises, SAATH, SNEHA, and Akanksha, for running their programmes. Korosec and Berman (2006) also mentioned that municipalities help social entrepreneurs by increasing awareness of social problems and by helping them to acquire resources, coordinate with other organisations, and implement programmes. Explaining the role of government in achieving sustainability in the services provided by the organisation, Armida Fernandez (founder of SNEHA, a charitable social enterprise) mentioned that it was only because it was working in partnership with government's existing infrastructure of health care that SNEHA was sustainable in providing services, despite being a financially sustainable organisation.

It was also found that many charitable organisations were using a combination of multiple strategies in order to face the sustainability issue for attaining the goal of sustainable development. Singh and Mofokeng (2014) studied three South African non-profit organisations and concluded that although non-profits have diversified their revenue sources, the revenue diversification does not necessarily ensure financial sustainability, as striking the right balance was still a major challenge. Further they mentioned that several other factors such as forming strategic alliances with key stakeholders, modernising the non-profit cause to meet the changing funder requirements, building the organisation's brand, and creating knowledge organisations contribute to the financial sustainability of non-profit organisations. They also suggested that for financial sustainability, non-profit organisations must look beyond a request for donations to other income-enhancing initiatives.

These findings indicate that alternatives and options are available for the existing charitable social enterprises which would help them to overcome the sustainability issue.

## Emerging research issue 3: *charitable vs. for-profit: which way to turn for sustainable development?*

The study showed that charitable social enterprises, which were dependent entirely on external grants, funds, and donations faced a financial sustainability problem. In the long run, all of them had to work on getting financial sustainability for their organisations. On the other hand, there were for-profit social enterprises, which did not face a financial sustainability problem. It was also found that due to the financial problem, the founders of charitable social enterprises (Dr Armida Fernandez, Shaheen Mistri, and Rajendra Joshi) and partly funded social enterprise (Geeta Ramanujam) were not found to be very excited and ambitious about the replication and scalability of their models in contrast to the founders of for-profit social enterprises. Does it mean that one should always opt for a for-profit model to get sustainability in their approach towards contributing to sustainable development? No, I am not recommending any particular approach; rather, I am presenting the options, which emerged from the study. These strategies can be used by those individuals who are interested in creating social enterprises within the not-for-profit sector only. These options include registration of an organisation under section 25 of the Companies Act 1956 (e.g. SammaaN Foundation), or making a profit-generating self-sustainable programme as a separate entity under section 25 or for- profit entity (e.g. SAATH); following hybrid models, i.e. creation of two organisations—one charitable and one for-profit (e.g. Kathalaya)—to substitute the funding of the charitable one or, within a for-profit legal framework, provision of services based on income segmentation of the beneficiaries (e.g. Narayana Hrudayalaya). Battilana, Lee, Walker, and Dorsey (2012) also observe that many non-profit organisations continue to seek ways to adapt their existing models to generate some revenue to be less dependent on donors. In this context, an introductory guide is available for people in non-profits who are interested in new methods of generating revenue for organisations via earned income. This guide assists an organisation, its leaders, and employees to tackle social enterprise, forming a sequence of steps and an action plan (www.socialenterprise.NET).

In the context of the hybrid model, it is worthwhile to discuss the case of Narayana Hrudayalaya. This is an excellent example of a hybrid model pursuing its social mission based on income segmentation of the beneficiaries. It is positioned between two extremes of charitable and for-profit social enterprises. Though registered as a for-profit entity, it developed separate packages for three different categories of patients: 1) those who can afford; 2) those who cannot afford but are insured under some government's micro health insurance programmes; and 3) those who can neither afford nor are insured under any of the government's health programmes. Despite owning different categories, the quality of health services is the same across all types of packages. Battilana et al. (2012, p. 55) mentioned: "hybrid entrepreneurs are opening the way for a reformulation of the current economic order, combining the principles, practices, and logics of modern capitalism with more inclusive humanitarian ideals".

The most important fact is that all the founders of profit-generating social enterprises in the study, whether registered as a Section 25 company or for-profit, believed that profit making is essential to get sustainability for the process of social value creation. Dr Devi Shetty clarified that charity is not scalable. Hence, for sustainable social value creation, the model should be based on good business fundamentals to generate profits. He said,

> First of all, we clarify to everyone that charity is not scalable. If we are going to do it free for ever, we are going to die. It has to be based on very good business fundamentals. We are one of the . . . perhaps the only organisation in the world, which has a balance sheet on a daily basis. We get a profit and loss account every day, which comes to my phone. All the senior administrators get a message about the previous day's revenue, expenses and a bit of margins. So, we respect money. All over the world people talk about the reducing the cost of health care, but nobody knows that how much money they are spending today. How are you going to reduce, if you don't know, how much is cost today? Our concept is, we have to be very vigilant about our revenues,

> expenses, how much money you spend, what is a wasteful expense, these things, you have to be very careful.

Similar to his opinion, Irfan Alam, founder of SammaaN Foundation, a section 8 company, also believed that making money by doing business on the one side and simultaneously passing benefits to the customers is social entrepreneurship. He had always been strictly against charity and taking donations from anyone. He said,

> This is what social entrepreneurship is. You are making it on one side is money by doing your business, on the other side, you are actually ensuring or retaining doing something good for your customers. This is what I want to prove. I might be the most hated person for the NGO sector people. I don't know about my image, but most of my awards have come from business world, corporate India, because I have been advocating for something that its all, at the end of the day is business. It's no more charity.

Thus, there is no black and white always, but grey area also exists. I suggest that rather than looking and comparing only two extremes of organisations for getting sustainability, one should look at other options also (discussed previously) while selecting a particular approach in order to make a sustainable approach towards sustainable development, depending on their purpose to create the social enterprise.

## Emerging research issue 4: *do only for-profits face the danger of mission-shift or mission-drift?*

The individuals interested in putting efforts towards sustainable development may doubt that there is a possibility of danger of mission-shift and/or mission-drift for the founders of for-profit social enterprises. However, when this issue was explored in the study, it presented findings different from this general misconception. The study found that not only the for-profit social enterprises but also the social enterprises in the not-for-profit sector, which were engaged in profit generation (SammaaN Foundation registered under section 25), accepted the existence of this danger. Declaring that he never faced the problem of mission-shift or mission-drift, Irfan Alam said,

> I never felt that [mission-shift or mission-drift]. Reason is that . . . you know, I was fortunate enough that I have seen lot of money before starting this venture. So, money is something which never ever attracted me. Never tempted me. And I know that money can . . . you know . . . money is just a tool, but what we are trying to do is . . . if I start making my enterprise's objective to maximise my profit, probably I will be making profit for my enterprise, but for social mission or social angle, what we are trying to do is actually we enhancing total market sise. By doing that there will be 10–20 or 100 companies like SammaaN Foundation who would love to come into the sector

> and domain to operate and they all will have their shares. At the end of the day, actually you are creating value. I mean, there are two things-value and wealth. So, strategically, we have chosen value than wealth.

In fact, all other social enterprises (NH—a hybrid organisation, Kathalaaya—sustainable with a combination of grants, donations, and income generated through own for-profit organisation), including the charitable social enterprises, mentioned that there is a danger of mission-shift and mission-drift even in their organisations. However, all of the founders included in the study realised that it is really the conscience and passion for social mission which prevented them from getting trapped in this danger. About Dr Devi Shetty, who followed a hybrid model to achieve his social mission, the General Manager, Corporate Relations, Narayana Hrudayalaya mentioned,

> Right from the beginning his philosophy is very-very clear. Whatever we do it, we should do it for the common man. At the same time, you know, we are not a totally charitable hospital, so that anybody, who comes in, will be done free of cost. The type of work that we are doing, I mean, we are getting the chairman, president of the companies for the type of work that we are doing and at the same time the janitor of the company also can walk in, get the treatment and if he cannot afford, the hospital will pitch in and see to it that he will be helped. This is the philosophy and we are continuing with the same. And we could do it, because of the volume we are doing. We are getting support from all and sundry.

Similar to the finding of this study, Jones (2007) also concluded that commercial ventures are only one among several paths to mission drift, even in non-profits that have no unrelated business activities, there is potential for mission-drift. The finding of the study supports the views that commercial and social dimensions within the enterprise may be a source of tension (Austin, Stevenson, & Wei-Skillern, 2006), and there is a potential risk of mission-drift within social entrepreneurial ventures Dorado (2006). Thus, I suggest that social entrepreneurs should not avoid the idea of following the for-profit route or the self-sustainable approach of the not-for-profit sector (section 25) completely in order to get sustainability in their efforts towards sustainable development, due to fear of mission-drift or mission-shift. It is not fair to link the danger of mission-shift and mission-drift only with the for-profit social enterprises or profit-generating social enterprises of not-for-profits.

## Conclusion

Recognising the importance of sustainable development to create an equitable society worldwide and the role played by social entrepreneurs in achieving the goal of sustainable development, especially in the poorer countries, in this chapter I tried to bring forth the sustainability issues in different types of social enterprises, ranging from charitable social enterprises of the non-profit sector to for-profit social enterprises. However, the chapter neither aims to evaluate the effectiveness of different types of social enterprises in achieving the goal of sustainable development nor gives a recommendation for any particular type of social enterprises for contributing effectively towards sustainable development. The purpose of this chapter was to present various research issues related to sustainability in the efforts of social entrepreneurs to attain the goal of sustainable development. The multiple cases included in the case study provided context to discuss these issues. Several research issues emerged from the data of these cases. The problems faced by different types of social enterprises in order to make a sustainable approach towards sustainable development and strategies adopted by them have been discussed. To summarise, it can be said that no particular approach of social entrepreneurs is good or bad. The choice of adopting a particular approach towards making sustainable development entirely depends on the individual's conscience, purpose of starting a social enterprise, context, and career choices. The emerged research issues provide a starting point for further discussion, debate for the scholars, and needs more exploration, which would provide future scope for studies in social entrepreneurial research focusing on achieving the goal of sustainable development. This knowledge, in turn, would surely guide social entrepreneurs in deciding their approaches and adopting strategies to get sustainability in their efforts in attain the goal of sustainable development.

## Notes

1 Ashoka Innovators for the Public is the global association of the world's leading social entrepreneurs—men and women with system-changing solutions that address the world's most urgent social challenges.
2 Section 25 is revised to 'Section 8' in the new The Companies Act 2013.

## References


Ashoka. (n.d.). *Social entrepreneurs: Doing sustainable development*. Retrieved March 9, 2013 from www.ashoka.org/files/ashoka_0.pdf

Austin, J., Stevenson, H., & Wei-Skillern, J. (2006). Social and commercial entrepreneurship: Same, different, or both? *Entrepreneurship Theory and Practice*, *30*(1), 1–22.

Battilana, J., Lee, M., Walker, J., & Dorsey, C. (2012). In search of the hybrid ideal. *Stanford Social Innovation Review*, Summer, 49–55. Retrieved July 16, 2015 from www.ssireview.org/articles/entry/in_search_of_the_hybrid_ideal

Burkett, I. (n.d.). *Sustainable social enterprise: What does this really mean*? Retrieved August 9, 2013 from www.socialtraders.com.au/sites/www.socialtraders.com.au/files/Sustainable%20Social%20Enterprise%20-%20Ingrid%20Burkett.pdf

Christie, M. J., & Honig, B. (2006). Social entrepreneurship: New research findings. *Journal of World Business*, *41*, 1–5.

Dale, A., & Sparkes, J. (2011). The "agency" of sustainable community development. *Community Development Journal*, *46*(4), 476–492.

Diesendorf, M. (1999). *Sustainability and sustainable development*. Retrieved August 10, 2013 from www.isf.uts.edu.au/publications/CorpSust.pdf

Dorado, S. (2006). Social entrepreneurial ventures: Different values so different process of creation, no? *Journal of Developmental Entrepreneurship, 11*(4), 319–343.

Foster, W. L., Kim, P., & Christiansen, B. (2009). Ten nonprofit funding models. *Stanford Innovation Review*, Spring. Retrieved July 10, 2015 from www.ssireview.org/pdf/2009SP_Feature_Foster_Kim_Christiansen.pdf

Grenier, P. (2006). Social entrepreneurship: Agency in a globalizing world. In A. Nicholls (Ed.), *Social entrepreneurship: New models of sustainable change* (pp. 119–142). New York: Oxford University Press.

Haldar, S. (2019). Towards a conceptual understanding of sustainability-driven entrepreneurship. *Corporate Social Responsibility and Environmental Management*, 1–14. https://doi.org/10.1002/csr.1763

Ireland, R. D., Hitt, M. A., & Vaidyanath, D. (2002). Alliance management as a source of competitive advantage. *Journal of Management, 28*(3), 413–446.

Jones, M. B. (2007). The multiple sources of mission drift. *Non Profit and Voluntary Sector Quarterly, 36*(2), 299–307.

Korosec, R. L., & Berman, E. M. (2006). Municipal support for social entrepreneurship. *Public Administration Review*, May/June, 448–462.

Ly, P. (2012). The effect of ownership in NGO's commercial ventures. *Annals of Public and Cooperative Economics, 83*(2), 159–179.

Martin, R. L., & Osberg, S. (2007). Social entrepreneurship: The case for a definition. *Stanford Social Innovation Review*, Spring, 29–39.

Nicholls, A. (2006). Introduction. In A. Nicholls (Ed.), *Social entrepreneurship: New models of sustainable change* (pp. 1–35). New York: Oxford University Press.

Pandey, A., Mukherjee, G., & Kumar, S. (2009). Creation of economic and social value by social entrepreneurship for sustainable development. *International Journal of Human and Social Sciences, 4*(13), 938–944.

Pritchett, L. (1997). Divergence, big time. *Journal of Economic Perspectives, 11*(3), 3–17.

Qizilbash, M. (2001). Sustainable development: Concepts and rankings. *The Journal of Development Studies, 37*(3), 134–161.

Schaltegger, S., & Wagner, M. (2010). Sustainable entrepreneurship and sustainability innovation: Categories and interactions. *Business Strategy and the Environment, 20*, 222–237. https://doi.org/10.1002/bse.682

Schorr, J. (2011). The holy grail for nonprofits. Book review (*Nonprofit sustainability: Making strategic decisions for financial viability* (Jeanne Bell, Jan Masaoka & Steve Zimmerman, 2010). *Stanford Social Innovation Review*, Summer. Retrieved July 10, 2015 from www.ssireview.org/book_reviews/entry/nonprofit_sustainability_jeanne_bell_jan_masaoka_steve_zimmerman

Seelos, C., & Mair, J. (2004). *Social entrepreneurship: The contribution of individual entrepreneurs to sustainable development.* Working Paper, WP No. 553, IESE Business School, University of Navarra.

Seelos, C., & Mair, J. (2005a). Social entrepreneurship: Creating new business models to serve the poor. *Business Horisons, 48*, 241–246.

Seelos, C., & Mair, J. (2005b). *Sustainable development: How social entrepreneurs make it happen.* Working Paper, WP No. 611, IESE Business School, University of Navarra.

Shao, G., Li, F., & Tang, L. (2011). Multidisciplinary perspectives on sustainable development. *International Journal of Sustainable Development & World Ecology, 18*(3), 187–189.

Shepherd, D. A., & Patzelt, H. (2011). The new field of sustainable entrepreneurship: Studying entrepreneurial action linking "what is to be sustained" with "what is to be developed". *Entrepreneurship Theory and Practice*, 137–163. https://doi.org/10.1111/j.1540-6520.2010.00426.x

Singh, A., Saini, G. K., & Majumdar, S. (2015). Application of social marketing in social entrepreneurship: Evidence from India. *Social Marketing Quarterly*, 1–21. https://doi.org/10.1177/1524500415595208

Singh, S., & Mofokeng, M.-A. (2014). An analysis of what makes a nonprofit organisation sustainable: Specific reference to revenue diversification. *Interdisciplinary Journal of Contemporary Research in Business*, *6*(2), 393–424. Retrieved July 10, 2015 from http://journal-archieves37.webs.com/393-424jun14.pdf

Sriram, M. S. (2011). *Profit or purpose: The dilemma of social enterprises*. Indian Institute of Management, Ahmedabad. W.P. No. 2011–08–02. Retrieved July 16, 2015 from www.iimahd.ernet.in/assets/snippets/workingpaperpdf/11519317320l1-08-02.pdf

United Nations. (2017). *Promoting entrepreneurship for sustainable development: A selection of business cases from the empretec network*. Retrieved August 6, 2019 from https://unctad.org/en/PublicationsLibrary/diaeed2017d6_en.pdf

WCED (World Commission on Environment and Development). (1987). *Our common future*. Retrieved August 10, 2013 from www.un-documents.net/our-common-future.pdf

Yin, R. K. (1993). *Applications of case study research*. Applied Social Research Methods Series, Vol. 35. London: Sage.

Yin, R. K. (2003). *Case study research: Design and methods* (3rd ed.). Thousand Oaks, CA: Sage.

# 2

# MADHAV SATHE

## Social entrepreneur seeking opportunity in problems

*Satyajit Majumdar and Bina Ajay*

### Rationale of case study in social entrepreneurship

Social entrepreneurship (SE) has drawn valuable attention among academics and researchers. It emerges as a possibility to encounter many socio-economic gaps created by the traditional models of economic development initiated by the state and also the market mechanisms created by the private enterprises. Over the years a significant amount of faith and hope has been generated in this field due to the historical evidence in countries like India—with wide geographical spread, diversified culture, and economic development status.

Though the practice of social entrepreneurship is age old, the field is new in scholarly inquiries. Academic programmes developed in this field in the last few decades emerged from various established disciplines such as social science, management, public policy, health systems, and technology. The wide research canvas not only provides multiple perspectives to conceptualise, explain, and theorise but also opens many questions on the established theories on entrepreneurship, management, development economics, political economics, sociology, and political science. Scholarly articles have also been written to theorise concepts like social innovation, social mission, social change, social value creation, and the social impact, based on case studies or small samples.

The scholarly advancement in social entrepreneurship is a function of the sensitivity of researchers to search for new knowledge and the theories with critical insights into the practice. Case study is an efficient method to search for knowledge in practice. Theorising new practices and developing scholarly insights are critical not only for theoretical generalisation but also for developing frameworks or points of view to question 'the future' wherein the scholarly research plays an important role.

## Background: narrative approach of the case study

In this case study we adopted a 'narrative' approach for developing the case study (Gartner, 2010) using the story of a social entrepreneur—Dr Madhav Sathe. While ours is an attempt to develop a case study, our ambition is also to develop some scholarly insights so as to create a theoretical basis of social entrepreneurial decision making. The case study is structured in three parts. We first report the background of the social entrepreneur and the social venture. We then elaborate on the opportunity-seeking key decisions our protagonist has taken over the years. Lastly, we explain the decision patterns.

Narrative is "a meaning structure that organises events and human actions into a whole, thereby attributing significance to individual actions and events according to their effect on the whole" (Polkinghorne, 1988, p. 19). Gartner (2010, p. 12) advocated the usage of narratives in entrepreneurship research, because "narrative scholarship can best address issues in entrepreneurship that are concerned with entrepreneurial intentions and actions and their interrelationships with circumstance". Garud and Giuliani (2013) also supported the same as it helps in reconciling the discovery and creation perspectives on the source of entrepreneurial opportunities. In sum, the scholars emphasised the need for using narrative in bringing a relational and temporal focus.

## Our protagonist social entrepreneur—Madhav Sathe

Madhav Sathe was raised in a large family which includes his grandparents, uncles, aunts, and cousins. His grandfather was a lawyer by profession and was passionate about causes such as local self-governance and education and financial independence for women. He was the inspiration for young Madhav to work in a manner that earns respect from the larger community.

In 1969, Madhav joined Vaishampayan Memorial Medical College in the Solapur District of Maharashtra (India). The medical college was managed by a charitable trust. Fees and the donations collected by the trust were made available as loans to run the college. It had a residential campus where students and professors stayed in close proximity and shared very good rapport. In 1972 the professors stopped receiving salaries due to a shortage of funds. That situation continued for many months, and as a result they went on strike, demanding legitimate salaries. Madhav, along with other students, came out openly to support them. Their efforts paid off, and the college agreed to settle the dues of the professors in a bid to salvage its reputation.

At the same time (while supporting the strike), Madhav got deeper insight into the workings of the college administration. He realised that under the loan-based funding model, the funds available with the college were insufficient to develop the necessary infrastructure to run a hospital accredited by the Medical Council of India.[1] Madhav decided to take the lead and proposed continuing the strike but this time for protecting the interests of (current and future) students. The purpose was to exert pressure on the trust (running the college) and pursue the government to take over the college.

This turned out to be an uphill task as the trust also tried to gather support from other colleges and the local community to oppose the students. Also the local government started suppressing the students' movement with police force. Despite such odds, Madhav and the students' group received greater support for their cause; they lead a large-scale protest outside the house of the Chairman of the Trust. Under the guise of participants, a few miscreants ended up creating a chaotic situation. The young students with almost no prior experience failed to handle this situation. The matter was viewed seriously by the local authorities, and as a consequence the students' movement was banned in the college. The local administration ordered the police to 'shoot on sight' if anyone attempted to violate the ban. Madhav and his team did not give up, and despite such restrictions, their movement gained further momentum. To avoid being arrested by the police, the students' leaders including Madhav went 'underground' and were forced to disguise themselves. The atmosphere of fear also forced many students to withdraw from the college, but Madhav's parents offered any possible help to support the movement, hence raising the morale of the movement. They were convinced that their son was fighting for a just cause. Around the same time, the youth wing of a large political party offered the students a silent support. This helped Madhav and his colleagues to strategise their activities.

One day, the General Secretary of the Students' Council of the College suddenly disappeared. Later in the evening, he issued a statement that the strike had been withdrawn following successful negotiations. Soon, Madhav and his friends realised that the person was forced to make such a statement by the college administration. The students then called a meeting and took a decision to remove the General Secretary from his position, rendering his statements powerless.

A day later, a member of the State Legislative Assembly invited Madhav and fellow students for a talk. Meanwhile, the youth wing of the political party that supported them took all credit for the success of the strike. It did not take much effort for Madhav and others to understand the political game being played by the political parties and the legislators. They took a firm stand that they would not accept anything less than a declaration by the government of its stand in the State Legislative Assembly. After waiting for a few days for the government to respond to their demand, Madhav and others marched to the capital city of the State of Maharashtra (India)—Mumbai—to meet the senior leaders of the state government. The meeting was successful, and the government announced that it would take over the college.

This experience in the college exposed Madhav to the interplay of vested interests when multiple stakeholders are involved (in any affair) and fear of being crushed through unfair and violent means. He also learnt the hard way how to deal with a large number of people. Those experiences were of immense help to him in the later part of his life.

## The Bombay Mothers and Children Welfare Society (BMCWS)

Madhav joined The Bombay Mothers and Children Welfare Society (BMCWS) in 1985 in the capacity of Joint Honorary Secretary. BMCWS, a public charitable trust, was established in 1919. Though located in Mumbai, the society was engaged with healthcare in general, childcare, education, and comprehensive rural development at many places in Maharashtra.

The funding requirements of the trust were primarily managed through donations. Availability of funds was always an issue due to ever-increasing expenses. In addition, in 1985, BMCWS was facing a labour dispute involving outstanding (from 1975) higher wages payable. The hospitals and other activity centres run by the trust were not generating enough to financially sustain, and higher wage payment was almost impossible. Considering the situation, the trustees were contemplating closing the trust's operations.

Madhav was then visiting doctor at the hospitals run by BMCWS. A group led by him witnessed the crisis and offered to take charge of the trust to safeguard its operations. The Bombay High Court, which was hearing the labour dispute, permitted this group to take over from the incumbent trustees. Madhav, the youngest and one of the most energetic members of the group, was asked to take charge as Joint Honorary Secretary. He was expected to come out with a plan to turn the situation around and hence save the trust from discontinuing its operations.

Madhav emerged as 'an entrepreneur' who was to save the organisation, redefine its operations with innovative approaches, and resolve the complex labour issues while taking the trust out of the financial crisis. Though he did not start a new venture, his emergence can easily be argued as 'entrepreneurial'; he was to act and take decisions as any entrepreneur does under stringent resource pressure and uncertainty.

## The social entrepreneur

Madhav was working as an anaesthetist in Mumbai, providing medical services at various hospitals in Mumbai for a fee. The hospitals run by BMCWS were the second source of income for him. His motivation to take charge of the trust was also to avert loss of his personal income. While he took charge of the trust, he was not too sure whether he would be able to do justice to his new role because he had no experience or adequate knowledge in finance, accounts, or administration. He almost challenged himself, decided to test his own capabilities for about a year, with fully committed efforts. He was willing to leave the new role being unsuccessful in his mission.

## Issues, entrepreneurial opportunities, and decisions

In his new role Madhav noticed that the Tilak Hospital, a maternity home in Worli (Mumbai) run by BMCWS, was not well maintained. The hospital used to charge the patients high fees, which lead to lower occupancy and hence insufficient fund collection to pay a regular salary to the staff. He soon found that the resident gynaecologist was involved in malpractices, which often resulted in leakage of funds. He did not take much time to ask her to leave after collecting evidence of malpractices. On the other hand, her husband, who was innocent and a committed individual, continued to work with the hospital. The family was also allowed to continue living in the quarters provided by the hospital within its premises. Considering that their only child was in the final year of high school, Madhav did not put undue pressure on the family by asking them to relocate.

As the next step, he had to do something to increase revenue collection. He was aware that any increase in patient fees might affect the number of patients—'a catch-22 situation'. Instead, he decided to reduce patient charges. For a normal delivery the charges were reduced from INR 1000 to INR 300 (Indian Rupees), while for a Caesarian section the charges were brought down from INR 3000 to INR 700. He realised that a strong signal of being an 'affordable hospital' was required to attract many patients. He also chose to use up a part of the trust's capital invested in the fixed deposits to improve the infrastructure and the visual appearance.

To cut the costs, he approached the Head of Housekeeping at the Taj Mahal Hotel in Mumbai with a request to provide the hospital with the old linens the hotel was proposing to donate to missionaries.

Madhav had another major challenge—to encourage and motivate the workers who were a party to the labour dispute with the trust. He chose to speak to them directly to explain the consequences of closing the trust: "if we proceed for closure, you won't have your jobs". Slowly they realised that their co-operation could indeed keep the trust and its activities alive while also ensuring regular income. He continued conversations with them, making them believe that the trust was interested in their welfare. He also disciplined the system to ensure that the workers were paid their dues on time. Monthly fee payment schedule from the (working) parents who kept their children at the day care centres run by the trust was also aligned with the wage payment to the workers. This improved the management of working capital.

## The social venture models

### *Convalescent home for cancer patients*

BMCWS had unused property at various locations which could be refurbished and put to use. Availability of funds was an issue. Madhav came up with an idea to address this problem after reading a newspaper article. The Lioness Club of Mumbai had collected INR 50,000 to build a cancer patients' home in Karjat (near Mumbai),[2] but that project could not materialise. The President of the club had once been his teacher. Madhav approached her with a request that the funds available with them be given to BMCWS to build a cancer patients' convalescent home within their (existing) premises in Mumbai. The club agreed with one condition—the home should be named as the Lioness Club Centre. Madhav faced some issues to convince the trustees of BMCWS about this arrangement. They felt that Madhav had given a large space in Mumbai in return for a paltry sum. He explained that that proposal was better than keeping the space idle. He also explained to them that once the convalescent home started generating some money to become sustainable, the trust would attain a better negotiating position. Finally, the trustees agreed; funds were provided by the Lioness Club, and the place was repaired to become habitable for the cancer patients, their relatives, and friends.

### *Day care centre*[3]

Around 1988, Madhav realised that one of the day care centres run by BMCWS was located in an area (Vile Parle in Mumbai) where people had better affordability due to their better earning capabilities. He held several rounds of discussions with the parents of the children enrolled there, requesting them to consider an increase in fees from INR 175 to INR 450 per month. He also explained to them that they earn well, and it would be an insult to them to subsidise the services. Subsidies are provided to those who cannot afford, and people with better earning capability should give it up in the interest of those who cannot. This appeal worked and the parents agreed for INR 375 per month and an annual increase of 10 percent to cover the rise in prices. Later, to cover up the fixed costs in providing better facilities, he also proposed a refundable security deposit system. This time around, there was no need to convince the parents as they had seen the results.

## Financial and investment decisions

Madhav was considering all options to cut his losses to work out plans for financial sustainability. He was actively considering options of closing down unviable establishments. As a result, he decided to close the day care centre at Nalasopara (in Mumbai) in 1989. He was sure that the trust could not become sustainable only with donations. He was, therefore, actively considering the options to move beyond the traditional donation model, normally practiced by the non-profit organisations. He also wanted to look for funding methods which would not become a burden on the trusts. In the early 1990s, he took a 10-year, unsecured interest-free loan from a construction company with an arrangement to construct a day care centre on the land available with BMCWS in Goregaon in Mumbai. The centre became operational in 1992, and the income received was used to repay the loan.

At the same time, construction of an additional floor at the Vile Parle (Mumbai) day care centre was initiated on assurance of a donation. In order to facilitate fast completion of work, the existing day care centre was temporarily shifted to an alternate leased location, but the donation was not received, creating a very stressful situation for him. He discussed this matter with his friend, who was running a hospital where he was associated as a visiting doctor. He requested the friend to suggest acquaintances who would be willing to donate some money to the trust. The next morning, the friend called up Madhav to know more about the project. Later he visited the site and expressed his willingness to donate INR 0.25 million. He offered to pay INR 0.07 million immediately and the balance at a later stage. The Governing Body of the Trust was sceptical about this deal and expressed doubts about the balance amount. Madhav assured them that the first instalment of INR 0.07 million was good enough to complete the first phase of the work and generate regular income.

Madhav did not give up his efforts and took another refundable interest-free loan in 2003–2004 for repairing the terrace of the Tilak Hospital. This was necessary to provide quality services to the patients. Interestingly, Madhav had no formal training in financial management; he was merely experimenting with new options.

## The labour issues

In 1992, the Bombay High Court (high court of the State of Maharashtra, India) ruled against BMCWS in the labour dispute that had continued since 1985. Madhav knew that this created a liability of almost INR 10 million to the trust. At that point in time the trust had only INR 0.04 million, and if it failed to comply with the ruling, its activities would be closed down. Madhav waited till the labour union leaders approached him for compliance with the court ruling, while knowing that the trust had no money to pay such a big sum. The union leaders were aware that closing down the trust's operations would lead to loss of jobs for the workmen. The leader appreciated that the trust had been running well and the workmen paid on time during the period 1985–1992. This was a puzzling situation. On the one hand, they were concerned about the trust's financial condition and potential loss of jobs. On the other hand, they were required to respect the court verdict. Some settlement was necessary to bring the issue to a closure. After several rounds of discussions, it was agreed that the trust would pay to each workman INR 10,000 instead of the awarded INR 0.01 million, in three installments.

Another problem surfaced for Madhav in the 1990s. The trust had seven workmen on contract for a fixed tenure working on a slum health programme (India population project) running in collaboration with Bombay Municipal Corporation (BMC) and Asian Development Bank (ADB), who were paid salaries by the BMC through the trust. In 1996, BMC stopped paying the trust their salaries without clearly stating that the programme was over. The workers demanded to work with the trust, to which Madhav stated that Trust was under no obligation to offer them alternate work or pay their salaries. A vice-chairman of the trust, with some political background, ordered that the trust pay these workmen. Madhav firmly opposed this order, stating that the trust was in no position to take on that additional financial burden. The vice-chairman mobilised local goons to threaten and pressurise him, who then sought police protection. The matter was resolved at the insistence of a senior trustee, who sought intervention from the chief of the political party with which the vice-chairman had close affiliation. Madhav simultaneously pursued the matter with the BMC to pay the workmen. Later BMC also formally communicated to the seven workmen that the project was closed.

## Organisation restructuring and growth

After the demise of BMCWS Chairman Dr Salaskar in 1998–1999, the trust was in search of a strong and morally upright personality to take over as Chairman. Madhav approached Mr. Soman, who had just retired from the Indian Police Service, with the request. He politely declined to take up the responsibility due to his commitments. As he was walking down the stairs after meeting Mr. Soman, Madhav met Mr. Hasan Gafoor (who later became the Commissioner of Police, Mumbai) and had a short discussion. Mr Gafoor advised Madhav to approach Mr. Julio Ribeiro, the high-profile and successful ex-Chief of Punjab and Mumbai Police, and offered to introduce them. Dr Sathe agreed and went along to meet Mr. Ribeiro on an appointed day. During that meeting, Mr. Ribeiro received a phone call from the Office of the Prime Minister of India with a request to become the Governor of Jammu and the Kashmir State of India, which he refused. Instead, he preferred to take up the role of Chairman of BMCWS. It is likely that Dr Sathe's passionate description of the trust's activities spurred Mr. Ribeiro's interest, and his association with BMCWS continues till the time this case was documented in 2017.

The trust has been working very effectively. In 2017, it employed 150 people, with many rural residents and the beneficiaries of the education and skill development programmes run by BMCWS. Most of the trust's activities are self-sustaining while some are also generating surplus as illustrated in Table 2.1 that provides a comparison of the trust's activities and finances in 1985–86 and 2014–15.

**TABLE 2.1** Comparison between 1985–1986 and 2014–2015

| *Particulars* | *1985–1986* | *2014–2015* |
|---|---|---|
| Staff | 99 | 150 |
| Hospital Indoor Admissions | 1809 patients (in five Hospitals) | 3009 patients (in three Hospitals) |
| Number of children in four day care centres | 255 | 907 |
| Income (INR) | 1,048,690 | 48,093,007 |
| Expenditure (INR) | 1,344,987 | 45,303,009 |
| Surplus/(Deficit) (INR) | (296,297) | 2,789,998 |
| Funds and Liabilities (INR) | 3,416,612 | 22,915,688 |
| Valuation of Physical Assets (INR) | 739,864 | 16,373,332 |
| Investment (INR) | 715,237 | 26,673,645 |
| Equipment and Stocks (INR) | 209,485 | 10,895,305 |
| Hospital Revenue Collection (INR) | 327,952 | 15,838,102 |

*Source*: Internal data from The Bombay Mothers and Children Welfare Society, Mumbai, Maharashtra, India. Used with permission.

## Research point of view

The case study attempts to trace the journey of a social entrepreneur, over the last 30 years, to understand the process adopted in understanding and tracking opportunities and the logic used to exploit them in key decisions along the way. We find evidence of both the views on the nature of opportunities—existing and creation. We also find that a mix of inherent characteristics and learnt skills helped script a success story spanning three decades.

The long span of 30 years' journey to trace back the decision logics and the process captured in our study ensures that there were multiple opportunities and many decision points all along. We reconfirm that (social) entrepreneurship is not a single decision of founding a new venture. Instead, it is a series of steps taken to evaluate and exploit opportunities—discovered and/or created. Social entrepreneurship is continuous engagement with the stakeholders for creation of sustainable social impact. We, with the help of a case study while using a narrative, explained how a social entrepreneur engages for doing so.

Our protagonist social entrepreneur Dr Madhav Sathe is an anaesthetist by training and profession who also manages a charitable trust based in Mumbai (India). He, contrary to the popular approach to entrepreneurship, did not engage with idea generation and defining a clear roadmap for implementation of the managed trust. Rather, he took the responsibility to manage the trust because the prevailing circumstances almost enforced on him the need to innovate a venture model.

Seeking and exploiting opportunities is critical in entrepreneurship, and the success of entrepreneurs greatly depends on the process they adopt for identification of opportunity. Shane and Venkataraman (2000, p. 218) defined the academic field of entrepreneurship as "the scholarly examination of how, by whom and with what effects opportunities to create future goods and services are discovered, evaluated and exploited". This highlights three aspects of entrepreneurship: 1) presence of opportunities, 2) individuals/groups of individuals who discover, evaluate, and exploit them, and 3) how they do it (i.e. the decision-making process).

The extant literature contains two distinct views on entrepreneurial opportunities. The first view suggests that opportunities exist, waiting to be discovered by entrepreneurs (Kirzner, 1973; Casson, 1982; Shane & Venkataraman, 2000; Casson & Wadeson, 2007). Kirzner (1973) refers to opportunities being available in the market process, and how while entrepreneurs seised upon them, others remained ignorant about these opportunities. In a similar note, Casson (1982) explains that entrepreneurs intervene to correct a potential misallocation of resources. The implication thereof is that such opportunities are lying around. Casson and Wadeson (2007, p. 298) defined an opportunity as "an unexploited project which is perceived by an individual to afford potential benefit" while discovery was explained to be "identification of an opportunity by an individual (entrepreneur) who scans the set of possible projects". The second view on opportunities suggests that opportunities can be created by the actions of the entrepreneur (Sarasvathy, 2001; Korsgaard, Berglund, Blenker, & Thrane, 2015). In other words, entrepreneurs represent an active rather than passive set of actors. Korsgaard et al. (2015, p. 868) specifically re-examine the work of Kirzner and stated that "a broader reading of his work reveals not one but two different views of entrepreneurship". According to them, Kirzner's second view acknowledges the role of the entrepreneur in actively shaping the future.

There is a stream of research on individual differences and characteristics that separates entrepreneurs from non-entrepreneurs and more successful from less successful entrepreneurs (Shane & Venkataraman, 2000). Fagenson (1993) reported differences in the values (such as ambition, courage, and honesty) of the entrepreneurs vis-à-vis managers, while Forbes magazine (2005) found that individual characteristics of entrepreneurs (e.g. age, experience) determined the speed of decision making in new ventures, which in turn could influence the survival. Generally, the scholarly literature concludes that these differences are inherent and unchangeable, but it also proposes that training and education can help reduce these differences.[4]

Equally important is the decision-making process in exploiting opportunity. In this context Sarasvathy (2001, p. 245) reported that successful entrepreneurs use 'effectual decision processes', which she describes as "taking a set of means as given and focus on selecting between possible effects that can be created with that set of means". She posited this as the reverse of causal decision processes, which involves setting a goal and selecting a means to achieve it. However, Shepherd, Williams, and Patzelt (2015) in their studies concluded that entrepreneurial decisions involve either or both approaches. While in their argument they referred to literature on opportunity assessment, entry, exit, and opportunity exploitation under the broad theme of entrepreneurial decision making, they suggested more research on other entrepreneurial decision areas such as crowdfunding, user entrepreneurship, and social entrepreneurship. A paucity of longitudinal studies on decision making in entrepreneurship in general and social entrepreneurship in particular has been the highlight of the gap in the current literature.

We found evidence of opportunities that both existed (unused land, building) and opportunities that our protagonist Dr Madhav Sathe created (new funding models hitherto underexplored in social entrepreneurship ventures). We found that Dr Sathe had some values (e.g. courage, persistence) that distinguished him from others. However, he picked up many skills along the way (e.g. strategising, communication, negotiation, financial management). A combination of these factors assisted him in various decisions.

We also observed that Dr Sathe had used both causal and effectual processes. An example of causal reasoning would be setting himself a cost reduction goal and going about gathering resources at a low cost from unexplored sources (housekeeping team at Taj Mahal Hotel). Another example would be to close down hospitals/ day care centres to reduce losses. An example of effectual reasoning would be using the existing building and turning it into a cancer patients' convalescent home. In another instance, Dr Sathe reached out to his personal contacts (such as the teacher) to obtain monetary or other forms of support for BMCWS.

Thus, this case study not only brings together the three aspects of entrepreneurship implicit in the definition given by Shane and Venkataraman (2000), but it also throws light on the debates raging in the field—opportunity discovery versus creation; inherent versus learned entrepreneurial capabilities; and causal versus effectual decision processes. We were keen to understand how Dr Sathe handled his responsibilities at the trust along with his existing profession (a practicing anaesthetist).

## Future research avenues

Research in social entrepreneurship continues to remain a field of inquiry in specific acts, groups, micro-economic contexts, and specific domains; large data-based studies, models, and cross-sectoral studies are yet to emerge as research agenda. The attempt made in compiling emerging research papers is valuable and relevant in contributing to the literature. We hope such advancements and attempts would continue to open up contemporary and relevant fields for research and knowledge creation. We propose that future research may empirically examine the efficacy of this model of decision making among social entrepreneurial ventures.

### *Hybrid entrepreneurship and performance*

In their 2010 article, Folta, Delmar, and Wennberg mention a 'path to transition to full-time self-employment' as a rationale for hybrid entrepreneurship. Dr Sathe's initial idea was to work with the trust for a year and test the waters. This is similar to what they have proposed. In his case, however, we found that he continued as a hybrid entrepreneur instead of transitioning to full-time self-employment (as a social entrepreneur). We did not observe a negative impact of his existing profession on his involvement with the trust or the performance of the trust. Future research may examine the implications of continuing hybrid entrepreneurship on performance using longitudinal data on multiple entrepreneurs.

### *Model for managing social entrepreneurial ventures*

Dr Sathe has an administrative team of seven to eight people who look after implementation of his ideas. He also visits various activity sites to understand issues that need to be addressed. Thus, there is a clear separation of thought and implementation. Future research may be directed at empirically examining the efficacy of such a model in social entrepreneurial ventures.

## Notes

1 As per the requirements of the Medical Council of India, every medical college must have an attached hospital to enable students to engage in practice-based learning.
2 Mumbai has many cancer hospitals. Many cancer patients are brought to those hospitals from across the country for advanced treatment, which sometimes takes several months. The patients and their accompanying relatives/friends find it very expensive to stay in

hotels during the treatment period. To support them, many charitable and community-based organisations have set up low-cost shared residential accommodations within and at the outskirts of the city.

3 Day care centres are the places where small children are kept by the parents who go for work during the daytime. The place is designed in such a way that children have the necessary facilities to eat, sleep, and play under the care of trained personnel. Hygiene, safety, and security of children are critical in these places. In some places, trained teachers are engaged to teach the children. The parents of the children pay for such services.
4 Palich and Bagby (1995) in a study concluded, "if certain aspects of cognition are different for entrepreneurs, or more successful entrepreneurs, these processes can be learned or mastered through program".

## References


Casson, M. (1982). *The entrepreneur: An economic theory*. Totowa, NJ: Barnes & Noble Books.

Casson, M., & Wadeson, N. (2007). The discovery of opportunities: Extending the economic theory of the entrepreneur. *Small Business Economics*, *28*(4), 285–300.

Fagenson, E. A. (1993). Personal value systems of men and women entrepreneurs versus managers. *Journal of Business Venturing*, *8*, 409–430.

Folta, T. B., Delmar, F., & Wennberg, K. (2010). Hybrid entrepreneurship. *Management Science*, *56*(2), 253–269.

Forbes, D. P. (2005). Managerial determinants of decision speed in new ventures. *Strategic Management Journal*, *26*, 355–366.

Gartner, W. B. (2010). A new path to the waterfall: A narrative on a use of entrepreneurial narrative. *International Small Business Journal*, *28*(1), 6–19.

Garud, R., & Giuliani, A. P. (2013). A narrative perspective on entrepreneurial opportunities. *Academy of Management Review*, *38*(1), 57–160.

Kirzner, I. M. (1973). *Competition and entrepreneurship*. Chicago, IL and London: University of Chicago Press.

Korsgaard, S., Berglund, H., Blenker, P., & Thrane, C. (2015). A tale of two kirzners: Time, uncertainty and the "nature" of opportunities. *Entrepreneurship: Theory and Practice*, *40*(4), 867–889.

Palich, L. E., & Bagby, R. D. (1995). Using cognitive theory to explain entrepreneurial risk-taking: Challenging conventional wisdom. *Journal of Business Venturing*, *10*, 425–438.

Polkinghorne, D. E. (1988). *Narrative knowing and the human sciences*. Albany, NY: State University of New York Press.

Sarasvathy, S. D. (2001). Causation and effectuation: Toward a theoretical shift from economic inevitability to entrepreneurial contingency. *Academy of Management Review*, *26*(2), 243–263.

Shane, S., & Venkataraman, S. (2000). The promise of entrepreneurship as a field of research. *Academy of Management Review*, *25*, 217–226.

Shepherd, D. A., Williams, T. A., & Patzelt, H. (2015). Thinking about entrepreneurial decision making: Review and research agenda. *Journal of Management*, *41*(1), 11–46.

# 3

# BUSINESS SERVICES FOR SMALL ENTERPRISE DEVELOPMENT

## Emerging theory and practices

*Edakkandi Meethal Reji*

### Introduction

Micro and small enterprises (MSEs) represent a diverse group of economic activities involving small-scale farming as well as non-farm activities. The importance of MSEs as an agent of economic development is well recognised globally (DFID, 2005; Reji, 2018). Recognising the role of small enterprises in economic development, governments and agencies supporting small enterprises are advocates for effective strategies for small enterprise development. Over the last few decades, the small enterprise development field has undergone a remarkable change (Harper & Tanburn, 2005). The current small enterprise development field emerges from a range of approaches and initiatives including 'clusters and networks', 'local economic development', and 'subsector approaches' (Jones, 2012; Reji, 2013). Each of these approaches offers diverse theories and lessons in enterprise development. All of them recognise the limitations of traditional enterprise development strategies involving subsidised assistance to individual enterprises. Moving away from traditional approaches, Kula, Downing, and Field (2006) observe that since the 1990s, there is a shift in approaches in small enterprise development with emphasis on sustainable and cost-effective delivery of a range of critical business development services (BDS). The emerging approaches in small enterprise calls for broad changes in the environment in which enterprises operates. It calls for focused attention on addressing sector-specific systemic issues rather than addressing the issues facing individual entrepreneurs or enterprises. The emphasis is on BDS market development (Committee of Donor Agencies, 2001; Harper & Tanburn, 2005). In recent years, BDS market development is emerging as one of many tools for small enterprise promotion (Miehlbradt & McVay, 2004, 2005; Reji, 2018). In this context, it is important to understand the approaches in BDS market development and how these approaches foster small enterprise development. This chapter examines the emerging BDS market development and practices in design and delivery of BDS to small enterprises. The focus is on analyzing various business models through which cost-effective BDS are made available to small enterprises. It is expected that learning from these diverse models could provide practical insights on design and delivery of appropriate BDS to small enterprises cost effectively. The key sections of the chapter deal with 1) concept of business development services, 2) BDS market development, 3) strategies and approaches in BDS market development, and 4) BDS intervention models, practices, and emerging results.

## Business development services

There is an increasing recognition of the need and importance of specific business services for small enterprises. It is evident that access to business services improves enterprise competitiveness and the ability to reach higher value markets. However, small enterprises in general are constrained to access many of the essential business services required for them. This is caused by a variety of reasons, ranging from lack of efficient service providers to their lack of ability to purchase these services. Considering this reality, BDS provision—design and delivery of various business development services—is becoming an important component of current small enterprise development programmes (Halder, 2003). It is recognised that even small enterprises are also able to buy these business services, provided they are made available in a cost-effective manner. BDS stands for a wide range of services used by entrepreneurs to help them operate efficiently and grow their businesses (Goldmark, 1999; Magara & Were, 2014; Sandeep, Bruno, & Mark, 2018). Traditionally known as 'non-financial services', it originally deals with provision of training, consulting, and other services. Generally, these services addressed the internal constraints of enterprises, especially their lack of education and technical capacity. The BDS field is now becoming a specialised enterprise support strategy.

### *Typologies of business development services*

The BDS field consists of a variety of services required by small enterprises, including subcontracting, business-to business linkages, marketing services, and information resources (Committee of Donor Agencies, 2001; Okeyo, Gathungu, & K'Obonyo, 2014). Carney (1998) classifies BDS under five different asset categories that are critical for development of small enterprises: physical assets, social assets, natural assets, human assets, and financial assets. Specific BDS under each of these asset categories in order comprises: 1) provision of home-based business space, power, water, factory sheds, business incubators, land tenure, roadside rights, transport, and common service equipment; 2) development of co-operative, business associations, clusters, networks, franchising, chambers of commerce, assistance with information, and linkages to customers and suppliers; 3) promotion of sustainable use of raw materials, pollution reduction, and waste disposal; 4) training, advice, counseling, consultancy in technical skills, business management, and entrepreneurship;

and 5) linkage with financial institutions, subsidies, etc. The importance of business services has been well recognised by development practitioners, government, and donor agencies. Several donor agencies and governments work to develop cost-effective business services targeted to small and micro enterprises. The SEEP Guide to Business Development Services had identified seven categories of BDS: market access, input supply, technology and product development, training and technical assistance, infrastructure, policy/advocacy, and alternative financing mechanisms. Considering the relative importance of business services, the Donor Committee distinguishes BDS into operational and strategic services (Altenburg & Stamm, 2004). The operational services consist of accounting and taxation services, assistance in keeping records, obtaining a loan, and complying with regulations, etc. Providers of these services essentially assist small enterprises to comply with government regulations and legislative requirements and in the processing of various bureaucratic controls. On the other hand, strategic business services include business planning, marketing, product design, new product development, advertising, and promotion. The strategic business services basically are oriented towards helping a firm improve performance, grow, and innovate. Important distinctions are made between strategic and operational business services: while strategic services tend to be forward looking, the operational services are more focused on day-to-day functions.

## *BDS providers*

MSEs obtain BDS from a variety of sources including traders, business associations, chambers of commerce and industry, fellow entrepreneurs, agents, government, etc. Tomecko (2005) identifies three categories of BDS providers: private service providers, business membership organisations, and government service providers. Each of them has a distinct role in the design and delivery of business services. The private service providers consist of standalone service providers such as accountants or private enterprises that provide many smaller enterprises with embedded services such as quality control, market information, etc. In this case, the BDS offer might be in the form of specific market research related to commercialisation of the services, advertising, and promotion, to popularise the services, product development, capacity building, and advisory services; and in certain cases limited transport subsidies to encourage the service provider to explore more distant markets. In the case of Business Membership Organisations (BMO), no support is offered for developing commercial private business services. Rather, attention is directed to help them provide three sets of services: 1) advocacy, business linkages and networking, area or sector development or competitiveness and information; 2) fulfilling an agency function where the BMO offers a unique service to its members such as group insurance, bar coding, or acts as an agent for the government in matters like business registration; and 3) BDS takes the form of, for example, a referral system for legal and other business issues, quality certification, or advice on how to comply with international quality standards, etc. The government service providers emphasise public benefit services such as appropriate policies, regulations, or legislations, country/regional or sector promotion, and capacity building to strengthen these services. In some cases, where the public body is clearly aware of the differentiation of the role of facilitator and service provider, the government can be encouraged by the donor's facilitator to become a local facilitator itself.

Several mechanisms have evolved to obtain access to these services. Some of them are purchased, whereas others are provided on a commission basis (Anderson, 2000; Nagayya & Rao, 2011). A number of business services are embedded in business environment and business relationships. Services provided on a commission basis include those for which payment is incorporated into a commission fee. Services provided through business relationships are typically sold in a package of products and services and paid for through a mark-up on the final product. Finally, services provided by business environments are those that are channeled through informal networks, customer interaction, or through the media. The most well-understood method of paying for BDS is commercial purchase of services.

## BDS market development

In recent years, there is a shift in approaches in BDS to small enterprises (Harper & Tanburn, 2005). While the traditional approaches to BDS focused on standalone subsidised services to individual entrepreneurs, the emerging BDS field emphasises developing a market for business development services (Jones, 2012). The BDS market development approach is rooted in the experience of donors and development practitioners involved in small enterprise development. With the constitution of the Committee of Donor Agencies for Small Enterprise Development in 1995, there is increasing consensus among practitioners and donor agencies on the need for design and delivery of specific business services targeted to small enterprises (Committee of Donor Agencies, 2001; Harper & Tanburn, 2005). The Donor Committee also had constituted a working group on BDS and published the preliminary guidelines for donor interventions. Following the publication of the preliminary guidelines, a series of conferences were held in Harare (1998), Rio de Janeiro (1999), and Hanoi (2000) (Downing, 2001). These conferences provided a platform for sharing and learning from the experiences of several practitioners and other agencies. There is consensus that the traditional interventions by government and donors have failed to provide affordable, high-quality BDS to a large proportion of the target population of small enterprises. The BDS market development approach emerges from these Donor Committee conferences.

The BDS market development underlines a new approach to BDS design and delivery that has the potential to reach a large number of small enterprises in a cost-effective and sustainable manner. Moving away from traditional approaches in the provision of BDS, the BDS market development approach proposes a new vision for success, one that looks like a healthy, private-sector, business services market: numerous, competitive BDS suppliers who sell a wide range of BDS commercially, to large numbers and types of small enterprises (McVay & Miehlbradt,

2001). In explaining BDS market development, Gibson (2005) clarifies that market development interventions are aimed at the development of vibrant and competitive private-sector markets of relevant, differentiated services consumed by a broad range and significant proportion of small businesses. The definition distinguishes market development from other types of BDS interventions, mostly concerned with the more effective functioning of specific providers. Market development is focused on institutional development (market) rather than the better functioning of organisational partners per se. It is argued that achieving improved enterprises productivity and competitiveness is possible only by relying on the private sector to provide services, by viewing clients as customers, and by limiting the use of subsidies (Gibson, 2005). Markets are the core of the new market development approach, and the relationship with the entrepreneur is a transactional one, in which the entrepreneur is considered to be a customer willing to pay for services (Downing, 2001).

## BDS market assessment

The BDS market development demands a clear understanding of the existing supply of BDS from the private-sector, donor-supported programmes, government, and the market failures that lead to a gap between supply and demand for services. BDS market development is directed to overcome these market failures and capturing the opportunities for expanding the services market for small enterprises; and the desired result is building competitive private-sector suppliers of BDS so that small enterprises could purchase unsubsidised BDS cost effectively (McVay & Miehlbradt, 2001). A logical first step in the BDS market development process is the assessment of potential BDS markets. The objective of market assessment is to understand the existing BDS supplies, demand for BDS, and demand-supply gap. It also captures the constraints that hamper market development. BDS market assessment generally addresses the following questions: how developed are various BDS markets, the key similarities and differences across various BDS markets, how can organisations assess the potential for a BDS market, and how can market assessment data be used for programme design (McVay & Miehlbradt, 2001). BDS market assessment provides an understanding of the level of awareness of the BDS market, helping small enterprises to understand services, persuading them to try services and ensuring that they continue to use services.

## BDS programme design and products development

The inputs from market research are used in the programme design and product development processes. Hileman and Tanburn (2000) explain the experience of an International Labour Organisationi (ILO)-sponsored Farm Implements and Tools (FIT) programme in the use of market research for design of innovative products and services. The products and services designed by FIT mainly included: enterprise visits, commercial training, and facilitation. Enterprise visits (study tours) were recognised as an effective tool for networking, developing new markets, and exchanges of technologies and skills for MSEs. The market research identified a demand from small business owners to learn from others. FIT then developed and tested study tours for MSEs to visit other businesses or commercial events in neighboring countries and other regions. The FIT programme was built on the willingness of MSEs to pay for some of the services. It also began supporting tour agencies to develop and sell such tours on a commercial basis. On the training front, the FIT programme developed and tested two training methodologies to help MSEs undertake practical marketing and demand-based product development. These products were tested first through traditional, donor-supported training channels and subsequently sold to commercial training businesses through training-of-trainer courses.

The Self Employed Women Association (SEWA) in India is another widely referred example of using market research for programme design and product development. SEWA conducts participatory sub-sector development programmes with poor, self-employed women (Chen, 1996). SEWA started its work by organizing self-employed women into groups according to the work they were involved in, such as incense making or dairy production. With these groups, SEWA used Participatory Rural Appraisal (PRA) techniques to identify immediately felt needs. These needs are the first to be addressed, but with the momentum of success, the groups go on to identify and tackle large issues. This approach led to SEWA's national dairy cooperative support project. The immediate need for women dairy workers was access to vaccinations and veterinary services. SEWA conducted a pilot effort to link women in the programme to services provided by the Ministry of Agriculture. Having demonstrated the viability and importance of supplying women with these inputs, SEWA built on that momentum to successfully advocate for women all over India to have access to government dairy support services (Chen, 1996).

## Strategies and approaches to BDS market development

### *Subsidised BDS provision*

Early efforts in BDS focused on subsidised provision of services to individual enterprises. The Gram Shree Mela, an exhibition cum marketing event targeted for the rural producers in India, offers a useful case in point in subsidised BDS provision (Kashyap, 1991). The Gram Shree Melas organised by the Council for Advancement of Participatory Agriculture and Rural Technology (CAPART) was a noteworthy marketing event to boost rural incomes through enhancing employment and opportunities for rural artisans in India. CAPART organised several exhibitions and short training programmes for the rural artisans who were the beneficiaries of the flagship self-employment programme, Integrated Rural Development Programme (IRDP) and Development of Women and Children in Rural Areas (DWCRA), programme supported by the United Nations Children Education Fund (UNICEF). These exhibitions helped the participants to directly interact with urban consumers and sell their products. CAPART met the expenditures for travel, accommodation, and food during the days of exhibitions, including their return travel ticket. Later the scope of these exhibitions has been widened to include buyer-seller meetings at which bulk contracts might be achieved by the participating groups. Seminars and workshops were also organised as part of these exhibitions. At the exhibitions, each group was provided with a 10-square-meter stall to display and sell their products. Publicity was arranged centrally by CAPART through attractive posters; brochures were directly mailed to potential buyers including shop owners, exporters, bulk buyers, and selected individuals. Press conferences were organised to ensure wide media coverage, and television stations were contacted to give exposure to these exhibitions. The participating groups received free marketing advice, and serious effort was made to bring producers and consumers into direct contact, thereby eliminating the ubiquitous middleman. CAPART invited several large institutions and helped them identify suitable products for bulk buying, negotiating terms and conditions of sale on behalf of the rural producer. The consumer and producer surveys carried out at the exhibitions have yielded a wealth of information, which helped in formulating an effective national marketing strategy. In order to institutionalise the support facilities to rural artisans in their locations, District Supply and Marketing Societies (DSMS) were created across the country. DSMS purchased raw materials in bulk and provided it to the rural artisans; purchased products from them and marketed in urban areas.

### Developing training market

Training is an important component of BDS targeted to small enterprises. A recent trend observed in training provision is developing a market for training products and services (Mole & Capelleras, 2018; Seo, Perry, Tomczyk, & Solomon, 2014). The government, donors, and private agencies are involved in developing training markets. In general, training is offered in two formats: embedded training programmes and standalone training programmes. In case of embedded training, the trainer has a business interest in developing the client, such as ensuring a supply of quality materials, expanding the business, and so on. More importantly, it is a means for the trainer to make more profit. The embedded training services have the strengths of affordability for the clients. The relevant and saleable skills taught during the training offers tangible benefits to the potential clients. Standalone private training is defined as training services which are operated on a fully commercial basis.

Private training provision is found to be more effective than a government training programme. Mckenzie (2001) illustrates the experience of International Finance Corporation (IFC)-supported Mekong Project Development Facility (MPDF) in training products in a Vietnamese market. MPDF began its programme by commissioning a market assessment, which revealed a strong need and demand by entrepreneurs for business management training. Based on the market assessment, MPDF developed high-quality training products tailored to the needs of the entrepreneurs. It gradually encouraged several new suppliers to enter the training development market. MPDF continued with its training activities for some time and made the courses affordable to a larger population in partnership with other agencies. Subsequently, MPDF partners began to use the training products in more lucrative training contracts with foreign and state-owned companies.

In Kenya, Tototo Home Industries is providing business training for women's groups (Walsh, Kevin, & Candance, 1991). In association with World Education, Tototo Home Industries has introduced an innovative participatory business training programme for women's groups in coastal areas of Kenya. Unlike the traditional approach to a training programme, this particular training programme was designed after extensive field research on the impact of enterprise activities on women in their household level. The training programme focused on three specific themes: profit, regular return, and financial records. Several participatory methods were employed to engage the trainees during the training programme. The overall impact of the training programme reflected on the financial performance of the members' group business.

Hileman and Tanburn (2000) narrate a successful example of developing a training market is the BDS under FIT programme. The FIT programme has designed and commercialised a range of innovative services using an action research methodology. This methodology tested both the products and commercial delivery channels that include enterprise visits and commercial training facilitations. Enterprise visits are a recognised and effective tool for networking, developing new markets and exchanges of technologies and skills for MSEs though they normally require high subsidies. The FIT programme identified a demand from small business owners to learn from others and experimented with national enterprise visits of MSE groups to meet their counterparts in other parts of the country. The FIT programme developed and tested two training methodologies to help MSEs undertake practical marketing and demand-based product development. These products were tested first through traditional, donor-supported training channels and subsequently sold to commercial training businesses through training of trainer courses in East Africa. These two products and another ILO-developed training product (grassroots management training) were eventually sold into the private sector where they were modified and adapted to meet the demands of the training market.

## *Vouchers programme*

Vouchers are generally recognised as a tool for facilitation of BDS development. Vouchers are partial transactional subsidy, which provides a currency of payment for services that might further reduce the risk of transaction to both service supplier and user (Philips, 2005). Hallberg (2006) provides the experience of one of the most ambitious and focused training voucher programmes, the micro and small enterprises training technology project in Kenya. The objective of the programme was to increase the demand for training by small business owners and to improve the sustainable supply of quality training programmes. Other major voucher programmes include Tanzania National Voucher Scheme, Hati Punguzo, the primary goal of which was to provide subsidised products to hard-to-reach consumers (Jones, Quijley, & Foster, 2006). One of the key objectives of the Tanzania voucher programme was to build on the burgeoning private sector for insecticide-treated net manufacturing and distribution, and to leverage delivery capacity of small businesses, thereby creating a win-win public-private partnership. The most important aspect of these programmes was the market linking and information service. The voucher users were paid the full cost of training in computer usage and business accounting. The service providers, meanwhile, valued their new relationship with the business associations that administered the program, because these associations kept them in touch with the requirements of their small enterprise customers.

## Matching grant fund

Similar to vouchers, the matching grant fund (MGF) is used to boost demand for services and encourage the suppliers to raise their fees for services. The rationale of the matching grant fund assistance is that the increased demand significantly reduces the supplier's risk and also encourages new entrants, which would lower fees in the long run. The MGF has been used in the form of a general market development fund, upgrading service providers to meet more sophisticated demand by user firms. A key feature of the donor-assisted market development fund is that the donor assistance flows not to a provider but to a facilitator, the fund manager. The purpose of the facilitator is not to provide technical services to enterprises but to mobilise the market, which could consist of both local and foreign service suppliers and local user enterprises. The approach included the provision of partial services, both to the demand side and to the supply side, to upgrade their services in response to meet the new demand.

The matching grant fund is increasingly used by the World Bank, the Inter American Development Bank (IADB), and other donors for creating markets for consulting and training capacity. Philips (2005) provides an evaluation of eight matching grant funds initiated by the World Bank. Most of these funds focused mainly on exports and provision of business services to boost productivity. In the case of export development, these services included: marketing research and planning, quality testing and certification, product adaptation, export fairs, and national/international marketing tours. In the case of business support, they included business strategy and planning, production management, product design, quality standards and control, productivity studies, information systems, and training.

Crisafulli (2000) discusses a matching grant scheme focused on technology diffusion and implemented by the Mauritius government with funding from the World Bank. The central objective of the project was development of the business services market. The programme promoted consulting services to help private firms improve quality, design, technology, or productivity. Under this programme, the government contracted a private agent to run the programme. The agent promoted the programme to potential clients; assisted them with planning; facilitated contact between firms and suitable private consultants; helped clients complete grant applications; advised them on maximising benefits from consulting services; and administered approvals and disbursement of funds. Matching grants had provided only mixed results (Crisafulli, 2000; Philips, 2005). Both authors agree that, if MGF are to fulfill their market creation and institution building potential, their design needs to be more carefully worked out and their operating guidelines improved.

## Franchising

Franchising is viewed as an instrument for enterprise transformation and entrepreneurship development. Business format franchising involves the owner of a proven business granting the right and providing the necessary assistance and support to another party to replicate his or her business. The franchiser provides the franchisee, not only with a business format, well-established brand names, equipment and supplies or raw materials, but also with training for the entrepreneur and his or her staff, support for the operations and setup and layout of facilities, as well as consultancies to ensure business success of the franchisee.

Choy and Goh (2005) describe two examples of franchise business format in Singapore. The first one, Econ-Minimart, relates to modernisation of a traditional local retail business. Franchising enables the entrepreneurs to hold their own business in the face of the competition from the entry of larger international retail businesses into the Singapore market. Under the franchise agreement, the franchiser extends help to modernise the shop floor in terms of proper ventilation, flooring, installation of fans, display racks, provision of electronic cash registers and weighing machines, etc. and training of staff, advertisement and business promotion, and supply of materials benefiting the advantage of bulk purchase. The franchisee needs to pay a fixed rate negotiated at the time of contract. The second case relates to overseas business expansion which involves the development of franchisee entrepreneurs abroad. To encourage the local business to expand overseas through franchising, the government operates a Franchise Development Assistance Scheme. This scheme helps the proven entrepreneurs in Singapore globalise their business by offering a business grant of 50 percent of the cost for consultancy and marketing abroad. The experiences of these franchise models suggests that franchising or franchise-like arrangements are not only beneficial to both franchisers and franchisees; they are also excellent vehicles for co-operation and development of entrepreneurs both internationally as well as within the country (Choy & Goh, 2005). Such business patterns transfers business knowledge and skills and methods to upgrade and thus develop the franchise entrepreneurs.

## Information communication technologies

Information and communication technologies (ICT) are increasingly used for delivery of BDS for small enterprises. ICT applications have enabled entrepreneurs to connect, communicate, and conduct business unhampered by space or location. Duncombe and Heeks (2001) describe a unique form of BDS delivery using ICT to bicycle manufacturers in Vietnam. The buyer in the UK established an internet link to send designs delivery box quantities, bar code labels, and production pipeline information. It was found that these market access and packaging services for small enterprise suppliers in Vietnam have reduced the assembly plant quality problems, production disruptions, and lead times. ICT enable small enterprises to access market information. For example, FIT-initiated commercial radio programmes provide market information and promote interaction among small enterprises and BDS suppliers (McVay, 2002). They have been instrumental in eliminating policy bottlenecks and opening markets for milk traders and fishermen, increasing safety and sanitation in physical markets, and reducing electrical and telecommunications costs.

McCarthy, Kumar, and Pavlovic (2009) share the experiences of ACDI/VOCA in India as it developed an ICT application to improve information flows and communication in a fresh fruit and vegetable value chain. The IGP India Program developed ICT-enabled wireless software applications, freshConnect, that are accessible on handheld devices. The applications enable field extension agents to address information gaps that constrain fruit and vegetable farmers and allow other supply chain participants to monitor and control both back- and front-end supply chain functions. The system makes it possible for a production sponsor (e.g. a fresh produce wholesaler and/or retailer, farmer organisation, or other intermediary) to schedule farmer production in advance of planting, as well as all other steps needed to ensure on-time delivery of the proper products to meet customer demand. IGP India's experience with freshConnect highlights the potential benefits that ICT applications can bring to both producers and suppliers by improving information flows and communication throughout a value chain.

## *Technology development*

Some BDS providers extensively use appropriate technology for product development and dissemination of BDS. For example, International Development Enterprise (IDE) has designed a 'treadle pump'—a manual water pump designed and adapted to various country contexts. It has now been disseminated in a number of countries in Asia and Africa, Bangladesh, Eastern India, Nepal, Kenya, Tanzania, and Uganda (McVay, 2000; Downing & Polak, 2001). The treadle pumps have been widely disseminated in African countries by ApproTech. Both organisations, IDE and ApproTech, focus on product development—manufacture, promote, and distribute the pumps—through the private sector. Their experience suggests that the private-sector businesses were willing to manufacture and sell pumps, but only if they could be assured of a sufficient volume of sales. Similarly, dealers were willing to sell pumps, but were less willing to risk investing in marketing and promotion of a new item and often needed credit to get started in pump sales.

Manaktala (2005) illustrates the unique market development strategies of IDE-India. IDE is promoting two key technologies: treadle pumps and drip irrigation. IDE works with local non-governmental organisations (NGOs). The IDE India staff clearly explains the market approach to partner NGOs and expect them to sell the pumps to local farmers and farmer groups. Realising poor response from women farmers in adopting the pumps due to the lengthy cylinders, IDE India subsequently made modifications to the pump to meet the needs of farmers in India. IDE India also initiated the process of identifying private supply-chain members, from manufacturers to distributors and retailers. IDE India staff ensured that the supply chain worked well (i.e. that a stock of quality pumps was available at the right place and the right price). IDE India had to maintain good relations with the manufacturers, train them further if necessary, appoint distributors and dealers in new areas, encourage them to stock pumps and spare parts, explain the business model to all providers, train mechanics in repair and maintenance, and finally, establish linkages between providers. IDE India branded the product as Krishak Bahandu (KB) and aggressively promoted the brand. The farmers started to demand KB products because the brand represented quality and affordability. Several demand-creation activities were also planned by IDE India. These activities consisted largely of several promotional and awareness campaigns in villages and rural weekly markets. In the maturity stage, the focus of IDE India has been to enhance product acceptance by reaching the next level of more risk-averse customers.

In Nepal, GTZ is focusing on product development and commercialisation in several business service markets (Tomecko, 2005). The strategy combines the development of new products, supplier technical assistance, and demand promotion with the aim of getting as many commercially viable products to the market for the least cost. GTZ focuses on many products and many suppliers. The emphasis is on 'product viability' rather than supplier sustainability. One of GTZ's first efforts was assisting a technical education facility. GTZ help the BDS providers to pilot innovative business-like BDS provisions. A successful case in this category is the support provided to a firm to develop the idea of selling training in basic auto maintenance to car owners or drivers. GTZ provided a brief orientation to the school's staff on how to conduct a market survey. The school surveyed potential students and then designed a pilot course. To reduce the school's risks, GTZ paid for initial advertising for the course. By 2001, the school was on its fifth training course; they were profitable and expanded to new business markets. Subsequent new products developed with GTZ assistance include: presentation skills, value-added tax services for the construction industry, basic banking for the garment/carpet industries, arbitration in the tourism sector, and using market research to increase profits and sales. Efforts to promote innovation among suppliers include: conducting a partially subsidised training course for suppliers on how to use market research tools to identify profitable new markets and develop and test new products; offering suppliers technical assistance in applying marketing research tools and developing new products; providing suppliers with market information from GTZ's BDS market assessment and other market research that identifies potentially profitable market niches and describes consumers' desired service benefits and features.

### *Extension services*

Several models are emerging for private provision of extension services to small producers. Abdullayev and Mustafayeva (2005) illustrate the experience of Mercy Corps in facilitating the availability of high-quality and reasonably priced veterinary and animal husbandry services in the livestock and poultry subsectors in Azerbaijan. Mercy Corps is stimulating demand for veterinary services by organizing clients into groups and building awareness of available services and providers. They are also strengthening the business and marketing capabilities of veterinarians through training and networking. The programme enables networks of trained veterinarians to expand their client base and improve services. A typical private vet in the region is usually male, uses a mobile phone from which he receives calls from clients, and travels using a car or a motorcycle that also serves as a mobile ambulance, complete with supplies and instruments. The vet visits farms and provides fee-based services. The mobile vet unit also coordinates with the State Veterinary Department on vaccination campaigns and disease outbreaks. In addition to traditional veterinarian services, vets also supply embedded livestock services, such as advice on animal breeding, feeding, and quality control, and links with potential animal buyers.

Similar programmes of private provision of extension services include the initiatives of Practical Action in Peru (Griffith & Rodríguez, 2005), the United States Agency for International Development (USAID), and Fintrac-supported Centro de Desarollo de Agronegocios (CDA) project in Honduras (Chalmers, Field, & Downing, 2005). Practical Action has worked with the livestock service farmers, called Kamayog, to identify appropriate extension products and services, and built the technical capacity of these community-based consultants. The Kamayoq earn a living selling inputs, such as veterinary products and providing technical advice, which farmers pay for in cash and kind. The CDA project in Honduras focused on technical assistance and market linkages and expanding market systems.

### *Improving sector competitiveness*

Some of the BDS programmes aim at improving sector competitiveness. A successful example of BDS market development with a focus on improving sector competitiveness is the Bangladesh Rural Advancement Committee (BRAC)'s poultry development programme (Newnham, 2001). The poultry sector in Bangladesh has been constrained by low productivity, a high level of mortality, and a lack of infrastructure. In order to address these constraints, BRAC designed a market infrastructure to provide necessary inputs and training to poultry producers and to assist in marketing eggs. This market system is made up of BRAC-subsidised services; BRAC sustainable business activities; and private-sector BDS suppliers. BRAC provides its members with: training, equipment, and the inputs of high-yield variety chicks, good-quality feed, and medical supplies. In addition to direct provision, BRAC also facilitates members to provide services themselves. Members are trained in basic veterinary techniques, chick rearing, feed production, or egg marketing. They provide inoculations, medicines, eight-week birds, feed, and marketing services to other BRAC members as well as the wider community. Newnham (2001) reports that BRAC's direct participation in the poultry sector has stimulated market development in rural areas, which has in turn increased demand for services to the poultry sector. It is also found that BRAC's facilitation of service providers has enabled the increasing demand for services and other inputs to be satisfied.

Similar to BRAC's poultry programme, the Kenya BDS programme works toward improving the competitiveness of Kenya tree fruit exports in global markets and increasing the participation of smallholders in the tree fruit value chain (Zandniapour, Sebstad & Snodgrass, 2004). The interventions focused on promoting commercially viable solutions to business constraints. The types of business solutions/services promoted include those related to product assembly and grading, such as including supply contracts, forward and backward linkages, and broker schemes. They also include quality assurance services related to crop husbandry skills such as post-harvest handling, certification, and traceability. Kenya BDS facilitates access to commercially viable material inputs as well as the development of commercially viable sources of market information, business skill development, and appropriate technology to upgrade products and production processes.

## Conclusion

The small enterprise development field is undergoing remarkable change. The change is triggered by the learnings and experiences of a number of approaches, including local economic development, cluster development, and subsector approaches. Business services are perceived as a missing link in small enterprise development. Learning from the experience of microfinance and similar programmes reveals that small enterprises also would be able to purchase the required business services provided they are made available in a cost-effective manner. Among other things, an important obstacle in access to business services that is recognised across the world is the lack of appropriate providers. The subsidised provision of business services proved to be less cost effective, lack quality, and not be made available and fall short of appropriate products and services meeting the demand for a variety of business services in different sectors.

The foregoing discussion reveals a paradigm shift in business services for small enterprises. The new paradigm focuses on the market development and serves to address a vital missing link in small enterprise development. The new paradigm of BDS market development has emerged from the practical experience of donors and practitioners over the years. Unlike the traditional approaches in BDS, like subsidised training and other services, the new approaches aim at creating a sustainable market. Various strategies used to promote business services to small enterprises include: offer vouchers and matching grants; provide information to consumers that aim to expand the demand for BDS by making small enterprises aware of available services and potential benefits; help small enterprises overcome diseconomies of scale in purchasing BDS by enabling them to purchase services in groups by operating in clusters and networks; create or expand BDS embedded within business relationships between SEs and other firms; build the capacity of new or existing BDS suppliers to profitably serve small enterprises through technical assistance; commercialize new products through existing suppliers by assisting with product development, market testing, and initial marketing of new products. It is found that the emerging BDS models provide access to business services to small enterprises in a cost-effective manner.

## References

Abdullayev, K., & Mustafayeva, N. (2005). *BDS market facilitation in Azerbajain: Veterinary services for small livestock holders.* Washington, DC: The SEEP Network.

Altenburg, T., & Stamm, A. (2004). *Towards a more effective provision of business services.* Discussion Paper 4. Bonn: German Development Institute.

Anderson, G. (2000). *The hidden MSE service sector—Research into commercial BDS provision to micro and small enterprises in Vietnam and Thailand.* Donor Committee Conference on Business Services for Small Enterprises in Asia: Developing Markets and Measuring Performance, April 2000. Retrieved October 10, 2016 from www.ilo.org/wcmsp5/groups/public/—ed_emp/—emp_ent/—ifp_seed/documents/publication/wcms_117727.pdf.

Carney, D. (1998). *Sustainable rural livelihoods: What contribution can we make?* London: Department Finance for International Development (DFID).

Chalmers, G., Field, M., & Downing, J. (2005). *Jump-starting agribusiness markets: How Centro de Desarollo de Agronegocios and USAID/Honduras helped small producers contribute to the rebirth of a sector.* Washington, DC: USAID.

Chen, M. (1996). *Beyond credit: A sub-sector approach to promoting women's enterprises.* Ottawa: Aga Khan Foundation.

Choy, C. L., & Goh, M. (2005). Franchising: A vehicle for entrepreneurship development in Singapore. In M. Harper & J. Tanburn (Eds.), *Mapping the shift in business development services: Making markets work for the poor* (pp. 67–73). Rugby, Warwickshire: ITDG Publishing.

Committee of Donor Agencies. (2001). *Donor committee guiding principles, 2001 SEEP guide to business development services and resources.* Small Enterprise Education and Promotion Network. Retrieved November 10, 2016 from www.enterprise-development.org/wp-content/uploads/BDS-Guiding-Principles-2001-English.pdf.

Crisafulli, D. (2000). Matching grant schemes. In J. Levitsky (Ed.), *Business development services: A review of international experience.* Rugby: Intermediate Technology Publications.

DFID (Department for International Development). (2005). *Making market systems work better for the poor (M4P): An introduction to the concept.* Discussion paper prepared for ADB/DFID joint workshop on Making Markets Work for the Poor, 15–16 February, Manila, Philippines.

Downing, J. (2001). Introduction: Business services for small enterprises in Asia. In J. Levitsky (Ed.), *Small business services in Asian countries: Market development and performance measurement* (pp. 1–21). Warwickshire, UK: ITDG Publishing.

Downing, J., & Polak, P. (2001). Commercialization of the treadle pump in Bangladesh: Product marketing on a mass scale. In J. Levitsky (Ed.), *Small business services in Asian countries: Market development and performance measurement* (pp. 234–245). Warwickshire, UK: ITDG Publishing.

Duncombe, R., & Heeks, R. (2001). *Enterprise development and information and communication technologies (ICTs) in developing countries: ICT-flyers.* Institute for Development Policy and

Management, The University of Manchester for DFID, March 2001. Retrieved October 5, 2016 from https://pdfs.semanticscholar.org/5947/be257a4f0f5d04375749611fb91fd784effb.pdf.

Gibson, A. (2005). Business development services: Core principles and future challenges. In L. M. Jones (Ed.), *Value chains in development: Emerging theory and practice* (pp. 83–95). Warwickshire, UK: Practical Action Publishing.

Goldmark, L. (1999). The financial viability of business development services. *Small Enterprise Development, 10*(2), 4–16.

Griffith, A., & Rodríguez, D. (2005). *The new Kamayoq: Developing farmer to farmer extension services in Peru.* Rugby, UK: Practical Action Publishing.

Halder, S. (2003). BRACS's business development services: Do they pay? *Enterprise Development and Microfinance, 14*(2), 26–35. https://doi.org/10.3362/0957-1329.2003.019

Hallberg, K. (2006). A retrospective assessment of the Kenya voucher training programme. *Small Enterprise Development, 17*(2), 56–67.

Harper, M., & Tanburn, J. (2005). *Mapping the shift in business development services: Making markets work for the poor.* New Delhi: ITDG Publishing.

Hileman, M., & Tanburn, J. (2000). *The wheels of trade: Developing markets for business services.* Rugby: ITDG Publishing.

Jones, L. M. (2012). *Value chains in development: Emerging theory and practice.* Warwickshire, UK: Practical Action Publishing.

Jones, L. M., Quijley, J., & Foster, G. (2006). Vouchers re-visited: Can small enterprises save government programmes. *Small Enterprise Development, 17*(4), 43–51.

Kashyap, P. (1991). Marketing rural products in India. *Small Enterprise Development, 2*(2), 51–56.

Kula, O., Downing, J., & Field, M. (2006). Value chain programmes to integrate competitiveness economic growth and poverty reduction. *Small Enterprise Development, 17*(2), 23–36.

Magara, V. P., & Were, S. (2014). Influence of business development services and policy factors on small and micro enterprise growth: A case of Nyakach constituency. *The Strategic Journal of Business & Change Management, 2*(2), 18–37.

Manaktala, S. (2005). *International Development Enterprises (IDE)'s twelve year journey towards facilitation.* Washington, DC: The Small Enterprise Education and Promotion (SEEP) Network.

McCarthy, S., Kumar, K., & Pavlovic, A. (2009). *New ICT solutions to the age old problems: Case of the IGP India project.* Washington, DC: The SEEP Network and ACDI/VOCA.

Mckenzie, J. (2001). Creating a market in management training for Vietnam's private sector. In J. Levitsky (Ed.), *Small business services in Asian countries: Market development and performance measurement* (pp. 118–131). Warwickshire, UK: ITDG Publishing.

McVay, M. (2000). *SME marketing programmes: Trends, lessons learned and challenges identified from an analysis using the BDS performance measurement framework.* Retrieved October 16, 2016 from http://bdsknowledge.org/dyn/bds/docs/110/mcvay.pdf.

McVay, M. (2002). *An information revolution for small enterprise in Africa: Experience in interactive radio formats in Africa.* Retrieved October 10, 2016 from www.ilo.org/public/libdoc/ilo/2002/102B09_97_engl.pdf.

McVay, M., & Miehlbradt, A. O. (2001). *Developing commercial markets for BDS: Can this give the scale and impact we need?* Second Annual Seminar, 10–14 September 2001, Turin, Italy.

Miehlbradt, A. O., & McVay, M. (2004). *Developing commercial markets for business development services.* BDS Update-2004. Turin, Italy: International Labour Organization.

Miehlbradt, A. O., & McVay, M. (2005). *From BDS to making market for the poor.* The BDS reader-2005. Turin, Italy: International Labour Organization.

Mole, K., & Capelleras, J.-L. (2018). Take-up and variation of advice for new firm founders in different local contexts. *Environment and Planning C: Politics and Space, 36*(1), 3–27. http://doi.org/10.1177/2399654417691514

Nagayya, D., & Rao, T.V. (2011). Enabling small and medium enterprises to target globalization. *The IUP Journal of Managerial Economics, 9*(4), 15–32.

Newnham, J. (2001). The BRAC poultry programme in Bangladesh. In J. Levitsky (Ed.), *Small business services in Asian countries: Market development and performance measurement* (pp. 220–232). Warwickshire, UK: ITDG Publishing.

Okeyo, W. O., Gathungu, J., & K'Obonyo, P. (2014). The effect of business development services on performance of small and medium manufacturing enterprises in Kenya. *International Journal of Business and Social Research, 4*(6), 12–26.

Philips, D. A. (2005). The market based approach to enterprise assistance: An evaluation of World Bank's market development grant funds. In J. Levitsky (Ed.), *Small business services in Asian countries: Market development and performance measurement* (pp. 103–115). Warwickshire, UK: ITDG Publishing.

Reji, E. M. (2013). Value chains and small enterprise development: Theory and praxis. *American Journal of Industrial and Business Management, 3*, 28–35. http://doi.org/10.4236/ajibm.2013.31004

Reji, E. M. (2018). Integration of small-scale handloom producers into global value chains: Insights from Kannur handloom cluster, India. *Enterprise Development and Microfinance, 29*(3 & 4), 209–226. https://doi.org/10.3362/1755-1986.18-00001

Sandeep, G., Bruno, S., & Mark, E. (2018). Business development services for micro, small and medium enterprises—Literature review of past trends and future directions. *World Review of Entrepreneurship, Management and Sustainable Development, 14*(3), 312–332. http://doi.org/10.1504/WREMSD.2018.091688

Seo, J. H., Perry, V. G., Tomczyk, D., & Solomon, G. T. (2014). Who benefits most? The effects of managerial assistance on high- versus low-performing small businesses. *Journal of Business Research, 67*(1), 2845–2852. http://doi.org/10.1016/j.jbusres.2012.07.003

Tomecko, J. (2005). Case studies of BDS market development interventions in weaker markets. In M. Harper & J. Tanburn (Eds.), *Mapping the shift in business development services: Making market work for the poor* (pp. 153–160). Warwickshire, UK: ITDG Publishing.

Walsh, M., Kevin, K., & Candance, N. (1991). A case for business training with women's groups. *Small Enterprise Development, 2*(1), 13–19.

Zandniapour, L., Sebstad, J., & Snodgrass, D. (2004). Review of evaluation of selected enterprise development projects, Microenterprise Report-3, Washington, DC: United States Agency for International Aid. Retrieved 15 April, 2020 from https://www.coursehero.com/file/7816929/Review-of-Evaluations-of-Selected-Enterprise-Development-Projects/

# PART 2
# Sustainability of community

The chapters in this section focus on the sustainability of community. 'Sustainable communities' are an integral part of sustainable development. Sustainability of communities implies a process in which members of a community come together to take collective action and generate solutions to common problems. A critical component of these initiatives is the community-based projects that address social, environmental, and economic issues. Many of these initiatives involve building local talents and skills, community participation, and empowerment of communities. The focus is on empowering individuals and groups with the necessary skills and competence to change their communities. Community development aims at achieving participatory democracy, sustainable development, economic opportunity, equality, and social justice.

In recent years there has been widespread acceptance of this terminology, 'sustainable communities', at the local, national, and international levels. Sustainable community initiatives have largely spread at various levels, including neighbourhoods and cities, in response to demand by various actor groups to create sustainable communities. The initiatives involve sustainability practices including land use and community design, transportation, energy efficiency, waste reduction, and sustainable consumption. The focus is on the environment and economic sustainability, social equity and well-being, and political empowerment. These initiatives are creating business models for sustainable living.

The idea of community development is part of social movements as well as economic planning. For example, in India, Mahatma Gandhi used the ideals of community development as part of the 'Swaraj Movement' aimed at interdependency of villages across the country. After independence, Jawaharlal Nehru, the first Prime Minister of India, had initiated a comprehensive community development plan as part of the First Five-Year Pan. In the 1970s and 1980s, community development had formed part of the Integrated Rural Development Programme—a development strategy initiated by the United Nations and World Bank.

# 4

# CASE STUDIES ON UTILISATION OF COMMUNITY RADIO IN ACHIEVING SUSTAINABLE DEVELOPMENT

*Amolina Ray*[1]

## Introduction

Controlling the media is one of the strategies employed by the authorities holding on to power. Hailed as 'manufacture of consent', the government tries to consolidate control over the media so that it can extinguish every possible voice of resistance. Community radio (CR) stations have emerged worldwide as a part of the resistance against the authorities by giving 'voice to the voiceless' and at the same time multiplying the many voices of resistance. This chapter deals with the role community radio stations in India play in bringing positive change into a community. To substantiate my argument, I have selected four community radio stations. These were selected on the basis of their year of operation, affiliation of the host organisation (non-governmental organisations, NGOs, or academic institute), and their geographical location. Community radio also marks the dissemination of power. While the power of decision making is concentrated in limited hands in mainstream media, in community radio, the decision-making power is with the community. It implies that the community will decide all the aspects such as the administrative, technological, and programming of the station. To attain sustainable development (SD), it is important for each and every individual to actively participate in the debates and decisions that affect their lives. On the one hand, they need to receive information, but on the other hand, they should voice their opinion. People at the grassroots level are often excluded from the developmental process because they lack the resources or skills that are necessary to be a part of this process. Community radio stations provide this platform.

This chapter draws heavily from theories related to development communication. Development communication has been defined as:

> Purposive communication intended to influence the developing areas of a nation or region in such a manner that the people of that area or region

> are socially, politically and economically transformed—their wellness being enveloped in an atmosphere of freedom where all citizens are free to pursue their noble goals in life without slavish subservience to the centres of authority. The purpose of development communication is to be stated in terms of desirable social change. Desirable social change includes better social relations based on equal or better sharing of the resources available in society in a dignified manner.
>
> *(Vilanilam, 2009, p. 97)*

Development communications has its roots in the Sender-Message-Channel-Receiver (SMCR) model. This model considers people as merely a passive audience that receives the intended message without questioning it and interpreting it in the exact desired way the sender(s) wanted it to be interpreted. Paulo Freire critiqued this model that saw the receiver or target audience devoid of any agency to cast their opinion. Freire engaged in activities that were aimed at raising critical awareness of mass media messages and content. As such, Freire developed a method of what he called 'education for critical consciousness among peasants learning to read'.

> What was special about Freire's approach was that it stressed active participation by students in the literacy process, a critical examination of their own situation of oppression, and the ultimate goal of empowerment instead of just learning the tools of reading and writing. It was a participatory method that advocated activism.
>
> *(cited in McAnany, 2012, p. 72)*

Paulo Freire emphasises to develop a strategy that involves the community people looking for ways and platforms to discuss issues that hold importance to them. In places where freedom of speech was restricted, a community radio station came into existence as a platform for those who were silenced for various reasons and to help make information available to them. People living in the periphery have always been at the crux of development discourse, but as the recipients of development measures rather than as active participants in the process. Also, many groups like women are kept silent by cultural traditions. Sustainable development can be achieved only when these oppressed people can control and manage their means of communication. Support for communication in the context of development does not just mean providing more information to poor people—it means giving them a 'voice' (Panos, 2007). It means enabling them to be the producers of information as well as to participate actively in decision making. Community radio, the third tier of broadcasting, employs the participatory method. Referring to the concept of participatory radio, Freire observed that as people actively participate in developmental processes, they will become liberated and empowered.

Gradually, communication for development became synonymous with notions such as alternative, participative, and horizontal. The participatory model projects the importance of the idiosyncrasies of cultural identity of local communities. The participation process takes place at three levels: national, local, and individual. This essentially means that any development communications activity or programme should cater to all three levels. This principle implies the right to participation in the planning and production of media content (Servaes, 2005). One of the prime examples in this area of communications for development as a participative approach is the establishment of community radio stations.

The principal task of community radio is to empower the local community and foster their participation in a two-way communication process (Gayen, 2012). Community radio follows an individual approach that is being specifically adapted to the wants and needs of the particular community. According to Salazar and Hammer (2008), the community radio station is inextricably linked to the particular community that developed it and is tailored to the culture, concerns, history, and current events of the community it serves.

One of the goals of development communication is to enhance the quality of life of populations, including mental wellbeing, eradicate social injustice, and promote freedom of speech. Community radio stations can play an important role in achieving United Nations Sustainable Development Goals (SDGs). Community radio stations can broadcast programmes on issues that will impact activities relating to the eradication of extreme poverty, achieving universal primary education, promoting gender equality, reducing child mortality, combating HIV/AIDS, ensuring environmental sustainability, and developing international partnerships for development (Gayen, 2012).

Community radio came into existence in India in 2004. There are 214 operational community radio stations in India as of December 2017. Books and articles have been written on the potential of community radio in India and issues related to making it self-reliant. One of the most referred books in this field is *Other Voices: The Struggle for Community Radio in India* (Pavarala & Malik, 2007), which focuses on the comparative study of the policy of community radio in other democratic countries. At the time of publication of the book, non-governmental organisations (NGOs) did not operate community radio stations. Some interested NGOs bought time slots in All India Radio (AIR) and broadcast their programmes. The book also analysed four such community radio projects. Another book, *Self-Sustainability of Community Radio: Stories from India* (Singh, 2016), deals with two models of community radio stations in revenue generation.

This chapter deals with the potential of community radio in bringing about positive change and development for the grassroots people. Through case studies of four community radio stations in India, this chapter documents the decade-long journey of community radio in India and analyses the potential of community radio as an agent for bringing sustainable development. The chapter is organised as follows. First, it reviews the key concepts and definition of community radio. This is followed by a description of community radio stations in India. The third section provides the methodology of the study, followed by results and discussion in the fourth and fifth sections.

## Review of literature

### *Community radio: definition and concept*

The seed of community radio was present in the MacBride Report, published by UNESCO in 1980. The Report analysed the negative aspect of a one-way flow of communication and information moving from richer countries to poorer countries and on a national level from those in power to those on the periphery (UNESCO, 1980). As defined by the Association of Community Radio Broadcasters (AMARC), community radio has three aspects: non-profit, community ownership and control, and community participation (Pavarala & Malik, 2007). In its aim and objectives, it is different from other forms of radio. Community radio emphasises freedom of speech, which is in direct contrast to state-owned or commercial radio which disseminates the viewpoint of the state or the capitalist society. The focus is on equal access and participation to all community members. It is managed by its own community and ensures active participation in the overall management of the station. A community radio station is considered successful when it operates on a non-profit model and has community ownership without any external interference. It acts as an independent voice and is accountable only to its community (Salazar & Hammer, 2008). Free from the coercive power of advertisers and commercial interests and owned, managed, and run by local communities, community radio stations open up the space for local talk by local people on issues of local interest and concern. In doing so, community radio represents a key element in the empowerment, development, and consolidation of local communities—a key element in other words of community development (Gaynor & O'Brien, 2011).

Community radio stands in sharp contrast to commercial radio and public-service radio. A community radio station mainly relies on government-sponsored projects, public interest advertisements, and limited advertisement for its sustenance. Because community radio does not depend on advertisements for its survival, advertisers also have no say in the programming. The management structure is also less complex and hierarchical than either commercial or public-service radio. This helps a community radio station to remain true to its ideology and help in voicing the concerns of its people without any bias. Community radio operates with very few paid staff. It relies mainly on volunteers. It endorses participatory decision-making practices, which is in contrast to the other tiers of broadcasting.

One of the most useful aspects of community radio is that it also acts as a connecting link between different communities across the country. At a local level, it provides a platform to the marginalised communities to voice their concerns, whereas at a national level it brings different marginalised communities across the country together. The individual communities thus realise that they are not alone and there are other groups like them who share their concerns. It is at this stage that a sense of solidarity develops between them. This kind of solidarity may give birth to a movement, which will help them to improve their position within the current system, or it may give birth to a new system, which will be based on 'equality and freedom to all citizens.'

The usefulness of community radio is more than one factor: it can give voice to the voiceless, provide an alternative to mainstream media's monopoly, and reinforce democracy. Community radio is the mouthpiece of change in the hands of marginalised people. Technology plays an important role in making community radio an agent for sustainable development. Community radio is characterised by not expensive high-tech gadgets but low-cost innovations that help the urban and rural poor to broadcast their views. Unlike commercial or public-service radio, which is characterised by heavy-duty technology, studio costs, and expert voices, in community radio the emphasis is not on technology but on the message. The emphasis is on making members of the community interact, inform, and participate.

In order to fully utilise its potential, new technological innovations are needed in community radio that can change the landscape of grassroots media. The United Nations Educational, Scientific and Cultural Organisation (UNESCO) has supported several community radio projects across the world and encouraged the use of low-cost technology in broadcasting so that people at the grassroots level can own the media. In the 1980s, UNESCO helped develop the first 30W solar-powered transmitter used in several community radio projects. UNESCO also supported the development of a radio in a box—something that is small, effective, and can be repaired by people themselves. This 55- by 50-cm box contains a laptop, mixer, CD/cassette player, and a 30W FM transmitter and antenna. It is most useful in broadcasting to remote communities and in disaster-hit areas where broadcasting infrastructure gets destroyed.

Another innovation is the e-Tuk Tuk that is very popular in rural Sri Lanka. This is a self-contained mobile tele-centre and radio broadcasting unit set up in an autorickshaw, with a laptop, a battery-operated printer, camera, telephone, and scanner. It runs on a generator and the roof carries the broadcasting unit. The weekly route of the Tuk Tuk is broadcast beforehand, and people assemble to listen and participate in the programmes.

## Emergence of community radio in India

Community radio became operational in India after the introduction of the policy guidelines on community radios in the year 2002 (Government of India, 2002). India is diverse in terms of culture, language, and socio-economic backgrounds. There are many communities whose access to information and self-expression are not always guaranteed by the state-owned or commercial radio. The state-owned radio in India is to a large extent irrelevant to the concerns of the common people because it acts as a propaganda machine to distribute the viewpoint of the State, whereas commercial radio is truly 'mass' in terms of consumption, but it is extremely limited in terms of participation. At the very core, development—if it is to be sustainable—must be a process that allows people to be their own agents of change: to act individually and collectively, using their own ideas, practices, and knowledge and own their means of communication and participate in the decision-making process.

The community radio movement in India gained momentum after the 1995 judgment of the Supreme Court of India. The historical judgment of the Supreme Court that declared 'airwaves constitute public property and must be utilised for advancing public good' was set against a dispute between the Ministry of Information and Broadcasting and the Cricket Association of Bengal. The primary holding of the case was that airwaves were public property and hence there could be no monopoly over it by state-controlled media, like Doordarshan. While the judgment does not directly speak of community radio, there are important implications that the judgment makes for community radio. The court also reiterated the right of freedom of speech and expression enshrined in Article 19(1). The Supreme Court judgment led to the Bangalore Declaration of 1996, which formed the basis of advocacy for community radio. Policy planners and media professionals discussed the importance of community radio in India. The Bangalore Declaration on Radio of September 1996 has emphasised that community radio would, 'besides educating and entertaining people, connect people with people through participatory or circular communication, connect with organisations and communities, and finally, connect people with government and public service agencies' (http://www.dds india.com/ www/radiostn.htm).

The Supreme Court judgment paved the way for a Broadcasting Bill in 1997. The Bill seeks to set up an 'autonomous' Broadcasting Authority of India (BAI). It was decided that some of the major functions of the authority would be: 1) to ensure that a wide range of broadcasting services are available throughout India, 2) to ensure services of high quality and offer a wide range of programmes to appeal to a variety of tastes and interests, 3) to determine the programme code and standard, and 4) to take necessary action for violation of code or condition of license.

After the drafting of the Broadcasting Bill, UNESCO sponsored a workshop in Hyderabad and Pastapur (Andhra Pradesh) which published the 'Pastapur Initiative on Community Radio' in the year 2000, urging the government to create a three-tier structure of broadcasting in India: state-owned public radio, private commercial radio, and a non-profit community radio. In December 2002, the Government of India approved a policy for the grant of licenses for setting up community radio stations to well-established educational institutions. In 2004, Anna FM, the first community radio in India, saw the light of day. In the beginning only educational institutes of high repute were permitted to operate and own a community radio station. In 2006, NGOs and agricultural institutes were permitted to operate community radio stations. Sangham Radio, the first community-based radio station that was completely different from campus-based radio, was launched in 2008 in the Pastapur village, Andhra Pradesh, and was set up by the Deccan Development Society (DDS).

The World Association of Community Radio Broadcasters (AMARC) defines community radio as 'a station that responds to the needs of the community which it serves and that contributes to its development in a progressive manner promoting social change' (www.amarc.org). The then Minister of Information and Broadcasting said that:

> Community radio movement has a hugely important role to play. . . . those concerns are neither discussed, nor debated nor deliberated with the vigor which they deserve. Unfortunately, because some of those issues are extremely dry, they are extremely localised and obviously would not generate the kind of excitement which advertisers are looking for which essentially are the revenue model on which the broadcasting industry thrives. Therefore, they do not find that kind of visibility or that kind of display on what we call the colloquially national discourse. Those are the real issues . . . issues of water, issues with regard to how the rural communities or farming community need to innovate and improve the techniques.
>
> *(http://edaa.in)*

Community radio in India can be operated by NGOs, educational institutes, and agricultural institutes, which are committed to air developmental, agricultural, health, educational, environmental, social welfare, community development, and cultural programmes. The programming should reflect the special interests and needs of the local community.

## Methodology

This chapter evaluates the impact of community radio stations in sustainable development in India. In the context of the research question, the case studies of selected radio stations have become integral to the study. To measure the impact of radio stations, case study was the most suitable method. Case study as a research method gives the opportunity to accommodate multiple perspectives and document the individual voices. To understand the impact, four case studies were done. The case studies of the radio stations mentioned were selected on the basis of their year of operation, affiliation to the host institute, and geographical location. In accordance with the policy guidelines for the community radio issued by the Ministry of Information and Broadcasting, Government of India, educational institutions, non-governmental organisations, and agricultural institutions are affiliated to host a community radio station. Since India is a heterogeneous country, it is interesting to study the different cultural practices and societal norms of different communities. It was mandatory to spread throughout the length and breadth of the country. If looked at from close quarters, it may be noted that representation from urban and rural India is also taken into account while selecting the stations, so as to see whether radio as a medium of dissemination is popular in both the regions. As in urban areas, the options are more in terms of commercial radio. Also, there are high-rises in urban India which pose problems in transmission. In this context, it is important to understand how does community radio overcome these impediments? In rural areas, were the people ready to make the transition from being recipients of information to makers of information was one of the key questions. The case studies of the community radio stations used in this chapter were funded by the project 'Community Radio in India' under the supervision of Prof Nilanjana Gupta, under University Grants Commission scheme 'University with Potential for Excellence-Phase II' housed at School of Media, Communication and Culture, Jadavpur University, and was carried out from January to November 2013. Table 4.1 provides the details of community radio stations included in this study.

The case studies included interviews with the head of the organisation, management staff, and listeners or performers of the radio stations. These interviews helped explore the level of involvement, ownership, and relationship of the community with the station and analyse the impact of the station on its community. The interviews were both structured and unstructured. The researcher conducted focus-group discussions and in-depth interviews. For each station, around 20 listeners/performers and all the management staff were interviewed. The interviews were mostly conducted inside the radio station and in the absence of any staff members. Some of the interviews were conducted outside of the radio premise. The focus group discussions took place during the time of field visit. For Anna FM and Puduvaai Vaani, the researcher relied on a translator as the language that most of the local people speak was not known to the researcher. To avoid any type of bias, it was kept in mind that the translator should not be in any capacity linked with the radio station. The management team of all the radio stations cooperated. The researcher categorically made it clear that the singular purpose of the study was to analyse the impact of the community radio stations and to document the impediments that stand in the way of utilising the full potential of the community radio stations. The study is not concerned in any way to evaluate the performance of these stations. These interviews were digitally recorded and transcribed on a computer.

Data was also collected through direct observation and content analysis of the programme schedules and selected broadcasts of the radio stations. The broadcast programmes were classified into four categories: education, information, social issues, and entertainment programmes. The respondents were selected on the basis

**TABLE 4.1** Details of community radio stations

| *Sl. No* | *Name of the Community Radio Station* | *Affiliation and Location* | *Year of Starting* |
|---|---|---|---|
| 1 | Anna FM | Anna University, Chennai (Tamil Nadu, Urban) | 2004 |
| 2 | Radio Banasthali | Banasthali Vidyapeeth, Vanasthali (Rajasthan, Rural) | 2005 |
| 3 | Puduvaai Vaani | Pondicherry University, Puducherry (Semi-Rural) | 2009 |
| 4 | Radio Namaskar | Young India, Konark (Odisha, Rural) | 2010 |

*Source*: Compiled by the author based on the interviews conducted

of their association with the station. In community radio, the line dividing the listener and the performer is blurred. Most of the performers of the stations were listeners at some time. True to the community radio ideology, the listeners double up as performers. Before starting the interview, the researcher introduced herself briefly and informed the respondents of the purpose of the study.

## Case studies on community radio stations

### *Anna FM*

Anna FM is the first community radio station of India. It started to function in 2004 at the campus of Anna University in Chennai. Being a technological university, the university wanted to use its technical expertise to train human beings so that they can express themselves and be useful for the society. It is a radio station situated on the campus but serving the nearby community. Anna FM has joined with both government and NGOs. Government organisations include the Chennai Police, National Council for Science and Technology Development (NCSTC), Department of Science and Technology (DST), Government of India, Department of Primary Education, Government of Tamil Nadu, Tamil Nadu Pollution Control Board, Tamil Nadu Science Museum, and the Saidapet Government Hospital. NGOs include The Banyan (an NGO for the mentally challenged), Ability Foundation (NGO for the differently abled), National Institute for the Visually Handicapped (NIVH), and Child Relief and You (CRY). Some of the programmes of the radio station are: a) *Magalir Neram*, scripted by the women's community. This programme has helped many women to speak about themselves and common issues that they face in their daily lives. The women not only produce and record the programme, but they also interview experts from the related field. It helps them to have a scientific outlook and educate themselves; b) *Muyarchi Thiruvinai Akkum*, a weekly programme for special children. The programme features interviews with special educators, the special students, teachers, parents, and volunteers.

### *Radio Banasthali*

Radio Banasthali is situated in Banasthali Vidyapeeth, which is a private University in the Tonk district, Rajasthan. The radio station started to function in 2005. The university was set up with the aim of community welfare and community development. It is one of the largest women's universities in the country. The main objective of the university is empowering the community and empowering women through education. As an extension of this objective, Radio Banasthali was set up to communicate with the community that resides outside of the campus. Radio Banasthali educates its community people and generates awareness about superstition through the radio programmes. The programmes focus on issues related to education, health, environment, agriculture, and rural and community development. The radio station collaborates with organisations like the United Nations

International Children's Education Fund (UNICEF), Pratham-Rajasthan, and Save the Children. It also bagged a project on Science for Women, which was funded by the Department of Science and Technology (DST), Government of India. A major focus of this community radio station is education and training. In collaboration with NGO Pratham, Rajasthan, Radio Banasthali has developed and produced 45 episodes on primary education. The programmes were designed in an informal format so that the students can easily understand the subject matter. The radio station is continuously training the women members in radio production so that they could gradually overcome their fear of the microphone.

## Puduvai Vaani FM

Puduvai Vaani is located in the campus of Puducherry University, Puducherry. It became operational in the year 2009. The main objective behind starting the radio station was to make the local people aware about their surroundings and improve their quality of life. The radio station was started after the disastrous tsunami that caused havoc in the year 2004. The university is situated near the coastal area. The fisherman community was largely hit by the tsunami. The radio station played an important role in rehabilitation of the fishermen. A sizeable amount of programmes were dedicated to the different government schemes related to rehabilitation. Education is another broad theme of the programmes of the radio station. Students from the university as well as nearby schools produce programmes on education. Information on different scholarship is given, celebrating important days like science day and youth day, where students participating are broadcast on air. Some of the programmes are: a) live programmes with varied topics related to health, road safety, and child labour that are discussed live with the participation of experts and community members, weekly. Listeners can phone in and participate in the programme; and b) *Unagalai Thed*, a popular cultural programme. The university is a central university where students from other states study. They participate and share their cultural practices. The students as well as members of the community come to know about different cultures of India. The programme is bilingual (Tamil and English).

## Radio Namaskar

Radio Namaskar is operated by the NGO Young India, Konark, in the State of Odisha. It started to function in the year 2010. The parent organisation works to bring critical awareness among people on self-governance, human rights, education, environment, health, gender, and cultural heritage. It works mainly with marginalised groups like tribals and dalits. As an extension of its parent organisation, the community radio station primarily focuses on local governance, agriculture, gender equity, human rights, and disaster management. It has collaborated with government organisations like the Ministry of Youth Affairs and Sports, Ministry of Information and Broadcasting, Government of India, Ministry of Environment and Forest, Government of India, and Department of Sociology, Utkal University, Bhubaneswar. NGOs like the Centre for Youth and Social Development (CYSD) and Action Aid, Bhubaneswar have also participated. Some of the programmes are: a) *Chala school ku jiba* (Let us go to school) is a programme based on student retention in primary school. This programme helped to achieve a zero dropout rate in the nearby villages; and b) *Chasa Basa Katha* is an interactive programme based on agriculture. Local farmers interview agriculture experts and seek their advice.

## Impacts of community radio

Community radio helps in connecting individual listeners to a broader community by bringing people of diverse socio-economic classes together. Madhevan, a listener and performer of Puduvai Vaani, spoke on how the radio station helped him to have a better understanding of the society in which he lives. Mr Madhevan shared that:

> Puduvai Vaani helped me and my friends, I know them personally and spoken to them [sic], to know my society because whenever we discuss about a situation or about like transportation situation or transportation problem, in live programmes. I started to get the news and views of people from the all levels of society like from people below poverty line, from various communities like teaching staff, non-teaching staff and student community. This helped me to know about my society and improve my decision-making qualities. I am really thankful to Puduvai Vaani . . . it told me that you are not only part of the society, there is much to explore, to learn. . . . consider everyone . . . consider the impact of the problem on everyone before taking a decision.

Jamaila, a participant of Anna Community Radio, believes that community radio not only helps in increasing self-worth, but it also helps in making different sections of the society sensitive to each other. She also hints at the level of belongingness of the community to the station. Ms Jamaila said that,

> I was really put back in my family. . . . I was being dumped. Anna CR brought me out. . . . whenever we come to Anna CR we feel we are in our mom's place. When we get married, we go to our husband place . . . then we come to our mother's place . . . we feel so comfortable, so secured. Anna CR is like that for us. And when I came to Anna CR, I was a mom for twins. . . . I used to feed here, students used to take care of them and I would produce programmes and that made me very satisfied, secured. . . . Anna CR made our life very comfortable and successful, too.

Lokesh Sharma, the Station Manager of Radio Banasthali, says that the impact of the community radio station can be measured by 'change of the mind-set of its member' towards social evils, social discriminations, and other problems related to their community. Community radio has helped them to question age-old practices and develop a scientific attitude. Mr Lokesh Sharma illustrates his point by giving the following example:

> We have a woman, Maya Sharma, in our community, who was a simple woman and not engaged in any other work other than home-life. So when she came to radio station she was shy and fear the microphone. She doesn't have any confidence. After few programs she was confident, and there was no any fear of the microphone. And gradually she started to present the programs on the issues of the community—social evil, social problems, and other things. She realised that social problems can be removed from the society if the people can be educated. Like, for example, uh, here in Rajasthan, we have a tradition that when a children is born, the people gives, you know, a . . . a spoon of tea to the child. And it is called *gutthi*. The name of this spoon is *gutthi*. But it is dangerous for the newborn children, because it is recommended that a newborn children should be given the milk of its own mother and such kind of *gutthi* are not suitable for the children. So this is a social evil in the many societies in the state, in the community. But when we produced some programs on this topic, and the health experts explained that this is a social evil—we must not go with this—then they realised yes, we must not adopt such kind of practices, this is a social evil. It may be harmful for our children. So they realised that we must educate the people in this sense.

Campus-based community radio stations are not always considered to be committed towards community development. One of the major accusations to campus-based community stations is that it acts as a media laboratory where students get practical training, and there is not much community involvement. Dr Arul Aram, Formal Director, Anna FM, owned by Anna University, reveals a different story:

> The Anna FM, though it is based on the campus we are not orienting towards the campus. We are orienting towards education. It is a radio situated on the campus but serving the community. We did a baseline survey and identified that the women are suppressed in the neighbouring areas. Men have work, many women do not have work and there is no parity of salary in the work and some men do not allow their women to work and some men are drunkards and even if the women work they take away the money and beat them up. And we have identified that. We carefully identified the neighbouring areas, where the standard of living is poor and we identified the women there and talked to them and we decided that on our community radio we will cater to their needs. Any institution has a need to save the local community apart from our higher education and we help the local community. Already the university has started a personal development program, unlike many other colleges, has made it mandatory for the first years, like NSS-National Service Scheme, Junior Red Cross and also Sports and NCC. And any one of these things should be mandatorily taken up by every student. Already our

> focus is to shape the individual with social outlook . . . to have a feeling that okay, we are fortunate to have been educated, we will serve the community.

Outreach and activism are the backbone of any community radio. It is not only about airing programmes. On-air programmes send across a message, but it may not translate awareness into action. That happens when there is inter-personal communication and off-air programmes involving the community people. Thus, community radio is owned by the community, managed by the community, and also programmed and participated in by the community. In the case of campus-based community radio, it is not owned and managed by the community; the university owns and manages it with active involvement of community people. Each community radio station has its own strategy for community participation which are unique to that radio station. There is no single solution which can tackle the complications faced by all community radio stations. There are a host of issues which need to be addressed. To quote Dr Aram:

> One thing I noticed, when you interact with people from the community it is tricky, and they have come from a different culture as our university culture is different. For instance mothers come with their children and the children might meddle with some wiring we would have to tell them to not bring their children. But they cannot put the children in the house and come, or there may be some worker talking to a colleague and it may have some repercussions also which depends on what is being said. Then as it is a paid thing one lady may say that the other lady is being paid more than her or getting more programming which may lead to a quarrel.

Community radio provides the platform where people irrespective of social status speak and discuss about the issues that exist in their lives, in their language. It makes its people more confident. For example, Radio Namaskar has succeeded in achieving a zero drop-out rate in primary school in the Konark area (http://radionamaskar.in). Rosalind, one of the staff members of the radio station, narrates the achievement:

> We requested our listeners to inform the station whenever they witness a case of a child not going to school. We repeated the message and the toll-free number at the end of each programme. Also the volunteers and members attached with the radio station were pro-active. Whenever we heard a case of a child dropping out of school, the volunteers would request and advise the parents and family members to send the child to school. With cooperation of the community, we have reached zero drop-out level in primary school, in our area.

It emphasises on extending communications rights to all members of the community while focusing on the importance of equality of access and participation.

Supriya Sahu, Joint Secretary, Ministry of Information and Broadcasting, commented that:

> Success of this movement will be when we will have community radio stations in every nook and corner of the country bringing the diverse culture, various languages of India together and when community radios are actually truly representing the community voices. The community actually participates in the entire management and governance of the community radio station. And raises issues and voices which are relevant, which are important and ultimately they lead our country to true development. That will be the day when we can call that this movement has been successful in India.

## Discussion and conclusion

Communication is recognised as an important tool for development. An inclusive and plural media has the potential of playing an important role in sustainable development. 'Inclusive' media means that media should accommodate different languages, issues, and voices of all the sections of the society, including the poor and the marginalised. 'Plural' media means that media should be diverse in audience, scope, and also ownership. Plurality of media is important because no single media can give space to all the voices of the society. Commercial and state-owned media have their own priorities and agendas. Community media can engage its members in the developmental process and make them agents of social change by designing their own unique strategy.

Community radio is not about individuals. It is concerned with the community. The community works for the upliftment and betterment of its members. They are the decision-makers. The power of change lies in the hands of the community. They will locate the problem and work together to find a solution for their problems. Along with freedom of speech and expression, which is guaranteed by the Indian Constitution, community radio also exercises the right to be heard. Community radio is not a matter of giving a platform to non-professionals to voice their concerns. Rather, it endorses two-way communication. The line that divides the listener and the performer is blurred, and both can effortlessly switch their positions as and when desired. Thus, community radio enables the individual to enter into public discourse and participate in the decision-making processes, thus directing to community in the path of growth and development. It endorses a bottom-up approach as opposed to a top-down approach of commercial and public-service radio. This also leads to a decentralised approach that supports dialogue and exchange. Through its programming, community radio constructs a collective sense of identity. What distinguishes community radio is the way in which the technical arrangements are rearranged and reconstructed to suit the particular and distinctive needs of local communities. By demystifying technology, making it low cost, community radio is changing the established concept of communication, making it the property of the common people so that they are agents of change. It highlights people's ability to alter and rearrange existing media structures to better suit their needs. In doing so, community radio demonstrates the possibility for alternative broadcasting structures, forms, and practices. As we have seen, the motive behind each of the community radio initiatives described here is rather similar, but the strategies used to realise the objectives are unique to each particular community.

## Note

1 **Acknowledgment:** The author is indebted to Professor Nilanjana Gupta of Jadavpur University for her constant encouragement and support, without which this study would have not been possible.

## References

Gayen, K. (2012). Community radio in Bangladesh: The policy and the spirit. *Media Asia, 39*(1), 32–39.

Gaynor, N., & O'Brien, A. (2011). Because it all begins with talk: Community radio as a vital element in community development. *Community Development Journal, 47*(3), 436–447.

Government of India. (2002). *Policy guidelines for setting up community radio stations in India.* New Delhi: Ministry of Information and Broadcasting, Government of India.

McAnany, E. G. (2012). *Saving the world: A brief history of communication for development and social change.* Urbana–Champaign, IL: University of Illinois.

Panos. (2007). *At the heart of change: The role of communication in sustainable development.* London: Panos Institute. Retrieved December 14, 2016 from http://panoslondon.panosnetwork.org/resources/at-the-heart-of-change/.

Pavarala, V., & Malik, K. (2007). *Other voices.* New Delhi: Sage Publications.

Salazar, L., & Hammer, C. (2008). Community radio: Supporting local voices through airwaves. In P. Mefalopulos (Ed.), *Development communication sourcebook* (pp. 180–194). Washington, DC: World Bank.

Servaes, J. (2005). Participatory communication: The new paradigm? In O. Hemer (Ed.), *Media and global change: Rethinking communication for development* (pp. 91–103). Buenos Aires: CLACSO—Consejo Latinoamericano de Ciencias Sociales.

Singh, A. K. (2016). *Self sustainability of community radio: Stories from India.* Lambert Academic Publishing. Retrieved December 15, 2016 from https://countercurrents.org/2016/08/25/self-sustainability-of-community-radio-stories-from-india/r.

UNESCO (1980). *Many voices: One world.* New York: UNESCO.

Vilanilam, J.V. (2009). *Development communication in practice.* New Delhi: Sage Publication.

## *Websites*

http://edaa.in/crsammelan2013/video. Retrieved September 20, 2017.

http://radionamaskar.in/. Retrieved February 20, 2018.

www2.amarc.org/?q=node/47. Retrieved September 22, 2017.

www.ddsindia.com/www/radiostn.htm. Retrieved September 22, 2017.

www.indiankanoon.org/doc/539407/. Retrieved February 20, 2018.

# 5

# SUSTAINABLE DEVELOPMENT AND INDIGENOUS ENTREPRENEURSHIP

## A case study of Santhei Natural Park

*Jackson Khumukcham, Satyajit Majumdar, and Samapti Guha*

Indigenous[1] people often inhabit areas of high biological diversity and share cultural, social, and economic relationships with their traditional lands, customary laws, customs, and practices (Collings, 2009). They have intimate knowledge to preserve the ecosystem and possess Indigenous knowledge that has the potential to deliver sustainable development (Onwuegbuzie, 2016) and have developed a variety of systems to govern their societies, their traditional and local economic systems that ensured sustainable utilisation of resources (Lasimbang, 2008). However, for a long time, they have been confronting environmental, social, and economic challenges. The environmental problems faced by Indigenous people are manifold, including climate change and dispossession of lands and natural resources (Collings, 2009). Further, it is evident that the social and economic disadvantage among the Indigenous population is a globally prominent problem (Hindle & Moroz, 2007a). Around the world, they are the most marginalised population (Subramanian, Smith, & Subramanyam, 2006) and the most vulnerable segments of the society (World Bank, 2001 as cited in Anderson, Honig, & Peredo, 2007). Besides such prevailing problems, in India where the Indigenous population constitutes a significant population,[2] they suffered from exclusion, deprivation, and discrimination (Xaxa, 2008). Specifically in the northeastern states of India (where Indigenous people are a majority population), they are still encountering socio-economic backwardness and disadvantages.

In recent trends, entrepreneurship has demonstrated abilities to resolve many such issues (See: Shepherd & Patzelt, 2011) and contributes towards economic development (both in the developed and developing world) (Kokkranikal & Morrison, 2002). With this conjecture, entrepreneurial actions of Indigenous people preserve ecosystems and also impact the socio-economic spheres. Their economic activities are embedded in cultural and social aspects, creating unique styles of entrepreneurship which can achieve sustainability (often community-oriented)

(Cahn, 2008; Bruton, Zahra, & Cai, 2018). In order to overcome socio-economic challenges, they continuously innovate and generate solutions to address their problems (Onwuegbuzie, 2016) by participating in economic activities (Peredo & McLean, 2006) by applying Indigenous knowledge that tends to generate grassroots innovation (Gupta, 2001 as cited in Onwuegbuzie, 2016). Considering the stated fact, this chapter explains the role of Indigenous entrepreneurship initiated and operated by the Indigenous community of a small village in the northeastern state of Manipur in India within the milieu of economic development and sustainable development, specifically from the aspect of the Triple Bottom Line (TBL). In this context, it is attempted to understand the impact and benefits towards the Indigenous community brought by the Indigenous entrepreneurship through the lenses of social, economic, and environmental dimensions.

We have conceptualised Indigenous people in the Indian context and Indigenous entrepreneurship in the first section. In the second section, a brief review of literature on the topic is discussed and a framework is outlined. Section three describes the methodology adopted in this chapter, and section four discusses the context of the site where research has been conducted. Section five furnishes the findings, and a discussion based on the study is presented in section six. The last section concludes the study.

## Literature review

In this section, a brief review of literature is discussed on Indigenous people, Indigenous entrepreneurship, sustainable development, and the Triple Bottom Line to understand the views of the existing authors about the role of Indigenous entrepreneurship in sustainable development.

### *Who are Indigenous?*

Defining "Indigenous people" is one of the most controversial issues (Abidin, 2015), heavily critiqued, debated, and one of the prevailing challenges in literature and practice (Dean & Levi, 2003). However, it is said that the term and the concept of Indigenous people emerged from the colonial experience (Alfred & Corntassel, 2005). Defining Indigenous people may vary from institution to institution, researcher to researcher (Anderson et al., 2007), and region to region, such as: "ethnic minorities (China, Vietnam, Philippines); tribes (Africa, Americas); hill tribes (Thailand); scheduled tribes or Adivasis (India); Native American, Indian or Amerindian (North and South America); Indigenous (Latin America); Aboriginal (Australia, Canada, Taiwan); and First Nations (Canada)" (Zeppel, 2006, p. 4). According to the World Bank (1991), 'Tribe', 'Aborigin', and 'Indigenous' present similar meanings. The term 'Indigenous people', 'Indigenous ethnic minorities', 'tribal groups', and 'scheduled tribes' describe social groups with a social and cultural identity distinct from the dominant society that makes them vulnerable to being disadvantaged in the development process (as cited in Hassan, 2016, p. 268).

UNESCO (2006, p. 16) acknowledges Indigenous people as:

> Specific social, cultural and economic and living conditions; distinct social, economic, cultural and political institutions and customs and traditions regulating their status; identification as "Indigenous" by others; self-identification as "Indigenous"; attachment to land and to a specific territory and special relationship with nature or the earth: and their cosmovision.

Scholars who work on Indigenous entrepreneurship, such as Patrinos, Skoufias, and Lunde (2007), gave four indicators to recognise Indigenous peoples: 1) they are the descendants of the original populations inhabiting in their lands at the time of conquest and identify as such; 2) they speak (or spoke) a distinct and native language, and typically aspire to remain distinct culturally, geographically, and institutionally rather than assimilate; 3) they have an affinity and attachment to the land; and 4) they tend to maintain distinct social, economic, and political institutions within their territories. Peredo, Anderson, Galbraith, Honig, and Dana (2004) observed three core elements they found commonly in the definitions of Indigenous peoples: 1) descent from populations inhabiting a region prior to later inhabitants, 2) geographical, political, and/or economic domination by later inhabitants or immigrants, and 3) maintenance of some distinctive social-cultural norms and institutions. They further added features of "attachment to ancestral lands and their resources, modern subsistence economic arrangements and distinctive languages". "Indigenous populations have also been associated with more sociological and psychological dimensions, such as a 'collective' or community-based orientation", "a sense of historical mistreatment by the dominant culture", a general desire to control their own economic resources", and "to participate in the general economy on their own terms".

According to Indian scholars such as Dash and Pati (2002), the word "Indigenous" is a state-imposed conception, etymologically refers to the natives, belonging naturally to the soil. In India, the phrase "Indigenous people" is not used in legal framework due to its inconvenience and complexity (like the impossibility to say who came first) (See: Kingsbury, 1998). However, Xaxa (1999) posited that social workers, administrators, politicians, and even scholars widely used the term to refer to a certain category of people that are "native equivalent". He added three aspects, which are central to the conceptualisation of the Indigenous people:

> First, the Indigenous are those people who lived in the country to which they belong before colonisation or conquest by people from outside the country or the geographical region. Secondly, they have become marginalised as an aftermath of conquest and colonisation by the people from outside the region. Thirdly, such people govern their life more in terms of their own social, economic and the cultural institution than the laws applicable to the society or the country at large. . . . the Indigenous are invariably seen

> as victims of conquest and colonisation from outside the region; hence the outsiders are easily identifiable.
>
> (*ibid., p. 3590*)

At present, the idea of "Indigenous people" is still an issue of considerable contention in India (Xaxa, 1999), and there is no common consensus on the definitions due to lack of uniformity and interpretation of the concept in two different ways[3] (Dash & Pati, 2002). Drawing from the different types of concepts/definitions given by authors and agencies, for this chapter, Indigenous people can be acknowledged as:

> the descendants of the original population inhabiting in their ancestral lands with special relationship with nature or the earth; having distinct social, economic, cultural, customs and traditions, living conditions and political institutions; are govern more in terms of their own social, economic and cultural institution than the laws applicable to the society or the country at large; aspire to remain distinct culturally, geographically and institutionally rather than assimilate; geographically, politically, and/or economically domination by later inhabitants or immigrants; and identification as "Indigenous" by others or self-identification as "Indigenous".

## *Indigenous entrepreneurship*

Entrepreneurship is not homogeneous around the world (Dana, Dana, & Anderson, 2007); it is diversified and multifaceted (Rønning, 2007) and still vague with no agreement on the definitions (Farrelly, 2012). Like nature and the universe, it keeps evolving in an endeavour to remain relevant and contextual (Rushesha & Mhaka, 2014). It is a universal construct, i.e. either applicable to any person, organisation (private or public, large or small), and nation (Morris, 1998); can be undertaken by a single individual or a set of people (by a team or a group) (Shane & Venkataraman, 2000), as in many Indigenous communities (Anderson, Dana, & Dana, 2006).

Entrepreneurial activities among the Indigenous community have a long tradition and are known as some of the world's oldest recorded business undertakings (Foley, 2011 as cited in Brueckner et al., 2011). In the context of New Zealand, Kawharu, Tapsell, and Woods (2017) mentioned that Indigenous entrepreneurship is based on the cultural values and that connects the entrepreneurship with resilience. According to Dana (2007), there is no one Indigenous worldview about entrepreneurship (even within Indigenous people) because of their rich heterogeneity and being far from identical in their respective values. Indigenous entrepreneurship is an emerging field of research (Hindle & Lansdowne, 2007), more holistic than mainstream theories as it focuses on both economic and non-economic goals (Lindsay, 2005). It is an enterprise-related activity carried out by Indigenous people (Peredo et al., 2004) that takes place within a particular cultural context (Maphosa, 1998; Lindsay, 2005), which incorporate entrepreneurial strategies originating in and controlled by the community and the sanction of Indigenous culture[4] (Lindsay, 2005). Dana (2005, p. v) defined "Indigenous entrepreneurship as 'self-employment based on Indigenous knowledge'" (as cited in Dana (2007, p. 4). Hindle and Lansdowne (2007, p. 9) gave a comprehensive definition that:

> Indigenous entrepreneurship is the creation, management, and development of new ventures by Indigenous people for the benefit of Indigenous people. The organisations thus created can pertain to either the private, public or non-profit sectors. The desired and achieved benefits of venturing can range from the narrow view of economic profit for a single individual to the broad view of multiple, social and economic advantages for entire communities. Outcomes and entitlements derived from Indigenous entrepreneurship may extend to enterprise partners and stakeholders who may be non-Indigenous.

Later, Hindle and Moroz (2007b, p. 25) brought a refinement definition and stated that: Indigenous entrepreneurship is an "activity focused on new venture creation or the pursuit of economic opportunity, or both, for the purpose of diminishing Indigenous disadvantage through culturally viable and community acceptable wealth creation". So, considering different concepts and definitions given by different authors, for this chapter, Indigenous entrepreneurship can be conceptualised as:

> An entrepreneurial initiative carried out by Indigenous people (a person or a team or a group) to bring social, economic, cultural, and environmental impact to their own community and controlled by the community itself; within a particular cultural context and sanction of Indigenous culture; through identifying and exploiting opportunities and locally available resources; involvement of self-employment, Indigenous knowledge, and innovation; where the fruit or outcomes derived from Indigenous entrepreneurship may extend to its partners and stakeholders who may be non-Indigenous.

## *Sustainable development and the Triple Bottom Line (TBL)*

Since the 1970s, sustainable development has emerged as a broader social goal, focusing on the need to integrate the pursuit of improved human wellbeing with the necessity of halting and reversing systematic ecological degradation (Parrish, 2010). Sustainable development as a complex concept (Parrish, 2008) gained popularity with the proposition of the need to change the destructive lifestyle of humankind and concerned with reducing the exploitation and consumption of natural resources at the World Commission on Environment and Development (WCED) in 1987, popularly known as the Brundtland Report.[5] The popular definition of "sustainable development" used by many authors such as Guillen-Royo (2016), İyigün (2015), and Cohen and Winn (2007) is propagated by the WCED (1987, p. 43) as "development that meets the needs of the present without compromising the ability of future generations to meet their own needs". Considerately, "the notion of sustainability has been evolving and is increasingly understood to encompass considerations of economic viability, as well as environmental sustainability and social responsibility" (Jamali, 2006, p. 809). It must be noted that both sustainability and development are necessarily human-centred concepts (Parrish, 2008) and have a vision for the long-term survival of humanity with a qualitative improvement in the human experience of life on earth (Malaska, 2001 as cited in Parrish, 2008). It is also associated with satisfying a national economy's needs for natural resources without compromising generations (Luke, 2013 as in İyigün, 2015). However, development is concerned with eliminating poverty, unemployment, and inequality (İyigün, 2015), and also with the improvement in the state of human wellbeing of a society over time (Sengupta, 2002).

'Sustainability' is often mentioned as a goal of businesses, non-profits, and governments in the past decade, but measuring the degree of being sustainable or pursuing sustainable growth is difficult (Slaper & Hall, 2011). With an aim to search for a new language to express the expansion of sustainable values in business practices, John Elkington in 1994 coined the concept "Triple Bottom Line" (TBL) (Majid & Koe, 2012). It is alternatively known as Triple P (Profit, Planet, People) (Slaper & Hall, 2011). Elkington explained the concept thoroughly in his book entitled *Cannibals with Forks: The Triple Bottom Line of 21st Century Business* in 1997 (Majid & Koe, 2012; Slaper & Hall, 2011). He propagated three main value-creating aspects of the sustainable conduct, namely: 1) economic prosperity, 2) environmental quality, and 3) social justice. Further, the concept has been developed into "3P formulation", which consists of "people, planet and profit" (Elkington, 2004 as cited in Slaper & Hall, 2011).

TBL as a concept includes three main dimensions which are closely related to each other, i.e. economic, environmental, and societal as a whole (İyigün, 2015). In this context, it can be considered as "an accounting framework that incorporates three dimensions of performance: social, environmental and financial" (Slaper & Hall, 2011, p. 4). It "requires for business ventures to be accountable not only for profit-related measures of success, but for social and environmental measures as well" (Gundlach & Zivnuska, 2010, p. 22) and serves as "a useful tool to be used by companies, non-profit organisations and government agencies to measure sustainability performance under the headings of environmental quality, social justice and economic prosperity" (Majid & Koe, 2012 as cited in İyigün, 2015, p. 1230). Cohen, Smith, and Mitchell (2008) posited that the TBL presents a useful foundation for a discussion of the balancing of multiple wants desired by entrepreneurs needed in society. According to them, proponents of the TBL suggest that for the sustainability of current and future generations, economic development must occur in a way (WCED, 1987) that meets the needs of the present without compromising the ability of future generations to meet their own needs.

According to Cohen et al. (2008), 'sustainability' value creation (i.e. the achievement of socio-enviro-economic objectives) lies at the intersection of all three components of the TBL. Depending upon circumstances, sustainability-motivated entrepreneurs seek to maximise, balance, and/or optimise economic, social, and environmental value creation. Jamali (2006) highlighted that the economic dimension encompasses issues of competitiveness, job and market creation, and long-term profitability; the environmental dimension focuses on (an organisation's) impact on living and non-living natural systems, including ecosystems; and the social dimension includes the expectations of diverse groups of internal and external stakeholders. It incorporates issues of community, skills, education, and equal opportunity.

The concept of "sustainability" and "triple bottom line" has created a platform for business, government, and civil society (İyigün, 2015). Interest in TBL is growing across for-profit, non-profit, and government sectors; many businesses and non-profit organisations adopted a TBL framework to evaluate their performance (Slaper & Hall, 2011). Nevertheless, the relationship between entrepreneurship and sustainable development has been addressed by various streams such as Ecopreneurship, Social Entrepreneurship, Sustainable Entrepreneurship, and in an indirect way also Institutional Entrepreneurship (Schaltegger & Wagner, 2011 as cited in Lundstrom, Zhou, Friedrichs, & Sundin, 2014). However, the literature on business and sustainability is comparatively inadequate (Cohen & Winn, 2007).

The flexibility of TBL makes it a suitable tool to be used by businesses, non-profit organisations, and government agencies to measure sustainability performance according to their specific needs (Slaper & Hall, 2011 as cited in Majid & Koe, 2012). At present, there is increasing use of TBL as a tool or device for sustainable reporting under the headings of environmental quality, social justice, and economic prosperity (Majid & Koe, 2012). In the domain of organisation, TBL captures the essence of sustainability by measuring the impact of an organisation's activities in the world, including both its profitability and shareholder values and its social, human, and environmental capital (Andrew, 2006 as cited in Slaper & Hall, 2011). From the corporate dimension, the TBL is now very much a feature of the reporting of corporate social, environmental, and economic performance in CSR (Lundstrom et al., 2014). Besides, many extant studies on sustainable entrepreneurship used the concept of TBL to describe what sustainable entrepreneurship is all about (Majid & Koe, 2012). However, there is still a gap in the literature where Indigenous entrepreneurship addresses sustainability development.

## Indigenous entrepreneurship and economic development: orientation towards sustainable development

Earlier "economic development" was referred to by quantifying macroeconomic indicators (most often through GDP per capita or economy). However, this concept got a qualitative perspective after World War II. There emerged a realisation that economic development[6] is inextricably linked to social development if we are to ensure an environment that is conducive to human existence and the creation of necessary conditions on the earth to improve the quality of life[7] (Scutaru, 2013). It can be pointed out that entrepreneurship influences economic development through employment, innovation, and welfare effects (Acs, Desai, & Hessels, 2008); identified inefficiencies in economies and mitigated (Baum, Frease, & Baron, 2007 as cited in Toma, Grigore, & Marinescu, 2014); constituted a major source for job creation (Toma et al., 2014); and its innovations create demand for new products and services that were not previously available (Kressel & Lento, 2012 as in Toma et al., 2014). Even, the Schumpeterians view that entrepreneurial process constitutes one of the key factors in the economic development of a region/country (Toma et al., 2014).

In this context, Morley (2014) mentioned that one key aspect of improving Indigenous economic development[8] is through Indigenous people operating their community-based enterprises. Many Indigenous leaders and community members viewed "economic development as one important avenue to achieve healthier and wealthier communities" (Kayseas et al., 2006 as cited in Conway, 2011, p. 1102). Authors like Galbraith, Rodriguez, and Stiles (2006) and Anderson et al. (2007) considered Indigenous entrepreneurial activities as the "second wave" of economic development. Indigenous people are engaging in economic activities as a coping mechanism to their issues (Hindle, Anderson, Giberson, & Kayseas, 2005). In the same way, it is said that through creating new ventures, new initiatives, and new wealth, entrepreneurship has the potential to enhance the economic development of Indigenous people, at all levels (individual, group, community and nation) (Government of Canada: RCAP Final Report, 1996; World Bank, 2005 as cited in Hindle and Moroz, 2007b). Even the comprehensive definition posited by Hindle and Lansdowne (2007, p. 9) indicates that Indigenous entrepreneurship has "the desired and achieved benefits of venturing can range from the narrow view of economic profit for a single individual to the broad view of multiple, social and economic advantages for entire communities". Such evidence leads Indigenous entrepreneurship to be defined as a minor subset of economic development (Hindle & Moroz, 2007b) and also considered as a contested aspect of Indigenous economic development (Gallagher & Lawrence, 2012).

Entrepreneurial activities provide multifaceted benefits for the entrepreneur, families, community, and the wider economic system (Lindsay, 2005). Likewise, the objective of Indigenous entrepreneurship is social improvement and empowerment through economic gain (Conway, 2011) and has the potential to overcome disadvantages of the Indigenous community (Hindle & Moroz, 2007b). In this context, Colbourne (2017) analysed that Indigenous hybrid ventures are the best models for value creation and addressing the challenges of the indigenous community. It has the potential to empower Indigenous people as economic agents in a globally competitive modern world (Hindle & Lansdowne, 2007); is a key tool by which Indigenous communities seek to achieve modern economic development, mostly on community-based economic development (Peredo et al., 2004); brings economic independence (Mapunda, 2007); and improves livelihood and alleviate poverty (See: Farrelly, 2012).

Furthermore, Cohen and Winn (2007), referring to Venkataraman's (1997) suggestion, agreed that the consequences of entrepreneurship can be economic and social in nature, and they added another category of environmental consequences. So, entrepreneurship can be viewed as a potential force for sustainability

(Salem, Anderson, & Dana, 2012), where sustainability dimensions include economic, environmental, and societal as a whole (İyigün, 2015). In this milieu, Indigenous entrepreneurship can be taken into consideration, where sustainability is intrinsically linked to the entrepreneurial activities of Indigenous communities (Gouvea, 2015). For instance, Indigenous entrepreneurs have an intimate knowledge of the ecosystem and understand how to preserve it (Onwuegbuzie, 2016) and learn to manage resources available in their environment in a sustainable way (Gupta, 1999 as cited in Onwuegbuzie, 2016). Among Indigenous people, the concept of sustainability is woven into their "way of living" (Lopik & Erdmann, 2013). While performing entrepreneurial activities, they tend to apply Indigenous knowledge[9] (Warren & Rajasekaran, 1993 as cited in Onwuegbuzie, 2016) and generate Indigenous/grassroots innovation[10] (Gupta, 2001 as cited in Onwuegbuzie, 2016), mostly environmentally friendly innovations that hold the potential of delivering sustainable development (Gupta et al., 2003). Furthermore, Indigenous entrepreneurship has the potential to reconcile sustainability ideas (Salem et al., 2012), is concerned with improving the wealth and wellbeing for the community,[11] and is generally environmentally sustainable (Dana, 2007). Above all, it contributes towards cultural sustainability (Foley, 2008 as cited in Farrelly, 2012), like enhancing the preservation of heritage (Lindsay, 2005) and strengthening traditional values (Anderson et al., 2006).

However, it can be noted that sustainability has been evolving and is increasingly understood to encompass considerations of economic viability, as well as environmental sustainability and social responsibility (Jamali, 2006), and the concept TBL has been popularly used by many scholars to explain sustainable development. Considering these discussions, the chapter seeks to illustrate empirical evidence about the dimensions of development brought by Indigenous entrepreneurship that contributes to sustainable development through the aspects of TBL. Hence, this chapter provokes the following question: 'How does Indigenous entrepreneurship bring economic development that has economic, social, and environmental impact and contributes towards sustainable development?'

## Methodology

The ethnographic approach can provide more sophisticated accounts of the ways individuals and communities negotiate with the notions of entrepreneurship (Farrelly & Vudiniabola, 2013). The ethnographic research method is adopted for this research. Another reason for adopting the ethnographic research method is its appropriateness in recording the entrepreneurship experiences of Indigenous people in their own words, with minimal cultural bias (Dana et al., 2007). The participant observation, which is an essential component of ethnographic research (Murchison, 2010), was adopted while conducting fieldwork. Although Indigenous people of the northeastern part of India have rich natural resources and traditional handicraft skill, which are sustaining since time immemorial, relatively little is known about the entrepreneurship on their own resources. The Santhei

Natural Park is one of them. For this research purpose, fieldwork was conducted by choosing and staying in the Andro village, and researchers experienced their economic activities and living style oriented with the business (family and community) of the Andro people. Data has been collected through participating and engaging in the social life of the Andro village (especially most of the time spent in the shop/stall near Santhei Natural Park). The information used in this chapter is gathered by using tools such as observation, field notes, informal conversations, and from the answers which came from the unstructured questions arising spontaneously during daily interactions. The duration for fieldwork was from June 2016 to November 2016.

The key respondents from which data are collected are: 1) volunteers: four volunteers who were actively involved in maintaining Santhei Natural Park; 2) Village Chief: present Andro village chief (one person) who sanctioned land for constructing Santhei Natural Park and has witnessed formation and transformation of the park; 3) Lampuba: the head of the management and control of village resources of the Santhei region; 4) the person who initiates: a person who was involved in initiating the Santhei Natural Park before even the name was not proposed; 5) self-employed entrepreneurs: four self-employed entrepreneurs who make and sell their own products; 6) four small-business owners who take products from others and sell in retail at Santhei Natural Park; and 7) three villagers who are still involved in local wine making but did not participate in business activities near Santhei Natural Park.

The criteria for selecting the key participants were based on importance, visibility, specialised knowledge, and recommendations. Through transcription and rechecking the data from field notes, observations, and informal interviews, themes and sub-themes were developed in an organised way. Considering the limitation of this research work, only those themes are used in this chapter, which is permitted by the objective and conceptual framework.

## *Understanding the site: Andro community*

Iankova, Hassan, and L'Abbe (2016) rightly pointed out that some of the Indigenous population are still conserving their original lifestyle and still live in remote geographical locations. The Andro Indigenous community is one of them. The Andro is the Indigenous population of the northeastern part of India, who are still inhabiting their ancestral land with a unique language, culture, and tradition. They are historically categorised under the Loi community. The term "Loi" is derived from the word "Loipot", which means the one who pays tribute (Devi, 2002). The Andro community falls under the category of "Phusaba Lois",[12] which means those Loi communities engage as "potters" and gave mudpots as a tribute to the King. For a long time, the Andro community as a Lois of Manipur had been encountered by both socially and economically backwardness. Devi (2002), in her book *The Lois of Manipur*, mentioned various types of challenges experienced by Lois: they were subdued people; considered to be an inferior class; kept isolated and were not allowed to take part in the general mainstream because of their indifferent attitude towards the King's religion of 'Hinduism'. At present they have started to merge with the general Meitei Society, but due to the difference in eating and drinking habits, the orthodox Hindus still look down on them (ibid.). In economic affairs, Lois isolation in the past still has an impact on their economic life. A majority of them live below the poverty line and re unemployed. The market of Andro bazaar is very small and mostly deals with vegetables, snacks, grocery, raw meat, and wine.

Despite their challenges, the Andro village has been tightly bonded with nature and the environment for centuries and produces a deep understanding of the environment surrounding them. Besides, local people have inter-relationships among the different elements of habitat with this village; everyone living in the village is considered to be as a brother (eyamba-enao), sister (echan-eche), mother (ema), father (pabung), aunt (ine), or uncle (mama-khura) to each other through the web of clan relationship. The community people have their own way of relating to ecological responsibility and respect their village god, locally known as "Panam Ningthou", which they consider as the supernatural one.

## *The Santhei Natural Park*

In the deep corner of the Andro village, near the Baruni hill (also called Nonmaijing Ching), there used to be a huge, dense, and grassy land at the foot of the hill, which was locally known as Santhei. The word "Santhei" means the place where cattle are directed. The villagers used this place as pastureland where cattle are grazed. In some rare occasions, people of the village or with friends from outside the village used to visit this place to organise a picnic or party, mostly during the festive season (but not frequently and not with a huge number of people). As time went on, members of the concerned youth club of this area called the Andro Western Baruni Road Youth Club (AWBYC), decided to rejuvenate this area for making comfort to the people, especially outsiders, in 2008. This was the beginning of the formation of the Santhei Natural Park. There was no official name given to the place during the early time when club volunteers (around 10 people) started to clean the dense green area of Santhei. They never anticipated the popularity which they got suddenly in just beginning the park. Many people started to visit the place frequently, especially in the festive season. By recognising such opportunity, those volunteers who were engaged in maintaining and cleaning the Santhei area named the place as Santhei Natural Park.

The Santhei Natural Park is covered and surrounded by beautiful trees and wild flowers which are grown naturally. The park has designated places for cooking food and getting together or enjoying or partying by the visitors. There is a garden with Indigenous flowers, a huge grass slope, a pond, and sitting stalls. At present, the Santhei Natural Park is under the control of a committee formed by the local people living within the Andro village. The committee is under the control of eight small localities from within the Andro village, especially by the elders. The small locality is called "Leikai Macha", and it is popularly known as Singlup. It can be said that Eight Singlup are controlling this park. From each Singlup (small locality), two or three people are nominated as representatives called "Lampuba". They are nominated to look after the hill, its natural resources, and also manage and control the administration of the Santhei Natural Park. Besides, there are 14 youth volunteers who are in charge of looking after the park. The task includes: taking charge of the booking counter, cleaning the waste, cleaning the park, and taking care of flowers, etc. They are maintaining this park from the earnings which are drawn out from the charges to visitors. The detail of the charges are: 1) if food from outside is brought inside, then INR 100; 2) for picnic purposes INR 200; and 3) for parking: two-wheelers INR 20, four-wheelers INR 50, and busses INR 200; and the voluntary maintenance charges that are taken from the visitors as per willingness. There is no single day where visitors do not visit this park. However, compared to other days, on Saturdays and Sundays people come in large numbers. In festival season, the park is flooded with an unexpected number of people. The timing of Santhei market (which is located on the street side which goes towards the Santhei Natural Park) depends upon the arrival and departure of the visitors. However, for regulation, in the summer season, it is open from 6 am to 5 pm and in the winter from 7 am to 4 pm.

## Findings

### *Socially motivated environment*

After the establishment of Santhei Natural Park, local people started to become aware of the opportunity and economic advantages which allow them to participate in economic activities. It is observed that the community people have developed an attitude where they are concerned with utilising and exploring the opportunity through economic activities which are provided by the Santhei Natural Park. They are mostly engaged in economic activities either as self-employed entrepreneurs or proprietors of stalls/shops. There is also an increasing interest in the environment to learn or teach the skill of those economic-oriented occupations like pottery making and local wine making. For instance, if a member of a family started to engage in making modern small earthen pots, then it influences another member of the family also, and in some cases, they insist on other members to join. Indirectly it also influences neighbours, cousins, and even other members in their own locality/community. Furthermore, other members of the community, by looking at the particular occupation and its demand in the market, got motivated and became a part of the occupation. Apart from traditional product-oriented businesses, people are also now bringing modern businesses such as ice cream shops, sugarcane juice machines, and selling machine-made products like toys and gift items outside the park.

The elders of the community, mostly those who make Andro traditional pots, are encouraging the youth to learn pottery. As there is a custom for not allowing members to make traditional Andro pots before marriage, and only married female members of the community are allowed to make them, by understanding such limitation, they give more focus on teaching the skill of making modern pottery items, which is not the traditional pot but small pots that can be easily made by any member of the community by creating a new design. Many youngsters are taking an interest in it and are learning the skill or through imitating, making small earthen products.

With this practise, there is also non-economic gain for the local people. They recognise the potters and consider those traditional Andro pot makers as their assets and valuable people. Besides, the village gives regards to those potters and business owners who are involved in economic activities. Those who work hard are highly regarded and achieve good status in the community. Visitors from various parts of the state are curious to know about the legends of Andro pottery and also prefer to buy unique and traditional Andro pots. Through such a process, the Andro potters are becoming famous and gaining recognition from outsiders, too.

Further, within the same village, it is also found that with the development of the concept of the park and its success, just near to the Santhei Natural Park, local people are now establishing an ecological park to generate economic opportunities for the community people. They keep the name of the park as "Panam Ningthou Garden", which was still under construction during the fieldwork period.

## *Changes in lifestyle*

With the establishment of Santhei Natural Park, there is a change in the lifestyle of the local people. From casual conversation with local people, it is obtained that before the park was established, the local people, especially those who are residing near the Santhei Natural Park, were living a rigid traditional lifestyle and had less interaction with outsiders. However, since the Santhei Natural Park started to boom and became popular, many categories of visitors from within the Manipur state started to visit the place. People visit the park every day, and there are no days when visitors do not come. It is observed that during the road bandh and blockade time in the state or some part of the state due to an unwanted law-and-order situation, visitors used to come. In normal days, people come in smaller numbers, but in the festival season or on any other occasion, people flood to this park in huge numbers, so that it is sometimes overcrowded and congested. Due to this phenomenon, the local villagers started to open up and show a welcoming nature towards the visitors.

As local people started to speak with outsiders, they have changed their behaviour and attitude to make visitors comfortable. Once, the village was known for being introverted to outsiders, but it is now people friendly. Locals started to mix with people from diverse backgrounds and from various places. This makes them understand the perspectives and expectations of outsiders. They realised that by making their place easy for the visitors, the more visitors might come, and it would lead to the development of their economy and the village. Many of them developed an attachment with outsiders.

Locals who are opening shops/stalls at the Santhei Natural Park also seem to have adapted and adjusted their lifestyle with the time and schedule of the park and its market. Despite different occupations and different ways of doing business, self-employed entrepreneurs and small business proprietors come to the park to open their stalls after finishing all the household works. As most of the proprietors of the stall/shop are female, they manage to do household work along with their business. However, some of them who have a daughter, daughter-in-law, and children get familial help in their business. When returning from the park, they return according to the time of the park and sometime when visitors go away. However, the time is flexible for everyone to come to the park and return according to their comfort. Most of them, after returning from the park, start the domestic chores. Those who get help from family members do not take the tension of the domestic chores.

## *The emergence of Indigenous ecotourism*[13]

The remarkable achievement of the Santhei Natural Park is the recognition of the park as one of the ecotourism spots by the people of Manipur. Due to this fact, the place attracts local news media and local film-making agencies. Many Manipuri film songs were shot in this spot. Such acts help in broadcasting the information of the park to the outer world and also in drawing the attention of outsiders. Visitors are now finding a scope to bring home souvenirs for self-use or to give someone or for decorative purposes.

Moreover, the Santhei Natural Park became a source of opportunity to the local people by providing revenue to local economies and generated employment for local people. Those traditional occupations which have been practiced for ages got a marketplace to survive and revive, and these local sellers also got an opportunity to innovate and renovate according to the changing time and demands. It also encourages local entrepreneurship (which will be discussed in a later section).

The Santhei Natural Park becomes a means of maintaining local resources and heritage. For instance, with the popularity of the park, the old heritages which were located within the Andro village also started to be recognised. There is a Laishang (place of god) for Panam Ningthou (village god), which has been preserved as a heritage site for many years. The specialty of this place is that the villagers are still keeping the ancient fire burning. Such heritage is also increasingly recognised by outsiders as a tourism spot.

Now, it is very clear that the Santhei Natural Park has become a popular eco-tourism spot. The Government of Manipur also recognises the potential in this place to be a tourism spot. Since then, the State Tourism Department, Government of Manipur, has been organising the state level festival, exhibitions, and trade fairs every year. Conducting the Manipur Sangai Festival[14] and World Tourism Day[15] at Santhei Natural Park of the Andro village are the best examples. The Santhei Natural Park is still maintaining its organic nature. Instead of getting some help from the local Member of Legislative Assembly (MLA) regarding construction of infrastructures like a road and rest house, the community is not ready and does not accept any form of partnership or investment from/with outsiders to scale up their entrepreneurship.

## *Market-oriented opportunity*

With the gaining popularity of the Santhei Natural Park, the area surrounding the park became a marketplace. The term "market" in Andro is locally known as "keithel". Historically, the Andro village has a community market (called Andro Bazaar or Andro Keithel) at the bus stand of the village. It is located within 500 meters from Santhei Natural Park. This community keithel has been the centre of economic exchange for the villagers for a long time. However, surprisingly, traditional pottery products of the Andro village were not sold in this market, but the sudden arrival of visitors from outside at the Santhei Natural Park created a marketplace for the Indigenous products and also for other outside products. On the street that goes towards the Santhei Natural Park, the village committee (represented by Lampuba) provides designated areas to the local people for opening their respective stalls/shops and to sell Indigenous products and other products that are brought from outside the village, mostly machine-made. The site has a designated area for the sale of respective products. The area which is designated for selling a specific traditional product is strictly maintained for that specific product only. It is not allowed to be mixed up with other products. Those individuals who sell traditional products are not allowed to open stalls at the designated place where other eatable products and machine-made products are sold and vice versa. Almost all the shops/stalls are made by using locally available material like bamboo and tin, etc. The three significant products that got a marketplace near the Santhei Natural Park are: 1) products oriented with earthen pottery: this product can be decorative items made of earthen clay as well as traditional pots; 2) products oriented with local wine: this product is mainly rice wine; and 3) products brought from outside the village or machine-made: this product is mainly soda, chips, plastic toys, and gift items, etc.

## *Employment of local people*

The park is now employing 14 youth volunteers from the community. Previously, when the park was just started, there were 10 volunteers, and now they have increased to 14 volunteers. Among the volunteers, those who are engaging at the booking counter and managing vehicle parking (three of them) got a salary of INR 3,000 (Rupees three thousand only) each per month on a regular basis. However, other remaining volunteers got a salary according to the total collected amount of the park. Their salary is not fixed and depends upon the season. During the normal season, on an average they got around INR 2,000 to INR 3,000 per month. However, during the festival season, when visitors come in a large number, they got a hike in their salary of INR 5,000 to INR 10,000 for that specific month. Besides, there are other contractual works which are continuously carried out inside the park. Such opportunity also provides the park committee to hire local people to engage in the works regarding construction and maintenance of infrastructures like a sitting area, shed, and road, etc. The salaries of these workers depend upon the project they are working on. On average, they got INR 500 for the day. Selections of contract labours are based on the respective skills possessed by local people.

Furthermore, many local youths are now attracted towards the occupation that is on demand like modern pottery making. Apart from pottery, the involvement of local people to engage in the production of local wine is increasing. From youth to elder people, many of the local people are engaging in this occupation. However, it can be noted that the local wine of the Andro has been very popular among the population of Manipur. It is locally known as "Kalei", and sometimes people also refer to it as "Andro". The demands for the local wine make people set up the stall at the designated place in the Santhei Natural Park.

## *Rise of self-employed entrepreneurs*

The park provides an opportunity to the local people to initiate any form of economic activity. Those local Indigenous people who have been engaging in the traditional pottery occupation and Andro traditional wine making are recognising this opportunity and getting ready to explore it. Further, some of them make local rice wine at home and also open stalls/shops at the Santhei Natural Park to sell modern earthen pottery products. There are business owners who utilise locally available resources and make the products and do business in new ways. Such individuals are self-employed entrepreneurs as they recognised the opportunity and understood to exploit it; they can take risks and challenges to come forward, and do their business in a new way. Some of them extend the involvement of their family members in the process of their business. Mostly in the pottery occupation, it is evident that there is an innovation in producing a modern form of pottery products. The entrepreneurs in this occupation tried to bring new ideas and designs in their earthen products that suit the present time. Such new products become the choices of the visitors and create demand. Their search for new designs is still going on, and according to them, they will not stop till they are engaging in this occupation.

In the local wine production also, a large number of youth are involved. Many of them are taking the contract from outsiders, and many are doing business within the village. For making wine, they produce their own rice, but for contract one, the rice are purchased from outside the village. Comparatively, a large number of villagers are attracted towards wine production because through this, earning can be done quickly, and the labour which is required in making wine can also be managed by the youngsters. However, the elders who are used to making wine leave the occupation when they feel their health is not good, and many of the elders due to the requirement of manual labour which they cannot perform. Those who left the wine-cooking occupation are also found to engage in the pottery-making occupation.

### *New trend of doing business*

Santhei Natural Park brought a new way of doing business with the traditional products such as Andro pottery and local rice wine. However, the traditional way of doing business with pottery and local wine still exists. Both of the occupations are organic in nature as they have existed since the civilisation of this Indigenous community. The old occupation of Andro pottery existed for household and community consumption, and their houses or courtyard of the house were the selling point for their pots. The traditional pottery products were used in their daily life and also for ritual ceremonies related to instances of life from birth to death. Besides, a huge number of pots (called Yu Kharung) were used for local wine cooking. Some community people who do not have the skill of making the pots used to visit skilled potters, and they took the pots from them. Some potters used to exchange their pots with the agricultural products of neighbouring tribal villages, and some of them used to travel to the mainstream market of the Imphal city and sell their pots. However, after the establishment Santhei Natural Park, the traditional Andro pottery makers got a new direction of doing their business by innovating their products. Many youth and elders are now doing their business of modern earthen products by opening stalls/shops near the Santhei Natural Park, and many of them have become suppliers of the modern earthen products by having production units at home. Sometimes, visitors to the park also visited the homes of the traditional potters and bought their pottery products. Such a trend leads to change in the pattern of making pots. Apart from the traditional design of pots, the innovative designs adopted on modern pottery work are flower pots, piggy banks, and animals and flowers are added to this domain of pottery. These products tremendously attract the visitors.

The trend is also changing in the local wine-cooking occupation. With the civilisation of the Andro community, the tradition of wine cooking (Yu Thongba in local language) has been there since time immemorial. The Andro rice wine is famous throughout the Manipur region for its high distillation quality. Traditionally, the wine was cooked for an offering to their village god called "Panam Ningthou" and for consumption of the family members. However, as time passed, outsiders visited the houses where local wine was cooked, and they either drank it or took it home. Some outsiders outsourced to sell at Imphal and other parts of Manipur. However, within the village, the market of local wine was limited at home, and only a few small vendors were selling the same. At present, with the establishment of Santhei Natural Park, the local wine business has flourished by getting the opportunity to access the Santhei Natural Park where the entrepreneurs get their designated place for selling. They are opening a small vendor-type stall made of locally available material like bamboo, plastic, and tin. Along with their own local rice wine products, they are putting out foreign and Indian-made liquors. Visitors are now easily accessing the vendors. It also impacted the other nearby areas of the park. At the entrance of the park, near the Andro community bazaar, and in other corners of the Andro village, the local wine business is flourishing. In both the occupations, the pattern of such a new trend of doing business with their traditional products is found to be very similar. They also help each other to make new stalls and start businesses of the same or similar products.

## Economic independence

The Santhei Natural Park brought a remarkable economic impact on the local people of the Andro village. The primary beneficiaries of the economic impacts are those people and their families who are willingly participating in economic activities through opening stalls/shops. The impact is very holistic and can be seen in the following broad sectors: 1) maintaining household expenditures; 2) investing in the education of children; 3) investing in the local credit system; 4) the tradition of helping/giving monetary help; and 5) investing in personal health.

A majority of the business proprietors who open stalls are the women (except one man), and they invest in the maintenance of household needs and management. This includes buying rations for their family, purchasing or refilling Liquified Petroleum Gas (LPG) cylinders, and buying vegetables. Almost all of the women who own the businesses are married and have children (there are two women who do not have children). The money they earned is invested in maintenance of their children and also spent on payment of school fees for their children or for the payment of fees for boarding school. They also invested by participating in traditional rotating saving and credit associations (ROSCAs), commonly known as Marup.[16] They also spend money on giving a gift or monetary help to their relatives and friends for an occasion or family event, which is called "Potyeng", or help in the form of an object called "Potpang". They also spend money on their illnesses and medical treatment. Sometimes they are suffering from a common cold, headache, or stomach problem, and above that the occupation of local wine cooking and pottery leads them to suffer from eye problems and back pain. So, they spend a portion of their earnings on the treatment for such illnesses. However, the economic impact does not limit to the following evidences because according to their conveniences and their needs, they spend money in other sectors which are not accounted for and periphery in nature.

## Environmental concern

Besides the use of available natural resources in making Indigenous products like pottery and rice wine, the volunteers and the park management committee realised the fact that people from outside the village got attracted because of the indigeneity of the park (which they are maintaining). They always preferred Indigenous flowers and trees while decorating the park. While constructing a sitting shed and hut, they always preferred to use locally available wood or bamboo by adopting the Indigenous design and style. Many of the volunteers are still in search of ancient Indigenous designs so that people who visited the place can get the Indigenous touch and feel.

The Andro village since time immemorial follows "Chieftainship" as their political form, in which the village chief has the right to control and administer the village land. It is mutually legitimised by the community custom. From the casual conversation with the village chief, we came to know that besides the personal houses and agricultural field, he controls the terraced land, reserve land, wasteland, and the hill. According to him, anyone from the village can borrow the land from the village by taking permission with stating a specific purpose. She/he can cultivate that land or use it for other eco-friendly business purposes by giving a tax every year. By doing such acts of business, the environment and ecology will remain unchanged and healthy.

The case is also the same with Santhei Natural Park. The members of the Andro Youth Club during the time of establishment took permission from the village chief for the use of Santhei land and the land around the Baruni hillside where Santhei is located. The process of taking land from the village chief is locally known as "Lam Nijaba", where "Lam" means land and "Nijaba" means wish/pray, so it is to wish/pray for the land. They have ethical concerns towards utilisation of their natural resources. While using the land, they keep in mind the utilisation by future generations, and they do not use all the available land. The village chief also has the concern to reserve/preserve the land for future use, too. Therefore, he does not permit anyone to take the whole land, which is available. By accompanying some village members (mostly Lampuba and park volunteers), they visited the land near Baruni foothill, which they prayed for and kept a landmark to the area where the permission was given for the establishment of the park.

Further, while constructing Santhei Natural Park, the volunteers were very much concerned not to cut those trees and flowers which already existed in that area. It includes the Indigenous trees, the ponds, and the Indigenous flowers. Instead of thinking about profit making through the establishment of the park, they are more concerned about the sustainability of the local environment. The volunteers during the time of constructing Santhei Natural Park always kept in mind that the local people within the village have a profound coexistence with the surrounding natural environment. Besides, the park also has a big pond to store drinking water, which is flowing down from the small streams of Baruni hill. This adds to the beauty of the park. The area where the pond is situated is also popularly known as "Dam" because the water running from the hill is kept and reserved there. The village keeps a tough rule regarding the use of this pond water. The pond serves as the source of drinking water for the visitors while organising picnics and for cooking purposes. Nobody is allowed to go inside the pond, and it is under the serious surveillance of the park volunteers.

## Discussions

The Santhei Natural Park provides the context for Indigenous entrepreneurship where Indigenous people initiate and control entrepreneurial activities within a specific social, economic, cultural, and environmental context. Such initiative confirmed that: 1) the model itself is a subset of economic development (Hindle & Moroz, 2007b); and 2) it simultaneously contributes towards the sustainable development (WCED, 1987). The overall benefits provided by the Santhei Natural Park have affirmed the aspects of TBL, i.e., enhancing economic, social, and environmental sustainability, which are important components of sustainable development (Slaper & Hall, 2011; Guillen-Royo, 2016; Salem et al., 2012). This park exhibits the potential to utilise natural capital wisely and be reserved for the wellbeing of the future generations (WCED, 1987; Kumar, 2016). Besides, the identification of opportunities by the local people and the creation of enterprises to exploit (these) opportunities confirmed Anderson et al.'s (2006) argument. However, the pattern of opportunity recognition by the youth of the Andro community club and local people to open their respective stalls is consistent with the views by Dana (2015) that opportunity recognition is culturally determined.[17] This substantiates Lindsay's (2005) argument that what constitutes an opportunity among an Indigenous community differs from what constitutes an opportunity from a non-Indigenous perspective. With this stance, the research convinced to put forward the argument that the "cultural aspect is inherent in the Indigenous entrepreneurship which ultimately contributed as the fourth bottom-line or fourth dimension of sustainable development". To consider "culture" as the fourth pillar is crucial because sustaining traditional or Indigenous knowledge is important to prevent the loss of culture and to achieve harmony among cultural diversity, environmental responsibility, and economic viability (Nurse, 2006 as cited in Majid & Koe, 2012). The analysis evoked the model of Santhei Natural Park to go beyond the concept of Indigenous entrepreneurship and suggested a model of ecotourism that is consistent with Zeppel's (2006) case studies of Indigenous-owned ecotourism venture in his book *Indigenous Ecotourism: Sustainable Development and Management* and also with Kokkranikal and Morrison's (2002) case study on Indigenous entrepreneurship of the Kerala (small houseboat). However, the partnership and collaboration pattern of the Santhei Natural Park contradicted with both the model of Indigenous entrepreneurship of either Zeppel's (2006) case studies, where most of the Indigenous ecotourism mainly depend on donor assistance, support from conservation NGOs, and other foreign aid, or the case of Indigenous tourism of Kerela small houseboat where partnerships and outsiders are involved from outside the community (Kokkranikal & Morrison, 2002).

Further, the ecological sensitivity among the local Andro people was reflected in their perception and application of entrepreneurship (Salem et al., 2012), where they value their land as a capital for establishing the Santhei Natural Park (Anderson et al. (2006). This confirmed that in this era of modernisation and globalisation, they are still having a 'special relationship' with their land, and access to and use of the resources of the land (Berkes & Adhikari, 2006). But, the context where the Andro community initiates and controls their entrepreneurship cannot be generalised with the finding of Anderson et al. (2006), which stated that Indigenous people participating in the global economy had been accompanied by an ongoing struggle for land. Besides, the participation of local people in decision making regarding the management of Santhei Natural Park is consistent with Farrelly's (2012) study on ecotourism (i.e., Bouma National Heritage Park, Fiji), which reveals that in the governance and management process of ecotourism, all community members participate in the decision making.

Nevertheless, the revelation of women's participation in the economic activities and its benefits is aligned with Osinubi's (2007) case study of Indigenous women in development through participation in the market that contributed to the development through making an adequate profit from sales, healthy relationships with other traders, improvement of the family economy, and participation in the cost of children's education and making sufficient gains for personal consumption. However, the lack of a women's market union in Santhei Natural Park revealed dissimilarity with Osinubi's (2007) finding that women are involved in addressing different problems of the market (development) and those (financial) of individuals through market union activities. Further, the pattern of participating in economic activities is consistent with Dunlop's (1999) reports that "the biggest problem identified by the Small Business Enterprise Centre (SBEC) was the 'copycat' mentality of entrepreneurs where people set themselves up in the same business, selling an identical product, and often in the same locality" (as cited in Cahn, 2008, p. 9). Almost all the entrepreneurs who make and sell local rice wine and the potters who make and sell modern earthen products or traditional Andro pots showed the involvement of family (Cahn, 2008). Thus, among the Andro community, their business activities involve more than stakeholders (Lindsay, 2005).

The innovative and sustainability-oriented approach of Santhei Natural Park aligned with the findings of Kokkranikal and Morrison (2002). Innovation specifically in the traditional Andro pottery is aligned with Szirmai, Naudé, and Goedhuys' (2011) assertion that it involves the development of new products, new processes, new sources of supply, and exploitation of new markets to contribute in economic development. However, considering the declining demand of traditional Andro pottery products and its uses, Johnson's (2001, p. 140) submission that "innovation and entrepreneurship can occur without threatening the core product or service base" is found contradictory. Further, the findings showed that the recognition and status gained by local people who are engaging in economic activities mostly among the traditional pottery occupation is contradicted by Cahn's (2008) finding that rural people often choose to trade off potential economic business success in order to ensure their family's status is not harmed in any way, and their place in the family, their social identity, and their security is not jeopardised. Again, the author's finding is contradictory in the sense that people may be reluctant to actively market their products due to a fear of being seen as disrespectful or 'flaunting' themselves, which is not an accepted way to behave. Besides economic activities, the finding has revealed that changes in the perception of local people who are residing near Santhei Natural Park and engaging in economic activities is aligned with Moghavvemi, Woosnam, Paramanathan, Musa, and Hamzah's (2017) study on the perception of residents living in a tourism destination where local people displayed a welcoming nature, sympathetic understanding, emotional closeness, and community commitments.

## Conclusion

This chapter contributed towards the literature where Indigenous entrepreneurship addresses sustainable development. The research study has showed two relevant aspects of Indigenous entrepreneurship where the Santhei Natural Park overcomes the socio-economic challenges of the Andro community and sustainability development. The foundation of such an entrepreneurship model is based on the specific natural environment and control/initiated by the Indigenous community can be replicated and can substantially contribute to this goal of sustainable development. While replicating such a model and initiating a partnership and collaboration with the state government, private partners, and NGOs, there must be concern for the Indigenous people, their culture, and heritage, and their values and beliefs must not be ignored. The chapter is a snapshot of a very early-stage Santhei Natural Park, which is why the positive impacts overwhelm the negative part. So, there is a scope for future assessment on the sustainability, observation, and critical research on the development cycle. Further research can be done on the negative impact and also compare the positive and negative impacts of the park.

## Notes

1 As a mark of respect to all Indigenous peoples, the word "Indigenous" is used with a capital "I" throughout this chapter (Hindle & Moroz, 2007a, p. 1).
2 An estimated 90 million Indigenous people live in India, where they are often referred to as "scheduled tribes" or Adivasis. They live in many parts of the country but are much more numerous in some Indian states than in others (Subramanian et al., 2006, p. 1795).
3 First, the Indian Council of Indigenous and Tribal Peoples (ICITP) presented its statement at the UN Working Group on Indigenous People at the 9th session, 22 July to 2 August 1991. It is also associated with the statement made by Mr. Prabhu Dayal on behalf of the delegation of India (Permanent Mission of India to the United Nations Office. Geneva) in the working group on Indigenous Populations, 31 July 1991. The second type of body is none but the anthropologists who have been actively engaged in the study of the tribal situation in India. Coming to the viewpoints of the first group, one finds a lot of different ones (Dash & Pati, 2002, p. 10).
4 Culture is the collective programming of the mind that distinguishes the members of one category of people from another. It can be measured in terms of power distance, individualism-collectivism, uncertainty avoidance, masculinity-femininity, and long-term versus short-term orientation. Culture influences attitudes and behaviors, which vary within and across nations and within and across ethnicities and is strongly embedded in Indigenous communities (Lindsay, 2005, p. 1).
5 The World Commission finds then the need to change destructive lifestyles, especially in industrialised countries, by adopting concrete measures such as reducing the exploitation of raw materials and reducing energy, water, mineral products, and other natural resources consumption. At the same time, it requires a global spread of eco-technologies, facilities purification, and recycling techniques. On this occasion was expressly stated the interdependence between economic development and environmental protection (Scutaru, 2013, p. 37).
6 It is a complex process that combines economic issues with the sociological, psychological, and political aspects of human life and society (Scutaru, 2013, p. 36).
7 After World War II, taking into account the accelerating population growth and consumption of non-renewable resources, with increasing incomes and living standards. In 1972, at the Stockholm Conference on the Environment initiated by the U.S. and

Scandinavia, for the first time is presented the deterioration of the environment due to human activities, which endanger the future of the planet, and it is emphasised that economic development is inextricably linked to social development if we are to ensure an environment that is conducive to human existence and creation of the necessary conditions on Earth to improve the quality of life. On this occasion the decision was made to establish a UNO Environment Programme under the auspices of the United Nations General Assembly (Scutaru, 2013, p. 36).

8 He referred to the HRSCATSIA (2008) definition of Indigenous economic development "as the involvement of Indigenous people in employment, business, asset and wealth creation in the communities and regions where they live" (Morley, 2014, p. 2).

9 A systematic body of knowledge acquired by local people through the accumulation of experiences, informal experiments, and an intimate understanding of the environment in a given culture (Warren & Rajasekaran, 1993 as cited in Onwuegbuzie, 2016, p. 106).

10 Indigenous entrepreneurs, who use Indigenous knowledge, tend to generate grassroots innovations, which are defined as need-based, simple, cost-effective, and sustainable solutions, generated to address problems faced by Indigenous communities (Gupta, 2001 as cited in Onwuegbuzie, 2016, pp. 106–107).

11 Kaupapa Maori Entrepreneurship can be described as a 'social entrepreneurship', in that it is entrepreneurial activity, but it is underpinned by social objectives to improve the wealth and wellbeing of the community, rather than just the individual (Cant, 2007, p. 466).

12 Phusaba Lois are inhibited in those villages which are categories and engaged as "potters" and gave mudpots as a tribute.

13 Indigenous ecotourism includes a nature-based product, Indigenous ownership, and the presentation of Indigenous environmental and cultural knowledge. Ecotourism includes Aboriginal people and their traditions because of the strong bond between Indigenous cultures and the natural environment. This includes cultural, spiritual, and physical links between Indigenous peoples and their traditional lands or natural resources (Zeppel, 2006, p. 11).

14 Sangai Festival has been held to display the uniqueness of the shy and gentle Brow-Antlered Deer, popularly known as the Sangai Deer, which is found only in Manipur at the floating Keibul Lamjao National Park in Loktak Lake, and to further promote Manipur as an excellent tourism destination.

15 World Tourism Day is being organised by the Department of Tourism, Government of Manipur with a motive of promoting tourism in the state and its villages.

16 Marup literally means 'friendship' in Manipuri. Marups are Indigenous unorganised rotating savings groups/schemes where women take turns monthly to receive the joint pool, thus enabling each woman to meet urgent expenditures or affect personal savings.

17 It can be said that opportunity recognition is therefore culturally determined because different cultures have different goals and culturally specific needs. If person A wants to eat meat and person B comes from a vegetarian culture, person B may not perceive an opportunity to go hunting as an opportunity having utility. Yet for person A, hunting is a means of attaining the goal of subsistence (Dana, 2015, p. 165).

## References


Abidin, H. (2015). *The protection of indigenous peoples and reduction of forest carbon emissions: The REDD-Plus regime and international law*. Boston, MA: Brill, Nijhoff.

Acs, Z. J., Desai, S., & Hessels, J. (2008). Entrepreneurship, economic development and institutions. *Small Business Economics, 31*(3), 219–234.

Alfred, T., & Corntassel, J. (2005). Being indigenous: Resurgences against contemporary colonialism. *Government and Opposition, 40*(4), 597–614.

Anderson, R. B., Dana, L. P., & Dana, T. E. (2006). Indigenous land rights, entrepreneurship, and economic development in Canada: "Opting-in" to the global economy. *Journal of World Business, 41*(1), 45–55.

Anderson, R. B., Honig, B., & Peredo, A. M. (2007). Communities in the global economy: Where social and Indigenous entrepreneurship meet. In C. Steyaert & D. Hjorth (Eds.), *Entrepreneurship as social change: A third new movements in entrepreneurship book* (pp. 56–78). Cheltenham: Edward Elgar Publishing.

Berkes, F., & Adhikari, T. (2006). Development and conservation: Indigenous businesses and the UNDP Equator Initiative. *International Journal of Entrepreneurship and Small Business, 3*(6), 671–690.

Brueckner, M., Pearson, C. A., Chatterjee, S., Wise, G., & Marika, B. (2011). *Indigenous entrepreneurship: Closing the gap on local terms.* The 12th International Conference of the Society for Global Business & Economic Development, 21 July 2011. Singapore: Society for Global Business & Economic Development (SGBED).

Bruton, G. D., Zahra, S. A., & Cai, L. (2018). Examining entrepreneurship through indigenous lenses. *Entrepreneurship Theory and Practice, 42*(3), 351–361.

Cahn, M. (2008). Indigenous entrepreneurship, culture and micro-enterprise in the Pacific Islands: Case studies from Samoa. *Entrepreneurship and Regional Development, 20*(1), 1–18.

Cant, G. (2007). The South Pacific: Australia, New Zealand and the Pacific Islands—Insights into the theory and praxis of indigenous entrepreneurship. In L. P. Dana & R. B. Anderson (Eds.), *International handbook of research on Indigenous entrepreneurship* (pp. 459–469). Cheltenham: Edward Elgar Publishing.

Cohen, B., & Winn, M. I. (2007). Market imperfections, opportunity and sustainable entrepreneurship. *Journal of Business Venturing, 22*(1), 29–49.

Cohen, B., Smith, B., & Mitchell, R. (2008). Toward a sustainable conceptualisation of dependent variables in entrepreneurship research. *Business Strategy and the Environment, 17*(2), 107–119.

Colbourne, R. (2017). Indigenous entrepreneurship and hybrid ventures. *Hybrid Ventures (Advances in Entrepreneruship, Firm Emergence and Growth), 19*, 93–149. DOI: 10.1108/S1074-754020170000019004

Collings, N. (2009). Chapter III, The environment. In Department of Economic and Social Affairs (Ed.), *State of the world's indigenous peoples* (pp. 84–127). New York: United Nations. Retrieved from www.un.org/esa/socdev/unpfii/documents/SOWIP/en/SOWIP_chapter3.pdf.

Conway, D. M. (2011). Promoting indigenous innovation, enterprise, and entrepreneurship through the licensing of Article 31 Indigenous Assets and Resources. *SMUL Review, 64*, 1095–1126.

Dana, L. P. (2007). Towards a multidisciplinary definition of indigenous entrepreneurship. In L. P. Dana & R. B. Anderson (Eds.), *International handbook of research on Indigenous entrepreneurship* (pp. 3–7). Cheltenham: Edward Elgar Publishing.

Dana, L. P. (2015). Indigenous entrepreneurship: An emerging field of research. *International Journal of Business and Globalisation, 14*(2), 158–169.

Dana, L. P., Dana, T. E., & Anderson, R. B. (2007). A theory-based empirical study of entrepreneurship in Iqaluit, Nunavut (formerly Frobisher Bay, Northwest Territories). In L. P. Dana & R. B. Anderson (Eds.), *International handbook of research on Indigenous entrepreneurship* (pp. 366–377). Cheltenham: Edward Elgar Publishing.

Dash, J., & Pati, R. N. (2002). The indigenous and Tribal people to-day: Issues in conceptualisation. In R. N. Pati & J. Dash (Eds.), *Tribal and indigenous people of India: Problems and prospects* (pp. 3–14). New Delhi, India: APH Publishing.

Dean, B., & Levi, J. M. (Eds.). (2003). *At the risk of being heard: Identity, indigenous rights, and postcolonial states.* Ann Arbor, MI: The University of Michigan Press.

Devi, L. B. (2002). *The lois of Manipur: Andro, Khurkhul, Phayeng and Sekmai.* New Delhi, India: Mittal Publications.

Farrelly, T. (2012). Community-based ecotourism as indigenous social entrepreneurship. In A. Holden & D. A. Fennell (Eds.), *The Routledge handbook of tourism and environment* (pp. 447–459). Oxon: Routledge.

Farrelly, T. A., & Vudiniabola, A. T. (2013). Kerekere and indigenous social entrepreneurship. *Sites: A Journal of Social Anthropology and Cultural Studies, 10*(2), 1–29.

Galbraith, C. S., Rodriguez, C. L., & Stiles, C. S. (2006). False myths and indigenous entrepreneurial strategies. *Journal of Small Business & Entrepreneurship, 19*(1), 1–20.

Gallagher, B., & Lawrence, T. B. (2012). Entrepreneurship and indigenous identity: A study of identity work by indigenous entrepreneurs in British Columbia. *International Journal of Entrepreneurship and Small Business, 17*(4), 395–414.

Gouvea, R. (2015). Sustainability and entrepreneurship: Fostering indigenous entrepreneurship in the Brazilian Amazon region. In Information Resources Management Association (Ed.), *Economics: Concepts, methodologies, tools, and applications* (pp. 228–246). Hershey, PA: IGI Global.

Guillen-Royo, M. (2016). *Sustainability and wellbeing: Human-scale development in practice*. London: Routledge.

Gundlach, M. J., & Zivnuska, S. (2010). An experiential learning approach to teaching social entrepreneurship, Triple Bottom Line, and sustainability: Modifying and extending Practical Organisational Behaviour Education (PROBE). *American Journal of Business Education, 3*(1), 19–28.

Gupta, A. K., Sinha, R., Koradia, D., Patel, R., Parmar, M., Rohit, P. . . . Vivekanandan, P. (2003). Mobilising grassroots' technological innovations and traditional knowledge, values and institutions: Articulating social and ethical capital. *Futures, 35*(9), 975–987.

Hassan, A. (2016). A composition of variable economic activities: Cases of three groups of Indigenous people of South Asia. In K. Iankova, A. Hassan, & R. L'Abbe (Eds.), *Indigenous people and economic development: An international perspective* (pp. 267–282). New York: Routledge.

Hindle, K., & Moroz, P. (2007a). Defining indigenous entrepreneurship as a research field: Discovering and critiquing the emerging canon. *Frontiers of Entrepreneurship Research, 27*(9), 1–16.

Hindle, K., & Moroz, P. (2007b). *Indigenous entrepreneurship as a research field: Developing a definitional framework from the emerging canon in BCERC 2007*. Proceedings of the 2007 Babson College Entrepreneurship Research Conference, Babson College, Babson Park, MA, pp. 1–54.

Hindle, K., Anderson, R. B., Giberson, R. J., & Kayseas, B. (2005). Relating practice to theory in Indigenous entrepreneurship: A pilot investigation of the Kitsaki partnership portfolio. *The American Indian Quarterly, 29*(1), 1–23.

Hindle, K., & Lansdowne, M. (2007). Brave spirits on new paths: Toward a globally relevant paradigm of Indigenous entrepreneurship research. In L. P. Dana & R. B. Anderson (Eds.), *International handbook of research on Indigenous entrepreneurship* (pp. 8–19). Cheltenham: Edward Elgar Publishing.

Iankova, K., Hassan, A., & L'Abbe, R. (Eds.). (2016). *Indigenous people and economic development: An international perspective*. New York: Routledge.

İyigün, N. Ö. (2015). What could entrepreneurship do for sustainable development? A corporate social responsibility-based approach. *Procedia-Social and Behavioural Sciences, 195*, 1226–1231.

Jamali, D. (2006). Insights into triple bottom line integration from a learning organisation perspective. *Business Process Management Journal, 12*(6), 809–821.

Johnson, D. (2001). What is innovation and entrepreneurship? Lessons for larger organisations. *Industrial and Commercial Training, 33*(4), 135–140.

Kawharu, M., Tapsell, P., & Woods, C. (2017). Indigenous entrepreneurship in Aotearoa New Zealand. *Journal of Enterprising Communities: People and Places in the Global Economy, 11*(1), 20–38.

Kingsbury, B. (1998). "Indigenous peoples" in international law: A constructivist approach to the Asian controversy. *The American Journal of International Law, 92*(3), 414–457.

Kokkranikal, J., & Morrison, A. (2002). Entrepreneurship and sustainable tourism: The houseboats of Kerala. *Tourism and Hospitality Research, 4*(1), 7–20.

Kumar, K. S. K. (2016). Economics of sustainable development. *Economic and Political Weekly, 3*, 34–36.

Lasimbang, J. (2008). Indigenous peoples and local economic development. *Indigenous Peoples Local Economic Development, 5*, 42–45.

Lindsay, N. J. (2005). Toward a cultural model of indigenous entrepreneurial attitude. *Academy of Marketing Science Review*, 1–17.

Lopik, W.V., & Erdmann, S. J. (2013). Indigenous entrepreneurship and sustainability: A case study-college of Menominee nation campus grind coffee shop. In K. K. White (Eds.), *America goes green: An encyclopedia of eco-friendly culture in the United States, Vol. 1: Thematic entries* (pp. 236–241). California: ABC-CLIO.

Lundstrom, A., Zhou, C., Friedrichs, Y.V., & Sundin, E. (2014). *Social entrepreneurship: Leveraging economic, political, and cultural dimensions*. Heidelberg, Germany: Springer.

Majid, I. A., & Koe, W. L. (2012). Sustainable Entrepreneurship (SE): A revised model based on Triple Bottom Line (TBL). *International Journal of Academic Research in Business and Social Sciences, 2*(6), 293–310.

Maphosa, F. (1998). Towards the sociology of Zimbabwean indigenous entrepreneurship. *Zambezia, 25*(2), 173–190.

Mapunda, G. (2007). Entrepreneurial leadership and indigenous enterprise development. *Journal of Asia Entrepreneurship and Sustainability, 3*(3), 1–27.

Moghavvemi, S., Woosnam, K. M., Paramanathan, T., Musa, G., & Hamzah, A. (2017). The effect of residents' personality, emotional solidarity, and community commitment on support for tourism development. *Tourism Management, 63*, 242–254.

Morley, S. (2014). *Success factors for Indigenous entrepreneurs and community-based enterprises*. Volume: Closing the Gap Clearinghouse, Canberra, A.C.T. Retrieved from www.aihw.gov.au/reports/indigenous-australians/success-factors-for-indigenous-entrepreneurs-and-c/formats

Morris, M. H. (1998). *Entrepreneurial intensity: Sustainable advantages for individuals, organisations, and societies*. Westport, CT: Quorum Books Quorum Books.

Murchison, J. (2010). *Ethnography essentials: Designing, conducting, and presenting your research* (Vol. 25). San Francisco, CA: John Wiley & Sons.

Onwuegbuzie, H. (2016). A 21st century paradigm for entrepreneurs and policy makers: Applying modern scientific methods to indigenous innovation. In J. Liddle (Ed.), *New perspectives on research, policy & practice in public entrepreneurship* (pp. 103–126). Bingley: Emerald Group Publishing Limited.

Osinubi, T. S. (2007). Women in development: The case of Bodija market in Ibadan, South Western Nigeria. *International Handbook of Research on Indigenous Entrepreneurship*, 46–59.

Parrish, B. D. (2008). *Sustainability-driven entrepreneurship: A literature review*. Sustainability Research Institute (SRI), School of Earth and Environment, The University of Leeds, UK, pp. 1–57.

Parrish, B. D. (2010). Sustainability-driven entrepreneurship: Principles of organisation design. *Journal of Business Venturing, 25*(5), 510–523.

Patrinos, H. A., Skoufias, E., & Lunde, T. (2007). *Indigenous peoples in Latin America: Economic opportunities and social networks*. Working Paper No. 4227. Retrieved from Worldbank.org: http://documents.worldbank.org/curated/en/608351468091486766/pdf/wps4227.pdf

Peredo, A. M., Anderson, R. B., Galbraith, C. S., Honig, B., & Dana, L. P. (2004). Towards a theory of indigenous entrepreneurship. *International Journal of Entrepreneurship and Small Business*, *1*(1–2), 1–20.

Peredo, A. M., & McLean, M. (2006). Social entrepreneurship: A critical review of the concept. *Journal of World Business*, *41*(1), 56–65.

Rønning, L. (2007). Entrepreneurship among Sámi reindeer herders. In L. P. Dana & R. B. Anderson (Eds.), *International handbook of research on Indigenous entrepreneurship* (pp. 232–245). Cheltenham: Edward Elgar Publishing.

Rushesha, S. T., & Mhaka, W. N. (2014). Afrintuneurship: Towards integral African enterprise development. In E. Mamukwa, R. Lessem, & A. Schieffer (Eds.), *Integral green Zimbabwe: An African phoenix rising* (pp. 133–154). New York: Routledge.

Salem, A. A. H., Anderson, R., & Dana, L. P. (2012). Entrepreneurship and sustainability. In C. N. Madu & C. Kuei (Eds.), *Handbook of sustainability management* (pp. 291–312). Hackensack, NJ: World Scientific.

Scutaru, L. (2013). Economic development versus sustainable development. *Ecoforum Journal*, *2*(1), 35–40.

Sengupta, R. (2002). Human well-being and sustainable development. *Economic and Political Weekly*, *37*(42), 4289–4294.

Shane, S., & Venkataraman, S. (2000). The promise of entrepreneurship as a field of research. *The Academy of Management Review*, *25*(1), 217–226.

Shepherd, D. A., & Patzelt, H. (2011). The new field of sustainable entrepreneurship: Studying entrepreneurial action linking "what is to be sustained" with "what is to be developed". *Entrepreneurship Theory and Practice*, *35*(1), 137–163.

Slaper, T. F., & Hall, T. J. (2011). The triple bottom line: What is it and how does it work? *Indiana Business Review*, *86*(1), 4–8.

Subramanian, S. V., Smith, G. D., & Subramanyam, M. (2006). Indigenous health and socioeconomic status in India. *PLoS Medicine*, *3*(10), 1794–1804.

Szirmai, A., Naudé, W., & Goedhuys, M. (Eds.). (2011). *Entrepreneurship, innovation, and economic development*. Oxford: Oxford University Press.

Toma, S. G., Grigore, A. M., & Marinescu, P. (2014). Economic development and entrepreneurship. *Procedia Economics and Finance*, *8*, 436–443.

UNESCO. (2006). *Guidelines on intercultural education*. Paris: UNESCO. Retrieved from http://unesdoc.unesco.org/images/0014/001478/147878e.pdf.

World Commission on Environment and Development (WCED). (1987). *Report of the World Commission on Environment and Development: Our common future*. Retrieved December 7, 2016, from www.un-documents.net/our-common-future.pdf.

Xaxa, V. (1999). Tribes as indigenous people of India. *Economic and Political Weekly*, *34*(51), 3589–3595.

Xaxa, V. (2008). *State, society, and tribes: Issues in post-colonial India*. New Delhi: Dorling Kindersley (India).

Zeppel, H. (2006). *Indigenous ecotourism sustainable development and management*. Wallingford, UK: CABI.

# 6

# NAPASAR

## An approach to sustainable livelihood

*Anu Sharma,*[1] *Simmi Bhagat, and Mona Suri*

The handloom sector is the second largest employer in India, providing employment to about 6.5 million people as per the report of the Ministry of Textiles (2010). The sector represents the continuity of the age-old Indian heritage of hand weaving and reflects the socio-cultural tradition of the weaving communities. Although the Government of India has been creating and implementing policy for encouraging the handloom sector since 1947, there is still a demand for charting a sustainable path for development of handloom clusters as per the market trends.

The real India consists of 80 percent of the population residing and working from villages. India is a country where technology and traditions are practised concurrently (Balaram, 1998). After post-modernism, the progress in science and technology established deviations to traditional practices and its products, leading to an increase in industrialisation at the cost of reducing the number of artisans practising traditional crafts.

Currently, the younger-generation artisans study in schools. The schools are teaching various subjects, which have no relevance to their family or traditional crafts. This type of education further alienates the artisans from their family craft, and finally, they lose respect for the craft, which has been practised for generations in their family. In addition, they grow up seeing the hardships the family has to endure, while practising a craft. They desperately want to try something else for a sustainable and worthy livelihood. As a result, the artisan families have greatly reduced in number and their art has declined, even sometimes died altogether or is ready to die.

While the population of India is increasing at an enormous pace, along with its associated human needs, the artisan/craftsman communities are ironically dwindling at almost the same pace. The skilled artisans are leaving their family professions of countless generations and turning to other jobs. The jobs are of unskilled urban labour, but they yield a better income and offer better financial security, compared to their traditional skilled jobs. Some of these artisans migrate to towns and cities in search of jobs and find work as labourers, domestic servants, peons, and so on.

An added difficulty is that many of these Indian craft traditions are oral traditions. In the absence of any document, the oral traditions, once lost, can never be revived. Therefore, it is a permanent loss. The case with crafts, such as multi-layer weaving and camel hair fibre products in Napasar, is similar. Therefore, there is an urgent demand for reviving old craft traditions as they are not only sustainable but are eco-friendly as well, with a minimum incorporation of conventional chemical substances and processes.

Sustainable practices and protection of the environment are concerns that today's designer cannot ignore (Chapman & Gant, 2006). Therefore, currently the world is looking for eco-friendly and sustainable textiles which can help the craftsmen to work using traditional techniques, but with an innovation, either in design or techniques or both, incorporating sustainability as a core concept. Sustainable design is an unambiguous methodology which is followed while designing, sourcing, and creating objects, developing and fashioning experiences. Usage of local raw materials and skills are the other two aspects which form the backbone of the sustainable practices.

As there is no empirical research available on Napasar—a small village of Rajasthan, which is a hub of handloom weavers engaged in the traditional crafts of weaving and spinning since ages—this study aims to acknowledge these traditional textile crafts and practices that can provide a sustainable livelihood to this village. This study illustrates these issues through the current scenario of the artisans of Napasar, along with their dwindling traditional practices and crafts. It concludes with some constructive suggestions for providing sustainable methods and approaches for making the cluster self-sustainable.

## History and scenario of Indian handloom industry

The Indian handloom industry can be linked to the ancient Indus Valley civilisation, *Rig Vedas*, and *Mauryan* eras. A study dated to 327 B.C. indicated the presence of magnificently woven Indian textiles taken by Alexander to his country. The trade of Indian cloth to Romans in million sesterces is described in a book called *Natural History* dated 711 A.D. Many historic writers such as Chaolu Kua, Marco Polo, and Renaudot in the 12th century have mentioned in their annotations about the presence of the skilful textile industry in India, as stated by Soundarapandian (2002). Spinning and weaving became small-scale industries in the 13th century; however, as Das (2001) described, by the early 19th century this industry started seeing a downfall due to the invasion of British manufactured products and mill-spun yarns. However, in the 19th century, the Indian textile industry saw a sudden rise due to Gandhi ji's Swadeshi Movement, but in the latter half of the same century it lost its identity to mill-made products. In 1947, although the All India Handloom Board provided support in terms of raw material, finance, and marketing to the handloom industry, still the powerloom industry overpowered it (Ministry of Labour, GOI, 1988).

As per the August 2013 report of the Handloom Export Production Council (HEPC), the handloom industry is the second largest employment provider to rural Indians after the agriculture sector. It has engaged 4.3 million people with 2.3 million weaving looms and also contributes 15 per cent of the cloth production in India (www.ibef.org).

In the current scenario of the 21st century, the handloom sector has been suffering due to its unorganised and dispersed policies. Through studies on handloom clusters like Chanderi[2] and Kota Doria,[3] the government established reality trees highlighting the problems of these sectors, which include improper infrastructure, deficient skill up-gradation, low product innovations and interventions, low to nil sustainable approach, no value addition, threat by modernisation and globalisation, etc. Such reality trees also highlighted the weak points of the cluster, which required immediate attention by government and non-governmental organisations (NGOs) for their development and growth. The main issues emphasised through the reality trees were 1) low infrastructure, 2) technical problems, 3) inadequate knowledge about market and trends, 4) shortage of finances, and 5) dominance of the power loom in the market.

## Methodology

A qualitative methodology was adopted for the study. Qualitative data was collected through primary as well as secondary resources. The primary data were collected from weavers and spinners through in-depth interviews. The cluster of Napasar is very small in terms of population size, with approximately 100 weavers. A purposive sampling technique was used to select weavers and spinners. Based on various categories in terms of work status (freelancer, employed by an organisation or working for family unit) and age (under 40 years or above 40 years), in-depth interviews with 50 weavers and 25 spinners were selected. An interview guide was developed to conduct in-depth interviews with them. The qualitative data so collected was analysed using content analysis. Secondary data were collected through museums, archives, journals, and web resources.

## The research context

### *Brief profile of Bikaner district*

Bikaner is a district of the Rajasthan state in India, which is renowned for its time-honoured hand crafts like hand embroideries, hand block printing, and handloom weaving. The district Bikaner was established by Rathore Prince Rao Bikaji, the son of Rao Jodha ji of Marwar in 1488 A.D. After the introduction of the Ganga Canal in 1927 A.D., the Bikaner state territory was divided into four districts: Bikaner, Ganganagar, Churu, and Hanumangarh. Later on for smooth administration functioning and development purposes, the district was divided into eight subdivisions: Bikaner, Loonkaransar, Khajuwala, Kolayat, Nokha, Chhattargarh,

Dungargarh, and Pugal. There are overall 893 villages and 219 Gram Panchayats[4] in this district, as per the MSME (2011).

## *Location, geographical area, and topography*

Bikaner is one of the desert districts situated in the northwest of the Rajasthan state. It extends from 27°11' to 29°3' North latitudes and 71°54' to 74°22' East longitudes. It is surrounded by Ganganagar in the North, Pakistan in the West, the Nagaur and Jodhpur districts in the Southeast directions, and Churu in the East. The district has a complete geographical area of 30247.90 km$^2$, which is around 8.8 percent of the whole area of the state. The chief part of the district is desert and has arid regions as part of the Great Indian Desert of Thar. Sand dunes of 6 to 30 meters in height keep shifting in these desert areas throughout the year due to its topographical structure and arid zone (MSME 2011).

## *Climate and rainfall*

The district has an arid climate with a huge divergence of temperatures and scanty rainfall. The uppermost temperature is up to 48 degrees Celsius in summer and the lowest is 1 degree Celsius in winter season. The sand dunes also keep shifting due to driving, hot winds in summer, flouncing from one area to the other in the Bikaner district.

## *Details of artisan units in Bikaner district*

As per the statistics collected till 31 March 2011, there are no large-scale industries or public-sector undertakings in Bikaner. However, there are 2,123 textile micro units and small industrial organisations encompassing cotton, jute, silk, and wool with hosiery and garments, providing employment to 11,945 people with an investment of Rs.[5] 822.434 million within the Bikaner district MSME (2011). As an arid zone with low water resources and scanty vegetation, industrial expansion has always been low in the district. Due to harsh climatic conditions, livestock such as sheep, goats, and camels makes it a large wool production centre.

### *Napasar—a village within Bikaner district: the case description*

Napasar is one among the 893 villages of the Bikaner district. It's a weavers' hub on a road trip of 20 kilometres away from Bikaner city. There are private as well as government buses which connect this village to Bikaner city and further villages around it. In former times, camel carts were employed as transportation in the Bikaner district, but with the advent of technology, the public have now started using cars, bikes, and other transportation vehicles. Besides the road connection, the village also has a railway station, which links it through trains coming from diverse regions of India.

### Population

According to the population of India website (2014), the total population of Napasar is 19,500, out of which 10,101 are males and the rest 9,399 are females. In Napasar, the weaving craft is primarily done by males, while spinning is the vocation of females (www.populationofindia.co.in/rajasthan/bikaner/bikaner/.napasar).

### Literacy

Education at a higher level has never been a priority in Napasar. Males of the weaver's community are usually secondary school drop-outs. However, the research confirms that now the young-generation weavers are appreciating the importance of education and are efficiently working towards it. It's amazing to see that in comparison to males of the village, younger women are more educationally qualified.

### Family unit

Napasar has a tradition of living in joint families. A good number of weavers and spinners reside in large joint families, with their parents, brothers, sisters, and in-laws constituting a number of six or more family members. This is why most of the weavers have learnt the skill of weaving from their fathers or elder brothers and are now teaching it either to their sons or younger brothers if interested. The younger women in a family take care of the kids and household work while largely the elder women of the house spin fibres into yarn. After completing all the domestic chores, the younger women also join the elders in spinning the yarn. This is in reference to the Chanderi and Kota Doria cluster's reality tree, where the traditional process of weaving and spinning without modernisation has also been categorised as a weak point of the clusters.

### Overview of current Napasar's trade

The manufacturing sector of Napasar is called a Napasar handloom cluster, which produces pure hand-woven cotton fabrics for apparels and home, with 135 units in government records (MSME 2011) (Figure 6.1). Weavers of Napasar also weave woollen shawls and aasans[6] given by Khadi Gram Udyogs or Pratisthans.[7] This place has its identity in creating 100 percent pure hand-woven solid, chambray, warp or weft striped, and extra weft cotton fabrics produced on handlooms having four harnesses generally. The yarn for weaving fabric is sourced and dyed in Bikaner, which is the prime drawback for the weaver's community. The fabrics so produced are utilised for fashioning apparels as well as home products after stitching. Almost 95 percent of the products from Napasar are unstitched, which include products such as stoles, shawls, chindi dhurries,[8] single bed cotton linens, and towels. The chief markets for Napasar products are local, Ahmedabad, and Mumbai.

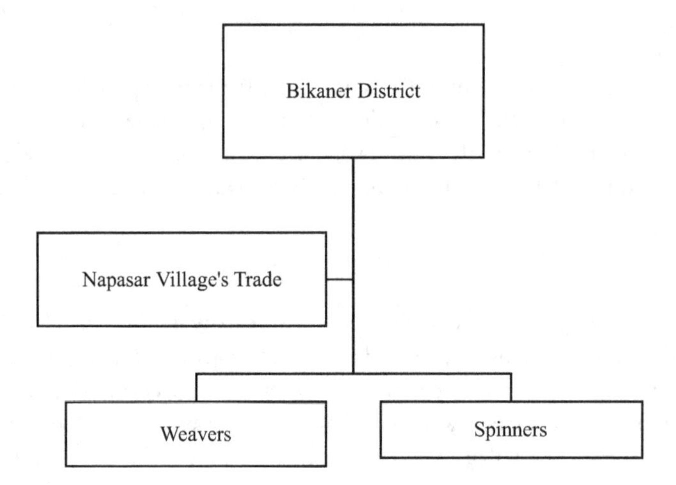


**FIGURE 6.1** Napasar organisational chart

*Source*: Prepared by the authors

Along with fabric weaving, the additional occupation of the villagers is the supply, production, and spinning of sheep wool. Bikaner district depends exceptionally on their livestocks, which include cattle, camels, goats, and sheep. Many villagers rear sheep for meat and wool, due to the harsh weather, topography of the district, and shortage of agriculture.

A sheep can yield approximately 1.3 to 4 kg of wool every year, which can materialise a key trade from Bikaner, but for this the villagers need training, knowledge, and better infrastructure facilities. This can elevate the employment opportunities for local people through development of woollen textiles industries such as woollen carpet, tufted carpet, felt, and other woollen textile items.

## *Primary dilemmas of the cluster*

1 The irregular and inadequate supply of raw materials, traditional technology, and low-quality standard products
2 Deficient infrastructure facilities
3 Unaware about government policies and schemes

## *Napasar spinner's community*

Weaving has been a forte of males in Napasar, while spinning has been a core area where women have excelled and ruled in this profession since ages. Every daughter and daughter-in-law of the village knows how to spin a yarn from the fibres on locally made spinning wheels called charkha.[9]

This instrument is made up of wood and iron and is locally made in the village. It's one of the main sources of income generation for the women of Napasar. Every woman learns to spin by the age of 12 to 16 years and becomes professional by the age of 18 years. Along with a sustainable mechanism, the raw materials which the spinners of Napasar spin are also natural and eco-friendly. A huge percentage of spinners are spinning locally sourced sheep wool for carpet and rug factories. The huge irony of this village's trade is that although Napasar is identified for its hand-woven cotton fabric, only few older women have spun cotton yarns in their pasts. In a place where the temperature is constantly soaring, currently every woman in the village spins sheep wool fibres for woollen shawls and aasans throughout the year. Apart from locally sourced wool fibres, these spinners sometimes also get 'merino wool' fibres to spin into yarn for creating shawls and other dress materials.

The wages of the spinners are entirely reliant on the production capacity of the yarn by a spinner in a day, which in turn depends upon the count of the yarn. The thicker the yarn, the smaller the count, and therefore more is the production, which means more wages for the spinners, or otherwise vice versa. Their package differs from Rs 1000 to Rs 6000 per month subject to these factors and the number of spinners in a family.

### *Napasar weaver's community*

Almost 70 percent of the weavers in Napasar have agricultural land, and they do farming besides weaving in the cultivation season. However, the climate of Napasar supports agriculture only for three to four months in a year. Therefore, nobody can depend entirely on farming as a profession. At present, there are almost an equal proportion of young weavers and old weavers in the village, which shows that although the younger generation is looking for new options of earning money, weaving is still being adopted as a profession in the same proportion as it was in the older generation. Every weaver in the village has at least one loom in his home, and weaving is the key profession for his income generation. As stated earlier, Napasar is still pursuing its tradition of living in joint families, and therefore almost 90 percent of weavers whether young or old have inherited the craft of weaving from their fathers or forefathers. As looms are available with the weavers at their homes, therefore many of them are working independently, while a few of them are working with an organisation and simultaneously freelancing as well. Few weavers of Napasar work in clusters or also groups.

The chief freelance job providers to weavers in the village are organisations like Deshnok Khadi Pratisthan, Khadi Sansthan, or Uni Sansthan. Some other important NGOs are Rangsutra and Desert Craft, which places orders for cotton and woollen fabrics at Napasar clusters to be stitched into apparels for Fabindia and their home brands, respectively.

The weaver either procures fibres from these organisations and then gets it spun at home or obtains spun yarn directly from the organisations for weaving. The warp beam is then attached to the loom, and after the drafting and denting of the warp yarns, fabric is woven. For this entire work the weaver earns an annual income which varies from Rs 50,000 to Rs 80,000. This income may be just adequate for a small family size but is surely not enough for a large family size to sustain, according to many weavers.

## Results and discussions: SWOC analysis of Napasar cluster

The SWOC means is used to analyse the strengths, weaknesses, opportunities, and challenges for a cluster. This analysis highlights areas which require improvement for the development of the cluster, keeping in view the cluster's strength and opportunities (Figure 6.2). This has been an intensive approach by most of the organisations like the United Nations Industrial Development Organization (UNIDO) and National Skill Development Corporation (NSDC) in India, for framing a diagnostic study of a cluster to fashion the right policies and right procedures leading to the development of the craft and the craftsmen. A similar approach has been applied in the study for framing the diagnostic study of the Napasar cluster.

### *Strength of the Napasar cluster*

#### *In-house weaving cluster*

Napasar is self-sustainable for creating fabrics of any amount, as even after the decline in the number of weavers from earlier years, there are still about 100 weavers who are involved in the weaving profession with full dedication. The strength of this cluster is self-dependency to produce any amount of fabric required and in providing employment to other clusters, as well as in places around the village if given a chance.

| STRENGTHS | WEAKNESSES |
|---|---|
| 1. In-house weaving<br>2. In-house spinning<br>3. Women Empowerment<br>4. Rising awareness about education<br>5. Availability of local raw material<br>6. A mix of all age weavers<br>7. Traditional craft practice<br>8. Availability of tools for fabric creation at home | 1. Loss of weaving interest<br>2. Forgotten craft of double cloth<br>3. No creation of old products<br>4. Lack of experimentation<br>5. Nil explorations<br>6. Lack of innovations<br>7. Lack of education<br>8. Lack of other skills |
| **OPPORTUNITIES** | **CHALLENGES** |
| 1. Community Synchronization<br>2. Available Government Schemes<br>3. Easy connectivity to Bikaner<br>4. Invitations for exhibitions and displays | 1. Rigid climate<br>2. Increasing powerlooms<br>3. Intervening middlemen<br>4. Sourcing of camel hair<br>5. Looking for more agencies other govt. agencies<br>6. Developing new marketing channels |

**FIGURE 6.2** SWOC chart of Napasar cluster

*Source:* Developed by the author

### In-house spinning cluster

As in weaving, this village is self-dependent for hand spinning as well. Women from young to old and from every household of Uttaradwas[10] and Goyallon ka Mohalla[11] of Napasar are part of the spinner's community. Similarly, as Rajasthan is famous for its banjara[12] clans, this profession also provides bread and butter to the women of these clans who come and stay in the boundary of this village for a temporary period, leading to an increase in the number of spinners for the Napasar village at any given point in time.

### Empowerment to women

All of the spinners are women, which gives the gender a power of earning money for themselves and their families. The spinning profession not only provides them the power to earn but also has given them the power to speak on the social matters of the family. Although men are the final decision makers of the family, yet females have their say in all the matters. This is vastly evident from the females outnumbering the males in achieving good and higher education in Napasar itself.

### Rising awareness about education among women

The research illustrated that although the older generation of females are completely illiterate, they are sending their daughters to achieve good education at the schools in Napasar. This awareness among women is clearly indicated by the higher percentage of literate women as compared to men and also that more young women than men hold higher educational degrees in Napasar.

### Availability of local raw material

Camel hair and varieties of sheep wool are available at Napasar and in the villages around it. Because of the hot and arid climate of Rajasthan, these two animals are cultivated the most. So using these available fibres and in-house spinners, the weavers of the Napasar handloom cluster can create new products by creating technological and design interventions.

### A mixture of all-age weavers

The best part of the Napasar handloom cluster is that there is an amalgamation of all the ages of weavers, from 19 to 70 years old. There are also weavers beyond the age of 70 years who are leading a retired life but are always available to share their experiences and guidance with the younger generation of weavers. Also the older weavers who are still practicing the craft are guiding and training the younger generation for this profession.

### *Traditional craft practice*

As the weaving and spinning craft is a traditional practice at Napasar, the importance of saving the handloom craft and keeping it alive is the main motto of this village. The craft practiced by all the weavers is inculcated in them from a very young age by their fathers and forefathers. However, many youngsters are moving towards cities and looking for other professions as their career, but they all know how to weave and are ready to join their family craft if they get good opportunities.

### *Availability of tools of fabric development at home*

The most important strength of Napasar is the availability of looms and hand-spinning machines in every house. As almost all the houses of Uttaradawas and Goyallon Ka Mohalla are involved in this profession, all these houses are well equipped with at least one loom in every house, and many among them even have two looms depending on the number of weavers in their family.

## *Drawbacks/weaknesses of Napasar*

### *Loss of weaving interest in younger generations*

The major snag of the weaver's community of Napasar is leaving behind their traditions and moving haphazardly without any focus of an aspiration to somehow earn more. A considerable number of budding generations below the age of 18 years do not appear to be fascinated by the traditional craft of weaving as their careers. Although as a tradition they are learning how to weave, after seeing the hardships of their families in sustaining, they are inclining towards opportunities of working outside the village, which according to them will fetch them continuous salaries and better livelihood.

### *Forgotten craft of double cloth weaving*

In bygone time, weavers of Napasar used camel hair and a double cloth technique for creating floor rugs to keep their home floors warm during winters (double cloth is a technique by which a weaver creates a double or multilayer fabric). This technique was used in Napasar to also create wider carpets. Today no one in Napasar uses camel hair fiber for weaving. Also the age-old technique and craft of double cloth has lost its identity and creation to the growing demands of the industry.

### *No production of rugs and carpets in Napasar*

Construction of rugs and carpets is evident via the Upanishads[13] reserved in the Bikaner State Archives, in which it is acknowledged that in the 18th and

19th centuries in Bikaner local jails, as a punishment all the prisoners were mandated to weave carpets and rugs. The trade of carpets and rugs was initiated with the tutoring of Persian weavers to the prisoners, but as time passed, some of the prisoners excelled in their weaving craft and they started training others. A special weaving technique known as double cloth weaving was employed in Napasar and Bikaner in the 18th and 19th centuries by Srivastava (1960–1961) for creating these products, which is now presently familiar to only three to four weavers in the village. This technique, along with camel hair, was also effective in fashioning wide carpets on smaller width looms. Along with the technique, the production of carpets and rugs are not practiced anymore in the houses of the weavers. Only if there is a demand, then chindi[14] rugs are created, but old carpets are limited to big textile factories of Bikaner and around.

## *Lack of experimentation*

Today most of the weavers of Napasar who are still continuing to weave handloom fabrics are weaving plain weave fabrics on four harness looms. They are creating fabrics which need more value additions before they can be sold off to a customer. There is a colossal need for experimentation and interventions in weaving designs and technology.

## *Less explorations done on camel hair and its usage*

Due to the hot, parched climate, agricultural yield is low in the village, hence the villagers rely heavily on livestock business for their livelihood. Due to a lack of water and scanty vegetation, livestock such as camels, goats, and sheep are preferred in the Bikaner district and its villages. As stated by Nagpal (2006), the camel is a valuable element of the desert ecosystem, where the agriculture could hardly fulfil the requirement of human food and energy. The acronym of CAMEL may be explained as 'C'—Carter, 'A'—Arid zone, 'M'—Multiuse, 'E'—Ecofriendly, and 'L'—Livestock (Bhakat and Sahani 2006). There are two varieties of camel from which the camel hair fibres are sourced: the *Camelus Bactrian* (double-humped) and the *Camelus Dromedary* (single-humped) camel.

Bactrian camels are found in the tremendously cold weather of Asian countries such as China, Mongolia, Iran, Afghanistan, Russia, New Zealand, Tibet, and Australia, while the Dromedaries exist in the hot climate of Arabian deserts (www.cashmere.com).

The republics of outer Mongolia and China were the major suppliers of camel hair used in the wool industry till World War II. However, currently Afghanistan, Iran, Iraq, Pakistan, and Syria are the chief suppliers of camel hair. The fibres of the Dromedary species are shorter and coarser in comparison to Bactrian camel hair, which are softer and finer in diameter. The camel population of the world is approximately 19.32 million and that of India is 1.03 million, which are mainly confined to northwestern states such as Rajasthan, Gujarat, Haryana, and Punjab

(93.12% of the total), with the highest density of population (70.13%) existing in 11 districts of Rajasthan (Bhakat and Sahani 2006).

The camel hair products provide a livelihood to the rural people of Rajasthan and Gujarat. They create handcrafted items such as blankets, bags, mattresses, ropes, floor rugs, etc. made up of these speciality fibres. The grading of hair, spinning, weaving, and embroidery with 100 percent camel hair or blending it with sheep hair provides income-generation opportunities to the women of handloom clusters of these states. The fine hair fibres (Bactrian camel hair) are used in overcoats, tops, coating, sportswear, and sports hosiery (Nagpal (2006).

In India the commercial use of camel hair, which is an eco-friendly and sustainable raw material, has not been explored exclusively. In other countries such as the United States, Germany, and England, camel hair is used in men's wear and high-grade overcoatings. The camel fleece and noils are blended with fine wool to spin the woollen yarn and to manufacture cloth for overcoats, knitwear, and rugs, whereas the tops are used to prepare worsted yarns for industrial conveyer beltings internationally. In India, this fibre is generally used to make carriage bags, animal clothing, and floor coverings and union-type blankets being prepared with cotton as warp and camel hair yarn as weft. The camel hair fibre available in India is very coarse in texture, so its application in the apparel and home industry has not been explored.

### *Lack of innovations in product design*

The product range of the Napasar cluster starts from unstitched base material for the apparel and home industry and limits itself to woollen shawls and aasans. Rajasthan is famous for its weaving, embroidery, and block printing crafts. However, this village is not exploring the other crafts and is only dependent on weaving and spinning, which is extremely basic in terms of its design and technology. The usage of sheep wool for creating products except aasans and shawls is also not been explored to its fullest. There is a huge scope of interventions and innovations for designing a new line of products using locally available sheep wool as in camel hair.

### *Lack of education*

One of the major causes of the backwardness of the clusters is illiteracy or less qualitative education. The education lack has led to unawareness about the scheme and policies launched by government, new marketing channels of consumers, consumer requirements, new technologies, and many more.

### *Lack of dyeing, printing, and tailoring expertise*

The cluster is dependent on other companies for yarn, dyeing, printing, and tailoring expertise. There are no yarn depots or dyers in Napasar, which is a huge drawback for a weaver's cluster. Similarly, after fabrication of the fabrics, the cluster doesn't have any tailoring personnel to provide them with good designs and silhouettes, making them dependent on other fashion brands like Fabindia, Madanaa, and Rangsutra for tailoring and selling their products.

## Opportunities

### Community synchronisation

There are still many more weavers around the two colonies that have been mentioned in the chapter, and therefore there is a strong requirement of handloom community synchronisation in Napasar. Many artisans from the two colonies of Napasar are working independently with an aim of earning more and expanding only their ancestral practices. Therefore, to create a strong platform, a huge programme of community synchronisation is required, which can make Napasar a good self-independent cluster.

### Government schemes

There are many government schemes for weavers and the handloom industry that have been announced by the state as well as central government of India in recent times, but it's a sheer irony that almost all the weavers and spinners of Napasar are unaware of these schemes and policies due to their lack of education and maybe due to a lack of proper advertising channels of the government agencies. There are opportunities by the government agencies which the cluster of Napasar needs to tap for their development.

### Easy connectivity to Bikaner and other cities

The rail track and road connectivity of Napasar to Bikaner is very short and approachable. The connectivity of this village to other parts of India via Indian railways is very good after the formation of a railway line and a station with the halt of two minutes for every express train. This makes life easier for the residents and people from around India or abroad to travel to this village.

### Exhibitions and displays

There are many NGOs like Dastakar which sponsor and provide space to handloom clusters for exhibiting and selling their products to consumers directly in metropolitan cities. Also, the government of India keeps announcing from time to time about exhibition venues and spaces at discounted rates for such clusters to display and market their products in every fiscal year.

## Challenges

### Climate

The biggest challenge of Napasar is the hot and dry climate. The temperature of this place is always beyond 40 degrees Celsius for more than eight months in a year, which makes the work environment tougher for the craftsmen and other people related to this industry to travel.

### Fight against power looms

The next biggest challenge for Napasar is to fight against the increasing demand of power loom machineries. In the process of creating more fabric and increasing the production process, many weavers at Napasar have converted their handlooms to power looms by attaching a local motor and self-throwing weft operating system. This develops a handloom's power a little closer to a power loom but in a desi[1] style.

### Sourcing of raw material, especially camel hair

The sourcing of raw materials like camel hair is a big problem at Napasar, because with the modernisation of transport vehicles and options of faster travel, the villagers have stopped cultivating camels. This is not only the situation in Napasar but is the same for all the villages around it. To improve on the condition, a Camel Breed Farm was created by the government to research camel breeds and its products for enhancing the idea of camel cultivation by the people of Rajasthan, but ironically still the numbers of camels are decreasing every year.

### Stop middlemen intervening

The middlemen have always made things costlier for any customers, wherein simultaneously the artisan has always been underpaid. The more middlemen there are, the larger are the gaps in money transactions. This can be controlled if the artisans can obtain direct opportunities to market their products to consumers.

### Looking for more agencies along with government agencies

The Napasar cluster requires understanding the importance, roles, and responsibilities of NGOs, various government agencies, self-help groups, and other organisations. For this, workshops can be organised by different agencies to make the cluster understand about the integrities of these organisations and adapt them as per their requirements for the growth of the cluster.

### Develop marketing channels

The marketing channels of the cluster need to be improved; there is an immediate necessity of the handloom cluster representatives to get in touch with the consumers directly and to serve them in all the corners of the country and the world. For this understanding of today's marketing channels via an institute or via government aid, workshops, training, and diploma courses are required. Younger educated males and females, who can take this as a continuous responsibility of updating and creating different marketing channels like e-retailing, online portals, blogs, etc., should be trained via these workshops and courses.

### *Language development*

The residents of Napasar, even after acquiring education till primary and secondary schools, are not able to communicate well in the English language, which is a weakness as well as a challenge for the cluster to develop so that they can easily tap all the opportunities on national and international platforms.

## Conclusion

Along with the sustainable raw material, sustainable techniques with interventions for the present market to create products keeping their traditions alive are of utmost requirement nowadays. The SWOC analysis of the Napasar cluster emphasised a few points such as education, awareness, empowerment of women, better marketing channels, language development, and many more, which are all interconnected. The results are in coordination with the diagnostic study done by the government agencies (Section 6.2.1). There are suggestions in the SWOC analysis which can be utilised to create new opportunities for the artisans and give them new avenues for growth. The aim of this whole research is to mark the possibilities which can provide Napasar a sustainable livelihood.

## Notes

1. *Napasar*: Name of a village in the Indian State of Rajasthan.
2. *Chanderi*: A hand-woven fabric from Madhya Pradesh, India, made up of silk.
3. *Kota Doria* is a unique hand-woven fabric from Kota Rajasthan, having a characteristic square-check pattern made up of silk and cotton.
4. *Gram Panchyat* is the cornerstone of a local self-government organisation in India of the panchayati raj system at the village or small town level and has a sarpanch as its elected head.
5. Rs. (Rupees) is Indian currency. Rupees 89.03 = 1 British Pound (as of 2 December 2018).
6. *Aasan* is a small prayer rug used during worshipping Gods in Indian homes.
7. *Khadi Gram Udyogs* and *Pratisthans* are government organisations dealing with handloom fabrics.
8. *Chindi dhurries* are rugs woven from left-over fabric swatches in weft and cotton threads in warp.
9. *Charkha* is a wooden-framed hand-spinning machine in Indian homes.
10. *Uttaradwas* is a colony in Bikaner where spinners reside.
11. *Goyallon ka Mohalla* is another colony in Napasar where spinners reside.
12. *Banjara* is a community in India who keep travelling from one place to another throughout their lifetime.

13 *Upanishads* are sacred Hindu treatises illustrating Vedas and written in the Sanskrit language.
14 *Chindi* refers to left-over fabric swatches after completing a product.

## References

Balaram, S. (1998). *Thinking design.* Ahmedabad: National Institute of Design.

Bhakat, C., & Sahani, M. S. (2006). Camel: A unique species in hot arid desert ecosystem. *Everyman's Science, 11*(6), 426–428.

Chapman, J., & Gant, N. (2006). *Designers, visionaries and other stories: A collection of sustainable design essays* (pp. 4–15). London: Earth Scan Publishers.

Das, S. K. (2001). *The warp and the woof: An enquiry into the handloom industry in West Bengal* (p. 19). Kolkata: K.P. Bagchi and Company.

Ministry of Labour, GOI. (1988). *Report on the working and living conditions of workers in the powerloom industry in India.* New Delhi. Retrieved November 20, 2013 from http://labourbureau.nic.in/MW_Report_2012. pdf.

Ministry of Textiles. (2010). *Guidelines of the Comprehensive Handloom Cluster Development Scheme (CHCDS).* Mega Handloom Cluster. Retrieved November 20, 2013 from http://handlooms.nic.in/writereaddata/1202.pdf.

MSME. (2011). *Brief industrial profile of Bikaner district.* Retrieved November 20, 2013 from http://dcmsme.gov.in/dips/DIPR_Bikaner.pdf.

Nagpal, K. (2006). *Assessment of physical properties of camel and goat hair.* Theses. Dharwad: University of Agriculture Science. Retrieved October 20, 2013 from www.uasbagrilibindia.org/cgi-bin/koha/opac-detail.pl?biblionumber=120357.

Sahani, S., Yadav, B., Mal, G., & Dhillon, R. S. (2003). Quality attributes of double-humped camel hair fibres, *Indian Journal Fibre and Textile Research, 28*, 227.

Soundarapandian, M. (2002). Historical growth of handloom industry in India. In *Growth and prospects of handloom sector in India* (pp. 3–22). Mumbai: National Bank for Agriculture and Rural Development.

Srivastava, V. S. (1960–61). *Catalogue of Ganga Golden Jubilee Museum.* Bikaner: Department of Archaeology and Museums, Government of Rajasthan.

## *Websites*

www.populationofindia.co.in/rajasthan/bikaner/bikaner/.napasar Retrieved May 17, 2014.
www.cashmere.com/ Retrieved October 20, 2013.

# PART 3
# Sustainability of development

The chapters in this section focus on sustainability of development. The current debates in sustainable development have emerged with the publication of the report of the World Commission on Environment and Development (Brundtland Commission) in 1987. The Brundtland Commission's report defined sustainable development as "development which meets the needs of current generations without compromising the ability of future generations to meet their own needs". Subsequently, the concept received international attention with the Earth Summit at Rio de Janeiro in 1992, which gave a boost to affirmative national and local action for sustainable development. Thereafter, several countries have constituted National Committees for Sustainable Development, and many corporations have lined up on the foray. The United Nations Commission for Sustainable Development started to examine the implementation of the Rio decisions at its annual meetings. In the context of combating global climate change and global financial crisis, this concept has emerged as more relevant and urgent. Both public and private sectors have been forced to critically review their strategies, policies, and commit affirmative action for 'sustainability' as an integral and essential foundation of survival and growth.

Ever since the term 'sustainable development' has emerged, it has been used in a variety of ways, with is social, economic, and environmental/ecological dimensions. However, the concept remained an oxymoron, with conceptual ambiguity on what is to be sustained and/or what is to be developed. The growing income inequality and declining social mobility have created social, economic, and political instability in many parts of the world. Several regions lag behind in development. Poverty and hunger is persistent globally. Around 836 million people are suffering from extreme poverty and hunger. More than a billion people worldwide have no access to an improved water source; more than 2.5 billion people do not have access to improved sanitation; one in four children under five years old worldwide has stunted growth. In addition, big gaps exist between the poorest and the richest households and between the rural and urban areas. Failure to address a growing sense of economic vulnerability is leading to a backlash against progress in sustainable development.

# 7

# ROLE OF SOCIAL ENTERPRISES IN THE CREATION OF SUSTAINABLE LIVELIHOOD

## The case of microfinance institutions in the slums of Mumbai

*Chandralekha Ghosh and Samapti Guha*

### Introduction

Sustainable livelihood (SL) is an integral part of sustainable development (SD) goals. Livelihood is a combination of capabilities and access to resources for making a living. SL can help to cope with economic shocks and vulnerabilities. Further, it enhances capabilities, so that opportunities can be given to the next generations (Patnaik & Prasad, 2014). For the last two decades, Sustainable Livelihood Approaches (SLA) have received a lot of attention in development practices and researches in order to understand the phenomenon of vulnerability and shift in livelihoods among the poor (McLean, 2015). It is not about the food security but about the poverty, development, etc. (Burchi & Muro, 2016). Although these approaches are criticised for ignoring power relations and inflexibilities, development practitioners and researchers still give importance to these approaches to bring about social change. In the development discourse, social entrepreneurship has emerged as an approach of bringing social change in an innovative way. Social entrepreneurs and social enterprises are trying to bring this change in a sustainable manner in every sector of society. The issues on sustainable development are addressed by these entrepreneurs and enterprises in order to meet the dire need of the marginalised sections of society in three ways: sustainable environment, sustainable economy, and sustainable society. In the area of sustainable economy, these enterprises are creating livelihoods in terms of wage employment and self-employment in the rural areas as well as in the urban slums of developing nations. For example, in India, Sampurn(e)arth has created wage employment for the rag-picker women in Mumbai, while Annapurna Mahila Mandal and the Self-Employed Women's Association (SEWA) have created self-employment in the urban slums of Ahmedabad, Pune, and Mumbai. In this context, Laeis and Lemke (2016) mentioned that a sustainable livelihood approach enabled an analysis of interrelations and interdependencies among various stakeholders and to visualise the way social entrepreneurs impact the livelihoods.

The major problem of these marginalised self-employed is a lack of access to resources such as credit, working capital, etc. Among all other resources, credit is also considered to be a coping strategy for the livelihoods of the marginalised section of people. Microfinance institutions as semi-formal[1] financial institutions have emerged as one of the important financial sources for these self-employed. In this chapter, we focus on the credit accessibility and usages of self-employed women who have established their micro-enterprises in the slums of Mumbai. Further, we have examined the role of social enterprises like microfinance institutions (MFIs) on creating sustainable livelihoods of these marginalised micro-entrepreneurs (MEs).

Looking at the growth of poverty and unemployment in developing countries, promotion of micro-entrepreneurship is found to be one of the avenues in the present context for creation of sustainable livelihood, especially in urban slums. The term 'micro-enterprise' refers to a very small-scale, informally organised business activity undertaken by poor people. According to Schreiner and Woller (2003, p. 1567), "Microenterprises are tiny businesses; most have one employee, the owner". According to Vasanthakumari (2012), micro-enterprise development has been considered as a tool for poverty alleviation and women's empowerment.[2] Interest in the promotion of micro-enterprise as an engine of growth (Pisani & Patrick, 2002) and as a poverty alleviation tool (Ortiz, 2001) in the developing world is gaining importance. The objective of micro-enterprise is to make the poor self-sufficient, whereas anti-poverty programmes are the means to support the poor to fight against poverty.

Promotion of micro-enterprises requires financial capital as one of the critical resources. The poor are the most disadvantaged in terms of access to credit through formal sources. Both market and government failed to provide access to credit to the poor. Stiglitz (1990) has explained why the formal financial sector is not able to cater to every section of the population in terms of credit. The formal sector is facing the problem of adverse selection[3] and moral hazard[4] in the credit market. Due to these problems, they are facing three major problems: screening problem,[5] incentive problem,[6] and enforcement problem.[7] According to Singh (2002), due to failure of the percolation theory of social development in India, poor people highly depend on the non-institutional sources of credit, and the microfinance sector has addressed the failure of the institutional financial sources and the exploitation attached to the informal system of credit.

Social enterprises like MFIs are providing collateral-free loans to the economically poor people. Most of the time, these semi-formal social enterprises try to design credit products according to the needs of marginalised people for their better livelihoods, as access to any resources is considered as access to intangible assets according to the SL framework. Although these social enterprises state that they are offering the collateral-free loans to these marginalised self-employed people, it is important to enquire about the factors which influence these social enterprises to offer these credit products. What are factors that indirectly influence the possibility of obtaining semi-formal and formal loans?

In this chapter, we identify the factors that influence the MFIs as agents of providing intangible assets to design the loan size for the MEs in the slums. In the process of research, we examine the loan profile of the MEs as providers of tangible assets and factors affecting the loan size.

## Brief literature survey

In this section, a survey of existing literature in the area of sustainable livelihood (SL), micro-enterprises (MEs), and microfinance institutions (MFIs) has been discussed. The concepts of sustainable livelihood framework and approach are used as macro concepts and the concepts of microfinance and micro-enterprises are used as micro concepts. While macro concepts help to understand the situation of poverty and vulnerability, micro concepts help to understand the complexities of the livelihood of the marginalised people.

### *Sustainable livelihood*

According to Chambers and Conway (1992),

> a livelihood comprises the capabilities, assets (stores, resources, claims and access) and activities required for a means of living: a livelihood is sustainable which can cope with or re- cover from stress and shocks, maintain or enhance its capabilities and assets and provide sustainable livelihood opportunities for the next generation; and which contribute to net benefits to other livelihood at the local and global levels and in the short and long term.
>
> *(p. 6)*

The authors have identified the four parts of the households' livelihoods: people, activities, assets, and gains or outputs. Among them, the portfolio of tangible[8] and intangible assets[9] is the most complex part. On a similar note, Patnaik and Prasad (2014) have reiterated the approach of SL offering principles which focus on intangible assets such as claims and access. They have mentioned that the single-sector approach to solve the complex problem of development is criticised, as it does not focus only on access but also capabilities to cope with the vulnerability and risks of daily life.

Apart from different definitions of sustainable livelihoods, over the years different approaches and frameworks of sustainable livelihoods have emerged. In Lyons and Snoxell (2005), according to the Sustainable Livelihood Approach (SLA) provided by the Department of International Development (DFID), it is mentioned that a combination of individual and collective actions is required in political empowerment and economic self-improvement. The bases of these actions are five assets: financial, human, natural, physical, and social.

Lienert and Burger (2015) have innovatively combined two approaches: the sustainable livelihood approach and capability approach to understand the means-ends relations in the context of usages of biological resources to give wellbeing to human beings. Further, the authors have discussed the dilemma in usage of the biological resources to reduce poverty as it also has repercussions on the ecosystem. In this discussion, they have attempted to analyse the relation between sustainable development and sustainable use of the biological resources. Nel (2015) has adopted an integrated framework and practice model of sustainable livelihoods and the asset-based community development approaches. This framework helps to understand the strengths and vulnerability of the community and make a plan for implementation of the sustainable development strategies. Though the authors made an attempt to apply this practice framework in South Africa and saw the success of bringing the marginalised people at the centre of the community development projects, it is hard to generalise the strength of this framework.

## *Micro-enterprises, microfinance institutions, and sustainable livelihoods*

From the prior discussion it is discerned that sustainable livelihoods create a bond between the people and the society. It does not only have impact on health, education, migration, etc., but also helps people to manage resources in a better way (Khosla, 2001). The success of sustainable livelihoods depends on: sustainable technology, sustainable enterprises, and sustainable economies. The author has stated that micro-enterprises which are going to use sustainable technology and local resources can produce goods and services which meet the needs of the local people without destroying the environment. So, these micro-enterprises can be considered as sustainable enterprises for sustainable livelihood. Agarwal (1990) has mentioned the coping strategies in the phase of transition in the industrial structure in India to improve the livelihoods. The author has divided these strategies into five categories: 1) diversifying sources of income, including seasonal migration; 2) depending on common resources like village common land, forests, etc.; 3) asset selling and adjustment of present consumption; 4) drawing upon social relationships—patronage, kinship, and friendship; and 5) informal credit. Among these strategies, the author has analysed that the most preferred strategy is availing credit from informal sources or semi-formal sources for maintaining livelihoods.

Presently, issues related to sustainable economic livelihoods have emerged from the mismatch between the growth rate of the industries and growth rate of the job creation. Moreover, in the era of Liberalisation, Privatisation, and Globalisation (LPG), most of the employment generated by the industrial sector is temporary in nature.[10] As a result, the security of these jobs is questionable. In the urban cities, the informalisation of work is prominent. As a result, a majority of the workforce in the urban sector is operating from slums either as wage labourers or as micro-entrepreneurs. This fact was also observed by Lyons and Snoxell (2005) in both North and South. They have mentioned that people in the slums are suffering from different livelihood-related problems such as congestion, land disputes, safety, and health hazards, etc. From their analysis, it is revealed that the survival of these self-employed people in the urban slums depends on financial management, adaptability of actions and products, finding a network in order to build social capital, etc. in Ghana and Nigeria. In the context of financial management, the authors have found that survival in business required long-term financial management in the form of savings, participation in decision making over trading practices, access to credit on time, and access to good customers or suppliers, and this is applicable across the genders of the self-employed. One of the constraints faced by the micro-entrepreneurs in the slums is the availability of credit. There are various sources of credit—namely, formal, informal, and semi-formal. There is a vast literature dealing with the sources of credit for micro-entrepreneurs. Olu (2009), Umoh (2006), Afrin, Islam, and Ahmed (2008) have analysed the different sources of credit available for the MEs. Ghosh and Guha (2014) have also identified the factors that lead to the choice of a particular source of loan for the MEs. In Malaysia, Amanah Ikhtiar Malaysia is providing assistance and development to micro-enterprises. Mamun, Saufi, and Ismail (2016) suggested that Amanah Ikhtiar Malaysia should design a flexible credit program, increase loan size, and form an advisory board to promote the micro-enterprises owned by the low-income households, as credit has a significant effect on the performance of these entrepreneurs.

Microfinance is the semi-formal source of funds available for the MEs. In Uganda, Jacobsen, Marshak, Oofri-Adjei, and Kembabazi (2006) have analysed the role of microfinance and micro-enterprises in livelihood promotion among the refugees. They have found that micro-credit has helped these displaced people to support their livelihoods, and MFIs have also provided the business development training for employment creation. The existing body of empirical literature suggests that a number of individual characteristics such as education and wealth or income are significant predictors of loan size taken from a microfinance institution. This suggests that lending institutions have adequate information to disburse loans that are related to a client's ability to repay. When borrowers receive smaller loans than what they had intended, they are recipients of loan-size credit rationing. Credit rationing may signify a lender's risk aversion due to inadequate information about borrowers or may imply a dearth of available credit. Empirical work on group loans suggests that indicators of household assets and wealth are strongly tied to a reported incidence of credit rationing.

Recent research has also suggested that the loan officers exercise important judgments about who should receive loans. They might discriminate according to personal biases based on sex, disability, or payment ability (Cramm & Finkenflügel, 2008; Agier & Szafarz, 2010) or to comport with institutional goals of targeting women over men (Barsoum, 2006). Female loan officers may be less inclined than their male counterparts to lend for risky projects and are also better able to keep track of their clients and encourage repayment (Beck, Behr, & Guettler, 2010). Therefore, it is possible that loan sizes may be related to the gender of the loan officer, and we would expect male officers to disburse larger loans than average.

So far in the context of India, there have been very few studies on self-employed such as micro-enterprises of the urban slums as well as studies of the factors that influence the loan size of the MEs as a source of livelihood. Most of the microfinance-related studies in the Indian context are on rural areas. For the present study, we have chosen Mumbai slums to find out the role of MFIs in creation of sustainable livelihoods for micro-enterprises in terms of loan disbursement.

## Conceptual framework

From the literature survey, it is found that a sustainable livelihood approach and framework provide a combination of tangible and intangible assets for earning a living standard and contributing to the ecosystem for the next generation. Among the tangible assets, income, food, and natural resources are important for a sustainable livelihood, and among intangible assets, access is the most important to create the tangible assets. In this study, micro-enterprise is considered as an agency of achieving tangible assets and microfinance institution is considered as an agency which provides intangible asset such as access to the financial and non-financial resources to the micro-entrepreneurs in order to achieve the tangible assets. The conceptual framework for this study is shown in Figure 7.1.

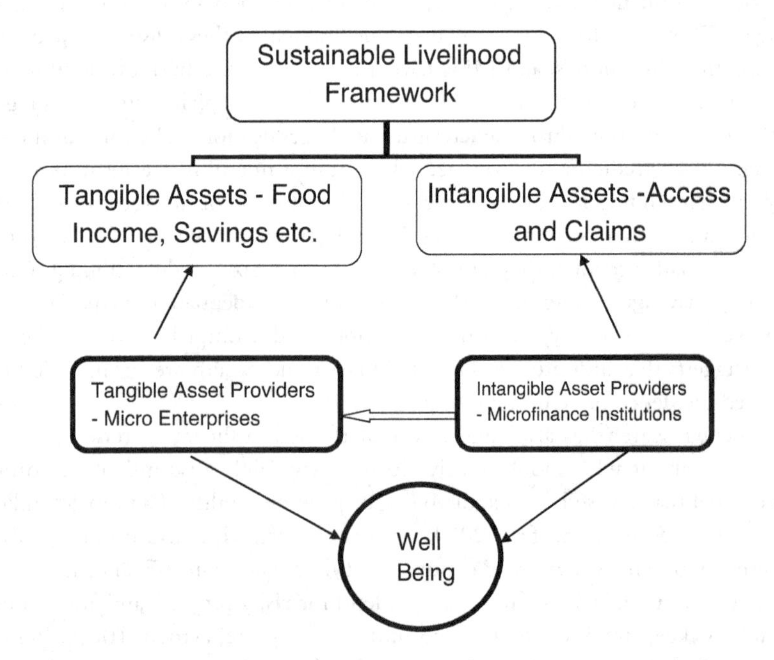


**FIGURE 7.1** Conceptual framework developed by the authors

*Source*: Prepared by the authors

## Context of the study

In Mumbai, 51 percent of people are living in 1,959 slums according to the 2001 census. Around 30 percent of people in the slums are self-employed (Risbud, 2003). Most of the people in the slums have migrated from different parts of India for their livelihoods. The National Sample Survey Office defines that there are two types of slums in India: those that are declared by the state authority and undeclared by the state authority. In Mumbai, among the declared slums, Dharavi is one of the largest slums in Asia. Apart from established slums, different slums in this city are under threat of demolition, as most of these settlements are considered to be illegal by the state agencies. Here, we consider these slums as the marginalised slums. It is important to study how these people achieve their tangible assets such as income, employment, credit, etc. and which agencies provide the intangible assets such as access to resources to them. It seems that MEs in these slums highly depend on semi-formal financial sources like MFIs and informal money lenders operating in these slums.

## Objectives of the study

Given this background, the main focus of the study is to identify the determinants of loan size of the micro-enterprises operating from different types of slums in Mumbai and the role of microfinance institutions in this regard. Here, access to loans is considered as one of the sources of a sustainable livelihood. The main objectives are as follows:

- To study the sources of financial service available in Mumbai slums.
- To study factors which influence the micro-entrepreneurs to borrow.
- To study the loan profile of the micro-entrepreneurs operating from different slums of Mumbai.
- To study the determinants of loan size of micro-enterprises operating from different types of slum, namely established and marginalised slums.
- To study the determinants of the loan size taken from microfinance institutions.

## Research methodology

### *Research design*

The study is exploratory in nature. In this study, the major focus is on how MFIs are helping MEs to achieve the intangible asset such as access to credit for sustainable livelihoods. The dependent variable, access to credit, is visible and takes a standard definition. So epistemologically, a positivist approach is adopted. Accordingly, a quantitative research methodology is followed.

### Sources of data

Data is being collected from primary and secondary sources. To select the sample slums, information is collected from annual reports and other documents of the Mumbai Municipal Corporation. Primary data was collected from the microfinance institutions and their micro-entrepreneurs of the selected slums.

### Sampling method

A multistage sampling technique has been adopted to collect the data. In the first stage, some of the established slums and some of the marginalised slums were purposefully selected. In the second stage, the information from micro-enterprises was collected from the selected slums by adopting random sampling.

### Methods of data collection

For data collection from the micro-entrepreneurs, a survey method and focus group discussion method have been adopted to collect the information about the micro-enterprise development programme from the facilitating agencies in order to understand the role of these agencies.

### Methods for data analysis

Statistical and econometric methods have been adopted to analyse the data collected from the MFIs and micro-entrepreneurs. We have collected the data on loan size from these micro-entrepreneurs. All of the micro-entrepreneurs have not borrowed in the last year. So this sample is a classic example of censored data and OLS (ordinary least squares) method of estimation or any of its variants cannot be used, as they will give biased and asymptotically inconsistent estimates of the parameters. So we have chosen Tobit regression analysis.

## Empirical analysis

### Socio-economic profile of micro-entrepreneurs

The study is based on a random sample survey of 275 micro-entrepreneurs, conducted in four different slums of Mumbai—namely, Sathenagar, Dharavi, Vasinaka, and Chithacamp. We have used a structured questionnaire for the collection of data. Randomly, 27 micro-enterprises from Sathenagar, 73 micro-enterprises from Dharavi, 24 from Vasinaka, and 151 from Chithacamp have been chosen. Vasinaka and Dharavi are examples of established[11] slums and the rest are marginalised[12] slums. Mumbai is a place in India which is known as the financial capital of India and which provides employment opportunities to a large number of people. So several people have migrated from various parts of India to Mumbai and have taken refuge in the slums of Mumbai.

**TABLE 7.1** Socio-economic profile

| *Variable* | *Frequency* |
|---|---|
| Migrated from other parts | 118 |
| *Religion* | |
| Hindu: | 140 |
| Muslim: | 116 |
| Other: | 19 |
| *Among Hindu* | |
| SC: | 51 |
| ST: | 4 |
| OBC: | 46 |
| General: | 39 |
| *Family Structure* | |
| Nuclear: | 149 |
| Joint: | 126 |
| *Marital Status* | |
| Married: | 248 |
| Unmarried: | 10 |
| Widow: | 17 |
| Total Sample ME | 275 |

*Source*: Primary survey data

In Table 7.1, it is seen that less than 50 percent of respondents have migrated from different parts of India to Mumbai. Generally, migration took place due to marriage or for work purpose of any other member of the family. But, it is observed that almost all of the migrated entrepreneurs have migrated more than ten years ago. People in these slums are from different religions and different castes, but there is a social harmony among them. A majority of them are married and belong to a nuclear family. The mean age of the sample MEs is 39.06, including the oldest entrepreneur of 73 years.

Table 7.2 shows that out of 275 micro-enterprises, 64 percent of MEs do not possess any landed property. More than 50 percent have capital assets, and 46 percent have financial assets either sole or partial. It is found that most of these MEs have used their own savings for the business purpose. Less than 50 percent of MEs have borrowed from MFIs. In these slums, different MFIs are operating. For example, in Chitacamp micro-entrepreneurs are members of either Svasti or Annapurna Mahila Multi-State Co-operative Credit Society (AMCCSL), whereas in Sathenagar micro-entrepreneurs are members of AMCCSL. In Dharavi and Vasinaka, micro-entrepreneurs are members of either 'Bandhan' or 'Ujjivan'.

In most of the declared slums, alternative sources of finance are patpedhis, a form of rotating savings and credit association (ROSCA). Most of the residents

**TABLE 7.2** Asset and loan profile

| *Variable* | *Frequency* |
|---|---|
| *Ownership of Land* | |
| Full Ownership: | 46 |
| Partial Ownership: | 51 |
| No Ownership: | 178 |
| Ownership of Capital Asset: | 144 |
| Ownership of Financial Asset: | 128 |
| *Usages of Savings* | |
| Business Purposes: | 165 |
| Other Non-Business Purposes: | 100 |
| *Loans taken from* | |
| MFI: | 122 |
| Non-MFI: | 153 |
| ROSCA: | Not mentioned |
| Loan size: | Rs 5000 to Rs 35000 |
| Range of Interest Rate: | 15 to 28 percent |
| Total Sample ME | 275 |

*Source*: Primary survey data

have been living in these declared slums for two to three generations. These ROSCAs are also charging an interest rate ranging between 10 to 12 percent. These loans are treated as emergency loans. This model also has a savings component. Some of these MEs have access to the formal banking sector for savings. There are few MFIs operating in these declared slums, and most of them are non-banking financial companies (NBFCs). All of the sample respondents have not mentioned about the ROSCA loans.

## *Profile of enterprises*

Information on the type of micro-enterprises shows that there are various types of micro-enterprises, including tea stall owners, vegetable vendors, paper makers, tailors, paper bag makers, imitation jewellery sellers, saree[13] sellers, grocery sellers, fish sellers, shoe makers, beauty parlour owners, garland sellers, flower sellers, idli[14] sellers, etc.

From Table 7.3 it is observed that a majority of the micro-enterprises are individual-led microenterprises, and more than 50 percent eof nterprises are less than five years old followed by enterprises older than ten years. These enterprises are operating from three different places: public spaces, private spaces which they or their family own, and rented spaces. More than 60 percent of enterprises are operated from private places.

**TABLE 7.3** Enterprise profile

| *Variable* | *Frequency* |
|---|---|
| Individual-led enterprises: | 176 |
| Group-based or family enterprises: | 99 |
| *Age of the enterprises* | |
| Less than five years: | 133 |
| More than five years old but less than ten years old: | 78 |
| More than ten years old: | 63 |
| *Place of operation* | |
| Public space: | 42 |
| Private space: | 188 |
| Rented space: | 45 |
| *No. of manpower in the micro-enterprise* | |
| Single manpower | 166 |
| More than one manpower | 109 |
| Total Sample ME | 275 |

*Source*: Primary survey data

## Analysis of the result obtained from Tobit regression

Out of 275 MEs, 105 have borrowed in the last year, and we have data on loan size for these borrowers. It is already mentioned in the research methodology section that this sample is a classic example of censored data, and we have chosen Tobit regression analysis.

The socio-economic characteristics as well as the characteristics of the enterprises usually influence the loan sizes. There is a vast literature which shows that socioeconomic characteristics such as gender of the entrepreneur, age of the entrepreneur, reason for starting the business, family structure, number of school going children, possession of assets both financial and capital, and owning of land are influencing the loan size. The characteristics of the enterprise such as age of the enterprise, place of operation of the enterprise, enterprise type, and number of employees engaged are also considered. The description of variables is given in Table 7.4.

In the analysis, we have tested two Tobit models. In Model I, we have considered all 275 MEs (Table 7.5), and in Model II we have only considered MEs who have taken loans from MFIs to see the impact of MFI membership on size of loans as a coping mechanism of livelihoods (Table 7.6).

It has been observed that entrepreneurs who have chosen their own businesses are taking a lesser amount of loan compared to those who have been advised to take up businesses by the MFI operators, members of the family, etc. The entrepreneurs who own financial assets and capital assets either partially or wholly have a higher

**TABLE 7.4** Description of the variables

| *Dependent Variable-Loan Size* | *Loan amount taken by the MEs in last one year (in INR)* |
|---|---|
| Explanatory Variables | Description and justification of the variable. |
| Entrepreneur's Age | Age is in years. It is believed that with age the experience and expertise of the entrepreneur in a particular business increases. |
| Number of School going Children | This variable is important since we are considering woman entrepreneurs who have to combine entrepreneurship with household activities. Moreover, in many cases we have observed that loans are taken to finance the education of the children. |
| Family Structure | This is a dummy variable. It takes value one if the entrepreneur has a nuclear family and zero otherwise. This variable is important since in case of joint families the woman has to share a lot of household activities along with entrepreneurship. |
| Business Choice Code | This is a dummy variable. It takes value equal to one if the entrepreneurship is started solely because of earning money. It takes value zero for other reasons like the entrepreneurship idea was given by the MFI, or it is started because she has a certain skill like weaving or tailoring. The value one dummy indicates the urgency of the entrepreneur for starting this activity. |
| Capital Asset | This is a dummy variable. It takes value equal to one if the entrepreneur solely or partially owns some capital asset. This asset may act as pseudo-collateral in times of obtaining a loan (Mason, 2014; Paul, 2013). |
| Financial Asset | This is a dummy variable. It takes value equal to one if the entrepreneur solely or partially owns some capital asset. This asset may act as pseudo-collateral in times of obtaining a loan (Mason, 2014). |
| Land Dummy | It takes value equal to one if the entrepreneur owns any land. This variable acts as credit worthiness of the entrepreneur (Paul, 2013). |
| Enterprise-Related Variables | |
| Enterprise Age | The starting years of enterprise. |
| Private Place of Operation | This is a dummy variable. It takes value equal to one if the entrepreneur operates from a private place owned by the entrepreneur. |
| Public Place of Operation | This is a dummy variable. It takes value equal to one if the entrepreneur operates from a public place. This indicates vulnerability of the entrepreneur (Woodward, Rolfe, Ligthelm, & Guimarães, 2011). |
| Employee_ Dummy | This is a dummy variable. It takes value equal to one if the enterprise has at least one employee. It takes zero if the entrepreneur is the only person involved in the enterprise. |
| Enterprise_ Type | This is a dummy variable. It takes value equal to one if it is individual based, or takes value equal to zero if it is group based or family based. This variable is important since the decision making of the enterprise depends on the organisation of the enterprise (Janda, Rausser, & Strielkowski, 2013). |

*Source*: Compiled by the authors

**TABLE 7.5** Tobit Model I: determinants of loan size

| *Explanatory Variables* | *Coefficient* | *Level of Significance* |
|---|---|---|
| Entrepreneurs' Age | 864.972 | 0.240 |
| Number of School going Children | –3452.58 | 0.358 |
| Family Structure | 2205.417 | 0.851 |
| Business Choice Code | –36732.72*** | 0.077 |
| Capital Asset | 20886.1*** | 0.080 |
| Financial Asset | 23668.31** | 0.043 |
| Land Dummy | –11723.65 | 0.281 |
| Enterprise Age | –2007.065*** | 0.071 |
| Private_Place_Operation | 9134.628 | 0.317 |
| Public_Place_Operation | –17117.33 | 0.245 |
| Employee_Dummy | 12260.84 | 0.419 |
| Enterprise Type | 27281.05*** | 0.076 |
| BIC | 2857.038 | |
| AIC | 2806.403 | |
| Number of Observations | 275 | |
| Log pseudolikelihood | –1389.2016 | |
| F (12, 263) | = 1.67 | |
| Prob> F = 0.0728 | | |

*Source*: Primary data analysis

*Significant at 1% level, ** significant at 5% level, *** significant at 10% level.

**TABLE 7.6** Tobit Model II: role of MFI on loan size

| *Explanatory Variables* | *Coefficient* | *Level of Significance* |
|---|---|---|
| Entrepreneurs' Age | 291.4951* | 0.008 |
| Number of School going Children | –368.6806 | 0.546 |
| Family Structure | 2815.401 | 0.134 |
| Business Choice Code | –11088.43* | 0.0 |
| Capital Asset | 9029.387* | 0.0 |
| Financial Asset | 10621.75* | 0.0 |
| Land Dummy | –1265.636 | 0.483 |
| Enterprise Age | –33.30093 | 0.766 |
| Private_Place_Operation | –965.4302 | 0.623 |
| Public_Place_Operation | –2762.329 | 0.269 |
| Employee_Dummy | 3701.302 | 0.218 |
| Enterprise Type | 5880.752*** | 0.057 |

(*Continued*)

**TABLE 7.6** (Continued)

| *Explanatory Variables* | *Coefficient* | *Level of Significance* |
|---|---|---|
| BIC | 1592.392 | |
| AIC | 1631.649 | |
| Number of Observations | 122 | |
| Log pseudolikelihood | 0.0753 | |
| LR chi2(12) | = 127.46 | |
| Prob> chi2 | = 0.0000 | |

*Source*: Primary data analysis

Significant at 1% level, ** significant at 5% level, *** significant at 10% level.

probability of taking a higher size loan than the other micro-entrepreneurs. This may be the case, although the entrepreneurs are not asked for collateral for receiving the loan. These micro-entrepreneurs are taking loans from an MFI or from informal ROSCAs where having collateral is not essential, but still we observe that these assets act as pseudo-collaterals. We have dropped the MFI dummy because there is a strong association between possession of capital assets and financial assets and the MFI dummy (see Appendix: Table 7A.1, 7A.1a, and 7A.1b). Now we will focus on the entrepreneurs who are MFI members. Table 7.6 represents the Tobit regression analysis for MFI members.

In case of entrepreneurs, those MFI members possessing financial and capital assets either partially or wholly lead to a higher size of the loan. If the individual ME chooses her own business type, then the probability of taking a higher amount of the loan falls. This might happen because of three reasons: first, she does not have need for credit; second, she approached but could not get the loan; and third, she has external support or savings required for her business which reduces the need for MFI credit.

The higher the age of the ME, the greater is the probability of taking a higher sized loan. Some respondents who are members of an MFI mentioned that loan size increases over time. So as the years of membership increase, the loan size gets increased. The individual-led entrepreneurship has a higher probability of taking a larger sized loan than the group-based or family-based MEs. In the case of individual-based enterprises, the source of loans are limited since the owner does not have the support of family nor other partners in the enterprise, so the probability of taking a higher size of loan increases.

Another interesting observation is that the greater the age of the micro-enterprise, the less the probability of taking a higher amount of loan. Here, micro-enterprises are of a survival type. Most of the micro-entrepreneurs mentioned that they wanted to continue their enterprising activities till their children joined the job market. This is one of the reasons for this finding.

Moreover, individual-based micro-entrepreneurs are taking a higher amount of loan than family- or group-based micro-entrepreneurs. In case of entrepreneurs who are MFI members, the age of the enterprise does not matter, but the entrepreneurs' age matters.

### *Comparison of profitability between borrowers and non-borrowers*

Now we should compare the average level of profit and sales for the borrowers and non-borrowers. We observe that the average revenue of the borrowers is Rs 22597.32, whereas for the non-borrower it is 17469.46. In case of profit also the average level of profit for the borrowers is more than that of the non-borrowers. The values are Rs 8161.65 and Rs 6846.93, respectively. (See Appendix: Table 7A.1 for details about the descriptive statistics between borrowers and non-borrowers.)

In order to compare the income, profit level, and revenue level between borrowers and non-borrowers, we have to first undertake the normality test. We have carried out a Kolmogorov Smirnov test to check whether the income distribution, profit distribution, and revenue distribution are normally distributed or not. (See Appendix: Table 7A.2.)

This test shows that these variables are not normally distributed, so we have carried out a Kruskal Wallis median test to check whether the median level of income, profit, and revenue differ between borrowers and non-borrowers. We have observed that although the median level of income and revenue do not vary between them, the median level of profit is significantly different for borrowers and non-borrowers. (See Appendix: Table 7A.3, 7A.3a, 7A.3b.) In the case of borrowers, 56 percent of micro-entrepreneurs have a profit level greater than the median level, and in the case of non-borrowers about 42 percent have a profit level above the median level.

## Discussion and conclusion

According to the sustainable livelihood framework, acquiring different kinds of assets in terms of income, access, etc. is important to earn a meaningful livelihood and create an ecosystem for the next generation (Patnaik & Prasad, 2014; Chambers & Conway, 1992). In this chapter, we have focused on achieving access to financial resources by the marginalised people who have taken ME as self-employment. Among all of the resources, these MEs are facing severe challenges to access to financial resources (Olu, 2009; Umoh, 2006; Afrin et al., 2008). From the preceding analysis, stylised facts about the access to loan by the micro-entrepreneurs for their livelihoods have emerged. It has been observed that although owning assets is not looked upon as an essential criterion for assessing loans, it is observed that MEs who possess financial and capital assets have a higher probability of taking higher sized loans. This holds true both for MFI loans or informal loans issued by ROSCA. Even if MFI loans do not need any collateral or asset recognition of the borrowers, in reality we are observing assets act as pseudo-collaterals for providing higher sized loans.

Individual-based enterprises have a higher probability of taking a higher amount of loan than do group-based or family-based enterprises since the decision of loans is solely taken by the entrepreneur in an individual enterprise, and this entrepreneur usually does not have other support for the enterprise.

Our study also showed that MFIs have the potential to promote micro-enterprises to create sustainable livelihoods in terms of creating provision for access to financial products, but these institutions are not able to reach the marginalised section of MEs due to their limitation of operation. If social enterprises like MFIs are considered as a tool for livelihood creation in a sustained way among the marginalised section of MEs, then policy support to these institutions are very much required in terms of tax subsidies, subsidised interest rates, etc. so that microfinance can be transformed into livelihood finance.

# APPENDIX

**TABLE 7A.1** Descriptive statistics between MFI loans and informal loans

| *MFI_DUMMY* | *N* | *Mean* | *Minimum* | *Maximum* | *Range* | *Variance* | *Std. Deviation* | *Coefficient of Variation* |
|---|---|---|---|---|---|---|---|---|
| NON_MEMBER | 30 | 5.74E4 | 1000 | 500000 | 499000 | 1.061E10 | 102992.36 | 1.79 |
| MEMBER_MFI | 75 | 1.31E4 | 5000 | 35000 | 30000 | 5.512E7 | 7424.09 | 0.57 |
| Total | 105 | 2.58E4 | 1000 | 500000 | 499000 | 3.401E9 | 58321.67 | |

*Source*: Primary data analysis

**TABLE 7A.1a** Association between financial asset and MFI dummy

| *Chi-Square Test* | *Value* | *Df* | *Asymp. Sig. (2-sided)* | *Exact Sig. (2-sided)* | *Exact Sig. (1-sided)* |
|---|---|---|---|---|---|
| Pearson Chi-Square | 5.028[a] | 1 | .025 | | |
| Continuity Correction[b] | 4.497 | 1 | .034 | | |
| Likelihood Ratio | 5.037 | 1 | .025 | | |
| Fisher's Exact Test | | | | .029 | .017 |
| N of Valid Cases[b] | 275 | | | | |

*Source*: Primary data analysis

**TABLE 7A.1b** Association between capital asset and MFI dummy

| *Chi-Square Test* | *Value* | *Df* | *Asymp. Sig. (2-sided)* | *Exact Sig. (2-sided)* | *Exact Sig. (1-sided)* |
|---|---|---|---|---|---|
| Pearson Chi-Square | 1.410[a] | 1 | .235 | | |
| Continuity Correction[b] | 1.137 | 1 | .286 | | |
| Likelihood Ratio | 1.412 | 1 | .235 | | |
| Fisher's Exact Test | | | | .275 | .143 |
| N of Valid Cases[b] | 275 | | | | |

*Source*: Primary data analysis

**TABLE 7A.2** Descriptive statistics of profit level, revenue level, and income level

| *Loan_Dummy* | | *Income* | *Profit_Per_Month* | *Sales_Per_Month* |
|---|---|---|---|---|
| No Loan | N | 168 | 170 | 170 |
| | Median | 5000.00 | 5000.0000 | 10150.0000 |
| | Mean | 5675.60 | 6846.9294 | 17469.4588 |
| | Std. Error of Mean | 317.741 | 485.95807 | 1777.29924 |
| | Minimum | 1000 | 1000.00 | 1300.00 |
| | Range | 29000 | 56000.00 | 184700.00 |
| | Kurtosis | 8.324 | 23.426 | 23.709 |
| | Variance | 1.696E7 | 4.015E7 | 5.370E8 |
| Loan Taken in Last Year | N | 102 | 105 | 105 |
| | Median | 5000.00 | 6000.0000 | 10000.0000 |
| | Mean | 6026.47 | 8161.6476 | 22597.3238 |
| | Std. Error of Mean | 404.872 | 848.59676 | 3879.93025 |
| | Minimum | 1200 | 1000.00 | 1500.00 |
| | Range | 28800 | 59400.00 | 328500.00 |
| | Kurtosis | 11.729 | 23.393 | 35.368 |
| | Variance | 1.672E7 | 7.561E7 | 1.581E9 |
| Total | N | 270 | 275 | 275 |
| | Median | 5000.00 | 5000.0000 | 10000.0000 |
| | Mean | 5808.15 | 7348.9127 | 19427.3709 |
| | Std. Error of Mean | 249.715 | 442.59904 | 1846.27185 |
| | Minimum | 1000 | 1000.00 | 1300.00 |
| | Range | 29000 | 59400.00 | 328700.00 |
| | Kurtosis | 9.370 | 25.873 | 43.921 |
| | Variance | 1.684E7 | 5.387E7 | 9.374E8 |

*Source*: Primary data analysis

**TABLE 7A.3** Kolmogorov-Smirnov test of sales per month, profit per month, and income level

| *Test Statistic* | | *Sales_Per_Month* | *Profit_Per_Month* | *Income* |
|---|---|---|---|---|
| N | | 275 | 275 | 270 |
| Normal Parameters[a] | Mean | 19427.3709 | 7348.9127 | 5808.15 |
| | Std. Deviation | 30616.95500 | 7339.67477 | 4.103E3 |
| Most Extreme Differences | Absolute | .277 | .194 | .197 |
| | Positive | .265 | .192 | .197 |
| | Negative | –.277 | –.194 | –.121 |
| Kolmogorov-Smirnov Z | | 4.592 | 3.209 | 3.230 |
| Asymp. Sig. (2-tailed) | | .000 | .000 | .000 |

*Source*: Primary data analysis

**TABLE 7A.3a** Frequency distribution of sales per month, profit per month, and income level

| *Variables* | *Statistic* | *No Loan* | *Loan Taken In Last Year* |
|---|---|---|---|
| sales_per_month | > Median | 85 | 50 |
| | <= Median | 85 | 55 |
| profit_per_month | > Median | 73 | 59 |
| | <= Median | 97 | 46 |
| Income | > Median | 62 | 41 |
| | <= Median | 106 | 61 |

*Source*: Primary data analysis

**TABLE 7A.3b** Test statistics of sales per month, profit per month, and income level

| *Test Statistics* | | *Sales_Per_Month* | *Profit_Per_Month* | *Income* |
|---|---|---|---|---|
| N | | 275 | 275 | 270 |
| Median | | 10000.0000 | 5000.0000 | 5000.00 |
| Chi-Square | | .147 | 4.565 | .291 |
| Df | | 1 | 1 | 1 |
| Asymp. Sig. | | .701 | .033 | .589 |
| Yates' Continuity Correction | Chi-Square | .067 | 4.050 | .169 |
| | Df | 1 | 1 | 1 |
| | Asymp. Sig. | .795 | .044 | .681 |

*Source*: Primary data analysis

Note: Grouping Variable: loan_dummyA

## Notes

1 Semi-formal institutions have mixed characteristics of formal financial institutions and informal financial institutions. For example, like formal institutions, these semi-formal institutions are running their institutions and are registered under different acts such as the RBI Act (45B), Section 8 Companies Act, Cooperative Societies Act, etc. Like informal institutions, these institutions provide financial services at the doorstep and provide credit without collateral. The major problem of these marginalised self-employed is a lack of resources such as credit, working capital, etc. Microfinance institutions have emerged as a financial resource for these self-employed. In this chapter, we focused on the micro-entrepreneurs who are operating from the slums of Mumbai and studied their credit accessibility and usages. In the course of this study, we also examined the role of microfinance institutions as social enterprises in creating sustainable livelihoods for the marginalised micro-entrepreneurs.
2 Here, empowerment has four dimensions: economic, social, political, and legal.
3 Due to information asymmetry, it is difficult for the financial sector to choose safe borrowers during the credit disbursement. This is called the hidden information problem.
4 Moral hazard is called a hidden action problem. It is not easily discerned how borrowers are using their loans due to information asymmetry.
5 In the absence of information about the returns from projects of different borrowers, the cost of determining the extent of risk of default for each borrower is high. In the event of failure of a project, it is difficult to compel repayment.
6 It is costly to ensure that borrowers take actions which make repayment most likely.
7 In the event of failure of a project, it is difficult to compel repayment.
8 Tangible assets are Stores and Resources, where Stores are food stocks, stores of jewellery, and other financial assets, cash reserves, etc. and Resources are natural resources, livestock, machines, etc.
9 Intangible assets are Claims and Access. Claims are demands and appeals for material, moral, and physical supports and Access are the opportunities to use the resources, stores, or services to get the information, technology, food, income, etc.
10 For example, most of the jobs are created in the construction industry in India. Casual labourers are dominating this industry.
11 Established slums are declared by the State Government of Maharashtra. The state has provided basic amenities like water, electricity, etc. to the dwellers of these slums.
12 Marginalised slums are illegal slums. These slums are always under demolition threat from the state. People in these slums do not have access to basic amenities. For these services, private service providers are prominent in these slums.
13 Saree: Traditional dress of Indian women.
14 Idli: A very popular breakfast item in India.

## References


Afrin, S., Islam, N., & Ahmed, S. U. (2008). The effect of microfinance factors on women entrepreneurs' performance in Nigeria: A conceptual framework. *International Journal of Business and Management*, *8*(3), 169–185.

Agarwal, B. (1990). Social security and the family in rural India coping with seasonality and alamity. *Journal of Peasant Studies*, *17*(3), 341–412.

Agier, I., & Szafarz, A. (2010). *Microfinance and gender: Is there a glass ceiling in loan size*? CEB Working Paper No. 10–047, Universite Libre de Bruxelles.

Barsoum, G. (2006). Who gets credit? The gendered division of microfinance programs in Egypt. *Canadian Journal of Development Studies/Revue canadienne d'etudes du development*, *27*(1), 51–64.

Beck, T., Behr, P., & Guettler, A. (2010). *Gender and banking: Are women better loan officers*? European Banking Centre Discussion Paper No. 2009–19. Tilburg, Netherlands.

Burchi, F., & Muro, P. D. (2016). From food availability to nutritional capabilities: Advancing food security analysis. *Food Policy*, *60*(2016), 10–19.

Chambers, R., & Conway, G. R. (1992). *Sustainable rural livelihoods: Practical concepts for the 21st century*. Discussion Paper 296. Institute of Development Studies, Brighton, UK.

Cramm, J. M., & Finkenflügel, H. (2008). Exclusion of disabled people from microcredit in Africa and Asia: A literature study, Asia Pacific disability. *Rehabilitation Journal*, *19*(2), 15–33.

Ghosh, C., & Guha, S. (2014). Do micro enterprises choose microfinance institutions to meet their financial needs? Evidence from Mumbai slums. *Journal of Developmental Entrepreneurship*, *19*(3).

Jacobsen, K., Marshak, A., Oofri-Adjei, A., & Kembabazi, J. (2006). Using microenterprise interventions to support the livelihoods of forcibly displaced people: The impact of a microcredit program in IDP camps in Lira, Northern Uganda. *Refugee Survey Quarterly*, *25*(2), 23–39.

Janda, K., Rausser, G., & Strielkowski, W. (2013). *Determinants of profitability of Polish rural micro-enterprises* [online]. Retrieved January 10, 2014 from http://mpra.ub.uni-muenchen.de/52771/.

Khosla, A. (2001). Sustainable livelihoods: The central issue of human security and sustainable development, *Social Change*, *31*(1 & 2), 174–185.

Laeis, G., & Lemke, S. (2016). Social entrepreneurship in tourism: Applying sustainable livelihoods approaches. *International Journal of Contemporary Hospitality Management*, *28*(6), 1076–1093.

Lienert, J., & Burger, P. (2015). Merging capabilities and livelihoods: Analyzing the use of biological resources to improve well-being. *Ecology and Society*, *20*(2), 20. http://doi.org/10.5751/ES-07405-200220

Lyons, M., & Snoxell, S. (2005). Sustainable urban livelihoods and marketplace social capital: Crisis and strategy in petty trade. *Urban Studies*, *42*(8), 1301–1320.

McLean, J. E. (2015). Beyond the pentagon prison of sustainable livelihood approaches and towards Livelihood trajectories approaches. *Asia Pacific Viewpoint*, *56*(3), 380–391.

Nel, H. (2015). An integration of the livelihoods and asset-based community development approaches: A South African case study. *Development Southern Africa*, *32*(4), 511–525.

Ortiz, J. (2001). Rethinking the approach to the microenterprise sector in Latin America: An integrating framework. *Journal of Microfinance*, *3*(2), 87–106.

Mamun, A. A., Saufi, R. A., & Ismail, M. B. (2016). Human capital, credit, and startup motives: a study among rural micro-enterprises in Malaysia. *The Journal of Developing Areas*, *50*(4), 383–400.

Mason, D. R. (2014). Who gets what? Determinants of loan size and credit rationing among microcredit borrowers: Evidence from Nicaragua. *Journal of International Development*, *26*, 77–90.

Olu, O. (2009). *Impact of micro finance on entrepreneurial development: The case of Nigeria*. The International Conference on Administration and Business, ICEA-FAA 2009, 14–15 November 2009. The Faculty of Business and Administration, University of Bucharest.

Patnaik, S., & Prasad, C. S. (2014). Revisiting sustainable livelihoods: Insights from implementation studies in India. *Vision*, *18*(4), 353–358.

Paul, S. (2013). *The Credit-worthiness of a borrower and the selection process in Micro-finance: A case study from the urban slums of India*. MPRA Paper No. 48116. Retrieved April 2, 2014 from http://mpra.ub.uni-muenchen.de/48116.

Pisani, M. J., & Patrick, J. M. (2002). A conceptual model and propositions for bolstering Entrepreneurship in the informal sector: The case of Central America. *Journal of Developmental Entrepreneurship*, 7(1), 95–111.

Risbud, N. (2003). *Understanding slums: Case studies for the global report on human settlements 2003: The case of Mumbai, India*. London: UN-Habitat. Retrieved October 14, 2013 from www.ucl.ac.uk/dpu-projects/Global_Report/cities/mumbai.htm

Schreiner, M., & Woller, G. (2003). Microenterprise development programs in the United States and in the developing world. *World Development, 31*, 1567–1580.

Singh, N. (2002). *Building social capital through micro-finance: A perspective on the growth of micro-finance sector with special reference to India*. Retrieved from www.sasnet.lu.se/EASASpapers/20NareshSingh.pdf.

Stiglitz, J. (1990). Peer monitoring and credit markets. *World Bank Economic Review, 4*(3), 351–366.

Umoh, G. S. (2006). Empirical investigation of access to micro-credit in an emerging economy. *Journal of African Business, 7*(1–2), 89–117.

Vasanthakumari. (2012). Economic empowerment of women through micro enterprises in India with special reference to promotional agencies. *Zenith International Journal of Multidisciplinary Research, 2*(1), 194–210.

Woodward, D., Rolfe, R., Ligthelm, A., & Guimarães, P. (2011). The viability of informal microenterprise in South Africa. *Journal of Developmental Entrepreneurship, 16*(1), 65–86.

# 8

# SOCIAL ENTREPRENEURSHIP THROUGH THE LENSES OF WELLBEING AND SUSTAINABLE DEVELOPMENT

## A critique

*Samapti Guha*[1]

### Introduction

Sustainable development (SD) is a contested concept as it is complex in nature. It addresses the most basic human condition of wellbeing and our position in nature (Parrish, 2008). Wellbeing of a person theoretically depends on his or her satisfaction of life or utility and the freedom he or she enjoyed (Dasgupta, 2005). It is difficult to measure wellbeing in terms of these theoretical constructs. The author has suggested that wellbeing can be measured by valuing the commodity determinants such as goods and services consumed, which give utility and are chosen freely by the person, and quantifying the outputs and inputs such as indices of health, real income, intellectual capital, etc. To achieve the sustainable development of any nation, inter-generational wellbeing has to be achieved. For this, institutions play an important role (Sengupta, 2002).

There are several approaches to achieve these goals. The approach of social entrepreneurship is an emerging approach to address these goals. This approach has been applied in micro settings to achieve macro goals of sustainable development in terms of education, health, asset creation, and livelihoods for better wellbeing.

It is important to know how the idea of sustainable development emerged. In this context, it was found that the idea of sustainable development received a global platform in 1972 at the United Nations Conference on the Human Environment in Stockholm, Sweden. In this conference, the outcome was to declare that the human society has a right to freedom, equality, and adequate condition of living. So, the production processes, which affected the environment and human society, had to stop. Since then, sustainable development has been drawing the attention of developed and developing nations. In 1992, the United Nations (UN) conducted an Earth Summit, which produced guiding principles for government and business to bring eco-efficiency to the countries across the globe. In the summit, Agenda 21: "a comprehensive programme of action for global action in all areas of sustainable development" (UN, 1992, p. 2) was adopted to change patterns of production to reduce the production of toxic components, to reduce fossil fuels by using alternative sources of energy, to increase awareness about scarcity of water, and to develop a culture of reliance on public transport, etc. The Earth Summit has influenced all conferences conducted by the UN which have connections to human rights, population, social development and women, and human settlements. Although Agenda 21 was weakened by the negotiation of developed nations such as the USA and European Union, it is still the most comprehensive agenda of the UN for sustainable development (Khor, 2012).

Across the nations, it is found that SD is a necessary condition to achieve sustainable growth. In developed nations, it is found that one in ten companies has achieved sustainable growth. Major reasons for unsustainable growth are market saturation, political and economic uncertainty, inequality, hunger, diseases, and human misery (Seelos & Mair, 2005b). The approach of social entrepreneurship can be a powerful instrument for developed countries as well as developing countries to bring sustainable development and to develop markets for creating comprehensive assets which can be accessed by all generations for their wellbeing. By adopting this approach, social entrepreneurs can work for inter-generational wellbeing by investing comprehensive capital such as reproducible capital goods, natural capital, population, intellectual capital, etc.

This chapter has made an attempt to study the potential of the social entrepreneurship approach in creating sustainable development, as an indicator of wellbeing in India. The first section introduces the concept of sustainable development, wellbeing, and social entrepreneurship. A brief literature review is given in the second section. The third section depicts the conceptual framework based on the literature review. The fourth section presents the case studies of social entrepreneurs to understand whether they have the potential to address issues related to wellbeing in India. The last section critically discusses the potential of the social entrepreneurship approach to create wellbeing for sustainable development and concludes the study.

## Sustainable development, wellbeing, and social entrepreneurship

Sustainable development demands maintenance of inter-generational wellbeing. At the very least, the living standard of future generations should not be declining over time. Sengupta (2002) has explained that SD is a concept of inter-temporal resource use, based on ethical theory. It means that this concept demands the present generation should use the natural, human-made, and human capital resources in such a manner so that future generations will attain the same level of social wellbeing. The concept of SD is multidimensional in nature: social, economic, and environmental. In the context of the economics of SD, the sustainability of an economy depends on the capacity to provide wellbeing (Arrow, Dusgupta, Goulder, Mumford, & Oleson, 2012; Kavi Kumar, 2016). Dasgupta (2005) has defined wellbeing as a combination of utility and freedom. This capacity to provide wellbeing depends on a productive capital base of the economy. The productive base includes marketed and non-marketed assets, which are called comprehensive wealth indicators. These authors have further stated that a productive capital base includes reproducible capital goods, natural capital or ecosystem, population, intellectual capital, and institutions which allocate the resources. A market for several assets such as water, air, etc. does not exist, for which shadow prices are used to assess the comprehensive wealth of an economy. Arrow et al. (2012) have suggested that to assess the sustainable development through the lenses of the comprehensive wealth, comprehensive investment is required. This investment is net addition to the stock of comprehensive wealth, holding the shadow prices constant.

The concept of wellbeing has been broadened by Dasgupta (2001). Sengupta (2002), by mentioning the work of Dasgupta (2001), has stated that the concept of wellbeing is broadened in order to accommodate the quality aspects of wellbeing such as civic and political life apart from material wellbeing or utility received from consumption of goods and services. Further, Thompson and Livingston (2016) mentioned that wellbeing is an important basis for addressing illness, crisis, and loss. Here, productive capital can be used to cover this aspect of wellbeing. So, a productive base of capital which creates comprehensive wealth is not only a combination of natural, human-made, and human capitals but also "institutions of the society and its cultural coordinates" (Sengupta, 2002, p. 4289). In order to use resources sustainably along with all forms of capital, institutions play a crucial role.

To understand the resources used for sustainable development, Sanwal (2012) has critically examined the Rio+20 UN conference and mentioned that this conference failed to address important issues such as sustainable resource use, production, and consumption, which can create the sustainable base of comprehensive wellbeing, The author has also stated that in the near future, India and China would become the largest users of natural resources, and to mitigate the conflict of resource uses among the countries including BRIC nations (Brazil, Russia, India, China), a global policy of sustainable development and distribution of scarce resources have to be designed by these countries, which they are negotiating now with the developed nations.

There is a strand of literature which also discusses how to achieve access to the comprehensive wealth which cannot be valued cardinally. It is the process of creation of many conditions so that inter-generations have access to comprehensive wealth. It is important to explore different models of development which have the potential to bring this access. In this context, Seelos and Mair (2005a) have studied the models of social entrepreneurship.[2] The authors have analysed that social entrepreneurs are successful in creating social and economic development in a poor country context. They have studied two social enterprises, BRAC and Grameen Bank, in Bangladesh. It is shown that these enterprises are successfully addressing various needs of the individuals, institutions, communities, and future generations. Further, the authors have recommended that after addressing the societal needs, it is important for social enterprises to focus on economic development, and to develop commercial enterprises to move the poor people out of poverty innovatively. They also discussed the example of "Telenor's joint venture with the Grameen Bank" (p. 12), in order to create an entrepreneurial economy. However, it is not clear from the study what steps these social enterprises have taken to create wellbeing in terms of freedom among the target group. Here, wellbeing is considered in terms of choosing one's own occupation or choosing the way of leading lives, etc. The approach is very top-down in nature; however, it has some benefits, too. Dey and Steyaert (2018) critically study the concept of social entrepreneurship. In their edited book, they analysed the dimensions of social entrepreneurship such as myth, political, constitutional, etc., in order to find the alternative democratic process and affirmation in social entrepreneurship for better wellbeing.

It is important to explore how social entrepreneurship addresses the issue of wellbeing to create a comprehensive wealth for SD.

In contrast to the previous author's view, in the context of Africa, the approach of social entrepreneurship is critically examined by Nega and Schneider (2014). The authors have analysed the developmental contribution of social enterprises such as microfinance institutions in Africa. On the one hand, they have mentioned that social entrepreneurship can play an important role in development by creating community-centred local organisations based on the local culture. On the other hand, they critically analysed that it does not have much impact on poverty and social transformation as this approach has a lack of political focus. The authors have felt that sometimes social entrepreneurship undermines the democratic state-led reforms which are required for social transformation and poverty alleviations, and the enterprises become the tool of corporations and the state to control the poor. They have suggested that in the presence of a corrupt state, social entrepreneurship should politically mobilise the people for sustainable development under a democratic developmental state.

In the Nigerian context, Obinna and Blessing (2014) have stated that social entrepreneurship, which is the application of entrepreneurship attributes of motivation, creativity, and innovation, tries to solve the pressing social problems in the society. The authors have studied the impact of social entrepreneurship on sustainable development in two states of Nigeria and found that it has not contributed to sustainable development due to a lack of innovativeness and creativity. This has adversely affected the development of women in rural areas. They have suggested that a government programme on entrepreneurship should focus not only on business and wealth creation but also on improvement of a citizen's creativity and innovativeness.

In this brief review of literature, several stands are taken by the authors regarding the approach of social entrepreneurship for creating wellbeing for SD. It is worth exploring the potential in this approach to achieve SD in an Indian context.

## Conceptual framework

From the brief review of literature, it is discerned that sustainable development and wellbeing are closely connected concepts. Social entrepreneurship is a process of

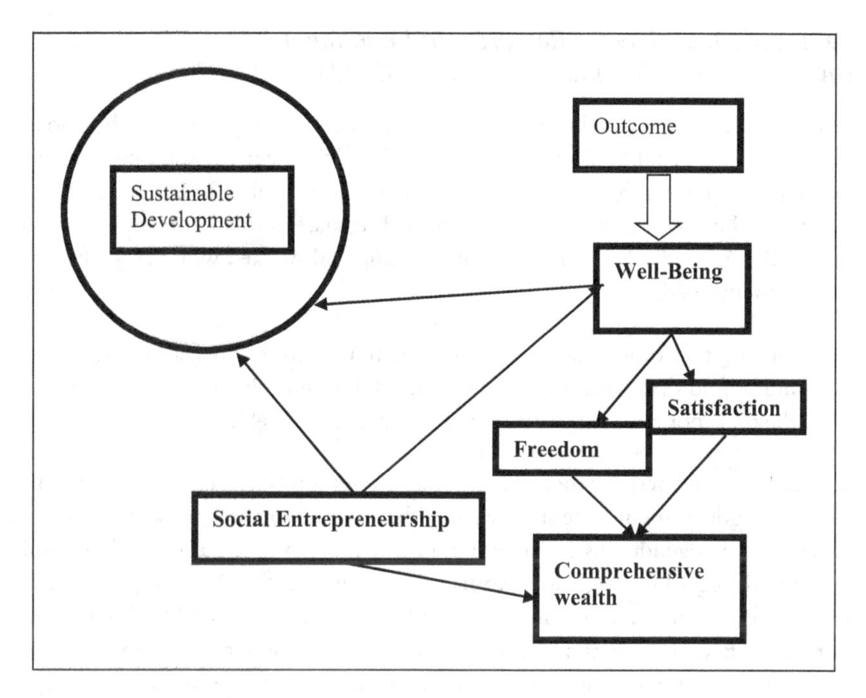


**FIGURE 8.1** Sustainable development, wellbeing, and social entrepreneurship

*Source*: Prepared by the author

developing the society's wellbeing. In the present study, a dimension of sustainable development is studied which advocates comprehensive wealth creation by comprehensive investment in order to bring sustainability into the economy. Where the outcome is to access the capability to provide wellbeing to the present and future generations, the study has attempted to learn the potential of the approach of social entrepreneurship in order to achieve this outcome in the context of India. Here, the concepts of wellbeing, sustainable development, and social entrepreneurship (Figure 8.1) and their relation are explored through the cases of social entrepreneurs in India in the following sections.

## Case studies

In this section, three case studies on social entrepreneurs and their enterprises are presented to understand how these entrepreneurs are working towards wellbeing of the communities to achieve sustainable development. These cases are selected purposefully as each of the cases intervenes to create integrated development for the marginalised community. Each case focuses on any of the three dimensions of sustainable development—social, economic, and environmental—or a combination of these dimensions.

### *Case study I: Society for Research and Rudimentary Education on Social and Health Issues (SRREOSHI)*

SREEOSHI, a women-led organisation, was founded on 27 May 2005 by a social entrepreneur, Ms. Sikha Roy, an Ashoka Fellow. She started working with the Development Research Communication and Services Centre (DRCSC), an NGO, in 1998 in the districts of Bankura, Birbhum, Purulia, South and North, Midnapur in West Bengal, India. She learnt organic farming and worked with marginal farmers. She mentioned:

> During that time I stayed with these families and found that women in the household shared their work load. They did most of the work for farming but they did not have rights to get the income of the field.

She realised that these women are not able to get any share of produce and any benefit of government schemes because they do not have any land right. She understood that gender discrimination is everywhere. Even she also faced discrimination with regard to wages as a woman worker in the NGO sector. She decided to work for women and their rights. In 2005, she started SRREOSHI to work with the indigenous women in villages in the Bankura district. She chose this area because it was her native place. She got the Ashoka fellowship to start working in the Saltora block in the Bankura district by forming ten self-help groups consisting of ten members per group. All women were land-less and had no rights. She started advocacy with Panchayat,[3] Land Department, Block Office and collected the information. As per the land rights of the indigenous community in India, 40 percent of total vested land should be distributed among women. In case of joint ownership, the woman's name should come first. She also received the training from a civil servant in the government of West Bengal about land rights. She started influencing the local governance system, block and district authorities for redistribution of the land rights among the women in Bankura. She took the help of the Minister of Land Reforms in West Bengal to influence these authorities. She also mobilised the women in these villages and brought the 'Jan Adalat', a type of local court, to register the cases in front of the District Magistrate, District Judge, and local Panchayat authority. She faced lots of obstacles in this process. She mentioned:

> Influential Political Parties in the villages were angry about me. I started to see the documents in the BDO office and found there no lands were in the name of the women. I asked the officer why vested land is in the name of the school teacher or panchayat leader. He also said that he did not know the rights. I also met the Panchayat Pradhan and villagers and I said that it is the Law of the Government not my own law. I helped the villagers for applying the getting joint patta. I found the Provision of Lok Adalat to achieve the success.

The women applied for joint ownership of the land, and after a prolonged fight, under SRREOSHI's supervision they got the land rights.

Ms. Roy did not stop there. She analysed the situation and decided to mobilise the women to promote their livelihoods. Because, after getting the land rights, these women should know how they can earn their livelihoods from the land. Her enterprise holds vast experience in formation of 300 women's self-help groups in 50 remote tribal villages in eight Panchayats in three blocks of two districts in West Bengal. These groups were facilitated to start integrated sustainable livelihood activities (products made of jute, bamboo, babui grass,[4] and khejur[5] leaves). The team of SRREOSHI has established a linkage with various marketing channels such as local markets, exhibitions, etc. They have realised that for marketing the products, training and capacity building are required. It can be possible if they link these women to the corporate sector under corporate social responsibility (CSR) programmes. One of such linkages is developed between the CSR team of IISCO steel plants and women's groups in Asansol. The CSR team supported the training and capacity building of these women's groups and SRREOSHI helped in marketing the products. Some of these women entrepreneurs who are promoted by SRREOSHI also won the fellowship of Confederations of Indian Industries (CII) for starting their business ventures on handicrafts. One of these women, Ms. Sundari Hembrom, mentioned:

> I was promoted by SRREOSHI for starting a new life. I also want to promote other women like me from indigenous communities so that we do not need to depend on anybody for our livelihoods and we can help our family. I feel empowered when I present my ideas in public forums.

Under the guidance of SRREOSHI, these women sold their products in the different markets in Kolkata, Mumbai, Asansol, and Durgapur. They received good responses from the corporate sector such as IISCO Steel, SAIL, etc., academic institutions like the Tata Institute of Social Sciences, and the local market.

SRREOSHI also realised that young women would not be able to achieve their rights if they were not oriented about these rights from early childhood. Presently, SRREOSHI has also addressed the sexual and reproductive rights of 2,000 adolescent girls in slums and 500 adolescent girls in schools under Asansol Municipal Corporation. The founder of SRREOSHI mentioned:

> We initiated this programme as we felt that girl children should know their rights at the tender age. It would empower them to lead their lives according to their choices as freedom is very important for them to make their own choices to understand the access to rights.

SRREOSHI also wants to set up a rural incubation centre for indigenous women so that women entrepreneurs can be created for positive social change. In this incubation centre, young women will be trained on business skills, and marketing of their products will be supported by the team of this proposed incubation centre. Ms. Roy remarked:

> We need to make a system which makes the women entrepreneurs independent so that they can sustain without our help. Their enterprises will be sustainable and addressing the issue of sustainable development.

## *Case study II: social security for people with disability*

Mr. Pradip Ghosh, Ashoka Fellow and founding member of OASiS, stated:

> In the World, very few nations are sensitive towards the people with disability. There is no availability of social protection measures for this section of population. Most of the insurance companies believe that people with disability is more prone to accidents and to health hazards. No insurance companies try to develop any innovative model of insurance to cover this section of population.

Mr. Ghosh visited an electronic shop in Bhopal where the shopkeeper appointed his son who was mentally disabled as a labourer. While repairing some electronic goods, that boy hurt his hands. The shopkeeper was not ready to pay a single penny for his son as he was mentally challenged. He informed Mr. Ghosh that his son did not have any insurance for accidents or for any other health problems. Mr. Ghosh visited Bajaj Allianz Insurance Company to know their policy about people with a disability. He came to know that there was no insurance policy for the disabled. He received a similar answer from other insurance companies. The common beliefs of these companies about people with a disability were: 1) they were not insurable; and 2) they were prone to accidents and health hazards.

As a first step of his experiment, Mr. Ghosh visited hospitals in Bhopal City in Madhya Pradesh, India to collect data on how many disabled persons were hospitalised in a year. He also visited police stations in the same city to collect data on the number of disabled people who had an accident within a stipulated time period. He found that an insignificant number of disabled persons had accidents within this time period. He again visited Bajaj Allianz to share this data about disabled people. However, he found that this company depended on the data published in the USA in 1951, and they were not ready to accept a proposal of insurance for disabled people. He approached other insurance companies, but none of them was convinced.

In 2005, Ashoka, a global organisation which promotes social entrepreneurs, organised a workshop on rights of the disabled. Mr. Ghosh requested Ashoka to invite him for this workshop. In this workshop, he met Ms. Anuradha Mohit, Chief Commissioner of Disability, Government of India, and Colin Gonsalves. He showed them the data which he collected from hospitals and the police station in Bhopal City. At the end of this meeting, it was decided to file public interest litigation (PIL) in the Supreme Court in India, demanding equal insurance rights for people with a disability in the country. He shared this information of filing PIL with the private insurance companies in Bhopal. These companies became soft, but they did not commit. New India Assurance Company Limited (NIACL) took the initiative and helped Mr. Ghosh to experiment with health insurance for people with a disability. This company wanted to insure not only the disabled but also their family members to spread the risk of insurance product. The first success of the project was achieved on 29 November 2005, when the first mentally challenged person in the country received health insurance without paying an extra premium. "NIACL also offered accidental insurance for the disabled for the first year on the basis of their perceived risk and subsequently after analysing the claim ratio for a year" (Ghosh, 2008). In December 2005, the Collector of Bhopal after seeing the success of this project announced in a press conference free health insurance for all economically weaker disabled people in this district. The premiums of this insurance would be paid by the district administration. In this way, OASiS brought change at the policy level.

From December 2005 to February 2006, OASiS mobilised NGOs which were working in the area of disability. Mr. Ghosh organised two workshops. One workshop on common diseases faced by disabled people and approximate medical expenses for these diseases and corrective surgeries, therapies, etc. was conducted by the dean of a medical college in Bhopal and his team. The objective of this workshop was to study the health expenditure pattern of disabled people. The second workshop was conducted by the District Civil Surgeon, and data was collected by the Panchayats.

In February 2006, a National Core Committee was formed on insurance for the disabled. This committee comprised Mr. Ghosh, the Chairperson of the National Trust for the welfare of persons with autism, cerebral palsy, mental retardation, and multiple disabilities, the Chief Commissioner of Disability, and commissioner of disabilities of ten states of India. In the first meeting of this core committee, an action plan was drawn. To implement this action plan, a taskforce comprising a three-member team of experts, including Pradeep Ghosh, Dr T. V. Ramesh of insurance brokering firm Alegion in Chennai, and Ms. Shyamala, director of Adi (formerly Spastic Society of Northern India worked on the insurance scheme with the actuaries of insurance companies).

Ms. Shyamala coordinated the data collection process. The final report on health problems, lifespan, corrective surgery, and the expenditure pattern of disabled people was submitted to the Insurance Regulatory and Development Authority (IRDA). One person from the IRDA coordinated with the insurance companies. In early 2007, the Chief Commissioner of Disability conducted two meetings: one with life insurance accentuaries and another with general accentuaries. The core group drafted a proposal under the guidance of the Chief Commissioner. He advertised tender for insurance companies. These companies submitted their quotation. Panchayat and the Ministry of Social Justice formed a committee to open the tender and declare the result.

On 28 March 2008, the National Trust launched 'Niramay', an insurance scheme for persons with autism, cerebral palsy, mental retardation, and multiple disabilities.[6] According to the National Trust, 400,000 mentally disabled people belonged to the economically weaker section. District Commissioners were told to find out 10,000 of such people from one district. The insurance product included hospitalisation, outpatient department services, medication, alternative medication, therapies, and corrective surgeries. The premium per annum per person was Rs. 99. In some states, the commissioner chose his/her own district, and in other states, districts were chosen based on the needs.

After one year of implementation, the premium was raised to Rs. 250 per annum for persons who belonged to richer sections, and the premium was funded by the individual. For the poor people, the National Trust funded the premium. For the first year of implementation, the National Trust appointed ICICI Bank, a private bank in India, to provide the insurance products. Although NIACL took the initiative of experiment on this project, they were not appointed by the National Trust. In the next year, the trust changed the insurance company for the same scheme. To provide this facility, the National Trust made the member NGOs as a nodal agency for coordination with the mentally disabled people. Presently, this scheme is implementing with the help of these NGOs.

Mr. Ghosh also critically looked at the policy. He mentioned:

> This scheme is only meant for a particular section of the disabled. I have mobilised the NGOs who were working in the area of disability to write to the Chief Commissioner of Disability to consider the insurance policies for all categories of Disabled persons. Till the date they have not received any commitment from him. Claim ratio was not high so premium was not modified. National Trust committed that it would pay if the claimed amount is higher than the premium. However, Insurance companies considered this commitment as baseless proof. Insurance companies were not ready to include corrective surgery in the policy as the cost of these surgeries was very high.

## *Case study III: Sampurn(e)arth Environment Solutions Pvt. Ltd.*

In a metropolitan city like Mumbai, waste generation is an alarming problem, which creates pollutions such as water pollution, air pollution, and affects bio-diversity. It is a threat to sustainable development. Jayanth Nataraju, Debartha Banerjee, and Ritvik Rao started their social venture, Sampurn(e)arth Environment Solutions Pvt. Ltd., to address the problem of waste management in Mumbai in 2012. After completion of their Graduation in Engineering degree, they came to Tata Institute of Social Sciences (TISS) to pursue an MA programme in Social Entrepreneurship. As a part of their curriculum, they launched a pilot project on waste management at the TISS campus. The success of their pilot accelerated the process of setting up Sampurn(e)arth Environment Solutions Pvt. Ltd to provide end-to-end environmental solutions to the customers. The operational process includes awareness about environmental problems, waste audit, and providing solutions to manage the waste. The organisation helps to segregate the wastes into biodegradable and non-biodegradable wastes. It also helps to develop a composting pit at the source if biodegradable wastes are generated in a small quantity, and if it is large enough, they help to set up a bio-gas plant. For electronic waste, the team of Sampurn(e) arth collects from the source and sends to the government-registered recyclers. For non-biodegradable wastes, they make paper products and a very small amount of waste which could not be recycled, they send it to the dumping ground. Their aim is decentralisation of the waste management system so that the overall pollution level of the cities can be reduced, and it also reduces the pressure on the dumping ground. They have felt that transporting a large amount of waste also creates air pollution. So, decentralisation of a waste management system reduces the carbon footprints.

For bio-gas plant, this organisation has collaborated with Bhaba Atomic Research Centre (BARC) for technology support. The founding members said:

> Collaboration and network play an important role to address this important socio-environmental issue. We do not have expertise in technology or human resource or accounting. We like to outsource to others who have the same expertise. When we were in TISS, we were working on a project given by Stree Mukti Sanghatana, an NGO who are mobilising women rag pickers for four decades. They introduced us to Scientists in BARC to know the technology of Bio-Gas Plant.

For recruitment of the waste managers, Debartha Banerjee, a founding member, mentioned in an interview with *Hindusthan Times*, a daily newspaper:

> We collaborated with Stree Mukti Sanghatana to employ our waste managers.
> *(www.sampurnearth.com/media/Hindusthan Times.JPEG)*

In this process of solving the problem of waste management, they have also addressed the problem of informal employment of the rag pickers. They found that waste is managed by informal workers such as women rag pickers. These workers are not working in a decent environment, and they do not have job security. One of the founding members, Mr. Jayanth, in an interview with *Indian Express*, a daily newspaper, in 2012 stated:

> The rag pickers make Rs. 100–150 daily but work is limited and cannot be guaranteed everyday. We plan to formalise their work and give them regular income and better working conditions. While the NGO will continue to organise them and take care of their health and education needs, the business end will be handled by us.
> *(Waste Business, Mumbai, 12 February 2012. Retrieved April 6, 2017 from www.sampurnearth.com/media/Indian Express.pdf)*

In the near future, they will start a community development project in Vashi, Bhav Nagar, and Govandi. For this initiative, they will collaborate with the corporate sector for funds under corporate social responsibility (CSR). The team of Sampurn(e)arth wants to support other firms who want to work in the area of waste management by providing technology, support, and information. For their future growth, they believe:

> there is a huge scope for development in Mumbai and they have opportunity to scale up at least 2000 times in Mumbai. We are not going anywhere from Mumbai any time soon.

## Discussion and conclusion

Three case studies on social entrepreneurship have brought very crucial points of discussion. It includes their approach of solving social problems, what kind of utility they are creating in the community, and what nature of comprehensive wealth as a measure of wellbeing they are creating. The study also critically analyses the potential of social entrepreneurship to contribute to the sustainable development and wellbeing.

### *Approach of solving social problems*

Three entrepreneurs have adopted different types of innovative process to address the social problems. While Ms. Roy challenged the state machinery about the land rights of the indigenous women in West Bengal, Mr. Ghosh appealed the state by showing his research output and by filing the PIL for the right of disabled people for accessing social products such as insurance, and the founding members of Sampurn(e)arth collaborated with an established research institute, BARC, for technology and Stree Mukti Sanghatana, an NGO, for accessing the community for their ventures. Each of the approaches is unique in nature to address the socio-economic and environmental problems. In each case, entrepreneurs tried to collaborate or develop networks to address the problem, as the volume of each problem is very high. It is impossible for an individual or an enterprise to address the problem without accessing any network. So, networks played an important role.

### *Utility or satisfaction created for wellbeing by social entrepreneurs*

Each of these social enterprises attempted to bring their target group in a satisfactory environment to access some of the comprehensive wealth (Arrow et al., 2012). For example, Ms. Roy has tried to give access to land rights to indigenous women, followed by sustainable employment which brings satisfaction in their lives. Mr. Ghosh has successfully convinced the state authority to give access to insurance to the disabled people in India. It does not only give satisfaction to the disabled people but also to their families and caregivers. The founding members of Sampurn(e)arth have attempted to give satisfaction to their customers by providing end-to-end environmental solutions as well as to women rag pickers whose informal employment is being transformed into formal employment. So, in a process, these entrepreneurs are successfully delivering some forms of comprehensive wealth in terms of natural capital, intellectual capital, economic capital, etc. However, for comprehensive wealth creation, people also need to be provided with choices of comprehensive wealth, including non-marketed assets, institutional capital, etc., which is limited in the context of social entrepreneurship as the premise of social entrepreneurship is micro in nature and based on local context. This aspect limits the creation of choices. Further, it will take a long time to create these choices.

### *Freedom for wellbeing created by social entrepreneurs*

Freedom is considered as an important aspect of wellbeing. Dasgupta (2005) explained that positive freedom liberates people from destitution. For example, employment opportunity gives us the autonomy and it helps us to understand where our interests lie. SRREOSHI has created a space for women entrepreneurs to liberate them from the clutches of poverty. It also successfully oriented the target group to train the women who belong to an indigenous group for accessing freedom through capacity building. OASiS has tried to create better resource allocation through an insurance product which liberates disabled people from the clutches of health inequalities. It created a provision of a better life and better freedom of accessing insurance products. Sampurn(e)arth, on the one hand, liberates their customers and rag pickers from the unhealthy environment, and on the other hand, this organisation is providing freedom to waste managers by generating formal employment. Although these social enterprises have made an attempt to provide sustainable wellbeing in terms of freedom, there is a limited scope in this study to understand the nature of the freedom enjoyed by the target group. Also, it is not clear from the interviews about their future steps on creating comprehensive wealth which help the target group to access freedom, autonomy, and inter-generational wellbeing. The perspectives of the target group about the freedom are also beyond the scope of this present study.

### *Nature of the comprehensive wealth created by social entrepreneurs*

To create sustainable wellbeing, comprehensive wealth has to be created. All three social enterprises aim to achieve this goal of creating comprehensive wealth amongst the target groups. Some of the dimensions of comprehensive wealth specially marketed assets are created by them such as economic capital, generation of reproductive capital, intellectual capital, etc. Some of them also created non-marketed assets such as sustainable environment, sustainable health, etc. However, it is not clear whether the created marketed assets are sustainable in nature or not and whether this access to marketed assets is inter-generational in nature or not.

## *Critiquing the approach of social entrepreneurship*

The study has made an attempt to understand the suitability of approach of social entrepreneurship in order to provide wellbeing for sustainable development. By adopting this approach, social entrepreneurs are successfully addressing social problems in the local context. Each of these social problems is connected to the global context. Presently, social entrepreneurs are unable to focus on this inter-relationship. If they do not pay any attention to this relationship, all of their attempts would be restricted to local solutions to a small dimension of the problem, almost like a bandage on a wound. To attain the issue of sustainable development, social entrepreneurs need to conceptualise wellbeing and comprehensive wealth much before their future interventions.

Social entrepreneurs are focusing on social mobilisation to address the issues which have political connotation such as land rights, worker's rights, right to access to social products, etc. The approach is very top-down. It is important for social entrepreneurs to focus on the process of political mobilisation, which can create a democratic state. This type of state can take the bigger responsibility of offering comprehensive wealth than the individual social entrepreneur (Nega & Schneider, 2014). The present study concludes on a positive note that the approach of social entrepreneurship has a lot of potential to address the issue of wellbeing for sustainable development. These social enterprises have just started to intervene by taking up the social problems in the local context. They need to connect these issues to the global context for better sustainability and creation of comprehensive wealth. For the same reason, along with social mobilisation, political mobilisation is required for creation of a better state to deliver this wealth for sustainable wellbeing.

## Notes

1 Acknowledgement: The author is grateful to all three social enterprises and Ms. Sikha Roy, Mr. Pradeep Ghosh, Mr. Jayanth Nataraju, Mr. Debartha Banerjee, and Mr. Ritvik Rao for allowing her to use their case studies in this study. She is also thankful to Dr Archana Singh for permitting her to use some documents on Sampurn(e)arth which are submitted by a group of students for their assignment at TISS as a TISS mimeograph.
2 The concept of social entrepreneurship has evolved as a means of creating social value, which can generate welfare of the marginalised section of the society. Social mission is the central point in the social entrepreneurship framework.
3 *Panchayat* is a local governance system at the village level in India.
4 *Babui* grass is a type of grass which is common in Bankura, Asansol, and Durgapur.
5 *Khejur* is a local name of date palm tree in West Bengal.
6 See http://thenationaltrust.in/NewWeb/Schemes.html

## References

Arrow, K. J., Dusgupta, P., Goulder, L. H., Mumford, K. J., & Oleson, K. (2012). Sustainability and the measurement of wealth. *Environment and Development Economics*, *17*(3), 317–353.

Dasgupta, P. (2001). *Human Well-Being and the Natural Environment.* Oxford University Press, Delhi, 2001.

Dasgupta, P. (2005). *An inquiry into wellbeing and destitution.* Oxford, UK: Clarendon Press.

Dey, P., & Steyaert, C. (2018). *Social entrepreneurship: An affirmative critique.* Cheltenham, UK: Edward Elgar Publisher.

Ghosh, P. (2008). *Health insurance for the disabled: Nirmaya.* Retrieved April 4, 2015, from https://drive.google.com/file/d/0B2f9FS3y4k0vQVgzLUQtYXBrMnc/edit

Kavi Kumar, K. S. (2016). Economics of sustainable development. *Economic and Political Weekly, II*(3), 34–36.

Khor, M. (2012). Rio+20 Summit: Key Issues. *Economic and Political Weekly, 47*(24), 1–7.

Nega, B., & Schneider, G. (2014). Social entrepreneurship, microfinance and economic development in Africa. *Journal of Economic Issues, 47*(2), 367–376.

Obinna, I. C., & Blessing, N. N. (2014). Social entrepreneurship and sustainable development. *Journal of Poverty, Investment and Development—An Open Access International Journal, 5*, 126–129.

Parrish, B. D. (2008). *Sustainability-driven entrepreneurship: A literature review.* Sustainability Research Institute, March 2008, No. 9, The University of Leeds, UK, pp. 1–57. Retrieved April 3, 2017 from www.see.leeds.ac.uk/fileadmin/Documents/research/sri/ . . . / SRIPs-09_01.pdf.

Sanwal, M. (2012). Global sustainable development the unresolved questions for Rio+20. *Economic & Political Weekly, 47*(7), 14–16.

Seelos, C., & Mair, J. (2005a). *Sustainable development: How social entrepreneurs make it happen.* WP No 611, October, 2005. Retrieved March 11, 2017 from https://papers.ssrn.com/sol3/papers.cfm?abstract_id=876404&rec=1&srcabs=1553072&alg=1&pos=7.

Seelos, C., & Mair, J. (2005b). Sustainable development and sustainable profit. *EBF, 20*, 49–53.

Sengupta, R. (2002). Human wellbeing and sustainable development. *Economic and Political Weekly, 37*(42), 4289–4294.

Thompson, N., & Livingston, W. (2016). Promoting well-being. *Illness, Crisis and Loss, 26*(2), 98–110.

United Nation. (1972). *Report of the United Nations Conference on the human environment.* Stockholm, 5–16 June 1972. Retrieved March 29, 2017 from www.un-documents.net/aconf48-14r1.pdf.

United Nation. (1992). *UN conference on environment and development.* Retrieved March 11, 2017 from www.un.org/geninfo/bp/envirp2.html.

Waste Business, Mumbai, 12 February 2012. Retrieved April 6, 2017 from www.sampurnearth.com/media/Indian Express.pdf.

# 9

# SUSTAINABLE DEVELOPMENT AND GREEN FINANCING

## A study on the banking sector in Bangladesh

*Dewan Muktadir-Al-Mukit and M. Ashraf Hossain*

### Introduction

It is said that developing countries are most vulnerable to climate change and global warming. Because environmental issues play a significant role in sustainable development, countries, especially developing ones starving for sustainable development, must adopt the policy considering an environmental scenario. In this context, in the economic development process, banks play a pivotal role through properly transforming and utilising resources. Therefore, banks are expected to ensure banking practices through their financing and investing activities in such a way that will protect the environment from deterioration and at the same time, can contribute towards sustainable development of the country.

Access to credit has a positive impact on the growth of the economy. Economic activity cannot function properly without the continuing flow of money and credit, where banks are the primary means of facilitating this flow of credit (Omankhanlen, 2012). Besides, the economic progress of a country is a function of advancement and growth of the banking industry (Agu, 1988; Nwankwo, 1994). In the economic progress, banks are considered as a major source of financing, and a major proportion of this financing is made to the industries which are responsible for carbon emission to a greater extent. Thus, banking sectors have a major responsibility to formulate policy and to conduct it in such a way which supports the environment-friendly sustainable economy while ensuring substantial reduction in carbon emission. And for this to happen, banks are expected to finance green technology, product, process, and pollution-reducing projects.

The sustainable economic growth of developing countries can be achieved through green products and activities that are not destructive to the environment. In this process, the financial sector can facilitate to build a low-carbon-based green industry through its green financing activities, which will help to build a green economy ensuring sustainable development. Green financing is a part of green banking activities where investing and financing decisions should be made considering social, ecological, and environmental issues in order to protect the environment and nature and to ensure proper utilisation of natural resources. The commercial banks are expected to take necessary measures in protecting the environment while financing new projects.

Developing or least developed countries are the worst victims of environmental pollution through industrialisation of the Western countries. Besides, developing countries face greater structural obstacles in preventing and cleaning up environmental pollution due to resource problems. Companies from developing countries have to manage their limited funds in production purposes, and there is no separate fund allocated for controlling pollution and reducing the amount of wastage created through the production process. Very few companies consider this issue and try to control pollution in their own interest. And people from the least developed countries are not much anxious or informed about this issue because of social structure, and therefore they are not much interested to impose regulation on their industries. They believe that rapid industrialisation will foster the economy to grow further, which will help them to be financially sound in the future. But in reality, rapid industrialisation may bring economic prosperity, but it may not be sustainable because of environmental issues. On the other hand, responses from developed countries which are mostly accused for environment degradation through patronising carbon-emitting industry are not satisfactory. At this situation, governments from many developing countries are taking initiatives to protect the environment from pollution mainly caused by industrialisation. Due to the funding constraints, governments of these countries fail to provide companies with the financial incentive to clean up the environmental cost of pollution or to adopt the technology for controlling pollution. But still many developing countries are trying to protect the environment from further degradation and to reduce carbon emissions.

Bangladesh is one of the developing countries that is exposed to the risk of vulnerability because of climate change and global warming, along with a lack of awareness of general people. On the other hand, as major funding in the process of industrialisation are made through financial assistance of commercial banks, so financial sectors of the country cannot deny their responsibility in protecting the environment from degradation and pollution. Bangladesh Bank, the central bank of Bangladesh, being the regulator of the money market, has taken some major initiatives towards substantial reduction of carbon emission and protecting environmental degradation through introducing green banking concepts in 2011. Green banking activities require all banks to allocate and to utilise separate funds in three segments: 1) green finance, 2) climate risk fund, and 3) green marketing, training, and capacity building. This study focuses on the major segment of green banking activities, i.e. green financing activities of the banks in Bangladesh. The study discusses the overall picture of green financing activities and present status with an implementation scenario of such green financing programmes.

There are not many literature studies regarding this issue, which indicates that no significant work has been done on this topic so far, especially from the perspective of a developing country. The discussion of the chapter on this contemporary topic may create a new platform where the issue of sustainable economic development can be addressed, incorporating environmental aspects with green financing activities.

The rest of the chapter proceeds as follows: section two discusses objectives, section three presents the methodology of the study, section four provides a theoretical framework on the issue, and section five demonstrates the empirical findings with analysis. The last section of the chapter provides concluding remarks along with limitations and future research direction.

## Objectives

The objectives of the study are:

- To explore the Bangladesh Bank policy guidelines for green banking and green financing.
- To analyse the green financing activities by banking industry in Bangladesh.
- To conduct a comparative analysis of green financing activities among state-owned, private, and foreign commercial banks operating in Bangladesh.

## Methodology

The study is mainly based on secondary data. Secondary data sources are the green banking reports of Bangladesh Bank and 47 listed banks, various seminar information, and other relative information published on websites. In addition to this, the data is also collected through the bank's annual report, daily newspaper, and different journals and articles. As the green banking policy was adopted in 2011 and there is only one published complete report available on the implementation scenario up to 2012, the study focuses primarily on 2012 and in some cases on 2011. The analysis is descriptive in nature, and all the data have been processed by using Microsoft Excel 2010 software.

## Theoretical framework

### *Financial sector and banking industry in Bangladesh*

Bangladesh is one of the developing nations, with around 154 million population where per capita income is $850. The country's economy is of $116.4 billion GDP with a growth rate of around 6 percent. The financial sector of Bangladesh consists of 56 scheduled banks, 31 non-banking financial institutions (NBFIs), 62 insurance companies, and two capital markets. Besides, a number of institutions from semi-formal and informal sectors also contribute to the financial system of

Bangladesh (www.bangladesh-bank.org/). The major segment of the financial sector of Bangladesh consists of 56 scheduled banks which operate under full control and supervision of Bangladesh Bank, the central bank of Bangladesh. These 56 scheduled banks are four state-owned commercial banks (SCBs), four specialized development banks (SDBs), 39 private commercial banks (PCBs), and nine foreign commercial banks (FCBs).

## *Green banking policy of Bangladesh Bank*

Green banking is nothing but conducting normal banking operations while considering the environmental aspects of business activities. The idea of green banking urges the banks to consider environmental and ecological factors in their operations and to formulate policies in a way which can protect the environment from further degradation. The bank can implement green banking practice through in-house activities and also by changing its lending policy by forcing industry to adopt environmentally friendly production processs and appropriate technology protecting the environment. Green banking activities are divided into two segments: in-house green banking activities and green banking activities other than in-house. First, green banking requires banks' in-house practice of green activities by adopting an appropriate policy of utilising renewable energy, conserving natural resources, and other actions to minimise carbon footprint from banking activities. Second, all banks should adopt environmentally responsible financing decisions considering environmental risks of projects and should support environmentally friendly green projects (Islam & Das, 2013).

## *In-house green activities*

In-house green activities are those activities involved with performing internal and official functions of banks by efficient use of renewable, non-renewable, human, and natural resources. These activities include efficient use of electricity, water, paper, and reuse of equipment, emphasizing online communication rather than printed documents for office management, installation of energy-efficient electronic equipment, using energy-saving bulbs and energy-efficient cars for employees, reducing paper waste by printing paper on both sides, promoting e-banking and mobile banking, using more daylight instead of electric lights, proper ventilation in lieu of using air conditioning, use of solar energy, and relying on virtual meetings through the use of video conferencing in lieu of physical travel and so on.

## *Green activities other than in-house*

These activities are involved with allocation and utilisation of separate mandatory budgets in three segments: 1) budget for green finance, 2) budget for climate risk fund, and 3) budget for green marketing, training, and capacity building.

**TABLE 9.1** Utilisation of fund for green banking (amount in million Taka)

| *Area* | *Utilisation of Budget* |
|---|---|
| Green Finance | 270921.53 |
| Climate Risk Fund | 258.89 |
| Marketing, Training, and Capacity Building | 90.42 |
| Total | 271270. 84 |

*Source*: Annual report on green banking, Bangladesh Bank, 2012

Note: Conversion rate: 1 $US = 78 Taka

Table 9.1 shows the utilisation of budget for green banking by all banks operating in Bangladesh in 2012.

### *Three phases of time frame for green banking policy*

Bangladesh Bank has formulated a green banking policy which needs to be covered through time frame work, which will be segregated into three phases:

Phase I: Banks are to develop green banking policies and to show a general commitment on the environment through in-house performance. The time lining for the actions to be taken under Phase I should not exceed 30 June 2014.

Phase II: A system of environmental management should be in place in a bank before 31 December 2014.

Phase III: It requires banks to address the whole ecosystem through environment-friendly initiatives and introducing innovative products. Standard environmental reporting with external verification should be part of the phase. The time lining for the actions to be taken under Phase III should not exceed 30 June 2015.

Figure 9.1 shows a three-phased strategy framework of green banking activities.

### *Green financing as a part of green banking*

This requires that during financing, eco-friendly business activities and energy-efficient and less environmentally hazardous industries will be given preference by the commercial banks, and at the same time, environmental infrastructure such as renewable energy projects, clean water supply projects, wastewater treatment plants, solid and hazardous waste disposal plants, biogas plants, and bio-fertiliser plants should be encouraged and financed by banks.

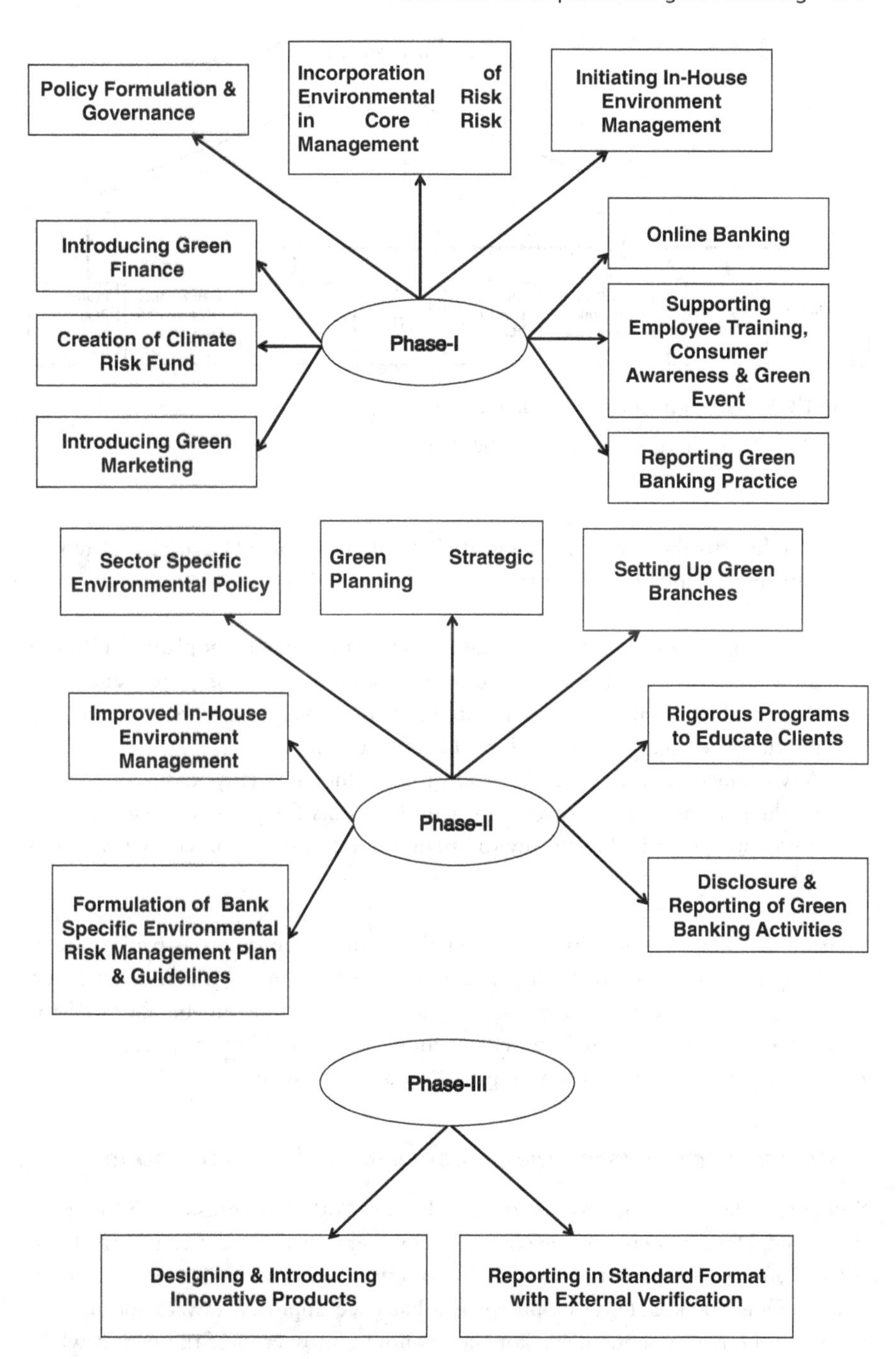


**FIGURE 9.1** Three phases of green banking policy implementation

*Source*: Annual report on green banking, Bangladesh Bank, 2012

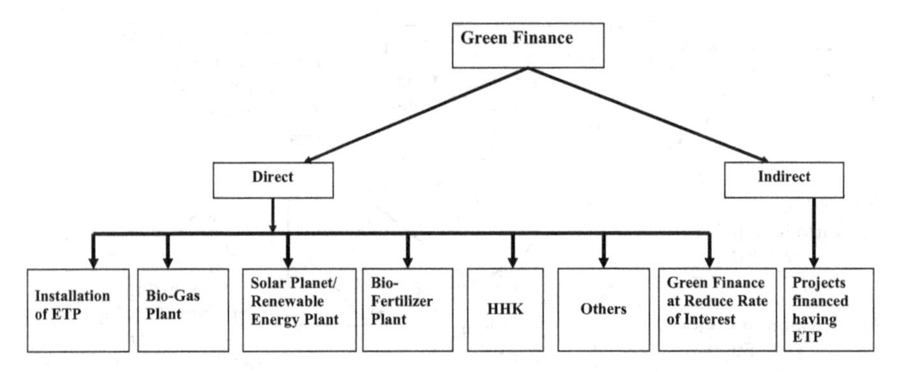


**FIGURE 9.2** Green financing at a glance

*Source*: Annual report on green banking, Bangladesh Bank, 2012

According to the policy of Bangladesh Bank, components that are related to green finance include the following:

1 Financing green projects/events such as an effluent treatment plant (ETP), and projects having ETP, biogas plant, bio-fertilizer plant, solar panel/renewable energy plant, solar irrigation pumping station, solar home system, solar PV module assembling plant, or Hybrid Hoffman Kiln (HHK).
2 Any project/event financed by banks for producing energy resource-efficient products or any project/event financed by banks for possible safeguards and mitigating hazards due to environmental conditions or climate change and others.

Figure 9.2 shows the activities of green financing by commercial banks. Green financing involves two broad categories: direct green financing and indirect green financing. While direct green finance requires a bank's funds to be allocated for renewable energy and environment-friendly projects, indirect green finance requires financing the projects having ETP or a similar system.

## *Sustainable development, the environment, and green financing*

Sustainable development was first defined by the World Commission on Environment and Development in 1987 as "Development that meets the needs of the present without compromising the ability of future generations to meet their own needs." Thus, sustainable development is a balanced approach toward social, economic, and environmental needs for the economic prosperity of the nation while aiming at the conservation of nature and natural resources (Figure 9.3). Sustainable development requires managing development in an ecologically sustainable manner so that we can move towards an energy- and resource-efficient economy through proper allocation of natural resources between present and future generations while

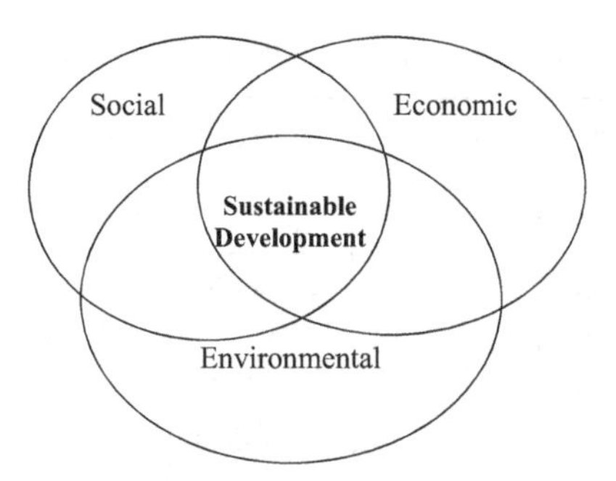


**FIGURE 9.3** Three domains of sustainable development

*Source*: Developed by the authors

protecting the climate. Sustainable development constantly seeks to achieve social and economic progress by formulating appropriate policies aiming at fulfilling the economic and social needs without disregarding the future and deteriorating the environment. Environment is considered as one of the most fundamental parts of sustainable development, which is related to the issue of biodiversity, natural resources, ecosystem integrity, clean air, water, and so on.

Economic development of a country is an outcome of rapid industrialisation, but economic progress through industrialisation depends on access to credit and continued flow of money. And in this process, the banking sector plays a major role through proper allocation of money to different economic entities. In the economic progress, a major proportion of a bank's financing is made to the industries which are responsible for carbon emission to a greater extent. So, the banking sector cannot deny its responsibility, which may indirectly contribute to environmental degradation. Thus, banking sectors also have a responsibility to formulate policy and to conduct business in such a way which will help to create an environmentally sustainable economy. Banks are expected to operate in such a way which will ensure the protection of the environment and natural resources while it can continue its normal course of business. Green financing is a part of that green banking activities, which allow traditional community banking while giving special attention to the social, ecological, and environmental factors aiming at the conservation of nature and natural resources.

## Analysis and findings

### *Allocation and utilisation of fund for green financing*

Banks are required to allocate and to utilise a considerable amount of funds for green financing under the green banking policy in their annual budgets. Table 9.2 and Table 9.3 consecutively show allocation and utilisation of funds for green financing by the banking sector of Bangladesh in 2012.

**TABLE 9.2** Allocation of funds for green banking and green financing in 2012

| *Bank Category* | *Budget Allocated for Green Banking (Million Taka)* | *Budget Allocated for Green Financing (Million Taka)* | *Percentage of Green Financing Budget* |
|---|---|---|---|
| SCBs | 7185.00 | 5000.00 | 69.59 |
| PCBs | 59760.24 | 58297.99 | 97.55 |
| FCBs | 41766.64 | 41712.92 | 99.87 |
| SDBs | 1800.30 | 1350.00 | 74.99 |
| Total | 110512.18 | 106360.91 | 96.24 |

*Source:* Annual report on green banking, Bangladesh Bank, 2012

Note: 1 $US = 78 Taka

**TABLE 9.3** Utilisation of funds for direct and indirect green finance in 2012 (amount in million Taka)

| *Bank Category* | *Direct Green Finance* | *Indirect Green Finance* | *Total Green Finance* |
|---|---|---|---|
| SCBs | 3513.10 | 2994.15 | 6507.25 |
| PCBs | 5623.74 | 173187.17 | 178810.91 |
| FCBs | 881.28 | 76517.03 | 77398.31 |
| SDBs | 1803.36 | 6401.70 | 8205.06 |
| Total | 11821.48 | 259100.05 | 270921.53 |

*Source:* Annual report on green banking, Bangladesh Bank, 2012

Note: 1 $US = 78 Taka

Table 9.3 shows that the highest contribution in terms of allocation of budget for green banking and green financing in 2012 was made by PCBs. Among the total budget for green banking, 96.24 percent was allocated for green financing only. As indicated in Figure 9.4 the highest proportion of green banking funds allocated for green financing activities was done by FCBs.

PCBs have utilised maximum (66%) funds for green financing as a whole. Further, PCBs stand first in terms of utilisation of funds for both direct green financing (47.57%) and indirect green financing (66.84%). It also reveals that FCBs are more interested in indirect green financing, whereas SCBs are more interested in direct green financing. Another interesting finding is that all banks have increased their contribution for green financing from the budget allocated in the initial period.

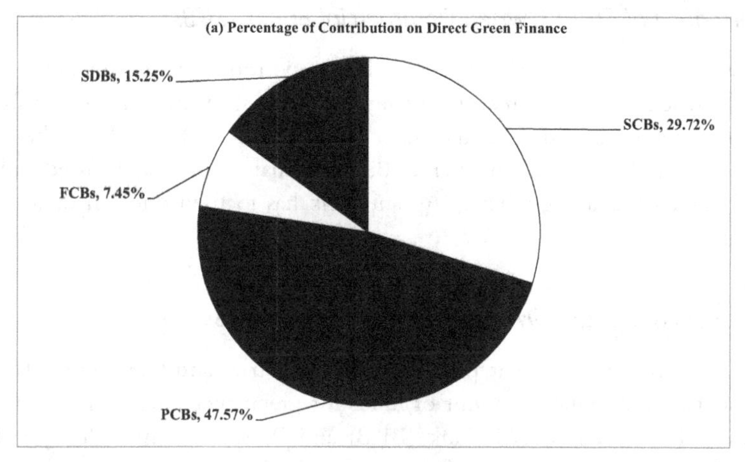


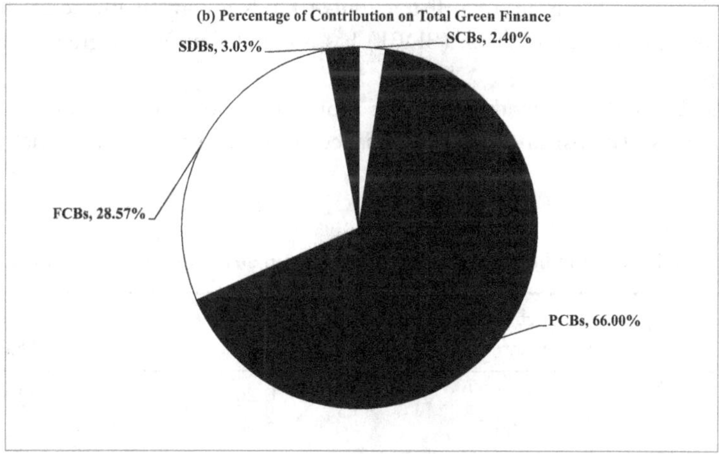


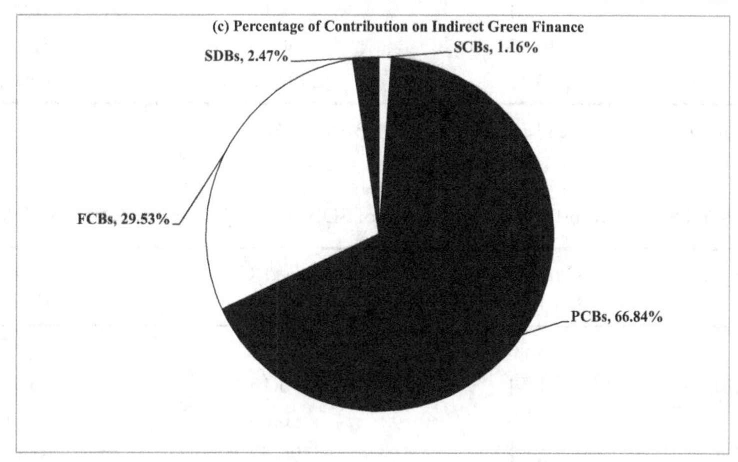


**FIGURE 9.4a, b, & c** Utilisation of funds for green finance

*Source:* Authors

### *Performance of State-Owned Commercial Banks (SCBs)*

Here we can see that Rupali Bank is in the top position among SCBs in terms of disbursement of fund for green financing, where most of the portion is disbursed for direct green financing. On the other hand, Sonali Bank has the highest contribution to indirect green financing. Besides, Janata Bank has focused only on indirect green financing, whereas Agrani Bank has focused only on direct green financing.

### *Performance of State-Owned Commercial Banks (SCBs)*

It is clear from Table 9.5 that Bank of Small Industries and Commerce (BASIC) has disbursed the highest amount of funds for green financing which is indirect in nature. Bangladesh Krishi Bank (BKB) and Rajshahi Krishi Unnayan Bank (RAKUB) have disbursed a small fraction of funds for green financing, though Bangladesh Development Bank (BDBL) has no contribution for green financing in this period.

Tables 9.6 and 9.7 provide the details about the performance of Foreign Commercial Banks (FCBs) and the performance of local private commercial banks, respectively.

**TABLE 9.4** Direct and indirect green finance of SCBs in 2012 (amount in million Taka)

| *Bank Name* | *Direct Green Finance* | *Indirect Green Finance* | *Total Green Finance* |
|---|---|---|---|
| Sonali | 373.64 | 2120.20 | 2493.84 |
| Janata | 0.00 | 23.06 | 23.06 |
| Agrani | 99.21 | 0.00 | 99.21 |
| Rupali | 3040.25 | 850.89 | 3891.14 |
| Total | 3513.10 | 2994.15 | 6507.25 |

*Source:* Annual report on green banking, Bangladesh Bank, 2012

**TABLE 9.5** Direct and indirect green finance of SDBs in 2012 (amount in million Taka)

| *Bank Name (SDBs)* | *Direct Green Finance* | *Indirect Green Finance* | *Total Green Finance* |
|---|---|---|---|
| BKB | 5.90 | 0.00 | 5.90 |
| RAKUB | 1.54 | 5.13 | 6.67 |
| BDBL | 0.00 | 0.00 | 0.00 |
| BASIC | 1795.92 | 6396.57 | 8192.49 |
| Total | 1803.36 | 6401.70 | 8205.06 |

*Source:* Annual report on green banking, Bangladesh Bank, 2012

**TABLE 9.6** Direct and indirect green finance of FCBs in 2012 (amount in million Taka)

| *Bank Name (FCBs)* | *Direct Green Finance* | *Indirect Green Finance* | *Total Green Finance* |
|---|---|---|---|
| Commercial Bank of Ceylon | 8.80 | 0.00 | 8.80 |
| Standard Chartered | 716.48 | 40674.89 | 41391.37 |
| State Bank of India | 0.00 | 2.85 | 2.85 |
| Citi N.A. | 20.00 | 34463.00 | 34483.00 |
| HSBC | 134.00 | 0.00 | 134.00 |
| National Bank of Pakistan | 0.00 | 0.00 | 0.00 |
| Habib Bank | 0.00 | 0.00 | 0.00 |
| Woori | 2.00 | 0.00 | 2.00 |
| Bank AL-Falah | 0.00 | 1376.29 | 1376.29 |
| Total | 881.28 | 76517.03 | 77398.30 |

*Source*: Annual report on green banking, Bangladesh Bank, 2012

**TABLE 9.7** Top six PCBs for direct and indirect green finance in 2012 (amount in million Taka)

| *Bank Name* | *Direct Green Finance* | *Indirect Green Finance* | *Total Green Finance* |
|---|---|---|---|
| EXIM | 1859.47 | 25748.24 | 27607.71 |
| Islami Bank BD | 168.37 | 27007.60 | 27175.97 |
| Eastern | 1.25 | 22264.00 | 22265.25 |
| AB Bank | 47.84 | 16218.07 | 16265.91 |
| Southeast | 0.00 | 15365.80 | 15365.80 |
| Bank Asia | 746.23 | 10393.60 | 11139.83 |

*Source*: Annual report on green banking, Bangladesh Bank, 2012

Among all FCBs, Standard Chartered has utilised the highest amount of Tk. 41391.37 million for green finance. The contribution of Citi N.A Bank is also significant. Both banks have emphasised indirect green financing. On the other hand, Habib Bank and National Bank of Pakistan did not contribute to green financing in 2012.

It is found that among all PCBs, EXIM Bank, Bank Asia, and Islami Bank have utilised consecutively the first, second, and third highest amounts of Tk. 1859.47, 746.23, and 168.37 million, respectively, for direct green finance, and Islami Bank, EXIM Bank, and Eastern Bank have utilised consecutively the first, second, and third highest amounts of Tk. 27007.60, 25748.24, and 22264.00 million, respectively, for indirect green finance. EXIM bank is in the top position for total disbursement of funds for green financing.

### *Sector-wise contribution of banks towards green financing*

The sector-wise contribution of banks towards green financing is provided in Table 9.8 and in Figure 9.5. Commercial banks undertook an initiative to implement green financing activities that was accomplished through paying low-interest loans to the customers who would like to set up solar equipment, effluent treatment plants (ETP), bio-gas and bio-fertilizer plants, Hybrid Hoffman Kiln (HHK), and so on.

**TABLE 9.8** Sector-wise contribution of banks towards green financing (amount in million Taka)

| *Green Projects/Events* | *SCBs* | *PCBs* | *FCBs* | *SDBs* | *Total* |
|---|---|---|---|---|---|
| ETP | 118.81 | 687.89 | 162.80 | 387.02 | 1356.52 |
| Projects having ETP | 2994.15 | 173187.17 | 76517.03 | 6401.70 | 259100.05 |
| Bio-gas plant | 9.73 | 283.82 | 0 | 606.32 | 899.87 |
| Solar/renewable energy Plant | 984.94 | 1685.56 | 718.48 | 249.39 | 3638.37 |
| Bio-fertilizer plant | 0.00 | 0.40 | 0 | 0 | 0.40 |
| Hybrid Hoffman Kiln (HHK) | 538.71 | 841.96 | 0 | 449.66 | 1830.33 |
| Others | 1860.91 | 2089.58 | 0 | 110.97 | 4061.76 |
| Reduced rate of interest | 0.00 | 34.26 | 0 | 0 | 34.26 |

*Source*: Review of CSR initiatives of Banks: 2012, Bangladesh Bank

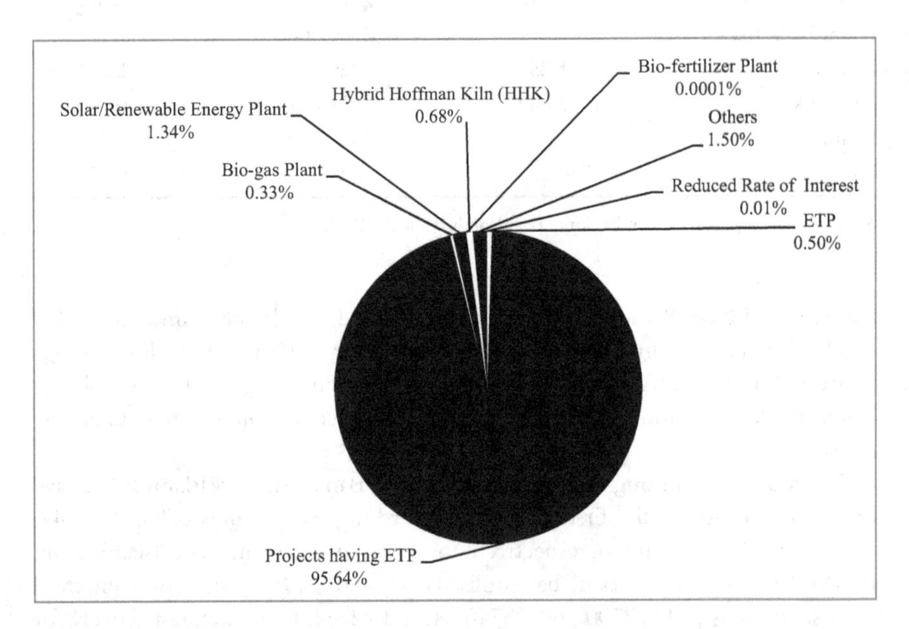


**FIGURE 9.5** Sector-wise contribution of banks towards green financing

*Source*: Authors

It is observed that the highest proportion of the funds have been disbursed for financing Effluent Treatment Plants (ETP). All categories of banks have allocated their maximum fund for this sector. The contribution of PCBs was highest for financing in all sectors except bio-gas plants, and the lowest financing was made to bio-fertilizer plants.

## *Financing projects after environmental risk rating*

According to green banking policy, projects which are eco-friendly and less hazardous to the environment will be given preference for financing by commercial banks. In this regard, commercial banks are expected to rate the projects considering environmental issues, and thus financing will be made according to the environmental risk rating (Table 9.9 and Figure 9.6).

Banks are now emphasising financing projects after conducting environmental risk rating. Banks have started environmental risk rating since July 2011. We see

**TABLE 9.9** Financing projects after environmental risk rating in 2011 and 2012

| *Year* | *2011* | *2012* |
|---|---|---|
| Number of projects rated | 4,394 | 12,088 |
| No. of projects financed after rating | 4,315 | 11,165 |
| Percentage of financed projects after rating | 98% | 92% |
| Amount disbursed to the rated projects (in million taka) | 270951.14 | 703633.21 |

*Source*: Annual report on green banking, Bangladesh Bank 2012

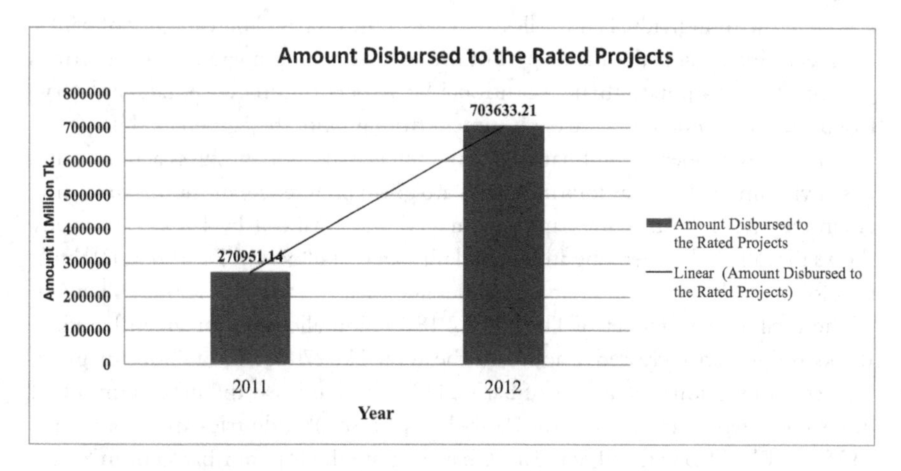


**FIGURE 9.6** Financing projects after environmental risk rating in 2011 and 2012

*Source*: Authors

there is an increase in rating projects over the period. Besides, disbursement for rated projects has also been increased.

### *Rankings of the banks based on allocation and utilisation of fund for green financing*

Figures 9.7 and 9.8 consecutively show the top 12 banks among all banks operating in Bangladesh, which allocated and utilised maximum budget for green financing.

From these figures, it is observed that in green financing, Standard Chartered, Eastern, and AB Bank are the top three banks which allocated more than Tk. 80,000 million for green financing. These three banks allocated Tk 41.67 billion, Tk 24.00 billion, and Tk 16.26 billion, respectively. It easily defines that Standard Chartered Bank's budget allocation is much higher than that of the other banks. On the other hand, Standard Chartered, Citi N.A., and EXIM Bank are the top three banks which have utilised the highest amount of funds for green financing. These three banks have utilised Tk 41.39 billion, Tk 34.48 billion, and Tk 27.60 billion, respectively, where Standard Chartered Bank's fund utilisation is much higher than that of the others.

## Conclusion

Being the guardian of the money market, Bangladesh Bank has taken some steps and formulated policy incorporating environmental issues into the operation of banking activities in Bangladesh. Now, commercial banks' in-house, office-based activities and business operations are being conducted following green banking regulations. The study attempts to discuss the issue of green financing as a part of green banking activities towards sustainable development of the country. It focuses on a theoretical framework as well as the present status of the implementation process, along with individual and collective contributions based on category of banks.

Green financing is the major part of the green banking operation where banks can directly incorporate their institutional borrowers (mostly corporate/industry-based clients) in protecting the environment through modified green lending policy and processes. Under green financing activities, eco-friendly business activities and less environmentally hazardous industries are given preference, and at the same time environmental infrastructures are encouraged and financed by banks. The study shows that all banks operating in Bangladesh together allocated Tk. 106360.91 million for green financing in their annual budget for 2012, which is about 96 percent of the total annual budget of Tk. 110512.18 million allocated for green banking. Banks utilised an increased amount of the total Tk. 270921.53 million for green finance. Among four categories of banks, PCBs have utilised the maximum (66%) funds for green financing. Rupali Bank, Bank of Small Industries and Commerce (BASIC), EXIM Bank, and Standard Chartered are the top four banks from SCBs, SDBs, PCBs, and FCBs categories that have utilised the maximum amount of funds for green financing under each category. Furthermore, among all banks of all

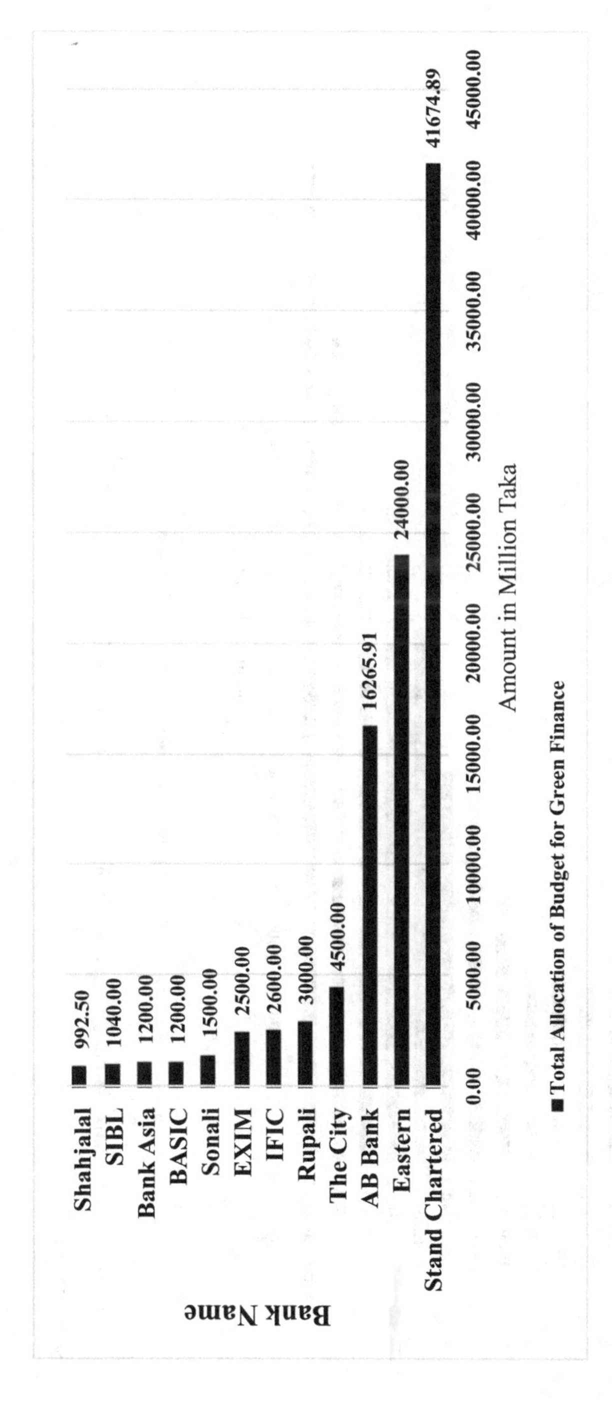


**FIGURE 9.7** Top 12 banks in allocation of budget for green finance during 2012

*Source:* Authors

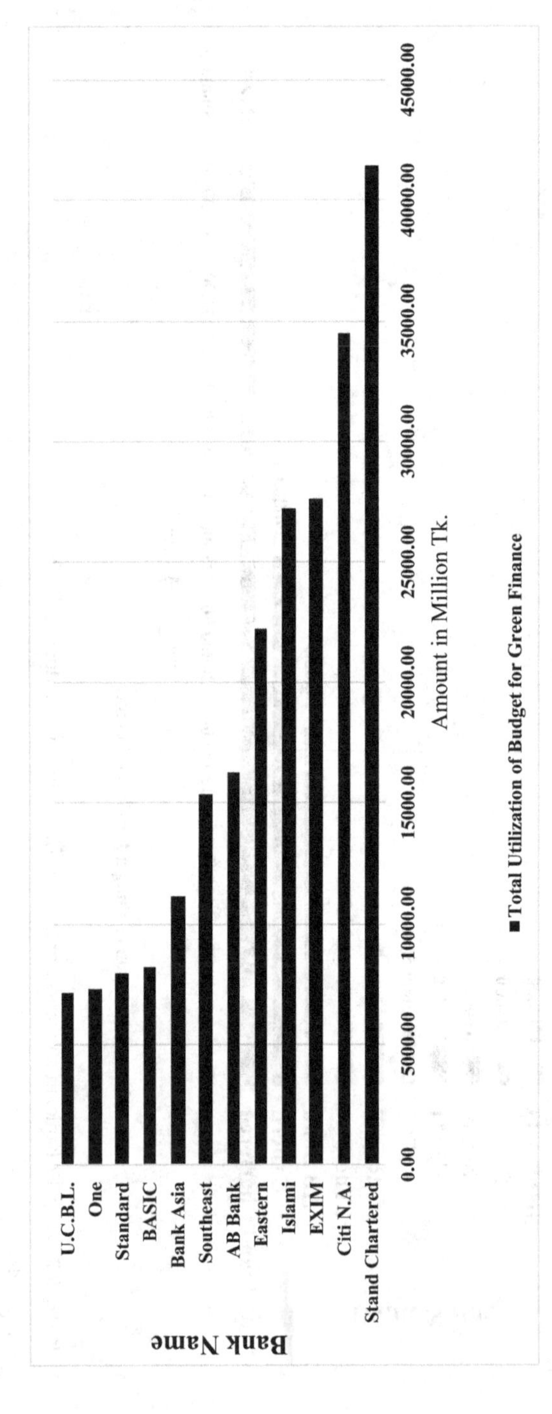


**FIGURE 9.8** Top 12 banks in budget utilisation for green finance in 2012

*Source:* Authors

categories, Standard Chartered Bank's allocation and utilisation of funds for green financing was the highest. In addition, the highest proportion of the funds has been disbursed for financing ETPs.

Bangladesh is one of the developing nations that is most vulnerable to climate change despite its small share of global greenhouse gas emissions. As the sustainability of economic and financial prosperity of the country is at stake, necessary steps should be taken to protect the country. In this regard, the government of Bangladesh is trying to formulate and implement different policies in order to handle the climate change risk which would have an adverse impact on the whole economic system of the country in the future. Green banking is such a proactive measure which requires financing by commercial banks addressing climate issues in business activities and through efficient use of resources in order to protect the environment. The economic development of the country is inevitably linked to its vulnerability to environmental degradation, so banks along with their stakeholders need to be aware and responsive to the green banking activities in order to protect the environment from degradation. Banks along with all the stakeholders should come forward and take a collective approach to make the world greener one and only then we can achieve our desirable sustainability of economic development. The Bangladesh Bank (www.bangladesh-bank.org) envisions the country as an advanced economy in 2050, with levels of human development and technological advancement sufficient to place her among leading Asian nations in terms of financial prosperity as well as social and environmental responsibility.

And in this sustainable economic development process, the banking sector is expected to play a leading role by promoting environmental and social responsibility while operating traditional banking activities.

The study is based on the ongoing implementation process of green banking which was initiated in recent time. Study on this issue using a longer time frame would produce better results. Moreover, due to the unavailability of data, the chapter fails to compare the findings of the study on Bangladesh with those of other developing nations.

The future research can consider additional factors which can be incorporated into green banking and green financing activities in Bangladesh and other developing countries. It can move further by using multivariate analysis to find out the impact of green financing activities on the economic development and sustainability of such progress.

## References


Agu, C. C. (1988). *Nigerian banking structure and performance: The banking system's contribution to economic development.* Onitsha: African-Fep Publishers.

Islam, M. S., & Das, P. C. (2013). Green banking practices in Bangladesh. *IOSR Journal of Business and Management, 8*(3), 39–44.

Nwankwo, F. O. (1994). *Rural savings mobilization.* Indigenous Savings and Credit Association in IMO State, Nigeria.

Omankhanlen, A. E. (2012). The role of banks in capital formation and economic growth: The case of Nigeria. *Economy Transdisciplinarity Cognition*, *15*(1), 103–111.

## *Websites*

www.bangladesh-bank.org/recentupcoming/news/oct022012newse_1.pdf. Retrieved April 17, 2019.

**PART 4**

# Sustainability of community and organisation interface

The chapters in this section focus on sustainability of community and organisation interface. Community and organisation interface is cited as critical for sustainable development. Both business and government often build collaborative relations with community organisations. These collaborative initiatives are aimed at improving the relations between them and community and implementing collaborative projects. These collaborative relations are central for co-creating shared value in a network of community and organisations. Such collaborative relations also help the business community and the general public to develop an awareness of the value of sustainable community development. These initiatives also provide opportunities to develop entrepreneurial and environmentally sound community-based projects and efficient use of resources.

# 10

# SOCIAL ENTERPRISES AND INCLUSIVE SOCIETIES

## A SAATH perspective

*Archana Singh, Gladwin Issac, and Shrinivas Sinha*

### Introduction

According to Chambers and Conway (1991):

> A livelihood comprises the capabilities, assets (including both material and social resources) and activities required for a means of living. A livelihood is sustainable when it can cope with and recover from stresses and shocks and maintain or enhance its capabilities and assets both now and in the future, while not undermining the natural resource base.
>
> *(p. 6)*

The idea of 'sustainable livelihood' was first introduced by the Brundtland Commission on Environment and Development in 1987 (Brundtland, 1987), advocating for the achievement of sustainable livelihoods as a broad goal for poverty eradication. According to Scoones (1998), five key indicators are important for assessing sustainable livelihoods: 1) poverty reduction, 2) wellbeing and capabilities, 3) livelihood adaptation, 4) vulnerability and resilience, and 5) natural resource base sustainability.

As a developing country, India places special priority on socio-economic development with the five-year plans (the Niti Aayog)[1] designed to accommodate social interests and promote sustainable development. However, public efforts have failed to reach its potential due to the sole reliance on traditional methods and lack of innovative strategies. Development is a complex process and cannot be 'programmed' through linear interventions (Easterly, 2001). The realisation that decades of experimentation and large-scale efforts of multilateral development organisations have not revealed any replicable designs that would enable sustainable economic development on a truly global scale reflects Brundtland's concerns at the lack of a 'blueprint for sustainability'.

Sustainable development is in need of innovative solutions and models for achieving sustainable livelihood. Anticipating the crises of the private and public sectors, Etzioni (1973) suggested that a new form of organisation would be needed to provide necessary innovations. That third alternative would combine the efficiency of the market and the welfare orientation of the state. It is the pattern-breaking change, the disruptive creation of new models and techniques, that is suitable to achieve sustainability.

In India, non-farm livelihood activities account for a significant portion of employment. Despite the potentially large employment numbers, gaps in capacity, infrastructure, access to finance, and technology diminish the potential of the sector. Within this context, it is pertinent to take note of the activities by social enterprises, in the livelihood sector, be it the promotion of such activities or directly aiding entities to address the gaps in the livelihood operations. Most economists and academics support the notion that entrepreneurship is becoming a crucial factor in the development and wellbeing of societies. Whether the entrepreneurial activities are practiced in factor-driven, efficiency-driven, or innovation-driven economies (Porter, Sachs, & McArthur, 2002), the ultimate results continue to exhibit: a) lower unemployment rates, b) increased tendency to adopt innovation, and c) accelerated structural changes in the economy. It offers new competition, and as such promotes improved productivity and healthy economic competitiveness (UNCTAD, 2004).

In this context, it is important to discuss all the related important concepts of 'social enterprise', 'social entrepreneur', and social entrepreneurship'. The concepts of social entrepreneurship and social entrepreneur are relatively new. Social entrepreneurship has emerged as a global phenomenon in the context of the increasing gap between social and environmental demand- and supply-side of resources (Nicholls, 2006). Social entrepreneurship is a process whereby an individual or a group of individuals identify a social problem as an opportunity, mobilise the resources, act innovatively to solve the identified problem, and create social value and bring about social change (Singh, 2016). These individuals are known as social entrepreneurs. Social entrepreneurs follow the entrepreneurial process to achieve their social mission. They drive the intentional social change process (Light, 2011), thus they are recognised as 'change agents' in the social sector globally. They solve systemic social problems, deliver sustainable social value, and bring about positive social change (Nicholls, 2006). They combine business techniques and private-sector approaches in order to develop solutions to social, cultural, or environmental problems, and do so in a variety of organisations (Marques, 2018). The organisations created by social entrepreneurs to achieve their social goals are known as 'social enterprises' (Singh, 2016). Like social entrepreneurship, social enterprise is also a contested concept (Teasdale, 2011). This conceptual confusion is because the concept of social enterprise is constructed by different actors promoting different discourses connected to different organisational forms. Social enterprise means different things to different people across time and context. The concept of social enterprise has been applied to worker co-operatives and employee-owned firms;

not-for-profit local regeneration initiatives; private-sector organisations that pay less than half their profits as dividends and self-identify as social enterprises; charities that earned income; and the privatisation of public services. In addition, these different organisational forms are linked to different practitioner discourses and explained by different academic theories (ibid.). For the purpose of this chapter, we have conceptualised 'social enterprise' as an organisation created by a social entrepreneur, who follows the entrepreneurial process to achieve his/her social mission irrespective of its organisational form.

Social entrepreneurs also contribute to achieve the goals of sustainable development. Seelos and Mair (2005) studied the cases of social entrepreneurship and found that social entrepreneurs who have created innovative organisations and service provision models succeed in creating social and economic development in a poor country context, and are contributing to sustainable development. They demonstrated how these social entrepreneurs cater to various levels of needs: the basic needs of individuals, the institutional needs of communities, and the needs of future generations. In this way, they contribute to sustainable development by meeting the needs of poor people (ibid.).

While the concept of social entrepreneurship and its reach in creating sustainable livelihoods is relatively new, initiatives that employ entrepreneurial capacities to formulate strategies for livelihoods are not. It involves acting as change agents for society, seizing opportunities which others have missed, and inventing new approaches and creating solutions to change society for the better. Social enterprises in the livelihood space can be broadly classified into two categories: first, entities that promote livelihoods; and second, entities that facilitate skill development. Livelihood promotion activities primarily include organising the informal non-farm/farm activities sector and facilitating market linkages. According to the Asian Development Bank's Report on the Social Enterprise Landscape in India (2012), skill development primarily includes enhancing the employability of unemployed youth through structured training courses. Social enterprises promoting livelihoods can be further classified based on their output, which could be a service or a product. Service-based enterprises provide impact in areas such as business process outsourcing (BPO), courier delivery, etc. Service-based entities train and employ rural youth for operations; eGramIT, Desi-crew, and Source Pilani are some of the entities that operate in this space. The product-based enterprises aggregate artisans (farmers for agriculture-related activities) and mainstream their operations by facilitating access to inputs, finance, and consumer markets.

It would be interesting to see how social enterprises active in this space promote non-farm sustainable livelihood activities to bridge the gap in India and create inclusive societies. The World Summit for Social Development (Copenhagen, 1995 as cited in DESA, 2009) defines an 'inclusive society' as a "society for all in which every individual, each with rights and responsibilities, has an active role to play" (p. 8). Such an inclusive society must be based on respect for all human rights and fundamental freedoms, cultural and religious diversity, social justice and the special needs of vulnerable and disadvantaged groups, democratic participation, and the rule of law. It is promoted by social policies that seek to reduce inequality and create flexible and tolerant societies that embrace all people. The detailed case studies of these social enterprises are crucial for their adaptation or replication at different places. It would also help practitioners interested in using a similar mechanism for creating sustainable livelihood for urban poor, and contributing towards creating inclusive societies. However, the absence of such case studies impedes the learning in this area.

To bridge this gap, the present study aims to examine one such innovative model of SAATH, a social enterprise based in Ahmedabad in the Indian state of Gujarat, which is engaged in creating 'inclusive societies' through promotion of sustainable livelihood among the urban poor. It explores how this model, engaged in promoting (non-farm) sustainable livelihood for the urban poor, is creating inclusive societies. In particular, it aims to understand their sustainability and scalability challenges, and also strategies adopted to face these challenges in order to create inclusive societies. Its specific focus on sustainability and scalability challenges and strategies used to deal with these for creating sustainable livelihood strategies for the poor would certainly benefit both academicians as well as practitioners.

This chapter is organised into five main sections. The introduction and research methodology is followed by a descriptive account of the creation of SAATH and its path towards inclusive development. The fourth section on the empirical findings and discussion are presented, further divided into five sub-sections. SAATH's successful need-based approach model is discussed in the first sub-section. The second covers the transition from a conventional charity-based organisation to a full-fledged social enterprise working with vulnerable communities. The third sub-section discusses its market-based approach towards providing solutions to the poor people. The fourth sub-section discusses the various hurdles faced by SAATH, since its inception to its sustainability level. The fifth sub-section deals with the scaling strategies along with expansion programmes adopted by SAATH. Finally, the fifth and the last section concludes the chapter.

## Research methodology

Recognising the contextual nature of social entrepreneurship and recognizing the objectives and exploratory nature of the research, case study research strategy has been used in the study. Case study covers both the phenomenon of interest and its context (Yin, 2003). SAATH, a social enterprise founded by Mr. Rajendra Joshi, engaged in promoting sustainable livelihood for the urban poor for creating inclusive societies, is selected purposely as a case. In the present study, the focus is on understanding the social enterprise's model, challenges, and its strategies, thus, 'social enterprise' is considered as the unit of analysis.

The data are collected from multiple sources, as it facilitates holistic understanding of the phenomenon being studied (Baxter & Jack, 2008). Primary data are collected from multiple stakeholders such as the founder, Mr. Rajendra Joshi; Associate Director, Mr. Neeraj Jani; three employees; and also from five beneficiaries through a series of in-depth interviews. All of the interviews were voice-recorded. In addition, information is also collected from secondary sources such as SAATH's website, brochure, and documents. To study the impact on the beneficiaries and operational model of SAATH, observation (participant as well as non-participant) is also used in the study. For knowing what people actually do, there is no substitute for watching them or studying their physical behaviour (Bernard, 2000). All of the data were collected during the period of March–August 2014.

Following Strauss and Corbin (1998) and Miles and Huberman (1984), all of the voice-recorded data were transcribed first and then coded to develop various sub-themes, themes, and categories for the final analysis.

## Case description of SAATH: the journey towards inclusiveness

SAATH is a non-governmental organisation (NGO), registered as a public charitable trust in Gujarat, India. The word SAATH denotes 'co-operation', which is the force that binds the organisation together. SAATH pioneered the Integrated Community Development Programme in 1989, an approach that seeks to turn slums into vibrant neighbourhoods. SAATH caters to the multiple needs of the poor at once by providing them with one-stop centres, through which slum residents have access to services such as health, education, employment, microfinance, and affordable housing. It invests in the human capacity of persons to manage SAATH programmes in their communities. SAATH Savings and Credit Cooperative Society Ltd. is another sister organisation of SAATH and was initiated to facilitate services for saving in a community-based model. As demand grew, SAATH came up with the Ekta and Sakhi credit co-operatives and established its operations in a more formal manner. In 2002, two co-operatives were formed to work in two different areas of Ahmedabad. In March 2010, all of the co-operatives came together to form SAATH Savings and Credit Co-operative Society Ltd. It was set up with a move towards institutionalisation of savings and affordable credit activities for increased reach and accessibility.

Since SAATH had a good experience working with vulnerable communities, it was decided to create a livelihood services provider that could address issues significant to the urban and rural poor.

In any urban setting of a developing country like India, the informal sector plays a vital role in generating economy. The sectors that account for a dominant share of informal employment are manufacturing and construction, and trade (wholesale and retail). They accounted for 76 percent and 72 percent respectively of all workers in the non-agriculture informal sector, in the rural and urban areas, as compared with 69 percent and 59 percent respectively of all workers in the non-agriculture sector (Census of India, 2011). Most of them live in slums and are included in mainstream society. They manage to earn only for their sustenance but still contribute a major share in the development of the country. There is an acute shortage of housing and health services. They have no access to credit and hence fail to receive the benefit of government services. SAATH focused on bridging this divide and fighting for the slum dwellers' right to get back what they give to society. SAATH's mission was to force society to give them a better deal.

Rajendra Joshi, the founder of SAATH, was inspired by the work of Julius Nyerere, whose practical approach to governance in his homeland of Tanzania promoted the idea of social inclusion. After his return to India, he was influenced by the works of Fr. Romero Eriviti, a Jesuit priest, who was involved in missionary activities and joined the slum education programme. Fr. Eriviti, who also was actively involved in working for the slum dwellers, told him "a sense of self-respect had to be built in its dwellers". After Fr. Romero's death, he along with his friends Robert David, who initially was with SAATH, and Pradeep Seth conceptualised SAATH. Mr. Joshi says:

> SAATH was born because for the majority of the houses that generate surplus incomes, the aspirations level are very high. And for the masses at the bottom of the pyramid, access to for quality services and goods was an issue which we endeavoured to provide at a minimal cost.

Its first strategic decision was to work with, not independently of, local government, and the second was to persuade private business to take its first steps towards corporate citizenship.

## Findings and discussion

### *The SAATH model—a need-based model*

In the process of establishing itself as a social enterprise, SAATH made sure that it adopted a need-based approach focussing on people's needs and subsequently creating an action plan to resolve those issues. Such an approach was crucial to the organisation's sustainability as well as in defining its purpose. The understanding of people's need, which is heterogeneous in nature, is essential for achieving the goals of inclusive development. As Mr. Neeraj Jani, the Executive Director of SAATH, recollects:

> From the very beginning, it was clear that we will adopt a need based approach since people's needs are diverse and not homogenous.

Mulgan, Tucker, Ali, and Sanders (2007) also mentioned that any successful organisation needs to be simultaneously focused on existing activities, emerging ones, and more radical possibilities that could be the mainstream activities of the future. In order to ensure the needs are met, SAATH adopted a target group mapping strategy to identify vulnerable communities both at the macro and the micro level and identifies their needs. The mapping programme brought three different segments of the society. These people were in need of the basic services. The first segment comprised people occupying the Bottom of the Pyramid (BOP), the poorest of the poor who barely manage to have two square meals a day and are the most vulnerable. The ethos of a social enterprise is most challenged since the clients cannot afford to pay for the services, and they look towards charity-based organisations. The next segment includes people who are poor in availing the services but are able to sustain their families with the wages they earn. These people are in a position to pay for the services given to them like vocational training and education. This segment forms the majority of the target group who can afford to avail services by any social enterprise. The third includes people who are well off but still continue to live in slums, who have a large share of the economy contributed by the slum dwellers. This segment focusses on raising the standard of living, and various schemes like housing loans would be of immense help to them. After identifying the needs of the services in the different segments of the society, SAATH formulated strategies to address those issues.

For example, in its endeavour to uplift the masses, it noticed that children in the villages in the age group of 3–6 years old do not go to school due to lack of a schooling facility in their area like Anganwadis,[2] or nursery school, and decided to educate slum children in the Juhapura area in Ahmedabad. To further its cause, it launched a programme named Balghar (educational centres for the children) for the same. It also focuses on allied services such as health and livelihood services in order to empower individuals to upgrade their standards of living. Housing is not the only solution to the population pressures on cities. People also need health care, education, financial services, jobs, infrastructure, and other services. A city should be made up of communities that offer these services in an integrated way. SAATH's urban programme operates with this very principle in mind, connecting slum communities to services and resources through one-stop service centres. As Mr. Jani recounts:

> If you are working with people to improve their health conditions but if you don't empower them for better livelihood, they will fall sick again and this vicious cycle will continue.

Based on their observation of 11 different social enterprises from around the world, Thompson and Doherty (2006) also mention: "The need to create and add value for customers and clients is always apparent, as is the need to find effective routes to market" (p. 361).

In order to encourage all-inclusive participation, there must be universal access to public resources and amenities such as community centres, recreational facilities, public libraries, resource centres with internet facilities, well-maintained public schools, clinics, water supplies, and sanitation. At the core of SAATH's functioning lies full participation in all aspects of life, which is supported by their programmes on overall development of the society.

## *SAATH Livelihoods—market-based approach: the transition from welfare-based entity to a social business entity*

SAATH was initiated as a welfare-based entity, but in due course of time, with the inception of the SAATH Livelihoods scheme, has evolved into a social enterprise though the identification of vulnerable communities and designing programmes for their betterment. A need was felt to create a financially sustainable system that would be a legal entity in order to reach a large-scale public, and thus SAATH Livelihoods came into the picture. Mr. Jani, the Associate Director of SAATH, says:

> At SAATH, we always were open to innovative solutions to societal problems so social entrepreneurship was always in our DNA.

SAATH Livelihoods grew as a not-for-profit company registered under Section 25 of the Companies Act 1956[3] on 12 February 2007. It contributes further to its vision of inclusive development. 'Inclusive development' is a pro-poor approach that equally values and incorporates the contributions of all stakeholders, including marginalised groups, in addressing development issues (Oxfam, n.d.).

SAATH identified the growing gap between communities and their accessibility to resources, available with the government in form of various schemes for training individuals. Mr. Jani says:

> We need to bridge the gap, the knowledge gap which hinders their ability to access these resources.

Thus, SAATH reaches out to those people who cannot avail themselves of government policies or subsidies. They identify communities where governmental policies have failed to reach hands, thus bridging the gap between the needy and the giver.

In order to achieve its goal of creating an inclusive society, SAATH focused on improving the quality of life of the marginalised people, which includes basic amenities like health, education, and sanitation. Its mission is to provide these services to the clients at an affordable cost. The BoP approach has contributed to shifting the prevailing view about poverty to see the poor as customers and not only as recipients of charity (Seelos & Mair, 2007). Mr. Joshi, the founder of SAATH, says:

> Our approach in treating people as customers/clients and not as beneficiaries has made all the difference.

For this, it relied more on income-generating activities rather than charity-based funding to sustain these programmes. In fact, social enterprises has been analysed as one of the market-based strategies for poverty alleviation (Cooney & Shanks, 2010). The need for innovative ways of addressing social problems rather than the traditional efforts such as development aid, donations, and charity, in the context of developing countries, has already been emphasised (Azmat, 2013).

In addition, market-based strategies of social enterprises can be used as a vehicle. While the government both at the centre as well as the state looked down upon slum dwellers, regarding them as *liabilities*, SAATH saw them as *assets* and made these basic services available to them at a nominal cost. SAATH's target group mapping programme helped SAATH in identifying not only needs of the different segments of the society, but also the affordability of their client base. It further helped SAATH to plan and develop their market-based solution to satisfy unmet needs of their customers. It is only through evaluating activities and operations based on profitability and mission impact that non-profits can develop strategic plans to manage short-term financial challenges while maintaining long-term mission goals (Sontag-Padilla, Staplefoote, & Morganti, 2011). While it is true that the charity-based model of non-profit organisations can also create social impact, social enterprise models (which can generate profit for the social purpose) have a stronger sustainable future with increased social impact, especially due to funding crunches faced by the non-profits.

In its seven years of existence, SAATH has strived to improve the quality of life of vulnerable urban and rural populations by actively encouraging livelihood options for them. Ravina, one of the beneficiaries, lives in Baroda with a family of four members. Before joining Umeed, the skill development programme run by SAATH, she was forced to drop out from school due to poor economic conditions. She learnt basic computer, spoken English, and life skills. Presently, she works for a company as a counsellor and is earning her livelihood. She says:

> Umeed did come into my life as a ray of hope, it has change my life completely. Earlier I was an introvert but the skill development training has increased my self-confidence. I have got a good job and with monthly salary of 6000 rupees I can financially support my family.

This discussion shows that due to SAATH's ability to assess the need, and also readiness to adopt innovative strategies such as a market-based approach, SAATH Livelihoods has been improving the quality of life of the people in a sustainable manner.

### Cross-sector partnerships and multi-stakeholder approach rooted in market-based solutions

SAATH's model of cross-sector partnerships rooted in market-based solutions has been successful in providing slum dwellers with clean and safe environments, electricity, access to credit, and vocational training. Scaling social impact is still one of the toughest challenges enterprises face in the longer run for sustainability. Most often the impact generated by any enterprise is too low in relation to the magnitude of problems they seek to address. The present situation calls for a collective action from all private, public, and social sectors for solutions with higher trajectories for growth and scale of impact. SAATH has gained the commitment of public, private, and voluntary organisations and carved a niche for itself in the social sector.

The partnerships with corporations constitute a well-suited locus to examine the normative influences faced and reinforced by social enterprises. Corporations are increasingly communicating about their social responsibility and tend to include the pursuit of social purposes in their declared missions. A social entrepreneur alliance could harness the power of collaborative creation of shared value to gain speed, scale, and sustainability while delivering on its primary purpose and promise of social impact (Barnabas, Ravikumar, & Narasimhan, 2020). This was seen in the form of ties with the electric utility and the community by, again, working as a broker in the Ahmedabad Slum Electrification Project. The slum electrification project was a result of a multi-stakeholder collaboration between Ahmedabad Municipal Corporation (AMC), which is responsible for the civic infrastructure and administration of the city of Ahmedabad, the United States Agency for International Development (USAID), and the Ahmedabad Electricity Company Ltd. (AEC). The AEC, sole distributor of electricity to the consumers in the city of Ahmedabad, was the lead project coordinator and supplier of electricity under this project. In addition, SAATH and another non-profit organisation, Gujarat Mahila Housing SEWA Trust (MHT), rendered strong support to the project by not only mobilizing the community, but also in helping the utility (i.e. the AEC) to implement the project effectively. The cost of providing electricity connections was brought down, slum inhabitants illustrated their ability to pay, and 80 percent of slums have now been electrified and electric company revenue increased substantially with the new customers. In pursuance of this objective, they also pressurised the government to streamline their programmes and make them accessible to the needy.

In addition, SAATH played a crucial role in convincing slum dwellers to become project stakeholders, rather than beneficiaries. It is rightly said that to achieve social integration, not only some but all members of society with different backgrounds must have a say and a stake in 'their shared society' (DESA, 2009). For example, Nirman, started in 2011, aims at improving the skills, working efficiency, and proficiency, enabling skills enhancement and perfection for the unskilled or skilled labourers in the informal sector. After completion of the requisite training, these individuals are placed as carpenters, plumbers, masons, and electricians. Mavijbhai, who attended the carpentry course conducted by Nirman, says:

> I learned in detail about the concepts of measurements, machine use, furniture production and the importance of savings. The programme gave me confidence to start my own workshop.

Similarly, other projects like Udaan (Employability Training Programme targeted for youth in the age group of 18–35 years from economically weaker sections and enables them to gain access to opportunities for sustainable livelihoods), R-Weaves (encouraging the two dyeing arts of Patola and Tangalia by supporting the artisans of the village of the Surendranagar district of the state of Gujarat; it provides them small capital for the procurement of raw materials, skill trainings to increase their productivity and diversify their product range, networking, and marketing for their products), and Urban Resource Centres (an information hub, which educates slum people about how to access various government services and other legal certificates or documents) also reflects the same philosophy of SAATH. In all of thee projects, the existence of cross-sector partnerships and multi-stakeholder participation rooted in its market-based solution is clearly evident.

## *SAATH'S sustainability model: withstanding the test of time*

To reach out to vulnerable communities, one requires resources at his/her disposal. The heavy reliance on resources from external agencies forces the organisation to prioritise and be selective, thus inhibiting inclusivity. Thus, to achieve the objective of an inclusive society, SAATH has partnered with the local government as well as the private players. However, it is necessary to maintain a balance among multiple partners to avoid conflicts. Establishing trust among the client base is equally important. Mr. Joshi says:

> Any social enterprise will only succeed if it has credibility based on relationship.

This can be established through networking and garnering the support of the key players in the different sectors, be it public or private.

Identification of social needs is most important to start with, but any social enterprise cannot wholly rely on governmental schemes and try to make it accessible to the masses. The reason, Mr. Joshi says, is because:

> There is no stability in terms of the design in schemes and the shift of power makes it unreliable.

In addition, social entrepreneurship has not been recognised as a legitimate field in India. Unclear rules and regulations hamper social entrepreneurs. Thus, social entrepreneurs have to generate their own strategies to combat social issues.

While designing and implementing solutions, flexibility is very important. This was realised with the slowdown associated with Balghar. After a few months of classes, parents stopped sending their wards to schools, because it was free of cost. Learning from his own experiences, Mr. Joshi says:

> Anything free is taken for granted.

SAATH resumed the programme by charging a nominal fee of Rs. 100. In this way every individual—be it the student or the parent or the service provider—becomes accountable. This paves the way for greater responsibility on parents as well as students, and makes the system more accountable and efficient. Further, it pushes the entity to develop a sustainable model, which makes a long-term impact. In the context of countries with emerging economies in Central and Eastern Europe also,

Cooney and Shanks (2010) mentioned that social enterprise must overcome cultural barriers to paying fees for services and the expectation that certain categories of disabled individuals are free from work. Social enterprises must orient the public to this kind of organisation (ibid.).

From a human resources perspective, the ability to attract top talent was always a major challenge for SAATH. These days, talented individuals look for something more than only impressive salaries and perks. Some want to start up their own enterprise, but SAATH takes this in a positive way. If any employee wishes to start up and work for impacting lives, then SAATH takes pride in it.

Lack of seed capital is an important aspect for the social enterprises. Generally, the social entrepreneurs run their business with their own funds or by raising funds from the local money lenders at a high rate of interest, which becomes a financial burden on them. The reason behind this approach is the bank's avoidance to providing loan facilities for social entrepreneurs given the various social complications attached to them. A hostile reaction from financial institutions and governments is another concern which forces social entrepreneurs to take what can be a more difficult path of approaching venture capitalist and philanthropic organisations. When SAATH was started, seed capital came in the form of grants and donations from international agencies and organisations, but now due to various geopolitical reasons, donors would rather invest in third world countries. However, with the inclusion of the provisions of corporate social responsibility, acquiring resources has become easy.

Finally, social enterprises in India often face policy and regulatory challenges. There are no specific legal frameworks for social enterprises. Like India, many other developing countries face problems of public authority, regulation, and oversight.

## *Scaling strategies: the road ahead*

Scaling is defined in terms of increasing impact of an approach to better match the magnitude of the social need or problem it seeks to address. Prior analyses of scaling up have identified three major patterns for widening the impacts of successful social entrepreneurship initiatives: 1) expanding coverage to provide services and benefits to more people, 2) expanding functions and services to provide broader impacts to primary stakeholders, and 3) activities that change the behaviour of other actors with wide impacts and so indirectly scaling up impacts (Uvin, 1995; Uvin, Jain, & Brown, 2000). Before scaling their approaches, social enterprises should have identified a precise definition of their mission and their core values as well as developed an established business model (Dees, Anderson, & Wei-Skillern, 2004). Furthermore, there must be an objective evidence of success, often referred to as "proof of concept", i.e. to emphasise the relevance of scaling to stakeholders and to obtain acceptance when targeting a new area (Roob & Bradach, 2009). If scaling takes place too early or too quickly and takes up too many resources of a social enterprise, there is a danger that advancing the enterprise's approach is sacrificed to maximise scale. Thus, it might be better to scale the approach to a limited extent in the first place. Dissemination, affiliation, branching, and franchising are the significant scaling strategies adopted by the social enterprises.

SAATH's scaling approach has been more of dissemination than any other type. At present, SAATH is working in three states with a move to expand to the state of Chattisgarh. With more than 25 years of experience of working with vulnerable communities, it has led to dissemination of information to other organisations who wish to adapt the SAATH model. Early-stage organisations require financial support as well as non-financial services and access to financial services. At the core of this strategy is the Aashray Incubation Centre launched for setting up of social enterprises and scaling up of innovative ventures and grassroots technologies. The Entrepreneurship Development Institute of India has agreed to be the nodal management agency with an aim to create an 'enabling and inclusive' ecosystem that can provide capacity building, handholding, and incubation support to emerging social entrepreneurs who are working towards creating appropriate, sustainable, and scalable social enterprises that have significant social impact. Social ventures are considered vehicles for mitigating social problems and market failures. The consortium will focus on building a pipeline of innovative business ideas for entrepreneurs.

The five-stage model for achieving the aim and objective of Aashray is identified. The first stage includes preparatory work in the form of incorporating the enterprise as a company through Section 25 of the Companies Act, which also includes establishing the infrastructure. The next stage involves identifying enterprises or entrepreneurs through crowdsourcing. The third stage involves incubation of ideas, which involves mentoring and peer learning and conduction of pilot tests wherever deemed necessary, followed by facilitating access to seed and venture funding. The final stage deals with the execution of the project and attracting promoters. Scaling will take place, when external investors are interested in investing capital to accelerate expansion/scaling up of an enterprise. With this concept, SAATH aims to help entrepreneurs to emulate the co-operative, collective ethos and many cross-sector partnerships, which it has built over these years. Mr. Joshi says:

> This is the real key to success especially insofar as reciprocity of knowledge is concerned.

The outcomes of the efforts are nonetheless successful in creating inclusive and more sustainable communities. McWade (2012) also argued that social investors have a crucial role to play by providing a greater inflow of capital into nascent and growing social enterprises in developing countries.

## Conclusion

The purpose of this research was to explore the innovative model of SAATH, a social enterprise founded by Mr. Rajendra Joshi, engaged in promoting sustainable livelihood among the urban poor for creating inclusive societies in the Gujarat state of India, and to find out the various challenges faced by the social enterprise for scalability and sustainability. The study shows that organisations like SAATH that initially worked as charity-based organisations have moved to a more rigid and complex structure of an enterprise in the social sector for attaining financial and structural stability. The mandate to sustain themselves in the social sector as well as maximizing the impact on vulnerable communities is the force behind the social enterprise ecosystem. Through their collective approach towards inclusive development, social enterprises like SAATH have contributed immensely in uplifting the socio-economic conditions of the urban poor. However, being a young entity, still in the process of establishing itself in the social sector, there is room for innovation and the extensive application of multidisciplinary approaches and entrepreneurial energy in the social sector. Gaining trust as an entity is imperative for an all-round impact, as well as acquiring seed capital for starting up, which can be established by creating partnerships with corporations to connect social enterprises with skilled labour. Corporate partners could offer employees to serve as consultants for a social enterprise for a period of time. Investors could consider extending grants alongside a financial investment or collaborating with a foundation the way SAATH did. It would require high levels of donor engagement and non-financial support for high-risk, high-impact potential social enterprises. Reforming sector-specific policies that restrict private-sector participation can be a step in the right direction. Also, more and more public-private partnerships can further alleviate these issues. Public-private partnerships for infrastructure development are key to building a business environment that can help social enterprises prosper. Thus, with reforms in the social sector, the overall operational effectiveness associated with an enterprise can be increased, which further translates into better sustainable livelihood services for the urban and rural poor. It is rightly said, "Social entrepreneurs, through their innovative approach have the potential to play a positive role in reducing poverty and sustainable development, even in the difficult contextual constraints of developing countries" (Azmat, 2013, p. 302).

## Notes

1 Niti Aayog, constituted in 2015, replaces the Planning Commission and is the premier policy think tank of the Government of India, providing both directional and policy inputs.
2 Anganwadi Centre is a part of the Indian public health care system, which provides basic health care in the villages of India. It also includes preschool activities.
3 The not-for-profit company registered under 'section 25' of the Companies Act 1956, is now known as a 'section 8 company' under the revised Companies Act, 2013.

## References

Asian Development Bank. (2012). *India social enterprise landscape report*. Maladuyong City, Manila.

Azmat, F. (2013). Sustainable development in developing countries: The role of social entrepreneurs. *International Journal of Public Administration*, *36*, 293–304.

Barnabas, N., Ravikumar, M.V., & Narasimhan, R. (2020). Social entrepreneur alliance: Collaborating to co-create shared value. In S. Majumdar & E. Reji (Eds.), *Methodological issues in social entrepreneurship knowledge and practice*. Springer Proceedings in Business and Economics. Singapore: Springer. https://doi.org/10.1007/978-981-13-9769-1_9

Baxter, P., & Jack, S. (2008). Qualitative case study methodology: Study design and implementation for novice researchers. *The Qualitative Report, 13*(4), 544–559.

Bernard, H. R. (2000). *Social research methods: Qualitative and quantitative approaches*. New Delhi: Sage Publications.

Brundtland, GH and World Commission on Environment and Development. (1987). *Our common future: Report of the World Commission on Environment and Development*. Oxford University. Retrieved November 8, 2016 from www.un-documents.net/our-common-future.pdf.

Census of India. (2011).

Chambers, R., & Conway, G. R. (1991). *Sustainable rural livelihoods: Practical concepts for the 21st century*. Discussion Paper 296. Brighton, UK: Institute of Development Studies. Retrieved November 8, 2016 from https://opendocs.ids.ac.uk/opendocs/bitstream/handle/123456789/775/Dp296.pdf?sequence=1&isAllowed=y.

Cooney, K., & Shanks, T. R. W. (2010). New approaches to old problems: Market-based strategies for poverty alleviation. *Social Service Review, 84*(1), 29–55.

Dees, J. G., Anderson, B. B., & Wei-Skillern, J. (2004). Scaling social impact: Strategies for spreading social innovations. *Stanford Social Innovation Review, 1*(4), 24–32.

DESA. (2009). *Creating an inclusive society: Practical strategies to promote social integration*. Retrieved December 31, 2015 from www.un.org/esa/socdev/egms/docs/2009/Ghana/inclusive-society.pdf

Easterly, W. (2001). *The effect of International Monetary Fund and World Bank programs on poverty*. Policy Research Working Paper Series, The World Bank 2517, The World Bank.

Etzioni, A. (1973). The third sector and domestic missions. *Public Administration Review, 33*(4), 341–323.

Light, P. C. (2011). *Driving social change: How to solve the world's toughest problems*. Hoboken, NJ: John Wiley & Sons, Inc.

Marques, J. (2018). Social entrepreneurship: Where sustainable leading meets sustainable living. In S. Dhiman & J. Marques (Eds.), *Handbook of engaged sustainability* (pp. 1–22). Cham: Springer.

McWade, W. (2012). The role for social enterprises and social investors in the development struggle. *Journal of Social Entrepreneurship, 3*(1), 96–112.

Miles, M. B., & Huberman, A. M. (1984). *Qualitative data analysis: A sourcebook of new methods*. New Delhi: SAGE Publications.

Mulgan, G., Tucker, S., Ali, R., & Sanders, B. (2007). *Social innovation: What it is, why it matters and how it can be accelerated*. Skoll Centre for Social Entrepreneurship.

Nicholls, A. (2006). Introduction. In A. Nicholls (Ed.), *Social entrepreneurship: New models of* sustainable change (pp. 1–35). New York: Oxford University Press.

Oxfam. (n.d.). *Inclusive development: Ensuring benefits for all*. Retrieved November 8, 2016 from www.oxfam.org/sites/www.oxfam.org/files/inclusive_development.pdf

Porter, M. E., Sachs, J. D., & McArthur, J.W. (2002). *Executive summary: Competitiveness and stages of economic development*. Retrieved November 8, 2016 from http://earthinstitute.columbia.edu/sitefiles/file/Sachs%20Writing/2002/WorldEconomicForum_2001-2002_Global CompetitivenessReport2001-2002_ExecutiveSummary.pdf

Roob, N., & Bradach, J. (2009). *Scaling what works: Implications for philanthropists, policymakers, and nonprofit leaders*. The Bridgespan Group.

Scoones, I. (1998). *Sustainable rural livelihoods: A framework for analysis*. IDS Working Paper 72. Institute of Development Studies (IDS), Brighton, UK.

Seelos, C., & Mair, J. (2005). *Sustainable development: How social entrepreneurs make it happen*. Working Paper No. 611, IESE Business School, University of Navarra. Retrieved March 31, 2017 from https://papers.ssrn.com/sol3/papers.cfm?abstract_id=876404

Seelos, C., & Mair, J. (2007). Profitable business models and market creation in the context of deep poverty: A strategic view. *Academy of Management Perspectives, 21*(4), 49–63.

Singh, A. (2016). *The process of social value creation: A multiple-case study on social entrepreneurship in India*. New Delhi: Springer.

Sontag-Padilla, M. L., Staplefoote, L., & Morganti, K. G. (2011). *Financial sustainability for nonprofit organizations: A review of the literature*. The Rand Corporation.

Strauss, A., & Corbin, J. (1998). *Basics of qualitative research: Techniques and procedures for developing grounded theory* (2nd ed.). London: SAGE Publications.

Teasdale, S. (2011). What's in a name? Making sense of social enterprise discourses. *Public Policy and Administration, 27*(2), 99–119. https://doi.org/10.1177/0952076711401466

Thompson, J., & Doherty, B. (2006). The diverse world of social enterprise: A collection of social enterprise stories. *International Journal of Social Economics, 33*(5 & 6), 361–375. https://doi.org/10.1108/03068290610660643

United Nations Conference on Trade and Development—UNCTAD. (2004). *World investment report 2004: The shift towards services*. Geneva and New York: United Nations. Retrieved November 8, 2016 from http://unctad.org/en/Docs/wir2004ch4_en.pdf.

Uvin, P. (1995). Scaling up the grass roots and scaling down the summit: The relations between Third World nongovernmental organisations and the United Nations. *Third World Quarterly, 16*(3), 495–512.

Uvin, P., Jain, P. S., & Brown, L. D. (2000). Think large and act small: Toward a new paradigm for NGO scaling up. *World Development, 28*(8), 1409–1419.

World Summit for Social Development, and United Nations. (1995). *World summit for social development: The Copenhagen declaration and programme of action*. New York: United Nations.

Yin, R. (2003). *Case study research: Design and methods* (3rd ed.). Thousand Oaks, CA: SAGE Publications.

# 11

# IS SERIAL SOCIAL ENTREPRENEURSHIP LEADING TOWARDS SUSTAINABLE DEVELOPMENT?

## A case of Annapurna Pariwar

*Samapti Guha, Medha Purao Samant, and Edakkandi Meethal Reji*

### Introduction

Sustainable development is gaining the imagination of world leaders both in politics and business (United Nations, 2015). Viewed from various disciplines including economic, environmental, and ecological, there are diverse perspectives on what constitutes sustainable development. Economists prefer to refer to sustainability as distributional equity, and there are contrasting views on whether this distributional equity is within the current generation or between the future generations (Solow, 1991). From an economist's perspective, development is viewed as progress in economic gains and very little emphasis is on environmental and ecological concerns. The relations between environment and economic development has been the subject matter of debate over the past decades, and there are views that development models with a greater emphasis on economic growth alone causes irreparable damages to the environment and ecology (Munda, 1997; Haque, 2000). They argue that the global warming and unprecedented natural disasters are direct consequences of the development process. This realisation pushes for a development model with greater emphasis on environmental and ecological concerns. Although this model of sustainable development brings out the environment-development linkages, it ignores other issues such as inequity, access to resources, and justice, etc. This leads to the need for a better conceptualisation of sustainability and sustainable development. The most widely discussed definition of sustainable development is "development which meets the needs of current generations without compromising the ability of future generations to meet their own needs" (WCED, 1987). Accepting this view, sustainable development, more often sustainability, is based on the principle of both inter-generational equity and intra-generational equity (Solow, 1991).

Sustainable development is foremost in the agenda of the United Nations since the 1970s. The concept received international attention with the Earth Summit at Rio in 1992, and thereafter pushing action-oriented plans such as Agenda-21, the Kyoto Protocol, the United Nations Framework Conventions for Climate Change Negotiations, and more recently the Sustainable Development Goals for bringing sustainability into practice (United Nations, 2015). We realise that amidst the rapid economic progress over the last several decades, humanity is confronted with a variety of development challenges, most of them human induced. These include widening inequality, extreme poverty and hunger, conflicts and violence, global warming, outbreak of epidemics, and unprecedented natural disasters. Global warming has become a reality with unprecedented consequences, such as natural calamities like drought, floods, and cyclones. As these challenges are global, not a single country alone can address any one or all of these challenges. It requires a local-global partnership and co-ordinated efforts. Realizing this need, the United Nations declared the year 2015 as the year of sustainable development and the member countries agreed upon sustainable development goals. Following this, the member countries are bound to critically review their strategies, policies, and commit affirmative action for 'sustainability' as an integral and essential foundation of survival and growth. The United Nations Declaration on Sustainable Development gives better clarity of thought on the issue, stating that:

> sustainable development is not a destination, but a dynamic process of adaptation, learning and action. It is about recognizing, understanding and acting on interconnections—above all those between the economy, society and the natural environment.
>
> *(United Nations, 2012; www.un.org/gsp/)*

Globally, around 1.2 billion people are suffering from extreme poverty and hunger; millions of people are affected by war, conflicts, and violence. Hence, sustainable development is also fighting against extreme poverty and hunger; ending terrorism, violence, and conflicts; and contending with epidemics and global warming. It is also about reducing inequality and bringing equity. There is increasing recognition that many of the problems facing humanity today can be addressed with simple solutions. For example, the experience of Grameen Bank has showed that the poor can access a range of financial services in a cost-effective manner (Yunus, 2009). A simple technology like a treadle pump has lifted almost 2 million marginal and small farmers out of poverty (Polak, 2008). It is worth noting that with pro-poor innovation and entrepreneurship, the entrepreneurs identify and pursue opportunities, mobilise the resources, and create value for themselves and society (Sarasvathy, 2001; Shane, 2000, 2004). This chapter examines the role of serial social entrepreneurship in creating sustainable social ventures and its contribution to sustainable development.

## Conceptualizing social entrepreneurship and serial entrepreneurship

### *Social entrepreneurship*

It is interesting to see the emergence of social entrepreneurship as a field of practice as well as academic discipline (Bornstein, 2004; Nicholls, 2006, 2010; Choi & Majumdar, 2014; Douglas & Prentice, 2019). Social entrepreneurship is viewed as innovative, social value-creating activity by integrating various elements such as the people, the context, the opportunity, capital, and social value proposition (Austin, Stevenson, & Wei-Skillern, 2006). In the absence of a unifying definition, social entrepreneurship is viewed as a cluster of concepts consisting social entrepreneur, social innovation, and social value creation (Choi & Majumdar, 2014). Accepting this view, social value creation is central to social entrepreneurship. The people's skills, attitudes, knowledge, contacts, goals, and values provide the resource mix that contributes to social value creation (Austin et al., 2006). Gartner (1985) integrates four major perspectives in entrepreneurship to provide a useful framework for new venture creation. These include: 1) characteristics of individuals that start the venture, 2) the organisation that they create, 3) the environment that surrounds the venture, and 4) the process by which the new venture is created (p. 698).

Over the past decades, social entrepreneurship has created a wave of optimism among the policymakers, practitioners, pro-poor advocates, and sustainability professionals to address many of the complex nature of social problems. It presents a new model of systemic social change (Bornstein, 2004; Nicholls, 2006), the solution to state failures in welfare provision (Aiken, 2006; Bovaird, 2006; LeGrand, 2003), a new market opportunity for business (Prahalad, 2005), a model of political transformation and empowerment (Alvord, Brown, & Letts, 2004), and a framework for emancipatory work (Chandra, 2017). An important contribution of the field is that social entrepreneurship enables us to view the world from multiple perspectives. Therefore, promoting a new generation of social entrepreneurs, development practitioners, and managers who can respond to the diverse development challenges in the age of sustainable development is very important.

### *Serial entrepreneurship*

Serial entrepreneurship is an emerging field of practice and research (Nahata, 2019; Shantana, Hoover, & Vengadasubbu, 2017; Parker, 2013, 2014). Serial entrepreneurs are entrepreneurs who exit their prior business and start a new venture or number of ventures (Westhead, Ucbasaran, Wright, & Binks, 2005; Parker, 2013). In recent years, there is considerable interest in understanding the differences in characteristics between novice and serial entrepreneurs (Westhead, Ucbasaran, & Wright, 2003, 2005; Parker, 2013, 2014). A fundamental difference between serial and novice entrepreneurship is that in serial entrepreneurship, the entrepreneurs recognise and exploit multiple businesses in sequence and contribute to substantial value creation (Parker, 2014). Recent studies have recognised serial entrepreneurship's potential for fostering wealth creation (Scott & Rosa, 1996; Westhead et al., 2005), job generation (Westhead et al., 2005), and economic performance (Westhead et al., 2003, 2005; Colombo & Grilli, 2005).

One of the major foci of studies in serial entrepreneurship is to understand the behaviours of entrepreneurs in their occupational choice and prior entrepreneurial and managerial experience (Westhead et al., 2005; Parker, 2014). Studies using the occupational choice model (Parker, 2014) show that an individual's formal education, managerial, and entrepreneurial experience have a significant effect on their entrepreneurial behaviour. These studies also contribute to our understanding on other aspects of an individual's motivation to serial entrepreneurship, including a desire for independence, autonomy, and wealth creation (Scott & Rosa, 1996; Westhead et al., 2005). Studies also highlight distinct features with regard to key entrepreneurial skills: opportunity recognition and exploitation. The study by Ucbasaran, Wright, and Westhead (2008) highlights the role of human capital in the development of serial entrepreneurship. It is argued that, as a result of their prior experience, serial entrepreneurs have the advantages of better managerial and technical skills, networks of contacts, and access to specific information, making them better in the pursuit of identification and venture creation (Bosma, Van Praag, Thurik, & De Wit, 2004; Ucbasaran et al., 2008). It is also argued that, if individuals with higher entrepreneurial human capital decide to leave their firms, they are likely to continue in the same occupation, becoming serial entrepreneurs (Amaral, Baptista, & Lima, 2011). The entrepreneurial-specific human capital acts as critical resources by influencing how individuals seek information, create, or identify entrepreneurial opportunities (Shane, 2000, 2004)). Hence, it is argued that serial entrepreneurs endowed with entrepreneurial human capital feel better prepared to identify and pursue opportunities (Westhead et al., 2005; Stam, Audretsch, & Meijaard, 2008). Recent research on the entry mode in serial entrepreneurship shows that founding experience as a significant form of entrepreneurial-specific human capital that has a positive impact on entrepreneurial re-entry both through start-up or acquisition of a subsequent firm (Amaral et al., 2011).

The literature on serial entrepreneurship emphasises the emergence of new entrepreneurial opportunities, arguing that some people are better able than others to identify and exploit these opportunities (Shane, 2000, 2004). But the literature lacks a theory of opportunity recognition and exploitation, which explains occupational choices between novice and serial entrepreneurship. There are only a few studies exploring which people remain serial entrepreneurs and which remain novice entrepreneurs (Holmes & Schmitz, 1990; Carter & Ram, 2003). Researchers agree that as human capital associates business experience with economic returns in entrepreneurship (Shane, 2000, 2004), serial entrepreneurs can perform better since they learn from their past venturing experience (Parker, 2014).

## Context of the study

This study has been conducted in the urban slums of Mumbai and Pune. Mumbai and Pune are the well-known cities in Maharashtra where urbanisation has taken place very fast. With this development, the incidences of inequality, poverty, and marginalisation are prominent in these two cities. For example, in Mumbai 60 percent of the population is staying in slums, confronting a variety of problems including poverty, access to critical basic services such as housing, health, education, drinking water, sanitation, and financial services, discrimination, and violence induced by both the state and markets. In 1993, the founder of Annapurna Pariwar (*Pariwar* is a Hindi word, which means 'family' in English) started to mobilise the marginalised women such as vegetable vendors, saree sellers, etc. in the slums of Pune and Mumbai, as she found that these women were excluded from the formal banking sector. Later on these women in the informal economy started to share other problems of their lives with Annapurna Pariwar such as the problem of day care for the children of these working mothers, problem of health, problem of housing, etc. Each of these problems influenced Annapurna Pariwar to create different enterprises within the slums of Pune and Mumbai to create sustainable development of the marginalised women through socio-economic empowerment in the slums.

## Objectives of the study

- To examine the role of serial social entrepreneurship in creating sustainable social ventures.
- To analyse whether this approach contributes to a better understanding and addressing some of the most pressing social problems at the grassroots level and making development sustainable.

## Data and method

The approach of this research is qualitative in nature as the major aim of this study is to explore the approach of serial entrepreneurship in the area of social entrepreneurship in order to bring sustainable development. This study adopts a case study approach (Yin, 2009). The primary aim of this research is to explore the role of serial social entrepreneurship in creating social ventures leading to sustainable development. As compared to other research methods, such as survey or experiments, the case study approach (Yin, 2009) is found to be more suitable for exploring a contemporary phenomenon like this in its real-life context. The use of case study is justified, when the objective is to capture the circumstances and conditions of everyday or commonplace situations or on the ground of its revelatory nature (Yin, 2009). Purposefully, we have chosen Annapurna Pariwar for this study as this social enterprise has been working for the last four decades and has developed several models of social entrepreneurship in order to solve the social problems by adopting the approach of serial entrepreneurship. The data were collected from multiple units such as the founder, managerial staff, field staff, and clients. The in-depth interview method was adopted for data collection and a guided checklist was designed as a data collection tool. Based on the collected data, we developed a case study on Annapurna Pariwar, and qualitative content analysis (Schreier, 2012) was performed for analysing the data.

## Annapurna Pariwar: the case description

Annapurna Mahila Mandal was started as an organisation working for the mess-runners in Mumbai in 1975. It was founded by a well-known social worker Padmashree Prema Tai Samant. Mumbai was the centre of a thriving textile industry with the largest concentration of textile mills in India. During the 1970s, as a result of a sharp fall in the textile mills in Mumbai, mill workers faced harsh realities and distress. Annapurna Mahila Mandal was born in the process of mobilising the women members of the workers' families and helping them to become self-reliant. Later, the daughter of Mrs. Prema Tai, Mrs. Medha Tai Samant, and her husband Mr. Dada Purav Samant, a Marxist trade unionist, set up Annapurna Pariwar, a group of five sister organisations. Annapurna Pariwar has been working in Pune and Mumbai cities in the state of Maharashtra, India since 1993.

Annapurna Pariwar works with poor self-employed women (90%) and also men (10%) in the urban slums in Pune, Mumbai, and rural Maharashtra through a comprehensive package of services, including microfinance, micro-insurance, day care centres, educational sponsorship, and hostel accommodation for working women through its five constituent organisations. Annapurna aims to "empower" these poor self-employed women by providing a range of financial as well as non-financial services. The team of Annapurna Pariwar believes that the poor do not go to the bank or insurance company, hence, banks and insurance companies have to go to the doorstep of the poor. It was also felt that one enterprise cannot provide all need-based services in a sustainable manner. In order to address these issues, it has created four more social enterprises: Annapurna Pariwar Vikas Samvardhan; the Vatsalyapurna Service Co-operative Society; Annapurna Mahila Mandal, Pune; and Annapurna Mahilamandal, Mumbai. It believes that the poor cannot be empowered only with financial services, but they also need a variety of non-financial services to overcome the economic and social problems in their everyday life. Annapurna Pariwar offers an interesting case in serial entrepreneurship which shows how each need creates a specific enterprise to solve a particular social problem. Figure 11.1 illustrates the structure of Annapurna Pariwar.

### *Annapurna Mahila Multi-State Co-operative Credit Society Limited*

The Annapurna Mahila Multi-State Co-operative Credit Society (AMCCSL) was created to address the problem of informal borrowing practices among the women

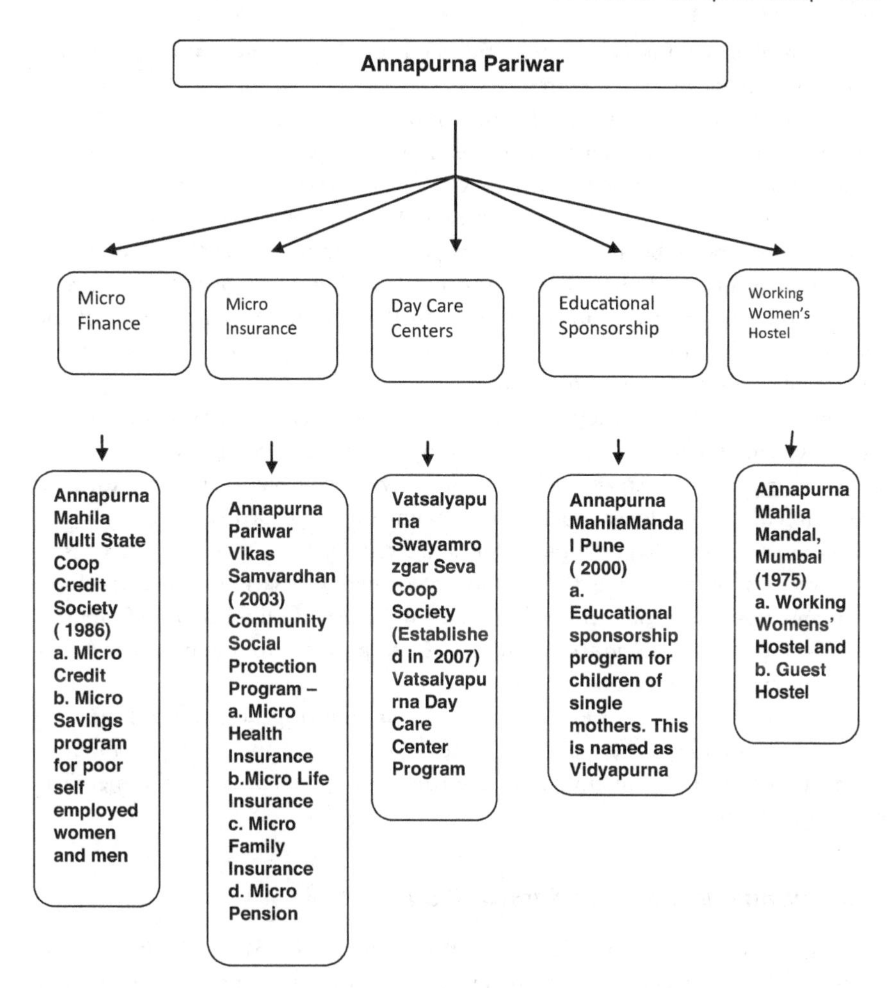


**FIGURE 11.1** Organogram of Annapurna Pariwar

*Source*: Prepared by the authors based on information compiled from Annapurna Pariwar Mandal, Pune

entrepreneurs such as vegetable vendors, saree sellers, etc. The founding member had witnessed the financial difficulties of these women micro-entrepreneurs in her hometown in Pune. In her narration, Mrs. Samant recalls that:

> I had a friendship with Savantabai, from whom I used to purchase the vegetable. I used to observe how Anna, an informal moneylender, operated in the vegetable market. I calculated the interest rate at which Savitabhai. It ranged between 15 to 20 percent per month. Shocking to me, at the end of the day these vendors had nothing to save. I wanted to make them free from the clutches of these informal moneylenders. That was the initial thought behind the micro credit activities.

As a banker, she found that microfinance had a lot of potential to address the problem of these micro-entrepreneurs. It was felt that setting up a co-operative society would not only solve the financial problem but also create a sense of ownership among these entrepreneurs. Hence, Annapurna Mahila Credit Co-operative Society was registered as a Multi-State Co- operative Credit Society. The society handles micro-credit and savings operations. All borrowers of Annapurna Mahila Credit Co-operative Society are the shareholders, and they elect their representatives of the Managing Committee of Annapurna Mahila Multi-State Co-op Credit Society. All important decisions are taken in the annual general meeting of the society through voting, and the profit earned by the co-operative is shared among the members in the form of dividends.

The society offers a variety of financial services to its members. These include business loans for setting up and expanding businesses; housing loans for construction, repairs, and expansion; loans for repayment of old debts; loans for asset creation; educational loans; micro saving with each type of loan; and voluntary saving in the form of recurring deposits and fixed deposits. Apart from credit services, other services such as the creation of compulsory saving with every loan, a community-based health mutual fund, a family security fund, and a life mutual fund for the borrowers and their families are also provided to the members. Annapurna adopts innovative practices such as community meetings, financial literacy trainings, regular loan recovery meetings, and an annual general meeting for the smooth functioning of the society. This creates knowledge and awareness about its products and services, functioning of the bank, and participation of the members in the governance.

## *Annapurna Pariwar Vikas Samvardhan*

During the delivery of microfinancial services, the AMCCSL has found that the micro-credit borrowers are subject to a variety of uncertainty and risk in their daily lives. Most of the time, these uncertainties push them into poverty. It was realised that, if they have access to insurance products, they might be able to improve their situation. Annapurna Pariwar Vikas Samvardhan (APVS) was born out of this thought. It is a not-for-profit company incorporated under Section 25 of the Companies Act, 1956. APVS provides access to insurance services to the members and their families. It runs a community-based insurance program. When AMCCSL gives micro loans to members, APVS does the enrolment of families of the borrowers under the community-based insurance programme. The contributions are collected at the time of loans and kept in separate bank accounts. The signatories to the bank accounts include members' representatives as well as staff working for this program.

In an interview, Mrs. Medha Tai narrated the background of the establishment of the community-based insurance programme and establishment of APVS. Annapurna started giving micro loans and collecting small savings from poor vegetable vendors in Pune in 1993. It started with a group of nine women.

By the year 1997, Annapurna had 1,500 members. Annapurna lost two members in 1997, due to sudden and untimely death. At that time all of the group members contributed rupees two to five and repaid the loans of these members. Therefore, the need was felt that insurance cover was required for all members. Annapurna joined the Janashri group insurance scheme of LIC in 1998 and continued till 2008. In the meantime, Annapurna Pariwar had grown to such a size that it could afford to house its own community-based life insurance scheme. In June 2009, Annapurna started its own Life Mutual Fund, and the members were covered for their life insurance. This is a self-owned and self-managed scheme of members of Annapurna Mahila Co-op Credit Society. Under this scheme, the entire loan ranging between Rs. 10,000 to Rs. 150,000 will be written off and Rs. 15,000 is given to the nominee of the member in case of death of the member.

There is an incidence about how members of the AMCCSL felt the need for health insurance. In 2000, one of the members of Annapurna, a domestic worker, died at the age of 29 due to a cardiac ailment, leaving behind three small children and a husband who was a rickshaw driver. After long discussions with them with community meetings and deliberations in the annual general body meetings, around 3,000 members of Annapurna expressed the need for health insurance coverage for them and their families within an affordable insurance premium. Members also expressed a need for proper health guidance. After exploring the available health insurance schemes, Annapurna Pariwar discovered that no commercial insurers offered an affordable package with proper medical guidance especially to build health awareness among the poor, who are mostly illiterate and have little formal education. In the formal sector, most insurers had commercial motives and were making profits from even the poor clients. The premiums were high, unaffordable, and there was no guarantee of claim settlement. If the clients did not fall sick in one year, the premium paid added to the profits of the insurance company. This was not acceptable to the members of Annapurna Pariwar. They wanted an assurance that if they or their family members had an unforeseen sickness anytime in the future, they should get even a higher amount of claim from their accumulated premium. Although the need was genuine, starting an insurance company was not so simple. It needed at least Rs 1 billioncapital for registering an insurance company under the Insurance Regulatory Development Authority (IRDA). Annapurna Pariwar could not gather the required capital from its poor borrowers. Hence, it decided to set up a not-for-profit company, namely APVS, to house its own community-based insurance.

The members of AMCCSL also felt the need for family insurance when Annapurna Pariwar lost one of its members, Dagdabai Kalein, in 2004. The family members had no money to pay the hospital bill as well as for the funeral ceremony. The hospital refused to hand over the body to the family of the dead person unless the bill was cleared. With the intervention of AMCCSL, the dead body was handed over to the relatives by the hospital, and then the family members could perform the last rites.

Further in 2005, five to six family members of borrowers of AMCCSL had gone for a Manderdevi Yatra pilgrimage. There was a stampede at this pilgrimage, in which hundreds of people died. In the same mishap, many relatives of members of Annapurna Pariwar had died. Annapurna's staff and members were very upset with this incident. The members contributed and collected money for helping the families for the funerals. Thus, the concept of giving immediate help to the borrowers at the time of death in the family was born. APVS gives an emergency help of Rs. 1000 to the member in whose family a death has occurred. APVS provides the following services to its members:

*Health Mutual Fund (HMF):* All of the borrowers of ACCSL and their families are members of this fund. For a contribution of Rs. 120 per head per year, they are insured up to Rs. 15,000 per head per year for hospitalisation plus free health advice and health check-ups.

*Life Mutual Fund (LMF):* All of the borrowers are members of this fund. For a contribution ranging from Rs. 80 to Rs. 800 covering all loan amounts and tenures, they are insured up to Rs. 15,000 for financial help in case of death, plus a refund of savings to the member's nominee and the entire loan outstanding is written off.

*Family Security Fund (FSF):* All of the borrowers are members of this fund. For a contribution ranging from Rs. 60 to Rs. 80 per head per year, they receive up to Rs. 3,000 as financial help, and three loan instalments are waived off for the death of a spouse, and Rs. 1,500 is provided as financial assistance in case of the death of a family member. Also, food grains, utensils, and clothes are given in case of an accident or a calamity in the house/community.

*Non-Financial Services*: Medical officers at Annapurna Pariwar run free guidance centers at branch offices, connect with hospitals and private practitioners for health services at low costs, and are available 24/7. APVS have Memorandum of Understanding (MoU) with good hospitals which form a network of health care providers and medical practitioners as well as diagnostic centers and chemist shops for giving low-cost services to Annapurna's members. So, in addition to giving financial assistance for medical expenses, Annapurna also connects the members with quality health care. There are specially appointed and trained health service staffs at APVS who guide and help the members to take the right medical treatment at the network hospitals. They also conduct regular awareness programmes for the members.

Along with these services, APVS has also developed customised software in-house for management of claims from the insured members and for their medical validation. Health cards are provided to each member, with the family photograph and information on it. This card is used at the time of hospital admissions, to get appropriate concessions and immediate care. The community representatives pass or reject claims in a meeting held on the 7th of every month in Pune and Mumbai.

So there is complete ownership of the community, leading to transparency and thus very high client satisfaction.

The claim ratio has never crossed 95 percent in the last 10 years since 2003 when the company was formed. Since all the claims are settled by the representatives of members who form the managing committee of APVS, this reinforces the community spirit as the groups are tied down to the community. The motto of the program is "our health in our hands". In the oath that is taken by all members at every meeting, a pledge is taken that it will be everybody's duty to maintain the health and hygiene of their families and the community by increasing their knowledge about health and avoiding sickness.

## *Vatsalyapurna Co-operative Society day care services*

There was a case of rape of a six-year-old girl in 2003 in Karvenagar, Pune, where Annapurna's community office is situated. Following this incident, the members of Annapurna Pariwar have expressed their fear and concern about the safety of their young daughters while they are away from home for work. The women members have also shared that the children are unattended and unsafe or attended by an elder sibling, mostly a girl when they are out of the home for work. As a result, the education of the eldest girl child usually suffers because she has to look after her younger siblings. They also expressed their concern that their unattended children pick up bad habits and grow up to be bad citizens or are exposed to various risks like sexual abuse, fights, riots, etc. It is dangerous to neglect these children.

In response to this incident, Annapurna Pariwar started the first day care centre at Karvenagar, Pune, in the year 2003. The Times Foundation offered financial support for setting up the first day care centre in 2003 and continued the support till 2005. Inter Aide, France gave technical and financial support to the programme from 2005 to 2010. As of 2016, Annapurna Pariwar has 17 day care centres in Pune and four in Mumbai. In the day care centres, the children are trained on scientifically developed games and developmental activities that lead to their overall growth and formation of creative ideas. Each day care centre is managed by a conductor and a helper—two women drawn from the same slum who are at the most educated up to 10th grade of school. These women are trained at a local women's university, every month, on topics like child psychology, hygiene, nutrition, language development, social development, and group activities. A separate co-operative society, Vatsalyapurna Swayamrojgar Service Co-operative Society, is registered with these women conductors.

Each day care centre charges fees ranging between Rs. 400 to Rs. 450 per month for 10 hours of child care daily. These costs of day care services and other rules are explained to the parents in quarterly parents' meetings. By charging a fee for its services, the day care centres are financially self-sustainable up to 70 percent. In order to support these centres, Annapurna Pariwar has secured corporate help under Corporate Social Responsibility (CSR). The corporate organisations like Barclays Bank and Garware Group have come forward to support these centres.

Annapurna Pariwar has also received contribution from OID, Germany in support to this and an Educational Sponsorship Program in 2013. The members of Annapurna Pariwar admit that enrolment of their children into day care centres lead to a 60 percent increase in their income. Mothers admit that it provides a safe environment. Hence, they are less worried while at work. Some households shared the fact of being more peaceful and organised. They vouch that there is an improvement of children's behaviour at the day care centres. They learn good and new habits. Mothers also noticed improvements in terms of autonomy, rhythm of life, language, and eating habits. Children in day care centres are eating better and alone. Moreover, the frequency of light respiratory infections is reduced.

## *Vidyapurna—Annapurna Mahila Mandal, Pune*

The following two stories of the members of AMCCSL narrate the reason for starting Vidyapurna at Annapurna Mahila Mandal, Pune:

> Ramdas Waghade was a tailor. He had a small shop in Dahanukar colony in Pune. In 1998, he became a member of Annapurna when he borrowed a sum of Rs. 2,000 for his business. As his repayments were on time, he could borrow a higher amount each time and this helped him increase his business. However, in 2003, during Ganesh Chaturthi he was forced to contribute a high donation for putting up the Ganesh Mandal. But as he could not afford the amount and refused to pay the money demanded. This led to the local youths beating up Ramdas leading to his death. After Ramdas's death, the entire family responsibility fell upon his wife, Mamta Waghade. Despite of being in pain, she repaid the entire loan taken from Annapurna without default. She later borrowed more money in her name to run the business. In order to help her out of difficulties, Annapurna offered to sponsor the entire education of her children. This was the beginning of the Vidyapurna program.
>
> Kanta Sapkal was a widow. She had two children. She was a cook and also worked as a caretaker of children. She had taken a loan of Rs. 3,000 and in order to pay her children's school fees, she wanted a bigger loan. As per the rules of the organisation, a second loan cannot be taken when an earlier loan is outstanding. However, in order to help her continue the children's education, Annapurna decided to help with the sponsorship of her children. Annapurna's timely help prevented the children from becoming school drop-outs and helped them complete their education.

Vidyapurna, the Educational Sponsorship Program of Annapurna Pariwar, is a financial assistance programme for the education of children of single mothers who are borrowers of AMCCSL. Annapurna Pariwar had conducted a survey of its members which showed that 10 to 12 percent of its members are single. In June 2014, Annapurna Pariwar gave assistance to 1,372 children amounting to Rs 3.5 million mostly collected from contribution from high income-earning people.

### *Annapurna Mahila Mandal, Mumbai—working women's hostel and guest hostel*

Annapurna Pariwar noticed that a safe place to stay is essential for single women who are working or are students, especially in big cities like Mumbai and Pune. This is one of the most important requirements of single women. Realising this, Annapurna Pariwar started its working women's hostel in Vashi, Mumbai in the year 1990. This hostel has the capacity to provide a safe and clean shelter for 125 single women. It also runs a guest hostel in New Mumbai in which 75 persons can stay. The hostel provides facilities such as shared rooms with a safe and clean environment; 24-hour generator back-up and aqua guard for purified drinking water; morning tea and canteen facilities in-house; solar power backed-up hot water supply for bathing; clean and adequate number of toilet blocks; regular pest control and water tank cleaning; a separate TV room for entertainment; a separate study room; a separate cafeteria; and 24-hour security services. This programme is self-sustainable and working on a non-profit basis. Many women from all over India who are coming to Mumbai as strugglers get safe and clean shelter in the hostel run by Annapurna Pariwar.

## Discussion

In this section, we examine serial entrepreneurship in Annapurna Pariwar followed by an analysis of its contribution to sustainable development, motivation of entrepreneurs for opportunity identification, and value creation (Parker, 2014; Westhead et al., 2003, 2005).

### *Annapurna Pariwar—a case in serial social entrepreneurship*

#### *Occupational choice*

Serial entrepreneurship involves creation of a series of entrepreneurial ventures by an individual or group of entrepreneurs in pursuit of opportunity identification and exploitation (Shane, 2000, 2004; Parker, 2014). It is found that the occupational choice of the serial entrepreneurs is influenced by the experience gained through previous employment or entrepreneur ventures (Parker, 2014). The founder of Annapurna Pariwar is a former banker who has gained substantial experience in her chosen field of entrepreneurship. The founder also benefits out of social capital through her socio-economic familial background, industry experience, and community engagement for social cause. Being associated with a family of well-known trade union leaders and social workers in the region, the founder of Annapurna made a conscious decision to quit her previous job in the bank and follow their family tradition of social work to bring positive social change among marginalised people. Parker (2014) has found that the individual's formal education, managerial, and entrepreneurial experience has a significant effect on their choice of entering and exiting entrepreneurship, as well as their performance as entrepreneurs. As a result of their prior experience, the serial entrepreneurs are expected to have better managerial and technical skills, networks of contacts, and access to specific information, making them better equipped with specific knowledge of business dynamics, opportunity identification, and in the process of setting up and running the new venture.

### *Entrepreneurial motivation*

While an individual's motivation to entrepreneurship may involve a desire for independence, autonomy, and wealth creation (Scott & Rosa, 1996; Westhead et al., 2005), the social entrepreneurs are motivated to bring social change and social impact (Nicholls, 2006). As the change-maker orientation is fundamental in social entrepreneurship, the social entrepreneurs are motivated by a compelling vision of transforming the world (Bornstein, 2004). Personal communication with the founder reveals her motivation to start Annapurna Pariwar. It originates from compassion for fellow human beings and the innate urge to help the poor and marginalised to lead a decent and respectful life. Three main reasons for creating this social enterprise were: 1) the founding members, with their Marxist background, wanted to work with workers and people at the margin; 2) am opportunity to work with poor people as they lack a banking facility; and 3) the founders felt the need to help the poor to access financial services by setting up a banking system for the poor. The vision is to bring the desired social change by transforming the institutional structures and social norms that inhibit the poor to access financial and other non-financial services. Social entrepreneurship literature identifies compassion as one of the unique motivating factors in social entrepreneurship (Dees, 2007; Mair & Marti, 2006).

### *Opportunity recognition and exploitation*

The discovery of entrepreneurial opportunities are influenced by possession of prior information necessary to identify an opportunity and the cognitive properties necessary to value it (Shane & Venkataraman, 2000). Social entrepreneurs go beyond the conventional method of opportunity identification and turn their attention to the social arena to identify venture opportunities. It is clear that the founders felt the need to create an institution for financial services for the poor out of their intimate relations with and compassion towards them. Compassion ignites the cognition process and directs people towards social problem identification and venture creation (Dees, 2007; Mair & Marti, 2006). Being a trained banker, the founder of Annapurna is aware of the problem of 'exclusion of the marginalised and poor' in access to formal financial services and also its potential for empowering them. Annapurna Mahila Mandal was created out of the aspiration of addressing the problems faced by the self-employed women by providing sustained access to financial services to them at an affordable rate of interest. Here, the founders adopt a problem-centric approach to opportunity identification and venture creation. Having realised that as the women are facing multiple problems, mere financial assistance alone is insufficient to bring desirable social change and quality of life for these women, the founders created a series of ventures for providing social security and life-long support to their clients. The founders were able to achieve this by leveraging their strength of human and social capital. It is well established that the entrepreneurial-specific human capital and social network influences how individuals seek information, create, or identify entrepreneurial opportunities (Shane, 2000, 2004).

## *Serial social entrepreneurship and sustainable development*

### *Inclusion and access to services*

Annapurna Pariwar is also a case in inclusive development through serial social entrepreneurship. This is achieved through clear targeting and identification of clients. The target clients of Annapurna Pariwar include economically active women workers and self-employed women. Annapurna Pariwar identifies and mobilises these marginalised women workers and self-employed women in urban slums through a group process for accessing financial as well as several non-financial services. The financial services are offered in the form of savings, credit, and insurance products. The non-financial services include day care facilities, rest houses, financial literacy training, and sensitisation on issues related to nutrition, child care, social security, gender, and women's empowerment (Guha & Ghosh, 2015). All of these services are provided with an objective of empowering the community with sustained social and economic outcomes. Olu (2009) has found that sustained access to financial and non-financial services plays a critical role in improving the productivity of micro-enterprises as well as the socio-economic development of the members. In the case of Annapurna Pariwar, a total of 0.15 million women members have access to a variety of financial as well as non-financial services from the Pariwar, most of them are repeat borrowers. Prior research has shown the failure of formal financial institutions to provide services to these women because of problems related to incentives, enforcement, and adverse selection (Stiglitz, 1990; Ghatak & Guinnan, 1999; Roy, 1998; Guha & Marakkath, 2015). Annapurna Pariwar overcomes these issues by adopting innovative lending practices such as self-selection, peer monitoring and group lending, and product innovation.

### *Equity and participation*

Equity is fundamental to sustainable development. Equity means opportunity for the members to access the services offered by the organisation. As a democratic, voluntary, and autonomous entity, co-operatives have the distinction of being the ideal entity for promoting equity and wellbeing of its members. Being a member-based, voluntary, and autonomous organisation formed on the principle of self-help and co-operation, Annapurna provides equal opportunity for all its members to access its products and services. The members are the primary shareholders of the Pariwar. Each member has a right to exercise her power in the selection of their representative in the general body of the society. The society functions on democratic principles and ensures participation of all members in its activities. The members elect their representative of the management committee that executes the decisions of the general body. This gives them a unique sense of ownership and control of the activities of their society. It is evident that this sense of belonging and ownership, as revealed from the interaction with several of its clients, acts as the foundation for success of Annapurna Pariwar.

### *Empowerment*

The root cause of the disempowerment of women is the patriarchal social system where men are treated as superior and they own and control the resources, leading to domestic violence, work burden, disrespect, humiliations, and lack of ownership of resources (Guerin, Kumar, & Ageir, 2013). Annapurna Pariwar started its journey in order to empower the women in slums in Mumbai and Pune. The objective of women's empowerment is embedded in all activities of this organisation. Each enterprise was created to make the women self-reliant. For example, microfinance services aimed at empowering women economically in terms of creating businesses, creating investment for the production, taking economic decisions, etc. For social empowerment, Annapurna Pariwar created separate enterprises for children of single parents, a fellowship programme for the children, and financial literacy training for their members so that women members can concentrate on work by getting new skills.

### *Sustainability*

Along with inclusion, equity, and access, another important aspect of Annapurna is its approach to sustainability. According to Ayayi and Sene (2010), an MFI could achieve sustainability by three means: improving management and governance practices, designing a portfolio of products, and deciding an appropriate rate of interest. Annapurna ensures that all of its activities are self-sustainable. Core to its sustainability is its unique approach to institution building. Annapurna Pariwar as an umbrella organisation provides leadership and direction to its constituent entities. Being a member-based co-operative entity, Annapurna instils a sense of ownership and control by its members in all its activities. This has been revealed in several interactions with the members of various entities, management, and staff of Annapurna Pariwar. To improve the credit portfolio, Annapurna uses peer monitoring and self-selection tools when choosing clients and monitoring repayment.

Annapurna adopts a life cycle approach in the design and delivery of its products and services. Realising the fact that access to financial services alone is insufficient to address various issues facing their clients, it provides a series of products and services that include savings, credit, insurance, financial literacy, day care facilities, and hostel facilities for the working women and self-employed. These products are designed with a conscious effort and keeping in mind the various requirements of their clients in the course of their life. Annapurna adopts a market-based approach for the delivery of its products and services. Interestingly, none of its activities are subsidised. The members pay the full cost of services either in terms of interest payment or subscription fee, depending on the nature of products or services.

An organisation could sustain in the long run provided they reduce dependency on grant or subsidies (Ayayi & Sene, 2010). Annapurna mobilises a substantial portion of its financial resources in terms of borrowing from a variety of institutions, including commercial banks and development banks. These are all at commercial interest rates. Since its inception, it was able to create credibility among the community as well as other key stakeholders, including government and financial institutions. This improves its ability to mobilise resources at a reasonable cost. One of its core activities is to instil a savings habit among its members. A majority of credit products provided by Annapurna Pariwar are for asset creation, including business loans, purchase of assets, and home loans. This ensures a regular flow of resources both for the client and the institution. The repayment of the loan is based on the financial flow from income-generating activities and their ability to repay. The clients pay the commercial interest rate on their loans. The loan repayment is on regular weekly or monthly instalment depending on the nature of the cash flow from income-generating activities. Annapurna ensures regular repayment of loans from its borrowers. This is achieved through a process of community engagement involving the clients and the staff members of the society. Interestingly, it claims zero percent non-performance assets (NPA) over the past 10 years, which is unheard of in Indian commercial lending. Besides, Annapurna adopts a professional approach in all its operations. Its operations are handled by a bunch of trained staff, most of whom are women who were recruited locally. All staff members are trained on all aspects of the activities of Annapurna Pariwar with an emphasis on co-operative values and principles. This helps the staff members to effectively deal with clients and creating a homely working environment.

## Conclusion

Our study reveals that Annapurna Pariwar has adopted the approach of serial entrepreneurship to address the complex social problems which are linked to each other. This approach has helped Annapurna Pariwar to create entrepreneurial ventures to address the complex issues of the slum community. Our analysis has brought to light several important aspects of operations of Annapurna, questioning the stereotypical beliefs of our society such as that poor women can't be empowered economically as they are illiterate, they cannot be bankable, their children cannot get good protection and education, etc. The study shows that serial entrepreneurship could play a crucial role in making development more inclusive.

## References

Aiken, M. (2006). Towards market or state? Tensions and opportunities in the evolutionary path of three types of UK social enterprise. In M. Nyssens (Ed.), *Towards market or state? Tensions and opportunities in the evolutionary path of three UK social enterprises* (pp. 259–271). London: Routledge.

Alvord, S., Brown, L., & Letts, C. (2004). Social entrepreneurship and societal transformation: An exploratory study. *Journal of Applied Behavioral Science, 40*(3), 260–283.

Amaral, A., Baptista, R., & Lima, F. (2011). Serial entrepreneurship: Impact of human capital on time to re-entry. *Small Business Economics, 37*(1), 1–21.

Austin, J., Stevenson, H., & Wei-Skillern, J. (2006). Social and commercial entrepreneurship: Same, different, or both? *Entrepreneurship Theory and Practice*, January, 1–22.

Ayayi, A. G., & Sene, M. (2010). What drives microfinance institution's financial sustainability. *The Journal of Developing Areas, 44*(1), 303–324.

Bornstein, D. (2004). *Social entrepreneurs and the power of new ideas*. New York: Oxford University Press.

Bosma, N., Van Praag, M., Thurik, R., & De Wit, G. (2004). The value of human and social capital investments for the business performance of startups. *Small Business Economics, 23*(4), 227–236.

Bovaird, T. (2006). Developing new relationships with the "market" in the procurement of public services. *Public Administration, 84*(1), 81–102.

Carter, S., & Ram, M. (2003). Reassessing portfolio entrepreneurship: Towards a multidisciplinary approach. *Small Business Economics, 27*(4), 371–380.

Chandra, Y. (2017). Social entrepreneurship as emancipatory work. *Journal of Business Venturing, 32*(6), 657–673. https://doi.org/10.1016/j.jbusvent.2017.08.004

Choi, N., & Majumdar, S. (2014). Social entrepreneurship as an essentially contested concept: Opening a new avenue for systematic future research. *Journal of Business Venturing, 20*(2014), 363–376.

Colombo, M. G., & Grilli, L. (2005). Founders' human capital and the growth of new technology based firms: A competence based review. *Research Policy, 34*(6), 795–816.

Dees, J. G. (2007). Taking social entrepreneurship seriously. *Society, 44*(3), 24–31.

Douglas, E., & Prentice, C. (2019). Innovation and profit motivations for social entrepreneurship: A fuzzy-set analysis. *Journal of Business Research, 99*, 69–79. https://doi.org/10.1016/j.jbusres.2019.02.031

Gartner, W. B. (1985). A conceptual framework for describing the phenomenon of new venture creation. *Academy of Management, 10*(4), 696–706.

Ghatak, M., & Guinnane, T. W. (1999). The economics of lending with joint liability: Theory and practice. *Journal of Development Economics, 60*, 195–228.

Guha, S., & Ghosh, C. (2015). Institutional framework of MFIs and economic benefit to clients in Mumbai slums. *Economic and Political Weekly, L*(25), 151–159.

Guha, S., & Marakkath, N. (2015). Relevance of social enterprise for micro entrepreneurial; growth: A case based discussions on Indian micro finance models. In S. Majumadar, S. Guha, & N. Marakkath (Eds.), *Technology and innovation for social change*. New Delhi: Springer.

Guerin, I., Kumar, S., & Agier, I. (2013). Women's empowerment: Power to act, or power over other women? Lessons from Indian Microfinance, *Oxford Development Studies, 41*(1), 76–94. DOI: 10.1080/13600818.2013.781147

Haque, S. M. (2000). Environmental discourse and sustainable development. *Ethics and the Environment, 5*(1), 3–21.

Holmes, T. J., & Schmitz, J. A. (1990). A theory of entrepreneurship and its application to the study of business transfers. *Journal of Political Economy, 98*(2), 265–294.

LeGrand, J. (2003). *Motivation, agency, and public policy. Of knights and knaves, pawns and queens.* Oxford: Oxford University Press.

Mair, J., & Marti, I. (2006). Social entrepreneurship research: A source of explanations, prediction and delight. *Journal of World Business, 4*(1), 36–44.

Munda, G. (1997). Environmental economics, ecological economics, and the concept of sustainable development. *Environmental Values, 6*(2), 213–233.

Nahata, R. (2019). Success is good but failure is not so bad either: Serial entrepreneurs and venture capital contracting. *Journal of Corporate Finance, 58*, 624. https://doi.org/10.1016/j.jcorpfin.2019.07.006

Nicholls, A. (2006). *Social entrepreneurship: New models of sustainable social change.* Oxford: Oxford University Press.

Nicholls, A. (2010). The legitimacy of social entrepreneurship: Reflexive isomorphism in a pre-paradigmatic field. *Entrepreneurship Theory and Practice*, July, 613–631.

Olu, O. (2009). *Impact of micro finance on entrepreneurial development: The case of Nigeria.* The International Conference on Administration and Business, ICEA-FAA 2009, 14–15 November 2009. The Faculty of Business and Administration, University of Bucharest.

Parker, S. C. (2013). Do serial entrepreneurs run successively better-performing businesses? *Journal of Business Venturing, 28*(5), 652–666.

Parker, S. C. (2014). Who become serial and portfolio entrepreneurs? *Small Business Economics, 43*, 887–898.

Polak, P. (2008). *Out of poverty.* San Francisco, CA: Berret Kohler Publishers.

Prahalad, C. K. (2005). *The fortune at the bottom of the pyramid: Eradicating poverty through profit.* Philadelphia, PA: University of Pennsylvania, Wharton School Publishing.

Roy, D. (1998). *Development economics.* New York: Oxford University Press.

Sarasvathy, S. (2001). Causation and effectuation: Towards a theoretical shift from economic inevitability to entrepreneurial contingency. *Academy of Management Review, 26*(2), 243–263.

Schreier, M. (2012). *Qualitative content analysis in practice.* Thousand Oaks, CA: Sage.

Scott, M., & Rosa, P. (1996). Has firm level analysis reached its limits? Tine for rethink. *International Small Business Journal, 14*(4), 81–89.

Shane, S. (2000). Prior knowledge and the discovery of entrepreneurial opportunities. *Organisational Science, 11*(4), 448–469.

Shane, S. (2004). *A general theory of entrepreneurship: The individual opportunities nexus.* Cheltenham: Edward Elgar.

Shane, S., & Venkataraman, S. (2000). The promise of entrepreneurship as a field of research. *Academy of Management Research, 25*(1), 217–226.

Shantana, J., Hoover, R., & Vengadasubbu, M. (2017). Investor commitment to serial entrepreneurs: A multilayer network analysis. *Social Networks, 48*, 256–269. https://doi.org/10.1016/j.socnet.2016.10.002

Solow, R. M. (1991). *Sustainability: An economist's perspective.* Paper presented at the Eighteenth J Seward Johnson Lecture to the Marine Policy Centre, Woods Hole Oceanographic Institution at the Woods Hole, Massachusets, 14 June 1991.

Stam, E., Audretsch, D. B., & Meijaard, J. (2008). Recent entrepreneurship. *Journal of Evolutionary Economics, 18*(4), 493–507.

Stiglitz, J. (1990). Peer monitoring and credit markets. *World Bank Economic Review, 4*(3), 351–366.

Ucbasaran, D., Wright, M., & Westhead, P. (2008). Opportunity identification and pursuit: Does and entrepreneur's social capital matter?' *Small Business Economics, 50*(2), 153–173.

United Nations (2012). The future we want: Outcome document of the United Nations Conference on sustainable development. Retrieved April 17, 2020, from https://sustainabledevelopment.un.org/content/documents/733FutureWeWant.pdf

United Nations (2015). Transforming our world: The 2030 agenda for sustainable development. Retrieved April 17, 2020, from https://sustainabledevelopment.un.org/content/documents/21252030%20Agenda%20for%20Sustainable%20Development%20web.pdf

Westhead, P., Ucbasaran, D., & Wright, M. (2003). Difference between private firms owned by novice, serial and portfolio entrepreneurs: Implications for policy makers and practitioners. *Regional Studies*, *37*(2), 187–200.

Westhead, P., Ucbasaran, D., Wright, M., & Binks, M. (2005). Novice, serial and portfolio entrepreneur behaviour and contributions. *Small Business Economics*, *25*(2), 109.

World Commission on Environment and Development (WCED). (1987). *Report of the World Commission on Environment and Development: Our common future*. Retrieved December 7, 2016 from www.un-documents.net/our-common-future.pdf.

Yin, R. K. (2009). *Case study research: Design and methods*. New Delhi: Sage Publications.

Yunus, M. (2009). *Banker to the poor: The story of the Grameen Bank*. New Delhi: Penguin.

# 12

# INTEGRATING CORPORATE SOCIAL RESPONSIBILITY (CSR) AND SOCIAL ENTREPRENEURSHIP (SE)

## A conceptual framework for social value creation

*Archana Singh*[1]

### Introduction

Value creation has long been discussed in businesses (Porter & Kramer, 2011) as well as in the management research (Haksever, Chaganti, & Cook, 2004). Very conservatively, it is argued that the social responsibility of the companies is to increase their profits and benefit the owners or shareholders, and to create values for them only (Friedman, 1970). Moving away from this conservative perspective on corporate social responsibility, several authors (Haksever et al., 2004; Chatterji, 2011; Arora, 2013) emphasised a stakeholder approach to understand corporate social responsibility (CSR). They argue that an organisation must create value for all stakeholders, not merely for shareholders. Shareholders/owners are just one of the stakeholders. Other important stakeholder groups are employees, customers, suppliers, and the society at large, including the environment (Freeman, 1984). In fact, companies can create economic value by creating societal value as well, and that is why 'shared value' must be created by the companies (Porter & Kramer, 2006, 2011). Not only this, but for corporate sustainability also, companies have to perform on all the parameters of the 'triple bottom line' (TBL)—people (social), profit (economic), and planet (environment)—which will further contribute to sustainable development and inclusive growth of the countries, particularly under-developed and developing countries. Seelos and Mair (2005b, p. 49) clearly mention that: "Sustainable development and corporate profits are not incompatible goals". However, the reality is that businesses have rarely approached societal issues from a value perspective, and they have treated them as peripheral matters (Porter & Kramer, 2011). Businesses have increasingly been viewed as a major cause of social, environmental, and economic problems (Porter & Kramer, 2019). Thus, there is an urgent need to address this issue and inspire businesses to incorporate all three dimensions of sustainability—social, environmental, and economic—in their strategies, in a manner that generates shared value creation for all stakeholders, including the environment and society (Bocken, Rana, & Short, 2015). Thus, from the stakeholder view of CSR, social value creation (society at large, including environment) is one of the important aspects for corporate sustainability, which seeks immediate attention.

On the other hand, 'social value creation' is at the heart of social entrepreneurship (SE) (Dees, 1998; Singh, 2016). Social entrepreneurs use their creativity and entrepreneurial skills to solve social and environmental problems in a sustainable manner and to create social value (Nicholls, 2006). Through their innovative organisations and service provision models, they contribute to achieve the goals of sustainable development (Seelos & Mair, 2005c). However, most often, social entrepreneurs operate in a resource-constrained environment, and thus, within and cross-sector partnerships and networking play a very important role in SE (Singh, 2016).

Recognising the interface between CSR and SE on 'social value creation', and its importance for sustainable development, the present chapter proposes a conceptual framework for social value creation, integrating both CSR and SE. The proposed framework may provide guidelines for the companies that would like to improve their performance on social and environmental parameters also, apart from economic performance. It may also provide opportunities to both corporate as well as social entrepreneurs to collaborate, develop partnerships, network, and work together in an innovative and entrepreneurial way for social value creation, accepting and understanding each other's strengths and limitations, and may create a win-win situation for both.

## Understanding concepts

Since the chapter incorporates several concepts such as value, social value, corporate social responsibility, and social entrepreneurship, it is important to discuss these concepts first.

### *The concepts of 'value' and 'social value'*

The concept of 'value' is not clear in the literature (Singh, 2016), as it has been used in different disciplines such as sociology, management, etc. (Lepak, Smith, & Taylor, 2007). Scholars from different disciplines have tried to see it from different perspectives (Haksever et al., 2004; Lepak et al., 2007). Obviously, it leads to multiple meanings of the concept of 'value'.

For the purpose of this chapter, I have borrowed the definition of 'value' given by Haksever et al. (2004). They state: "Value is the capacity of the good, service, or activity to satisfy a need or provide a benefit to a person or a legal entity" (p. 292). The reason behind adopting this particular definition lies in its capacity to include all the tangible and intangible benefits (including quality of life, physical and financial security, knowledge, safety, nutrition, shelter etc.) contributing positively to satisfy a person's need or a legal entity.

As the aim of the chapter is to identify and discuss opportunities for combining CSR and SE for social value creation, it is important to conceptualise the concept of 'social value' as well. Adopted from Singh's (2016) conceptualisation of 'social value', I have broadly defined 'social value' as

> Creating desired positive social impact, bringing desired social change, which includes a range of impacts, from creating awareness, empowering beneficiaries, bringing behavioural, attitudinal, perceptional changes and institutional changes, to creating socio-economic benefits for beneficiaries and impacting their lives positively.

It may also include creating 'environmental value'. The social value creation should be sustainable.

## *Corporate social responsibility (CSR)*

The primary role of business is to produce goods and services that society wants and needs Cannon (1992), but there is an interdependence between business and society in the need for a stable environment with an educated workforce (Moir, 2001). As corporations derive wealth from society, create wealth for society, and earn profit by dealing with the wealth of the society, in the larger perspective it is society that actually gives permission to business to operate in society and earn money. Thus, CSR is the responsibility of the corporations to fulfil (Chatterji, 2011). Wood (1991) also states:

> the basic idea of corporate social responsibility is that business and society are interwoven rather than distinct entities.
>
> *(p. 695)*

However, there is no universal definition of CSR (Chahoud et al., 2007; CII, 2013). The social responsibility has been conceptualised in a variety of ways (Carrol, 1979). The extreme conservative view focuses on maximising shareholders/owners' value. It argues that the social responsibility of the companies is to increase their profits and benefit the owners or shareholders (Friedman, 1970). Several other scholars, such as Carroll (1979) and Fauzi, Svensson, and Rahman (2010), discussed an integrated model of CSR. Carroll (1979) defines social responsibility as a four-stage continuum. In his model, *economic* (business has responsibility to produce goods and services that society wants and to sell them at a profit), *legal* (society expects business to achieve its economic mission within the framework of legal requirements), *ethical* (apart from economic and legal responsibilities, there are also ethical responsibilities, which are additional behaviours and activities that are not necessarily codified into law, but nevertheless are expected of business by society's members), and *discretionary* goals (these roles are purely voluntary, and a decision to assume them is guided only by a business's desire to engage in them; social roles are not mandated, not required by law, and not even generally expected of businesses in an ethical sense, e.g. philanthropic contributions) are integrated. Further, he outlined a 'corporate social performance' (CSP) framework, which included a philosophy of responsiveness, social responsibility categories, and the social issues involved.

Fauzi et al. (2010) extended the concept of CSP to consider the aspects of people (social) and planet (environment) as important parts of a company's performance. They focus on an extended corporate performance labelled as 'triple bottom line' (TBL) as 'sustainable corporate performance' (SCP), including three interlinked measurement elements: 1) financial, 2) social, and 3) environmental. The concept of CSP, in which the environmental aspect is included, is synonymous with CSR and socially responsible behaviour (ibid.).

In recent years, measuring corporate performance on all three parameters of the TBL—economic, social, and environmental—has also been emphasised by the scholars (Savitz & Weber, 2006; CII, 2013; Bocken et al., 2015) for corporate sustainability.

> Corporate Sustainability essentially refers to the role that companies can play in meeting the agenda of sustainable development and entails a balanced approach to economic progress, social progress and environmental stewardship.
>
> *(CII, 2013, p. 7)*

Thus, all three forms of value creation—economic, social, and environmental—are equally important for corporate sustainability in the long run. Bocken et al. (2015, p. 67) state:

> Pressures on business to operate sustainably are increasing. This requires companies to adopt a systemic approach that seeks to integrate consideration of the three dimensions of sustainability—social, environmental, and economic—in a manner that generates shared value creation for all stakeholders including the environment and society. This is referred to as sustainable business thinking.

It clearly indicates the importance of value creation for all the stakeholders for corporate sustainability. In addition, most shareholders are absentee owners, and their livelihoods do not entirely depend on the performance of the firm (Haksever et al., 2004). Other stakeholders, such as employees, managers, suppliers, and local communities, have much more at stake than investment capital; their livelihoods are tied to the firm (Beauchamp & Bowie, 1993). This could be the reason behind universal acceptance of Freeman's concept of the 'stakeholder' (Freeman, 1984). Freeman (1984, p. 46) defines a stakeholder in an organisation as "any group or individual who can affect or is affected by the achievement of the organisation's objectives". The five groups, namely owners/shareholders, employees, customers, suppliers, and the society at large, constitute a fairly comprehensive set of stakeholders (Haksever et al., 2004). Both the concepts of CSR and stakeholder are interrelated, because if CSR aims to define *what* responsibilities business ought to fulfil, then the stakeholder concept addresses the issue of *whom* business is or should be accountable to (Kakabadse, Rozuel, & Lee-Davies, 2005; Jamali, 2008). Thus, businesses must create value for all stakeholders. The stakeholder approach to CSR has attracted the attention of scholars like Jamali (2008).

The sustainable company conducts its business so that the benefits flow naturally to all stakeholders, including employees, business partners, the communities in which it operates, and also shareholders: "Sustainable companies find areas of mutual interest and ways to make 'doing good' and 'doing well' synonymous, and thus avoiding the implied conflict between society and shareholders" (Savitz & Weber, 2006, p. 21). A sustainable corporation creates profits for its shareholders while protecting the environment and improving the lives of those with whom it interacts. It operates so that its business interests and the interests of the environment and society intersect. Sustainability respects the interdependence of living beings on one another and on their natural environment (ibid., p. x). Porter and Kramer (2011) also emphasised the concept of 'shared value creation', which focuses on identifying and expanding the connections between societal and economic progress. They (2002) argued that even corporate philanthropy, i.e. their charitable efforts, can be used to improve their competitive context—the quality of the business environment in the location or locations where they operate. Using philanthropy to enhance context brings social and economic goals into alignment and improves a company's long-term business prospects. The context-focused philanthropy can be used to achieve both social and economic gains.

The literature discussed herein shows that with the changing contexts and time, the concept of CSR has evolved from the conservative approach, philanthropy, and now incorporates all related concepts such as the triple bottom line, corporate sustainability, stakeholder, shared value, and also business responsibility. The newly evolved CSR model encompassing Carroll's (1979) four-stage continuum model of CSR, Freeman's (1984) stakeholder approach, corporate performance on the TBL, and Porter and Kramer's (2011) concept of shared value creation is presented in Figure 12.1.

## *Social entrepreneurship (SE)*

Social entrepreneurship is the process wherein an individual or a group of individuals identifies and exploits opportunity in a social problem, mobilises resources and acts innovatively to solve a social problem, creates social value, and brings about positive social change (Singh, 2016). Social entrepreneurship combines the resourcefulness of traditional entrepreneurship with a mission to change society (Seelos & Mair, 2005a). Social entrepreneurs are best known as 'change agents' in the social sector (Nicholls, 2006). Thus, social value creation is central to the

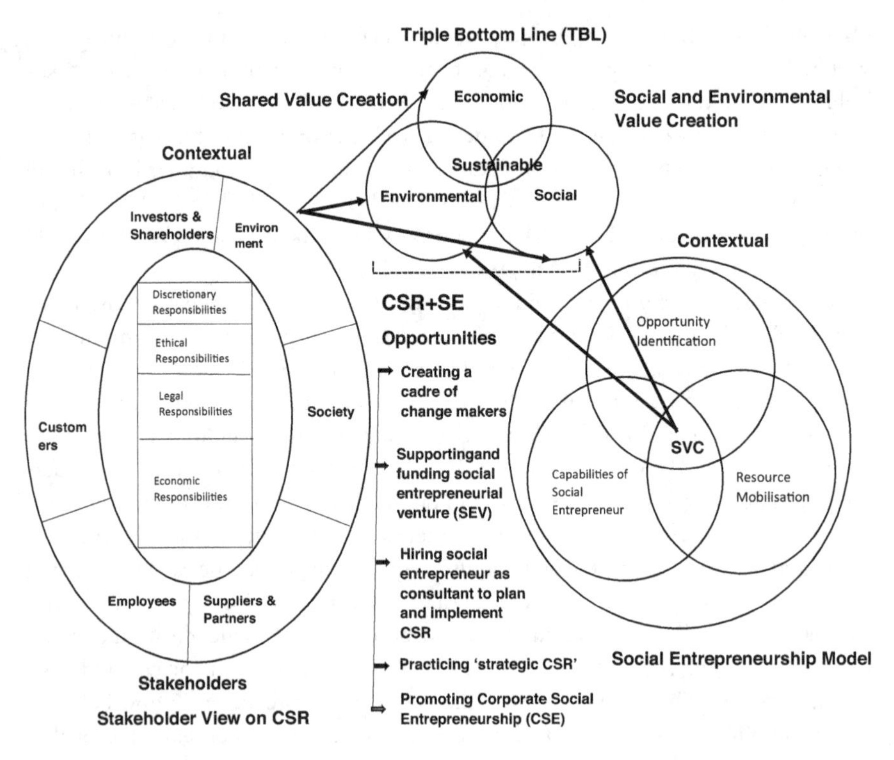


**FIGURE 12.1** Conceptual framework: integrating CSR and SE for social value creation

*Source*: Developed by the author

process of social entrepreneurship (Singh, 2016). Dees (1998, p. 3) mentioned: "For social entrepreneurs, the social mission is explicit and central". Like corporate enterprise, any social enterprise creates value for all its stakeholders—employees, suppliers, beneficiaries, funders, etc. (Dees, 2001), but the beneficiaries are always the intended target of value creation (Lepak et al., 2007). Social entrepreneurs have created models for efficiently catering to basic human needs that existing markets and institutions have failed to satisfy (Seelos & Mair, 2005a). Most often social entrepreneurs work in a resource-constrained environment to create maximum social impact. Thus, networking and partnership play a very important role in the process of social value creation in social entrepreneurship (Singh, 2016).

Social entrepreneurship can emerge across all the sectors—non-profits, public, for-profit, and cross-sector partnerships (Nicholls, 2006). Hybrid organisational forms of social enterprises can develop within and across all three sectors (Mair & Noboa, 2003; Neck, Brush, & Allen, 2008), with the condition that its primary focus is on a social mission, not on the economic value creation or profit maximisation.

> The business model of social enterprises is characterised by unique strategies based on the competencies of the entrepreneurs, and is not aimed primarily

> at the maximisation of profits, but rather at carrying out goals for the benefit of society.
>
> *(Szegedi, Fülöp, & Bereczk, 2016, p. 1504)*

The process of social value creation is highly contextual (Singh, 2016). The social entrepreneurship conceptual model adopted from Singh (2016) is incorporated in in Figure 12.1.

## Interface between CSR and SE

It is already discussed that economic/financial value creation is the primary focus of corporate, shared value creation, i.e. convergence of social and economic interests, is very important for corporate sustainability, and thus creating value for the society at large (including the environment), one of the stakeholders, becomes an important responsibility for the businesses. In addition, CSR also enhances a company's reputation; provides greater employee loyalty and retention; maintains trust, support, and legitimacy with the community, government, and employees; and thus benefits businesses (Moir, 2011). As they often lack expertise in this context, they may need help to create social and environmental value.

CSR refers to "the active behaviour of a company, by which it can create new solutions to meet the needs of society, either on its own or in cooperation with other social stakeholders" (Szegedi et al., 2016, p. 1504). In this context, it makes sense to discuss social entrepreneurship as 'social value creation' that is at the heart of 'social entrepreneurship' (SE) (Dees, 1998), and as networking, collaborations, and partnerships also play a significant role in social entrepreneurship because of resource constraints. There is the potential to combine both for social value creation. Social entrepreneurship can be used as a powerful tool for corporations to gain entry into and build loyalty in developing markets (Seelos & Mair, 2005b).

Recognising this potential, I propose a conceptual framework for social value creation, integrating both CSR and SE (see Figure 12.1).

Figure 12.1 shows that the stakeholder view of CSR focuses on creating value for all the stakeholders, not only for shareholders, which is contextual in nature. It implies convergence of social interest and economic interest, and achieving the goal of creating value on all three parameters of the triple bottom line for corporate sustainability. Companies have expertise in creating economic value, but they may lack the same expertise in creating social and environmental value.

Figure 12.1 also presents social entrepreneurship as a contextual and multidimensional concept. The three important dimensions are resource mobilisation, opportunity identification, and capabilities of the social entrepreneur. All three dimensions are directed towards social value creation that occupies a central position in the model. Social entrepreneurs, using their abilities, creativity, and entrepreneurial skills, identify social problems as opportunities and mobilise resources to create social value (including environmental value). It shows an interplay between these dimensions in the process of social value creation, and it happens within a context.

Further, Figure 12.1 shows that social and environmental value creation are common goals for both CSR and SE. Due to this interface, it provides opportunities to combine CSR and SE. It further elaborates multiple ways of combining both for social value creation.

## Opportunities to combine CSR and SE for social value creation

### *Creating a cadre of social change makers*

Historically, CSR has been practiced mainly as corporate philanthropy in India (Afsharipour & Rana, 2014), but these days corporations are discovering and designing innovative models of CSR pro-activeness and reasonable experimentation, which provide them with unique competitive advantage (Majumdar & Saini, 2016). For example, DBS Bank India has developed a partnership with the Centre for Social Entrepreneurship, Tata Institute of Social Sciences (TISS), Mumbai to support start-up social ventures. TISS initiated a two-year Master's Programme in Social Entrepreneurship. The graduates are supported with the CSR fund as grant capital and also expert mentorship to launch social ventures to address complex social problems. Instead of supporting one social venture and addressing a single social problem, the bank chose to support a number of social ventures solving diverse social problems in different states of India, creating a cadre of social change makers. A few of the social ventures are Sampurn(e)arth Private Limited, providing a decentralised waste-management solution to urban residents and businesses; Apni Shala, educating children about life skills; and Krishi Naturals Private Limited, promoting organic farming and helping framers in the Gujarat state of India. In similar ways, corporations have opportunities to develop partnerships with the institutions (e.g. non-profit incubation centres, like Aashray in Ahmedabad, for supporting budding social entrepreneurs and their social ventures), which creates a pipeline of social change makers and can help to create a cadre of social change makers. A similar opinion is expressed by Seelos and Mair (2005b). They suggested that companies can re-employ philanthropic community spending as 'social venture capital' to support early-stage social entrepreneurship initiatives that complement corporate resources and have the potential for future partnerships. Such innovative models of CSR will certainly help corporations to enhance their reputation and also solve social and environmental problems.

### *Supporting and funding social entrepreneurial ventures*

With the implementation of the Companies Act 2013, India has become the first country in the world to make CSR mandatory for companies. Under this act, companies must spend at least 2 percent of their average net profits made during the three immediately preceding financial years in every financial year on CSR. The CSR rules provide several different acceptable methods through which companies can undertake CSR activities. One such method is conducting CSR through a third party. It is clarified that CSR activities may be undertaken through a registered society or trust or a section 8 company (i.e. a non-profit company) under the Companies Act so long as such entitled have a track record of three years in undertaking similar projects or programmes (Afsharipour & Rana, 2014). It provides opportunities for corporate and social enterprises to collaborate. Due to unavailability of a clear legal framework for social enterprises in India, social entrepreneurs are free to register their social ventures as a society or trust or a section 8 company (i.e. a non-profit company), or even as for-profit companies, depending on the contexts and the need. If companies feel that they have less expertise or competency for developing and executing CSR programmes, they can identify the existing social enterprises doing great work in their interest areas and support them financially and by providing mentorship as well. This could certainly be beneficial for the existing social ventures too, because of resource constraints and other limitations. With this support, using their own entrepreneurial skills, social entrepreneurs can solve social and environmental problems innovatively. Companies can also provide them with management skills and resources for scaling up, thus freeing the entrepreneur to start new ventures (Seelos & Mair, 2005b). Several social ventures, such as Akanksha Foundation, Mumbai (working in the education sector) and SNEHA, Mumbai (health care awareness), have been engaged in creating a meaningful impact on society with the support of CSR funds as well. In this way, not only companies' funds have been utilised to create meaningful social impact, but also social entrepreneurs addressed resource mobilisation challenges in the process of solving social problems. Crisan and Borza (2012) concluded that companies can sustain social entrepreneurship through collaborations and partnerships. Many such collaborations are needed in the process of social value creation. In addition, "Because it contributes directly to internationally recognised sustainable development (SD) goals, social entrepreneurship may also encourage established corporations to take on greater social responsibility" (Seelos & Mair, 2005a, p. 241).

### *Hiring social entrepreneurs as consultants to plan and implement CSR*

Companies also have the option of developing a CSR plan and carrying out their CSR activities through hiring existing social entrepreneurs as consultants. Social entrepreneurs can conceptualise, innovate, and implement CSR projects of the companies, and companies support them to achieve the social mission. Seelos and Mair (2005b) also mentioned that social entrepreneurs bring a lot to the table as partners for corporations. Social entrepreneurs who make it through the experimentation and failure phases have already removed significant uncertainty and risk. They act as change agents that enable the poor to participate in economic life, and they also invent business models that can be scaled up and replicated elsewhere. Seelos and Mair stated: "Social entrepreneurship initiatives also constitute local resources that lend themselves to new configurations for novel forms of value creation. All of this could be of great interest to corporations" (p. 53). For example, Ramana Babu Killi, a social entrepreneur and founder of Green Basics (greenbasics.co.in), successfully conceptualised and implemented major CSR projects in the agriculture and dairy sectors, for a central public-sector enterprise, Goa Shipyard Limited in Goa (India). Under CSR initiatives, collective farming cooperative societies were formed which benefited 724 households, till November 2013. Also, 80 micro-entrepreneurs/farmers were involved in the dairy projects (Killi, 2014). The company has won several CSR awards due to these initiatives. Aligning social and business interests and incorporating all stakeholders, this innovative model of CSR has been creating shared value on the triple bottom line. It indicates that a significant effort is being made to create an innovative and sustainable model (Majumdar & Saini, 2016). Seelos and Mair (2005b, p. 53) have gone so far as to say this: "Serial social entrepreneurs may be the best hope, both for the poor and for companies wanting to participate in new market development models".

## *Practicing strategic CSR*

Without any doubt, businesses are the economic engine of society, and making profits is a social responsibility of the companies (Carroll, 1979; Henderson, 2005), but companies today, in various contexts, are under intense pressure to rebuild public trust and stay competitive in a global economy (Jamali, 2007). A company's long-term value (e.g. brand, talent, relationships) is affected by rising expectations among shareholders about the social roles of business (Bonini, Mendonca, & Oppenheim, 2006). It has also been recognised that aligning business and social benefits, the stakeholder approach to CSR improves a company's long-term business prospects by providing competitive advantage to the firms (Porter & Kramer, 2006) and enhancing their reputation (Orlitzky, Siegel, & Waldman, 2011). In this way, strategic CSR not only fulfils the social responsibilities and contributes to development of the firms, but also contributes to create a sustainable society. Galbreath (2009, pp. 121–122) mentioned:

> Firms who better understand their social responsibilities and who begin to more adequately explore how they can build CSR into strategy are likely to reap the rewards of improved competitive positions in the future, to the benefit of their shareholders, but also to the benefit of society at large.

Thus, examining CSR in the context of firm strategy is increasingly necessary to develop competitive advantage in the current environment, as it contributes ultimately to good management practice, economic benefit, and societal welfare (Galbreath, 2009). Companies must see the social dimensions not just as risks, but also as 'opportunities' (Bonini et al., 2006). For example, HUL's CSR strategy is empowering the women and working for a social cause. Simultaneously, it is enhancing sales through their women representatives and reaching areas which were till now inaccessible to them (Dutta & Durgamohan, n.d.). The 'e-choupal' initiative of ITC Ltd. is another example of a successful strategic CSR project, initiated by the International Business Division of ITC in the Indian state of Madhya Pradesh in the year 2000 (Ramachandran, 2011). While studying this model, Ramachandran (2011) mentioned that 'response clarity' (i.e. 'sense and respond') and 'resource leverage' (i.e. 'execution') are two important dynamic capabilities, which play an important role in the success of strategic CSR. The 'sense and respond capability' refers to the ability of a project team to sense social conditions, identify a social issue to be addressed, and design a response to mitigate the issue and also contribute to improvements in a firm's relative cost or price position. The 'execution capability' refers to the ability of a project team to integrate internal and external resources into sub-combinations and combinations (ibid.). Hence, there are opportunities to integrate CSR and SE. Corporations can help social entrepreneurs to achieve their social mission by involving them in identifying social issues, designing, and executing the social programmes.

### *Promoting corporate social entrepreneurship (CSE)/ intrapreneurship*

Corporations can also be social entrepreneurs (Seelos & Mair, 2005b; Austin, Leonard, Reficco, & Wei-Skillern, 2006). Austin et al. (2006, p. 170) define the concept of corporate social entrepreneurship (CSE) as "the process of extending the firm's domain of competence and corresponding opportunity set through innovative leveraging of resources, both within and outside its direct control, aimed at the simultaneous creation of economic and social value". The main purpose of CSE is to accelerate companies' organisational transformation into more powerful generators of societal betterment (Austin & Reficco, 2009). Most importantly, the process of CSE is aimed at enabling businesses to develop more advanced and powerful forms of CSR (ibid.).

Creating an enabling environment, fostering corporate social intrapreneurs, amplifying corporate purpose and values, generating double value, and building strategic alliances are central elements to this process (Austin & Reficco, 2009). They further elaborated these elements and mentioned that for companies to move from their old approach to CSR to the CSE approach, they must adopt an entrepreneurial mindset and cultivate an entrepreneurial environment that enables fundamental organisational transformation. In the process of CSE, corporations need to be entrepreneurial in order to innovate and go beyond their traditional managerial approaches. Therefore, multiple change agents, i.e. corporate social intrapreneurs, play very important roles. These corporate social intrapreneurs are internal champions, good communicators, creators of innovative solutions (new resource configurations, actions, and relationships), not simply managers, but catalysts for change (who inspire and create synergies in the work of others), coordinators (able to effectively reach across internal and external boundaries, mobilising, and aligning interests and incentives), contributors (who support the success of others, team players who enable other groups), and also shrewd calculators (cost-conscious and mindful of the bottom line). As organisational change agents, they need to be able to assess how fast and far they can move the transformational process within the realities of the organisation. The corporate social intrapreneurs ensure that social value generation—fulfiling social responsibilities—is seen as an essential component in companies' mission and values statements. Overall, CSE aims to maximise returns to all the stakeholders, and thus create value for all of them, not only for the investors (Austin & Reficco, 2009).

CSE is not about managing existing operations or CSR programmes; it is about creating disruptive change in the pursuit of new opportunities, like all entrepreneurship (Austin & Reficco, 2009). Thus, companies need to re-think their current approaches to CSR and must tap the creativity of every individual. They can promote CSE, as it involves opportunity and innovation, corporate and social entrepreneurship.

## Conclusion

The concept of CSR has evolved from a traditional philanthropic and conservative approach to a multi-stakeholder approach. It is well recognised that the convergence of social and economic interests has become necessary for corporate sustainability, and corporations must create value for all stakeholders, not only for shareholders/owners. For this, they need to create values on all three bottom lines: social, environmental, and economic. In reality, few companies practice CSR, and for several possible reasons. One possibility is a lack of awareness of how to go about it. Companies may seek the help of others to create social and environmental value. On the other side, social entrepreneurs most often operate in a resource-constrained environment. The importance of innovation, creativity, networking, partnership, and an entrepreneurial way of solving social problems in social entrepreneurship may help and support corporations in creating social and environmental value.

Recognising the potential of social entrepreneurship in solving social and environmental problems innovatively and sustainably, the chapter develops a conceptual framework for social value creation (including environmental value) by integrating CSR and SE, and also discusses various opportunities to combine both CSR and SE in this process.

The proposed conceptual framework may provide guidelines for companies that would like to improve their performance on the other two parameters as well—social and environmental, apart from economic—for corporate sustainability. Companies need to understand that sustainable development and corporate profits are not incompatible goals, and both can be addressed simultaneously, but the reality is that social entrepreneurs and corporations still live in different worlds today (Seelos & Mair, 2005b). The proposed framework may provide opportunities to both the corporate sector as well as social entrepreneurs to collaborate, develop partnerships, network, and work together in an innovative and entrepreneurial way for social value creation, considering each other's strengths and limitations. It may create a win-win situation for both. It would ultimately contribute to sustainable development and inclusive growth of the country.

## Note

1 This chapter is based on a paper presented in the "The Twelfth Biennial Conference on Entrepreneurship" held during February 22–24, 2017 at the Entrepreneurship Development Institute of India (EDII), Ahmedabad, Gujarat, India.

## References


Afsharipour, A., & Rana, S. (2014). *Corporate social responsibility in India*. UC Davis Legal Studies Research Paper Series, Research Paper No. 399. Retrieved December 17, 2016 from http://ssrn.com/abstract=2517601

Arora, P. (2013). Incorporate corporate social responsibility strategy into business. *The SIJ Transactions on Industrial, Financial & Business Management (IFBM)*, *1*(2), 75–82.

Austin, J., & Reficco, E. (2009). *Corporate social entrepreneurship*. Working Paper 09–101, Harvard Business School. Retrieved December 18, 2016 from www.hbs.edu/faculty/Publication%20Files/09-101.pdf

Austin, J., Leonard, H., Reficco, E., & Wei-Skillern, J. (2006). Social entrepreneurship: It's for corporations, too. In A. Nicholls (Ed.), *Social entrepreneurship: New paradigms of sustainable social change*. Oxford, UK: Oxford University Press.

Beauchamp, T. L., & Bowie, N. E. (Eds.). (1993). *Ethical theory and business* (4th ed.). Englewood Cliffs, NJ: Prentice Hall.

Bocken, N. M. P., Rana, P., & Short, S. W. (2015). Value mapping for sustainable business thinking. *Journal of Industrial and Production Engineering*, *32*(1), 67–81. https://doi.org/10.1080/21681015.2014.1000399

Bonini, S. M. J., Mendonca, L. T., & Oppenheim, J. M. (2006). When social issues become strategic. *The McKinsey Quarterly*, *2*, 20–31.

Cannon, T. (1992). *Corporate responsibility* (1st ed.). London: Pitman Publishing.

Carroll, A. B. (1979). A three-dimensional conceptual model opf corporate performance. *Academy of Management Review*, *4*(4), 497–505.

Chahoud, T., Emmerling, J., Kolb, D., Kubina, I., Repinski, G., & Schlager, C. (2007). *Corporate social and environmental responsibility in India: Assessing the UN global compact's role*. Retrieved March 4, 2014 from www.google.co.in/url?sa=t&rct=j&q=&esrc=s&source=web&cd=1&cad=rja&ved=0CCUQFjAA&url=http%3A%2F%2Fwww.globalcompact.de%2Fsites%2Fdefault%2Ffiles%2Fjahr%2Fpublikation%2Fstudies_26.pdf&ei=CfEWU4KuHMGNrgf3s4DwCQ&usg=AFQjCNE1yvshOSK0WefZXrRik2zMqdZ0WA&bvm=bv.62286460,d.bmk

Chatterji, M. (2011). *Corporate social responsibility*. New Delhi: Oxford University Press.

Confederation of Indian Industry (CII). (2013). *Handbook on corporate social responsibility in India*. Retrieved March 4, 2014 from www.pwc.in/en_IN/in/assets/pdfs/publications/2013/handbook-on-corporate-social-responsibility-in-india.pdf

Crisan, C. M., & Borza, A. (2012). Social entrepreneurship and corporate social responsibilities. *International Business Research*, *5*(2), 106–113.

Dees, J. G. (1998). *The meaning of social entrepreneurship*. Retrieved December 12, 2016 from www.fntc.info/files/documents/The%20meaning%20of%20Social%20Entreneurship.pdf

Dees, J. G. (2001). *Social entrepreneurship: Mobilising resources for success*. Retrieved on October 10, 2011 from www.tgci.com/magazine/Social%20Entrepreneurship.pdf

Dutta, K., & Durgamohan, M. (n.d.). *Corporate social strategy: Relevance and pertinence in the Indian context.* Retrieved December 18, 2016 from www.iitk.ac.in/infocell/announce/convention/papers/Industrial%20Economics%20%20Environment,%20CSR-08-Kirti%20Dutta,%20M%20Durgamohan.pdf

Fauzi, H., Svensson, G., & Rahman, A. A. (2010). "Triple bottom line" as "sustainable corporate performance": A proposition for the future. *Sustainability*, *2*, 1345–1360. https://doi.org/10.3390/su2051345

Freeman, R. E. (1984). *Strategic management: A stakeholder approach.* Boston, MA: Pitman.

Friedman, M. (1970). The social responsibility of business is to increase its profits. *Times Magazine*, September 13.

Galbreath, J. (2009). Building corporate social responsibility into strategy. *European Business Review*, *21*(2), 109–127. https://doi.org/10.1108/09555340910940123

Haksever, C., Chaganti, R., & Cook, R. G. (2004). A model of value creation: Strategic view. *Journal of Business Ethics*, *49*(3), 291–305.

Henderson, D. (2005). The role of business in the world today. *Journal of Corporate Citizenship*, *17*, 30–32.

Jamali, D. (2007). The case for strategic corporate social responsibility in developing countries. *Business and Society Review*, *112*(1), 1–27.

Jamali, D. (2008). A stakeholder approach to corporate social responsibility: A fresh perspective into theory and practice. *Journal of Business Ethics*, *82*, 213–231. https://doi.org/10.1007/s10551-007-9572-4

Kakabadse, N. K., Rozuel, C., & Lee-Davies, L. (2005). Corporate social responsibility and stakeholder approach: A conceptual review. *International Journal of Business Governance and Ethics*, *1*(4), 277–302.

Killi, R. B. (2014). *Case study of NCSR Hub.* TISS-GSL Agriculture and Dairy Cooperative Project (Unpublished Case Study).

Lepak, D. P., Smith, K. G., & Taylor, M. S. (2007). Value creation and value capture: A multilevel perspective. *Academy of Management Review*, *32*(1), 180–194.

Mair, J., & Noboa, E. (2003). *The emergence of social enterprises and their place in the new organisational landscape.* Working Paper, WP No. 523, IESE Business School, University of Navarra.

Majumdar, S., & Saini, G. K. (2016). CSR in India: Critical review and exploring entrepreneurial opportunities. *Journal of Entrepreneurship and Innovation in Emerging Economies*, *2*(1), 56–79.

Moir, L. (2001). What do we mean by corporate social responsibility? *Corporate Governance*, *1*(2), 16–22.

Neck, H., Brush, C., & Allen, E. (2008). The landscape of social entrepreneurship. *Business Horizons*, *52*, 13–19.

Nicholls, A. (2006). Introduction. In A. Nicholls (Ed.), *Social entrepreneurship: New models of sustainable change* (pp. 1–35). New York: Oxford.

Orlitzky, M., Siegel, D. S., & Waldman, D. A. (2011). Strategic corporate social responsibility and environmental sustainability. *Business & Society*, *50*(1), 6–27. https://doi.org/10.1177/0007650310394323

Porter, M. E., & Kramer, M. R. (2002). The competitive advantage of corporate philanthropy. *Harvard Business Review*, December, 19–32.

Porter, M. E., & Kramer, M. R. (2006). Strategy and society: The link between competitive advantage and corporate social responsibility. *Harvard Business Review*, December.

Porter, M. E., & Kramer, M. R. (2011). The big idea: Creating shared value. *Harvard Business Review*. Retrieved December 12, 2016 from www.hks.harvard.edu/m-rcbg/fellows/N_Lovegrove_Study_Group/Session_1/Michael_Porter_Creating_Shared_Value.pdf.

Porter, M. E., & Kramer, M. R. (2019). Creating shared value. In G. Lenssen & N. Smith (Eds.), *Managing sustainable business*. Dordrecht: Springer. https://doi.org/10.1007/978-94-024-1144-7_16

Ramachandran, V. (2011). Strategic corporate social responsibility: A 'dynamic capabilities' perspective. *Corporate Social Responsibility and Environmental Management*, *18*, 285–293.

Savitz, A. W., & Weber, K. (2006). *The triple bottom line*. San Francisco, CA: Jossey-Bass.

Seelos, C., & Mair, J. (2005a). Social entrepreneurship: Creating new business models to serve the poor. *Business Horizons*, *48*, 241–246.

Seelos, C., & Mair, J. (2005b). In depth of social entrepreneurship: Sustainable development, sustainable profit. *EBF*, *20*, 49–53. Retrieved December 18, 2016 from http://christian-seelos.com/p49-53%20id%20seelos.pdf.

Seelos, C., & Mair, J. (2005c). *Sustainable development: How social entrepreneurs make it happen*. Working Paper No. 611, IESE Business School, University of Navarra. Retrieved from https://papers.ssrn.com/sol3/Papers.cfm?abstract_id=876404

Singh, A. (2016). *The process of social value creation: A multiple case study on social entrepreneurship in India*. New Delhi, India: Springer.

Szegedi, K., Fülöp, G., & Bereczk, A. (2016). Relationships between social entrepreneurship, CSR and social innovation: In Theory and practice. World Academy of Science, Engineering and Technology. *International Journal of Social, Behavioral, Educational, Economic, Business and Industrial Engineering*, *10*(5), 1504–1509.

Wood, D. J. (1991). Corporate social performance revisited. *Academy of Management Review*, *16*, 691–718.

# GLOSSARY

**aasan:** A small prayer rug used during worshipping Gods in Indian homes.

**Aashray Incubation Centre:** 'Aashray' is the name of Incubation Centre. 'Aashray' is the Hindi word, which means 'to support' in English.

**babui grass:** It is a type of grass which is common in Bankura, Asansol, and Durgapur in West Bengal, India.

**Banjara:** A community in India who keep travelling from one place to another throughout their lifetime.

**biodiversity:** The variation among living species encompasses microorganisms, plants, animals, ecosystems, and the ecological complexes of which they are part.

**biogas plant:** Plant in which biodegradable waste matter is converted into compost in the absence of air for the purpose of production of biogas as a sustainable renewable fuel.

**Business Development Services:** Business Development Services (BDS) refers to provision of non-financial services including training, design, market information, and other business advisory services for the development of small enterprises.

**causal and effectual entrepreneur and decision-making:** A causal entrepreneur starts by carrying out comprehensive market studies to identify market opportunity. The entrepreneur thus defines a goal and chooses among different alternatives to achieve the goal. In contrast, an effectual entrepreneur does not commit to a particular goal but rather utilises knowledge and network to find partners. An effectual entrepreneur adapts the goal considering the available resources and the network strength.

**central bank:** A national bank that provides financial and banking services through formulating monetary policy, issuing currency, controlling credit, and regulating member banks.

**chanderi:** A hand-woven fabric from Madhya Pradesh, India, made up of silk.

**charkha:** A wood-framed hand-spinning machine in Indian homes.

**chindi dhurries:** Rugs woven from left-over fabric swatches in weft and cotton threads in warp.

**chindi:** Left-over fabric swatches after completing a product

**climate change:** Climate change refers to long-term changes in the climatic condition,

**community radio:** Community radio refers to horizontal communication, where members of the community participate and engage in the overall functioning of the radio station.

**convalescent home:** A place where people stay when they need medical and nursing care but they are not sick enough to be in a hospital.

**credit:** Contractual agreement between two parties in which a borrower receives something of value now and agrees to repay the principal along with interest to the lender at some specific period in the future.

**Dastakar:** An NGO which supports craftsmen from all over India by exhibiting their products in Delhi.

**Deshnok Khadi Pratisthan, Khadi Sansthan:** Government organisations which gets handloom fabrics woven from Napasar weavers.

**desi:** Locally available.

**effluent treatment plant:** A treatment plant which is particularly designed to purify industrial waste water.

**franchising:** Franchising is as an instrument for enterprise transformation and entrepreneurship development. Business format franchising involves the owner of a proven business granting the right and providing the necessary assistance and support to another party to replicate his or her business.

**Goyallon ka Mohalla:** Another colony in Napasar where spinners and weavers reside.

**Gram Panchyat:** The local self-government organisation in India of the panchayati raj system at the village or small town level that has a sarpanch as its elected head.

**green banking:** Concept of conducting the banking business which requires the banks to consider environmental and ecological factors in their operations.

**green financing:** A policy which requires formulating financing decisions in a way where eco-friendly business activities and less environmentally hazardous industries will be given preference, and at the same time environmental infrastructure should be encouraged and financed.

**Hybrid Hoffman Kiln (HHK):** Energy-efficient technology used in the production of bricks and some other ceramic products.

**industrialisation:** The process of converting to a socio-economic order in which primarily an agriculture-based economy is transformed to a manufacturing one.

**informal credit:** The credit provided not by institutional sources.

**kalei:** Kalei is the name of local rice wine from the Andro community.

**Khadi Gram Udyog and Khadi Pratisthan:** Government organisations dealing with handloom fabrics.

**kota doria:** A unique hand-woven fabric from Kota Rajasthan, having a characteristic square-check pattern made up of silk and cotton.

**Leikai Macha:** Leikai Macha is known as a small locality within the village.

**Madanaa:** A local fashion brand in Bikaner.

**marginalised:** Social exclusion, or social marginalisation, is the social disadvantage and relegation to the fringe of society. This section of the population is deprived of the resources of the society.

**market development:** Market development refers to an approach aimed at the development of vibrant and competitive private-sector markets of relevant, differentiated services consumed by a broad range and significant proportion of small businesses.

**marup:** An indigenous unorganised rotating savings groups/schemes which involves taking turns monthly to receive the joint pool that enables people to meet necessary or urgent expenditures or affect personal savings.

**Matching Grant Fund:** The Matching Grant Fund is used to boost demand for services and encourage the suppliers to raise their fees for services. It is used in the form of a general market development fund, upgrading service providers to meet more sophisticated demand by user firms.

**micro-enterprise:** A micro-enterprise is an enterprise where investment in plant and machinery does not exceed Rs. 25 lakh (MSME Act, 2006).

**patpedhis:** A type of Rosca or a type of informal bank in Marathi.

**productive capital base:** It includes reproducible capital goods, natural capital or ecosystem, population, intellectual capital, and institutions which allocate the resources.

**Rangsutra:** A non-governmental organisation (NGO), community-owned craft company.

**SAATH:** In the Hindi/Gujarati language, 'Saath' means 'together, co-operation, a collective or support'. SAATH is an NGO, founded in 1989 and registered as a Public Charitable Trust. It is based in Ahmedabad, Gujarat (India).

**serial entrepreneurs:** Entrepreneurs who exit their prior business and start a new venture or number of ventures.

**slum:** According to the Census Definition, "A compact of at least 300 population or about 60–70 households of poorly built congested tenements in unhygienic condition usually with inadequate infrastructure, and lacking in proper sanitary and drinking water facilities."

**social entrepreneurship:** Social entrepreneurship can be defined as a process of social value creation. Social entrepreneurs use the entrepreneurial process to create social value.

**social innovation:** Social innovation refers to innovative activities and services that are motivated by the goal of meeting a social need and that are predominantly diffused through organisations whose primary purposes are social.

**social value creation:** Social value creation refers to the desired social change.

**society:** An organised group of individuals joining together for fulfilment of any purpose of literature, science, or charity.

**sustainability of the social enterprise:** Continuity of the social enterprise in the long run.

**sustainability:** Sustainability is often used interchangeably with sustainable development and refers to ecologically sustainable or 'environmentally sound' development.

**sustainable development:** Sustainable development refers to development which meets the needs of current generations without compromising the ability of future generations to meet their own needs.

**The Concept of Social Entrepreneurship:** The Concept of Social Entrepreneurship has evolved as a means of creating social value, which can generate welfare for a marginalised section of the society. Social mission is the central point in the social entrepreneurship framework.

**trust:** A legal entity created by an agency (or party) in which the second agency (or party) has rights to hold for the benefit of the third agency (party).

**trustee:** The second agency (party) in a trust (see *trust*).

**Uni Sansthan:** A government organisation which deals with woollen handloom woven fabric.

**Upanishads:** These are sacred Hindu treatises illustrating the Vedas and written in Sanskrit language.

**Uttaradwas:** A colony in Napasar where spinners and weavers reside.

**value chain:** Value chain refers to all functions such as design, production, marketing, and sales required to bring a product or service from its initial conceptualisation to the final consumption.

**vouchers:** Vouchers are a partial transactional subsidy which provides a currency of payment for services that might further reduce the risk of transaction to both service supplier and user.

**wellbeing:** Wellbeing of a person depends on his or her satisfaction of life or utility and freedom he or she enjoyed.

**yu kharung:** A particular variety of pot used for keeping local rice wine.

**yu thongba:** A local term used by the Andro community that refers to wine cooking.

# INDEX

Note: page numbers in *italic* indicate a figure and page numbers in **bold** indicate a table on the corresponding page. Page numbers followed by 'n' denote notes.


*Aasan* 129n6
Abdullayev, K. 65
aborigin 89
Academy for Story Telling 32
access to credit 170
adivasis 89
Afrin, S. 137
Agarwal, B. 136
Ahmed, S. U. 137
Alam, Irfan 36
Ali, R. 196
All India Handloom Board 116
All India Radio (AIR) 75
Amanah Ikhtiar Malaysia 137
Anand, S. 3
Anderson, R. B. 90, 95, 107
Andro Bazaar 102
Andro community 97–98; employment of local people 102–103; self-employed entrepreneurs, rise of 103; *see also* Santhei Natural Park
Andro rice wine 104
Andro village 97
Andro Western Baruni Road Youth Club (AWBYC) 98
Anganwadi Centre 204n2
Anna FM 81
Annapurna Mahila Mandal, Mumbai 133; working women's and guest hostel 219
Annapurna Mahila Multi-State Co-operative Credit Society Limited (AMCCSL) 14, 141, 212–219
Annapurna Pariwar *see* Pariwar, Annapurna
Annapurna Pariwar Vikas Samvardhan (APVS) 214–217
antimicrobial resistance (AMR) 6
anti-poverty programmes 134
Aravind Eye Care 12
Arrow, K. J. 157
Ashoka 10, 28, 29, 38n1, 162
Asian Development Bank (ADB) 47, 193
assets 141, **142**, 199
Austin, J. 237
Ayayi, A. G. 222

*Babui* grass 168n4
Bagby, R. D. 52n4
Banerjee, Debartha 165
Bangladesh 9; banking sector in 170–187; financial sector and banking industry in 172–173
Bangladesh Bank 171, 172, 184, 187; green banking policy of 173, 174; in-house green activities 173
Bangladesh Development Bank (BDBL) 180
Bangladesh Krishi Bank (BKB) 180
Bangladesh Rural Advancement Committee (BRAC) 12, 65, 157

*Banjara* 129n12
Bank Asia 181
Bank of Small Industries and Commerce (BASIC) 180
Battilana, J. 35
Berman, E. M. 34
Bhaba Atomic Research Centre (BARC) 165
Bhatt, Ela 13
Bikaner district: artisan units in 118–122; brief profile 117–118; climate and rainfall 118; location, geographical area, and topography 118
Blessing, N. N. 158
Bocken, N. M. P. 230
Bombay Mothers and Children Welfare Society (BMCWS) 44; convalescent home for cancer patients 45–46; day care centre 46; financial and investment decisions 46–47; labour issues 47–48; organisation restructuring and growth 48
Bombay Municipal Corporation (BMC) 47
Bornstein, D. 8
Borza, A. 235
British Council 11
Broadcasting Authority of India (BAI) 78
Brundtland Commission on Environment and Development 191
Brundtland Commission's report 92, 131
Burger, P. 135
business development services (BDS) 53, 54–56; asset categories 54; extension services 65; franchising 62; information and communication technologies 62–63; market assessment 57; market development 53, 54, 56–58; matching grant fund (MGF) 61–62; programme design and products development 57–58; providers 55–56; sector competitiveness, improving 65–66; subsidised BDS provision 58–59; technology development 63–64; training market, developing 59–60; typologies of 54–55; vouchers programme 60–61
business format franchising 62
Business Membership Organisations (BMO) 55

Cahn, M. 108
campus-based community radio stations 84
Cannon, T. 229
capital asset **150**
Carney, D. 54
Carroll, A. B. 229, 231
Casson, M. 49
Centro de Desarollo de Agronegocios (CDA) project 65
Chambers, R. 135, 191
*Chanderi* 129n2
change agents 1, 8, 192
charitable social enterprises 29–32, 34
*Charkha* 129n9
Chieftainship, Andro village 106
*Chindi* 130n14
*Chindi dhurries* 129n8
Choi, N. 7
Choy, C. L. 62
Christiansen, B. 26
climate change 6, 171
Cohen, B. 93, 95
Colbourne, R. 95
communication 86
community-based orientation 90
community radio (CR): definition and concept 76–77; emergence in India 77–79; impacts of 83–86; methodology 79–81; principal task of 75; in sustainable development 73–87; technology 77
community radio stations: Anna FM 81; case studies on 81–83; details of 80; Puduvai Vaani FM 82; Radio Banasthali 81–82; Radio Namaskar 82–83
Companies Act 2013, Section 8 38n2
Conway, G. R. 135, 191
Cooney, K. 202
Corbin, J. 195
corporate philanthropy 231
corporate social entrepreneurship (CSE) 237–238
corporate social performance (CSP) framework 230
corporate social responsibility (CSR) 14, 161, 166, 217, 227–239; plan and implement 235–236; practicing strategic 236–237; social entrepreneurship (SE) 231–233
corporate sustainability 230
cosmovision 90
Council for Advancement of Participatory Agriculture and Rural Technology (CAPART) 58, 59
'creating shared value' (CSV) concept 10
Crisafulli, D. 61
Crisan, C. M. 235
crop losses 5
culture 109n4

Dana, L. P. 90–92, 107
Das, S. K. 116
Dasgupta, P. 156, 157, 167

Datta, P. B. 13
Davis, S. 8
day care centres 46, 52n3
decision-making process 50
Dees, J. G. 8, 232
Delmar, F. 51
Department of International Development (DFID) 135
development 191; challenges 5–6; communication 73–75; process 2, 89
Devi, L. B. 97
Dey, P. 158
Dharavi 139, 140
Diesendorf, M. 26
distributional equity 2
District Supply and Marketing Societies (DSMS) 59
Doherty, B. 197
Dorado, S. 37
Dorsey, C. 35
Downing, J. 53
Duncombe, R. 62
Dunlop 108

earned income strategies 10
Earth Summit 155, 156
Eastern Bank 181
ecological sustainability 4
Econ-Minimart 62
economic competitiveness 4
economic development 3, 53, 94–96, 107, 177, 187; "second wave" of 95
economic growth 25
entrepreneurial economy 158
entrepreneurial efforts 7
entrepreneurs 7; *see also* indigenous entrepreneurs; social entrepreneurs
entrepreneurship 7, 9; *see also* indigenous entrepreneurship; social entrepreneurship
environmental problems 6
environmental sustainability 96
equity 4, 207, 221–222
essentially contested concept (ECC) 7
established slums 152n11
ethnic minorities 89
ethnographic research method 96
e-Tuk Tuk 77
Etzioni, A. 192
EXIM Bank 181

Fagenson, E. A. 50
Family Security Fund (FSF) 216
Farm Implements and Tools (FIT) programme 57, 58, 60
Farrelly, T. A. 108
Fauzi, H. 230
Fernandez, Armida 32, 34
Field, M. 53
financial asset **149**
financial inclusion 14
financial stress 5
financial sustainability 34
First Nations 89
Folta, T. B. 51
Forbes magazine 50
foreign commercial banks (FCBs) 178, 180, 181, **181**, 184
for-profit social enterprises 29
Foster, W. L. 26, 32
four-stage continuum model 231
Franchise Development Assistance Scheme 62
Freeman, R. E. 230, 231
Freire, Paulo 74

Gailey, R. 13
Galbraith, C. S. 90, 95
Galbreath, J. 236
Gandhi, Mahatma 8
Gartner, W. B. 42, 209
Garud, R. 42
gender bias 6
gender inequality 6
German Organisation for Technical Cooperation (GTZ) 64
Ghosh, C. 137
Ghosh, Pradip 162
Gibson, A. 57
Giuliani, A. P. 42
global greenhouse gas emissions 6, 187
global health threats 6
globalisation 9
global warming 6, 171, 208
Goedhuys, M. 108
Goh, M. 62
*Goyallon ka Mohalla* 129n11
Grameen Bank 157, 158, 208
*Gram Panchyat* 129n4
Gram Shree Melas 58
green banking activities 171
green banking policy 173, 174; three phases of time frame 174
green economy 12, 14
green energy technologies 12
green financing 170–187; allocation and utilisation, fund 177–181, **178**; budget allocation, banks **185**; budget utilisation, banks **186**; financing projects, environmental risk rating 183–184; fund allocation and utilisation, banks rankings 184; green activities 173–174;

methodology 172; objectives 172; part of green banking 174–176; sector-wise contribution, banks 182–183; sustainable development and environment 176–177; theoretical framework 172–177
Guha, S. 137

Habib Bank 181
Haksever, C. 228
Haldar, S. 26
Hallberg, K. 60
Hammer, C. 75
Hamzah, A. 108
Handloom Export Production Council (HEPC) 117
Hanoi 56
Harare 56
Hassan, A. 97
Health Mutual Fund (HMF) 216
Heeks, R. 62
Hileman, M. 57, 60
hill tribes 89
Hindle, K. 92, 95
Hinduism 98
Hindustan Unilever Limited (HUL) 14
*Hindusthan Times* 165
HIV 6
Honig, B. 90
HRSCATSIA 110n8
Hrudayalaya, Narayana 9, 12, 35, 37
Huberman, A. M. 195
human wellbeing 4
hybrid entrepreneurship and performance 51
hybrid model 35

Iankova, K. 97
idli 152n14
inclusive growth 25, 227, 239
inclusive societies 191–204
India 9, 11, 12, 115; population of 115
India Inclusive Innovation Fund (IIIF) 11
Indian Council of Indigenous and Tribal Peoples (ICITP) 109n3
Indian handloom industry: history and scenario of 116–117
indigenous ecotourism 110n13
*Indigenous Ecotourism: Sustainable Development and Management* 107
indigenous entrepreneurs 96, 110n10
indigenous entrepreneurship 88–110; definition 92; economic development and 94–96; methodology 96–99
indigenous knowledge 88, 89, 92
indigenous peoples 89–92, 95, 96, 103, 106; definitions 90; indicators 90
individual-based enterprises 148
individual-led entrepreneurship 146
information and communication technologies 62–63
innovation 77
innovative models 12, 14, 16, 194
Insurance Regulatory and Development Authority (IRDA) 163
intangible assets 152n9
Inter American Development Bank (IADB) 61
inter-generational wellbeing 156–158
intrapreneurship 7, 237–238
Islam, N. 137
Islami Bank 181
Ismail, M. B. 137
ITC's e-Chaupal initiative 14, 15

Jacobsen, K. 137
Jamali, D. 94, 231
Johnson, D. 108
Jones, M. B. 37
Joshi, Rajendra 32

Kathalaya 32
Kaupapa Maori Entrepreneurship 110n11
Kawharu, M. 91
Kembabazi, J. 137
Kenya BDS programme 66
*Khadi Gram Udyogs* 129n7
*Khejur* 168n5
Kikuchi, T. 9
Kim, P. 26
Kirzner, I. M. 49
Kokkranikal, J. 107–108
Kolmogorov-Smirnov test 147, **151**
Korosec, R. L. 34
Korsgaard, S. 50
*Kota Doria* 129n3
Kramer, M. R. 231
Kruskal Wallis median test 147
Kula, O. 53
Kumar, K. 63
Kyoto Protocol 208

L'Abbe, R. 97
Laeis, G. 133
Lam Nijaba 106
Lansdowne, M. 92, 95
Lee, M. 35
Leikai Macha 98
Lemke, S. 133
liabilities 199
Liberalisation, Privatisation, and Globalisation (LPG) 136

Lienert, J. 135
Life Mutual Fund (LMF) 216
Lijjat sisters 13
Lindsay, N. J. 107
Livingston, W. 157
loan profile **142**
loan size **145–146**
Loi community 97
*The Lois of Manipur* 97
Ly, P. 33
Lyons, M. 135–136

MacBride Report 76
Madhav Sathe *see* Sathe, Madhav
Mair, J. 157, 193, 227, 234–236
Majundar, S. 7
malaria 6
Mamun, A. A. 137
Manaktala, S. 63
Manipur Sangai Festival 101
marginalised slums 152n12
market-oriented opportunity 102
Marshak, A. 137
Martin, R. L. 26
Marup 105, 110n16
matching grant fund (MGF) 61–62
McCarthy, S. 63
Mckenzie, J. 59
McWade, W. 203
Meitei Society 97
Mekong Project Development Facility (MPDF) 59, 60
Mercy Corps 65
Micro, Small, and Medium Enterprises (MSMEs) Act 11, 118
micro and small enterprises (MSEs) 53, 55, 58, 60
micro-enterprises (MEs) 134–139, 141, 148; borrowers and non-borrowers, profitability 147; profile of enterprises 142, **143**; Tobit regression 143–147
micro-entrepreneurs 134, 136, 138, 140, 146; socio-economic profile of 140–142, **141**
microfinance 137
microfinance institutions (MFIs) 134–141, 148; dummy **149**, **150**; loans and informal loans **149**; slums of Mumbai 133–148
Miles, M. B. 195
Millennium Development Goals (MDG) 5
Ministry of Textiles 115
Mitchell, R. 93
Mofokeng, M.-A. 34
Moghavvemi, S. 108
moral hazard 152n4
Morley, S. 95
Moroz, P. 92
Morrison, A. 107, 108
mortality rates 5
Mulgan, G. 196
Musa, G. 108
Mustafayeva, N. 65

Nagpal, K. 125
Napasar, Rajasthan 115–130; agencies along with government agencies 128; all-age weavers 123; awareness about education, women 123; camel hair and usage, less explorations 125–126; case description 118; climate 128; community synchronisation 127; double cloth weaving, forgotten craft 124; dyeing, printing, and tailoring expertise, lack 126–127; exhibitions and displays 127; fabric development tools availability, home 124; family unit 119; fight against power looms 128; government schemes 127; in-house spinning cluster 123; in-house weaving cluster 122; lack of education 126; lack of experimentation 125; language development 129; literacy 119; local raw material availability 123; marketing channels 128–129; organisational chart *120*; population of 119; primary dilemmas 120; product design, lack of innovations 126; qualitative methodology study 117; rail track and road connectivity 127; raw materials like camel hair, sourcing 128; research context 117–122; rugs and carpets, no production 124–125; spinner's community 120–121; stop middlemen intervening 128; SWOC analysis of 122–129; trade overview 119–120; traditional craft practice 124; weaver's community 121–122; weaving interest loss, younger generations 124; women empowerment 123
narrative approach 42
National Bank of Pakistan 181
National Policy for Skill Development and Entrepreneurship, 2015 11
National Trust 164
Native American 89
*Natural History* 116
Naudé, W. 108
Nega, B. 158
Nel, H. 136
Nepal 9, 64

New India Assurance Company Limited (NIACL) 163
Newnham, J. 66
Niramay 164
Niti Aayog 204n1
Non-Financial Services 216
non-governmental organisations (NGOs) 63, 64, 75, 117
non-performance assets (NPA) 223
non-profit organisations 10, 34, 35
not-for-profit sector 29
not-for-profit ventures 8

Obinna, I. C. 158
Olu, O. 137, 221
on-air programmes 85
Oofri-Adjei, A. 137
operational services 55
opportunity recognition 110n17
Organisation for Awareness of Integrated Social Security (OASiS) 162, 163, 167
Osberg, S. 26
Osinubi, T. S. 108
*Other Voices: The Struggle for Community Radio in India* 75
oxymoron 2

Palich, L. E. 52n4
Panam Ningthou 98, 104
Panam Ningthou Garden 100
*Panchayat* 168n3
Paramanathan, T. 108
Pariwar, Annapurna 207–223; case description 212–219; empowerment 222; entrepreneurial motivation 220; equity and participation 221–222; inclusion and access to services 221; occupational choice 219–220; opportunity recognition and exploitation 220–221; sustainability 222–223
Parker, S. C. 219
Participatory Rural Appraisal (PRA) techniques 58
Patnaik, S. 135
Patzelt, H. 50
Pavlovic, A. 63
Peredo, A. M. 90
Philips, D. A. 61
Phusaba Lois 110n12
plurality of media 86
Poon, D. 10
Porter, M. E. 10, 231
Potpang 105
pottery 104
Potyeng 105
poverty 5
Prasad, C. S. 135
*Pratisthans* 129n7
private commercial bank (PCBs) 178, **181**, 184
protagonist social entrepreneur 42–43
'3Ps' (serving the 'people,' benefiting the 'planet,' and making 'profit') 12
Puduvai Vaani FM 82

Radio Banasthali 81–82
Radio Namaskar 82–83
Rajshahi Krishi Unnayan Bank (RAKUB) 180
Ramachandran, V. 237
Ramanujam, Geeta 32
Raven, R. P. J. M. 7
real-time information 15
research avenues 51; hybrid entrepreneurship and performance 51; social entrepreneurial ventures, managing 51
research issue 29–37; charitable social enterprises 29–34; charitable *vs.* for-profit 34–36; for-profit social enterprises 36; mission-shift or mission-drift, for-profits 36–37
Rio+20 UN conference 157
Rio de Janeiro 56
Rodriguez, C. L. 95
rotating savings and credit associations (ROSCAs) 105, 141, 142, 146, 147
Royakkers, L. M. M. 7
Rupees 129n5

SAATH 33, 191–204; case description of 195–196; cross-sector partnerships 199–201; livelihoods 198–199; market-based approach 198–199; multi-stakeholder approach 199–201; need-based model 196–197; research methodology 194–195; scaling strategies 202–203; sustainability model 201–202
Sahu, Supriya 86
Salazar, L. 75
Samant, Medha 14
Sampurn(e)arth Environment Solutions Pvt. Ltd 164–166
Sanders, B. 196
Sangai Festival 110n14
Santhei Natural Park 96–99; business, new trend 104–105; changes in lifestyle 100–101; economic independence 105; environmental concern 105–106; indigenous ecotourism, emergence of

101–102; market-oriented opportunity 102; self-employed entrepreneurs, rise of 103; socially motivated environment 99–100
Sanwal, M. 157
Sarasvathy, S. D. 50
saree 152n13
Sathe, Madhav 41–52; Bombay Mothers and Children Welfare Society (BMCWS) 44; financial and investment decisions 46–47; issues, entrepreneurial opportunities, and decisions 44–45; labour issues 47–48; protagonist social entrepreneur 42–43; research point of view 49–51; social entrepreneur 44; social venture models 45–46
Saufi, R. A. 137
scheduled tribes 89
Schneider, G. 158
Schorr, J. 32
Schreiner, M. 134
Scoones, I. 191
Seelos, C. 157, 193, 227, 234–236
SELCO 12
self-employed entrepreneurs 103
Self-Employed Women's Association (SEWA) 13, 14, 58, 133
*Self-Sustainability of Community Radio: Stories from India* 75
semi-formal social enterprises 134
Sen, A. 3
Sender-Message-Channel-Receiver (SMCR) model 74
Sene, M. 222
Sengupta, R. 156, 157
serial social entrepreneurship 207–223; data and method 211–212; objectives 211
Shane, S. 49, 51
Shanks, T. R. W. 202
Sharma, Lokesh 83, 84
Shepherd, D. A. 50
Shri Mahila Griha Udyog Lijjat Papad 13, 14
Singh, A. 229, 233
Singh, N. 134
Singh, S. 34
Singlup 98–99
small and micro enterprises 55; *see also* micro and small enterprises
Small Business Enterprise Centre (SBEC) 108
small enterprise development: business services 53–67; emerging theory and practices 53–67
Smith, B. 93
Snoxell, S. 135, 136
social activism 26
social business entity 198–199
social change 8, 13, 74, 133, 161, 192, 209, 220
social enterprise policy 11
social enterprises (SE) 10–11, 14, 26, 27, 29, 32, 38, 192; inclusive societies and 191–204; methods of data collection 140; research design 139; sampling method 140; sources of data 140; sustainable livelihood and 133–148
social entrepreneurial ventures 28
social entrepreneurs 1, 7–9, 14, 17n1, 26, 27, 37, 159, 168, 192, 193, 238; case studies on 159–166; comprehensive wealth nature 167–168; freedom 166–167; opportunity in problems 41–52; Sampurn(e)arth Environment Solutions Pvt. Ltd 164–166; social security for people with disability 162–164; Society for Research and Rudimentary Education on Social and Health Issues (SRREOSHI) 160–162; solving social problems approach 166; utility or satisfaction 166–167
social entrepreneurship 209; case study rationale 41; concept of 7–8; critiquing approach of 168; development of 8–11; methodology 28–29; narrative approach, case study 42; in sustainable development 12–15; theoretical underpinning 27–28; *see also individual entries*
social innovation 7, 11, 12
social justice 12, 93
socially motivated environment 99–100
social problems 6, 9
social responsibility 96
social value 8, 29, 228–229
social value creation 8, 227–239; cadre of social change makers 234; hiring social entrepreneurs 235–236; supporting and funding, social entrepreneurial ventures 234–235
social venture models 45–46
societal transformation 1
Society for Research and Rudimentary Education on Social and Health Issues (SRREOSHI) 160–162
socio-economic backwardness 88
Solow, R. M. 2, 3
Soundarapandian, M. 116
specialized development banks (SDBs) 184
Srivastava, V. S. 125
Standard Chartered 181

State-Owned Commercial Banks (SCBs) 178, 180, **180**, 184
Steyaert, C. 158
Stiglitz, J. 134
Stiles, C. S. 95
Stockholm Conference 109n7
strategic alliances 33
Strauss, A. 195
Stree Mukti Sanghatana 166
strengths, weaknesses, opportunities, and challenges (SWOC) analysis 122–129
strong sustainability 4
sustainability 4, 6–7, 26, 27, 29, 93, 94; community and organisation interface 189; of development 131–132
'sustainable corporate performance' (SCP) 230
sustainable corporation 231
sustainable development (SD): community radio in 73–87; concept of 25; indigenous entrepreneurship and 88–110; *see also individual entries*
sustainable development goals (SDGs) 5, 27, 29–32, 75
sustainable entrepreneurship 26
sustainable human development 2, 3
sustainable livelihood 115–130, 135–136, 191; conceptual framework 138, *138*; micro-enterprises and 136–138; microfinance institutions and 136–138
sustainable livelihood (SL): social enterprises and 133–148
Sustainable Livelihood Approaches (SLA) 133, 135
Sustainable Living Plan 14
sustained growth 2
Szirmai, A. 108

Tanburn, J. 57, 60
tangible assets 138
Tanzania 5
Tapsell, P. 91
Thompson, J. 197
Thompson, N. 157
Tobit regression 143–147; analysis 140
Tomecko, J. 55
tribes 89
triple bottom line (TBL) 89, 92–94, 96, 107, 227, 230
trusteeship, Gandhian Sarvodaya ideology 13
Tucker, S. 196

Ucbasaran, D. 210
Uganda 6
Umoh, G. S. 137
Unilever Sustainable Living Plan (USLP) 14
United Kingdom (UK) 10, 11
United Nations Brundtland Report 25, 26
United Nations Commission for Sustainable Development 131
United Nations Conference on Environment and Development, Rio de Janeiro 2
United Nations Conference on Sustainable Development 5
United Nations Declaration on Sustainable Development 4, 208
United Nations Development Programme (UNDP) 3
United Nations Educational, Scientific and Cultural Organisation (UNESCO) 77, 90
United States 10, 156, 162
*Upanishads* 130n13
*Uttaradwas* 129n10

value 228–229
value creation 227; interface between CSR and SE 233–234
variables **144**
Vasanthakumari 134
Vatsalyapurna Co-operative Society day care services 217–218
Venkataraman, S. 49, 51, 95
Vidyapurna-Annapurna Mahila Mandal, Pune 218

Wadeson, N. 49
Walker, J. 35
weak sustainability 4
weaving communities 115
welfare-based entity 198–199
welfare states 10
wellbeing 136, 155–168; conceptual framework 158–159; freedom 166–167; utility or satisfaction 166–167
well-developed ecosystem 10
Wennberg, K. 51
Westhead, P. 210
Williams, T. A. 50
Winn, M. I. 95
Witkamp, M. J. 7
Woller, G. 134
women 6; awareness about education 123; empowerment 13, 123; micro-entrepreneurs 213; union for poor self-employed women workers 13
Wood, D. J. 229
Woods, C. 91

Woosnam, K. M. 108
Work Integration Social Enterprises (WISE) 10
World Association of Community Radio Broadcasters (AMARC) 78
World Bank 61, 89
World Commission 109n5
World Commission on Environment and Development (WCED) 92, 176
World Health Organisation (WHO) 6
World Summit for Social Development 193
World Summit on Sustainable Development 2
World Tourism Day 101, 110n15
Wright, M. 210

Xaxa, V. 90

Zeppel, H. 107